teach yourself...

C++

FIFTH EDITION

Al Stevens

MIS:
PRESS

Henry Holt & Co., Inc. • New York

MIS:Press
A Subsidiary of Henry Holt and Company, Inc.
115 West 18th Street
New York, New York 10011
http://www.mispress.com

Limits of Liability and Disclaimer of Warranty

The Author and Publisher of this book have used their best efforts in preparing the book and the programs contained in it. These efforts include the development, research, and testing of the theories and programs to determine their effectiveness.

The Author and Publisher make no warranty of any kind, expressed or implied, with regard to these programs or the documentation contained in this book. The Author and Publisher shall not be liable in any event for incidental or consequential damages in connection with, or arising out of, the furnishing, performance, or use of these programs.

All products, names and services are trademarks or registered trademarks of their respective companies.

teach yourself… and the ty logo are registered.

Fifth Edition—1997

Library of Congress Cataloging-in-Publication Data

```
Stevens, Al.
Teach yourself--C++, by Al Stevens. -- 5th ed.
   p.  cm.
 ISBN 1-55828-552-0
 1. C++ (Computer program language)  I. Title.
QA76.73.C153S73  1997
005.13 3--dc21                                   97-23417
                                                    CIP
```

MIS:Press and M&T Books are available at special discounts for bulk purchases for sales promotions, premiums, and fundraising. Special editions or book excerpts can also be created to specification.

For details contact: Special Sales Director
                          MIS:Press and M&T Books
                          Subsidiaries of Henry Holt and Company, Inc.
                          115 West 18th Street
                          New York, New York 10011

10 9 8 7 6 5 4 3 2 1

Associate Publisher: *Paul Farrell*

Managing Editor: *Shari Chappell*   **Production Editor:** *Anthony Washington*
Editor: *Debra Williams Cauley*   **Technical/Copy Editor:** *Betsy Hardinger*
Copy Edit Manager: *Karen Tongish*

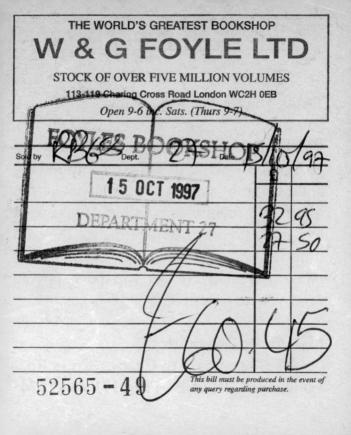

THE WORLD'S GREATEST BOOKSHOP
W & G FOYLE LTD
STOCK OF OVER FIVE MILLION VOLUMES
113-119 Charing Cross Road London WC2H 0EB

Open 9-6 inc. Sats. (Thurs 9-7)

FOYLES BOOKSHOP

Sold by RBG   Dept. 27   Date 15/10/97

15 OCT 1997

DEPARTMENT 27

32 95

27 50

£60 45

52565 - 49

Foyles' Mail Order Service

Thank you for visiting Foyles.

If you would like to order books from us by post, simply write or fax to the following address with as many details about the books you require as possible. If you wish to pay by credit card, please state the card number, expiry date and cardholder's name. Alternatively we will be happy to send you an order form.

Mail Order Department,
Foyles Bookshop, 113 Charing Cross Rd,
London WC2H 0EB. Fax 0171 434 1574

Dedication

This book is lovingly dedicated to:

Ji... ... (aka Buzz Lightyear)
Todd Little
Andy Peloso
Stuart Pond
Adam Shamban
JB West

And most especially...
John Rae-Grant
Each of you knows why.

Acknowledgments

Thanks are due to the companies and individuals mentioned here.

Cygnus (www.cygnus.com), which developed and distributes gnu-win32, a Win32 port of the GNU C++ compiler.

P.J. Plauger, whose implementation of the Standard C++ Library is the closest to the proposed standard of them all and who patiently answered my questions without complaint.

Herb Schildt, a fellow author and friendly competitor. We collaborated at length on the most appropriate strategies for dealing with moving targets.

Alexander Stepanov, who coauthored the Standard Template Library, made it available, and continues to provide guidance on its future and use.

Bjarne Stroustrup, who created C++ and continues as its staunch supporter and outspoken defender.

Contents

PREFACE XVII

CHAPTER 1: An Introduction to Programming in C++ 1
Who Are You? 2
What Do You Need? 2
A Brief History of C and C++ 3
C's Continuing Role 6
C versus C++ 7
A Brief Description of C++ 8
The main Function 11
Summary 12

CHAPTER 2: Writing Simple C++ Programs 13
Your First Program 14
    Line 1: The #include Directive 15
    Line 2: The using namespace Directive 15
    Line 3: White Space 16
    Line 4: The main Function Declaration 17
    Line 5: The main Function's Statement Block .17
    Line 6: Writing to the Console 17
    Line 6: Source-Code Comments 17
    Line 7: The return Statement 18
    Line 8: Terminating the Statement Block 18
Variations on main 18
Identifiers 19
Keywords 20
The Standard Output Stream 21
Variables 22
    The bool Type 22
    The char Type 23
    The wchar_t Type 25
    The int Type 26
    Floating-Point Numbers 28

Constants 29
    Character Constants 29
    Escape Sequences 29
    Integer Constants 31
    Floating Constants 32
    Address Constants 32
    String Constants 32
Expressions 34
Assignments 34
Comma-Separated Declarations 37
Operators in Expressions 37
    Arithmetic Operators 38
    Logical Operators 40
    Bitwise Logical Operators 41
    Bitwise Shift Operators 42
    Relational Operators 43
    Increment and Decrement Operators 45
    Assignment Operators 47
    Compound Assignment Operators 49
    Conditional Operator (?:) 51
    Comma Operator 53
Precedence and Associativity 54
    Associativity 55
    Precedence 56
When an Expression Is Not Evaluated 56
Initializers 57
Type Conversion 58
Console Input and Output 60
    The Standard Output Stream 61
    Formatted Output: Manipulators 61
    The Standard Error Stream 63
    The Standard Input Stream 63
Summary 65

CHAPTER 3: Functions **67**
The Function 68
    Remember the main 68
Arguments versus Parameters 69
Declaring Functions by Using Prototypes 70
    Unnamed Parameter Types 70
    A Typical Prototype 70
    Functions Returning void 71
    Functions with No Parameters 72
    Functions with Variable Parameter Lists 72
    Functions Returning Nothing and with No Parameters 72

Standard Library Prototypes 73
Functions without Prototypes 73
Defining and Calling Functions 73
Returning from Functions 74
Returning Values from Functions 76
Ignoring Return Values 77
Passing and Using Arguments 77
The Scope of Identifiers 79
Initializing with Function Calls 79
The Sequence of Initializer Execution 79
Passing Several Arguments 80
Function Calls as Arguments 81
Pass by Value 81
Type Conversions in Arguments and Return Values 81
Unnamed Function Parameters 82
Default Function Arguments 82
inline Functions 84
Recursion 85
Overloaded Functions 85
Overloading for Different Operations 85
Overloading for Different Formats 87
Type-Safe Linkages 88
Linkage Specifications 89
Summary 94

CHAPTER 4: Program Flow Control **95**
Statement Blocks 96
Nesting Depth 96
Indentation Styles 96
Selection: Tests 97
The if Statement 97
The if...else Statements 101
The else if Statements 102
The switch...case Statements 104
Declaration within an if Conditional Expression 105
Iterations: Looping 106
The while Statement 106
The do...while Statement 108
The for Statement 110
Declaration within a for Conditional Expression 113
Loop Control 113
break 113
continue 114
Jumping: goto 116
Invalid Uses of goto 117

C++ goto versus C goto 117
Fixing the Invalid goto 118
Should You Use goto? 119
Summary 120

CHAPTER 5: More About C++ Data **121**
Scope 122
Global Scope 122
Local Scope 123
The Global Scope Resolution Operator 125
File Scope 126
Scope vs. Lifetime 128
Storage Classes 129
The auto Storage Class 129
The static Storage Class 130
The extern Storage Class 131
The register Storage Class 133
Initial Default Values 134
Type Qualifiers 134
The const Type Qualifier 134
The volatile Type Qualifier 135
User-Defined Data Types 136
Declaring a struct 137
Defining a struct Variable 137
Referencing struct Members 138
Initializing a Structure 138
Structures within Structures 139
Passing and Returning Structures to and from Functions 141
The union Data Type 142
The enum Constant 146
Arrays 147
Declaring Arrays 147
Accessing Arrays with Subscripts 148
Initializing Arrays 148
Arrays of Structures 149
Multidimensional Arrays 150
Character Arrays: A Special Case 152
Pointers and Addresses 153
Pointers to Intrinsic Types 154
Pointer Arithmetic 156
Pointers and Arrays 159
Pointers to Structures 163
Pointers as Function Arguments 164
Returning Addresses from Functions 167
Pointers to Functions 169

Pointers to Pointers 172
Pointers to Arrays of Pointers 174
Pointers to const Variables 176
const Pointer Variables 177
void Pointers 179
The sizeof Operator 181
C-Style Typecasts 183
typedef 185
Command-Line Arguments: argc and argv 186
Program Memory Architecture 188
The Heap 188
The Stack 192
Recursion 193
A Simple Recursive Example 194
A Recursive Calculator 195
Reference Variables 200
The Reference Is an Alias 201
Initializing a Reference 203
References to Reduce Complex Notation 204
References as Function Parameters 206
Returning a Reference 210
Pointers vs. References 212
Summary 213

CHAPTER 6: Library Functions **215**
<cassert> 216
<cctype> 218
<cerrno> 219
<cmath> 220
<csetjmp> 221
<cstdarg> 224
va_list 225
va_start 225
va_arg 225
va_end 226
<cstdio> 226
Global Symbols 226
<cstdlib> 226
Numerical Functions 227
Memory Allocation Functions 227
System Functions 228
Random Number Generation Functions 228
<cstring> 230
strlen 231
strcmp 231

strcpy 232
strcat 232
strncmp, strncpy, and strncat 232
memset 233
<ctime> 233
asctime 234
ctime 234
difftime 234
gmtime 234
localtime 235
mktime 235
time 235
Summary 235

CHAPTER 7: The Preprocessor **237**
Preprocessing Directives 238
Including Files 238
#include 239
Macros 240
#define 240
#define with Arguments .242
Notation and Justification 249
The # "Stringizing" Operator 249
The ## Operator 250
#undef 252
Compile-Time Conditional Directives 252
#if 252
#endif 252
#if defined 253
#ifdef and #ifndef 254
#else 254
#elif 255
#error 256
Other Standard Directives 257
#line 257
#pragma 258
Summary 258

CHAPTER 8: Structures and Classes **259**
The C++ Class 260
The Characteristics of Data Types 260
Data Representation 260
Implementation 261
Behavior 261
Interface 261

User-Defined Data Types 261
   Abstraction 261
   What Are the Objects? 262
   Data Abstraction and Procedural Programming 262
   Data Abstraction and Encapsulation 265
Structures with Functions 265
   Adding Functions to Structures 266
   Multiple Instances of the Same Structure 267
   Different Structures, Same Function Names .268
Access Specifiers 271
Should You Use Procedural Programming? 272
The Class versus the Structure 272
Unions 274
Summary 274

CHAPTER 9: C++ Classes **275**
Designing a Class 276
   Class Declaration 276
   Class Members 278
   Object-Oriented Class Design 280
   The Scope of a Class Object 281
   inline Functions 281
Constructors 283
   Constructors with Default Arguments 284
   Default Constructors 285
   Overloaded Constructors 285
Destructors 287
Class Conversions 288
   Conversion Functions 288
   Converting Classes 292
   Invoking Conversion Functions 295
   The Contexts in Which Conversions Occur 297
   Explicit Constructors 299
   Conversion within an Expression 300
Manipulating Private Data Members 301
   Getter and Setter Member Functions 302
   const Member Functions 303
   An Improved Member Conversion Function 304
Friends 305
   Friend Classes 306
   Implied Construction 307
   Forward References 308
   Explicit friend Forward Reference 309
   Friend Functions 310
   Anonymous Objects 312

Nonmember Friend Functions .... .312
Using Destructors .... .314
Overloaded Assignment Operators .... .317
The this Pointer .... .320
   Returning *this .... .321
   Using this to Link Lists .... .326
Arrays of Class Objects .... .328
   Class Object Arrays and the Default Constructor .... .329
   Class Object Arrays and Destructors .... .331
Static Members .... .333
   Static Data Members .... .333
   Static Member Functions .... .336
   Public Static Members .... .339
Classes and the Heap .... .339
   Constructors and new; Destructors and delete .... .339
   The Heap and Class Arrays .... .340
   Overloaded Class new and delete Operators .... .343
   Testing for Exceptions .... .346
   Overloaded new and delete Exceptions .... .347
   Overloaded Class new[] and delete[] .... .347
Copy Constructors .... .350
References in Classes .... .354
Constructor Parameter Initialization Lists .... .356
A Brief Essay on const .... .358
Mutable Data Members .... .361
The Management of Class Source and Object Files .... .362
   Class Definitions in a Header .... .362
   Class Member Functions in a Library .... .363
Summary .... .363

CHAPTER 10: Overloaded Operators .... .365
To Overload or Not to Overload .... .366
A Case for Overloaded Operators .... .367
The Rules of Operator Overloading .... .368
Binary Arithmetic Operators .... .369
Class Member Operator Functions .... .370
Nonmember Operator Functions .... .373
Relational Operators .... .376
More Assignment Operators .... .378
Auto-increment and Auto-decrement .... .380
Unary Plus and Minus Operators .... .382
Subscript Operator .... .384
Pointer-to-Member Operator .... .386
Summary .... .389

CHAPTER 11: Class Inheritance 391
  Inheritance 392
    Why Inheritance? 395
  Specialized Data Abstraction Class Design 396
    The Base Class 397
    Designing for Efficiency 400
    Single Inheritance 404
    The Derived Class 404
    Protected Members 405
    Derived and Specialized Members 405
    Public and Private Base Classes 405
    Constructors in the Base and Derived Classes 406
    Specializing with New Member Functions 407
    Specializing by Overriding Base Class Member Functions 408
    Building the Program 409
    Scope Resolution Operator with Base and Derived Classes 410
    More Than One Derived Class 411
  Problem Domain Class Hierarchy Design 420
    C++ versus Pure Object-Oriented Design 422
    More Data Abstractions 423
    Overloading < and > 424
    SSN and Money: Two More Data Abstractions 427
    Including Headers 430
    The Standard C++ string Class 431
  Person: The Base Class 431
    Enums in a Class 435
    Virtual Functions 435
    Abstract Base Class: The Pure Virtual Function 436
    Two Ways to Display 436
  Derived Classes 436
    The Employee Class 436
    Overriding a Function Override 438
    The WagedEmployee Class 439
    The SalariedEmployee Class 440
    The Contractor Class 442
    Building Object Libraries 444
    Using the Problem Domain Class Hierarchy 445
    Calling Virtual Functions by Reference 449
    Calling Nonvirtual Functions by Reference 450
    Overriding the Virtual Function Override 450
    Virtual Functions without Derived Overrides 450
    Virtual Destructors 450
    Which Member Functions Should Be Virtual? 452
  Polymorphism 453
  Inheritance and Frameworks 455
  Summary 464

CHAPTER 12: Multiple Inheritance 465
  Multiple Base Classes 466
  Constructor Execution with Multiple Inheritance .468
  Destructor Execution with Multiple Inheritance 468
  Refining the Property System Design 468
  Overriding Members with Multiple Inheritance 470
  Ambiguities with Multiple Inheritance 471
    Ambiguous Member Functions 472
    Ambiguous Data Members 472
    Resolving Ambiguities in the Design 473
    Unavoidable Ambiguities 474
  Virtual Base Classes 474
  Implementing the Design 476
    The DisplayObject Class 476
    The Vehicle Class 477
    The Property Class 478
    The Asset and Expense Classes 480
    The Computer and Pencils Classes 481
    The CompanyCar and LeaseCar Classes 482
    The Application 483
  Some Practice 483
  Summary 484

CHAPTER 13: Templates 485
  Class Templates 486
    A Bounded Array Class Template 490
    When to Use Class Templates 493
    A Linked List Template 494
    A Linked List of Integers 501
    A Linked List of Dates 502
    Template Specialization 504
  Function Templates 507
    Sorting with a Template 509
  Summary 512

CHAPTER 14: Exception Handling 513
  Exception Handling in C 514
  Exception Handling in C++ 517
    The try Block 517
    The catch Exception Handler 518
    The throw Statement 519
    The try/throw/catch Sequence 519
    Exception Specification 523
    Unexpected Exceptions 523

Catch-all Exception Handlers 524
Throwing an Exception from a Handler 525
Uncaught Exceptions 527
Selecting among Thrown Exceptions 530
Exceptions and Unreleased Resources 532
An Improved Calculator Program 533
Summary 538

CHAPTER 15: ANSI/ISO Language Innovations 539
Namespaces 540
The namespace Definition 541
Explicit namespace Qualification 542
The using Declaration 542
The using Directive 543
The namespace Alias 543
The Global namespace 544
Unnamed namespace Definitions 545
Namespaces Summarized 545
New-Style Casts 547
dynamic_cast 548
static_cast 552
reinterpret_cast 554
const_cast 555
Runtime Type Information (RTTI) 557
Operator Keywords, Digraphs, and Trigraphs 559
Summary 562

CHAPTER 16: The Standard C++ Library 563
The string Class 564
Constructing Strings 565
Assigning Strings 565
Concatenating Strings 565
Subscripting Strings 566
Comparing Strings 566
Substrings 566
Searching Strings 567
String Operations 567
Input/Output Streams 568
Stream Classes 569
Buffered Output 571
Formatted Output 571
Output Member Functions 582
Input Member Functions 583
strstream 601
stringstream 612

The complex Class 615
The Standard Template Library 616
   STL Rationale 617
   Sequences 618
   Container Adapters 619
   Associative Containers 620
   Iterators 621
   Algorithms 622
   Predicates 625
   STL Summarized 630
Standard Exceptions 631
Summary 635

CHAPTER 17: Object-Oriented Programming **637**
The Basics 638
Procedural Programming 639
Object-Oriented Programming 640
   The Object-Oriented Program 640
   The Object 642
   Abstraction 642
   Encapsulation 644
   Methods and Messages 645
   Inheritance 649
   Class Relationships 650
   Polymorphism 651
Summary 652

APPENDIX A: Using Quincy 97 . . . .**653**
GLOSSARY **681**
BIBLIOGRAPHY **705**
INDEX **707**

Preface

This book is the fifth edition of *teach yourself C++*, a tutorial text with which programmers teach themselves C++. I wrote the first edition in 1990; subsequent editions came out in 1991, 1993, and 1995. Significant changes in the C++ language have influenced each edition. So has my own increased understanding of the language through programming and teaching C++.

The ANSI/ISO C++ Standardization Committee is close to approving a standard definition of C++. Most of the language and class library additions and changes defined in the current draft standard have been implemented in PC compilers. Those implementations represent the contemporary C++ language, which is available for use by programmers and which will undoubtedly become the approved standard language. That is the language taught in this book.

Readers of earlier editions of *teach yourself C++* will observe that the book gets bigger with each new edition. This growth reflects the growth in the language. C++ is a much larger language than it was when I wrote the first edition. As a result there are more things to learn, and this book adds chapters to cover new subjects.

NOT A C PROGRAMMER?

This edition of *teach yourself C++* does not assume that you already know C. I have included heavily updated and reorganized selections from an earlier book, *Al Stevens Teaches C*, so that this book stands alone as a complete tutorial in the C++ language.

Most books on C++ published in the past several years have assumed that the reader already knows C. But by now, most C programmers have learned C++. The principal audience for this book is, therefore, the programmer who knows neither language and wants to learn C++.

According to conventional wisdom, we should learn C first and then learn C++. That advice turns out not to be so wise after all. It is better to avoid learning the "C style" of programming lest we start out with a few unnecessary and unhealthy biases. If you do not already know C, you should wade right into C++, according to more current conventional wisdom. I decided, therefore, to turn this work into a full treatment of C++ aimed at those who understand programming but not necessarily any particular programming language. Of course, C programmers who want to learn C++ can use this book, too.

ALREADY A C PROGRAMMER?

It might seem to C programmers that Chapters 2 through 7 are mostly about the C language component that is built into C++. A C programmer might be tempted to skim these chapters, but I recommend that you read them carefully. Chapter 2, for example, provides an introduction to the C++ console input/output *iostream* objects, which C++ programmers use instead of the *getchar, putchar, gets, puts, printf,* and *scanf* family of Standard C functions. Also watch for subtle differences in other parts of the C++ language scattered throughout the text in these chapters. For example, the behavior of the C++ *goto* statement described in Chapter 3 is different from that of the C *goto*; a void pointer in C++ cannot be assigned to a pointer to a type without a cast; the *main* function cannot be called recursively in a C++ program; you must initialize a *const* object; variables cannot be implicitly declared as *int*; an enumerator is a type and not an *int*; and so on. I do not always highlight these differences. Instead, I tend to treat C++ as a completely new subject, so you should not depend on your C knowledge to let you neglect the lessons that the first seven chapters teach.

EXERCISES AND PROBLEMS

Beginning in Chapter 1, *teach yourself* C++ leads you through the C++ learning process with a series of exercises. Each exercise includes C++ source code that you can compile and execute. To get the maximum benefit from these lessons, you should load, compile, and run the exercises as you go along.

The exercises lead you through the subjects in a sequence that introduces simpler concepts first, using them in successive exercises as more complex subjects are developed. The exercises build upon preceding ones. Therefore, you should follow the exercises in the order in which they appear.

The exercise programs are small. They are not full-blown, useful programs that you take into the workplace, nor are they intended to be. Each exercise demonstrates a particular feature of C++. The exercises are complete programs in that they compile and link independently. Some programs combine code from several exercises. In these cases, the dependent code always follows closely behind the code it needs.

COMPILER INCLUDED

The CD-ROM in the back cover sleeve includes Quincy 97, a Windows 95-hosted C++ compiler system that you can use to compile and run the exercises. Quincy 97 leads you through the exercises by having you select from a list that corresponds with the exercise numbers and titles that appear in the book.

AN APPROACH TO TEACHING AND LEARNING

A complex subject such as a programming language often sends you into a learning loop. You cannot learn a lesson without knowing about a prerequisite lesson, which has some other prerequisite lesson, which in turn has the new lesson as a prerequisite. A case in point is the C++ *iostream* classes, which define objects that read from and write to the console. To understand them thoroughly, you must understand C++ classes and overloaded operators, both of which are advanced C++ topics. Yet to progress to those advanced topics, you must run exercises that use the keyboard and screen devices, which are implemented by the *iostream* family of classes. You must use the system-defined *cin* and *cout* objects with an unquestioning faith that what they do and how they do it will eventually make sense.

Because of this circular approach, a programmer who is already well versed in C++ might wonder about the organization of this book. Some exercises do not include code constructs that a seasoned C++ programmer would recognize as conventional, appropriate, or even necessary. These omissions are intentional and result from the learning sequence of *teach yourself C++*. Eventually the book covers those bases. Other omissions are due to the highly advanced nature of C++ and the kind of strange and exotic code that it permits. There are elements in C++ that a tutorial work should spare the newcomer. Later, when you have the language well in hand, you can study advanced books and push C++ to its limits.

Trust the book and be patient—everything eventually becomes clear. You will see many forward references to chapters when topics are mentioned that you haven't yet learned. If a discussion is unclear, make a note to yourself to return to the discussion after you've read more about the topic in the referenced chapter.

THE ORGANIZATION OF THIS BOOK

Chapter 1 introduces you to programming in C++. It explains what you should already know and what you need in order to use the exercises on the CD-ROM. The chapter includes a brief history of C++ and an overview of the C++ programming language with an introduction to the *main* function, the entry point of every C++ program.

Chapter 2 is where you begin writing programs. I teach you more about the *main* function, how to put comments in your code, how to include the header files of the standard libraries, and how to perform simple console output to view the results of your programs. You learn about C++ expressions and assignment statements. You learn how to read data from the keyboard and display information on the screen.

Chapter 3 is about functions. I show you how C++ programs declare, define, and call functions, passing parameter arguments and getting return values. You learn how C++ functions are arranged into nested blocks of code. You learn how to link C++ program modules with modules written in other languages, such as C.

Chapter 4 is about program flow control. You learn the *if...else, do, while, for, goto, switch, break, continue*, and *return* operators.

Chapter 5 teaches C++ data types, including characters, integers, and floating-point numbers. You learn how to use constants and pointers in your programs. You learn about the scope of variables. You see how to arrange data types into aggregates called *arrays, structures*, and *unions* and how to define new data type identifiers with the *typedef* operator. You learn about recursion and C++ reference variables.

Chapter 6 discusses some of the Standard C library functions. You learn how to use header files for the standard functions that your programs call. You learn about string functions, memory allocation functions, math functions, and others.

Chapter 7 is about the C++ preprocessor, which allows you to define macros and write compile-time conditional expressions that control how a program compiles.

Chapter 8 introduces the class mechanism by expanding on what you can do with the *struct*. You learn about the data abstraction properties of intrinsic and user-defined types, data members and member functions, and access specifiers.

Chapter 9 expands the discussion of classes by introducing constructors, destructors, conversion functions, assignment functions, arrays of class objects, and class object memory allocation.

Chapter 10 is about overloaded operators, a feature that assigns behavior to class objects to mimic the behavior of intrinsic data types when used in expressions that include arithmetic, relational, and other operators.

Chapter 11 is about class inheritance, which allows you to build object-oriented class hierarchies consisting of base and derived classes. You learn about the object-oriented property called *polymorphism.*

Chapter 12 is about *multiple inheritance,* a language feature that allows derived classes to inherit the properties of multiple base classes.

Chapter 13 is about templates, the C++ feature that allows you to build generic parameterized data types.

Chapter 14 is about exception handling, which allows a program to throw and catch exceptions in an orderly fashion.

Chapter 15 is about namespaces, casts, and runtime type information.

Chapter 16 is about the Standard C++ Library. You extend your knowledge of the *iostream* console input/output classes and learn how to read and write disk files. You learn about the standard *string* and *complex* classes and the set of container classes that is referred to as the Standard Template Library.

Chapter 17 describes object-oriented programming, relating what you know about the syntax and behavior of C++ classes to the object-oriented programming model.

The Appendix describes how to install and use Quincy 97.

The Glossary defines some common C++ programming terms. If I use a term in the book that you do not know, try looking in the glossary to see whether I've defined the term there.

The Bibliography lists books that you can read to further your C++ language education.

Al Stevens

astevens@ddj.com

Spring 1997

CHAPTER 1

An Introduction to Programming in C++

The C and C++ programming languages are, between them, older than many of their practitioners. C was originally developed in the early 1970s, and C++ saw first light in 1980. In the time since, C and C++ have evolved from a small tool that a programmer in a research laboratory built for himself and some colleagues into the worldwide object-oriented language of choice for several generations of programmers. C++ now has a published proposed standard definition; the C standard has been formal for several years; the proposed C++ standard definition is close to being approved. There are C++ compilers for virtually every computer and operating system, and C++ now enjoys the distinction of being the language with which most contemporary mini- and microcomputer applications are written. In this chapter you will learn:

1

- What you should have and what you should know to use this book
- A brief history of C and C++
- An introduction to the C++ language
- Writing the *main* function

WHO ARE YOU?

To understand this book, you should have some background in computer programming. You need not be a seasoned programmer, but you should know what programming is and how programmers write code that compilers compile and computers execute. You should understand typical programming issues such as expressions, operators, precedence, data types, constants, recursion, data files, and console input/output. You should be familiar with the different base notations—decimal, octal, hexadecimal, and binary—for representing numbers in a computer. You should be familiar with the common character sets used in computer programming, such as ASCII, EBCDIC, and UNICODE. Anyone with a knowledge of BASIC, FORTRAN, COBOL, Pascal, or any structured, procedural programming language should have no trouble following the lessons in this book.

If you do not have such a programming background, you can begin with my earlier book *Welcome to Programming*, published by MIS:Press. It uses the QBasic language to teach the fundamentals of programming. A student can move from that book to this one to learn C++ programming.

Unlike many C++ tutorial books (and the four previous editions of this one), *teach yourself C++ 5th Edition* does not assume that you already know the C programming language.

WHAT DO YOU NEED?

The companion CD-ROM (in a pocket on the inside back cover) and a Windows 95 PC are all that you need. The CD-ROM contains the source code for the exercises. Unlike most C++ books, which require the reader to provide a compiler, this one includes Quincy 97, a C++ compiler system that you can use to run the exercises and write your own C++ programs. Quincy's tutorial mode goes hand-in-hand with the tutorial exercises in the book. As you read the book, you can load the exercises, run them, change them, and see how the

C++ language behaves. The tutorial keeps track of your progress and always takes up where you left off.

Quincy 97 is a Windows 95-hosted integrated development environment (IDE) that uses the gnu-win32 port of the GNU C and C++ compilers, which implement all of Standard C and most of Standard C++. The Appendix to this book provides a complete user's guide for Quincy 97.

The C++ language is evolving, and the GNU C++ compiler does not yet implement all the newer C++ features, although it supports most of them. I have compiled and tested the exercises that demonstrate the non-GNU features with other compilers; the constantly changing state of commercial compilers—in view of the changing and emerging standard—does not ensure, however, that these tests will be valid in the future. They represent the language as we understand it today, in the first months of 1997.

If you do not use Windows 95 or prefer to use a different Standard C++ compiler, you can compile and run all the exercises with the compiler of your choice.

A BRIEF HISTORY OF C AND C++

In the early 1970s, Dennis Ritchie, a programmer at AT&T Bell Laboratories in Murray Hill, New Jersey, adapted BCPL—a *typeless* programming language with control structures similar to those in ALGOL—into the first version of what he named C. Ritchie's goal was to provide a language that would allow the programmer to access the hardware much as assembly language did, but with structured programming constructs similar to those found in high-level languages. He included integer and pointer data types that mapped directly over the hardware registers of the PDP-11 minicomputer, and he took advantage of the PDP-11's hardware stack architecture to support local variables and recursive functions.

C, as originally designed, ran on the AT&T in-house Unix multiuser, multitasking operating system, which ran first on the PDP-7 and then on the PDP-11. When Ritchie rewrote the Unix C compiler in C itself and when Unix developer Ken Thompson successfully rewrote Unix in C, they made programming history. Unix became the first major operating system to be written in something other than assembly language. When they ported the C compiler to other computers, the developers turned Unix into the first operating system able to run on many different platforms, a truly portable operating system. Porting Unix became a matter of porting the C compiler, rewriting a few assembly language operating system driver programs and interface functions, and recompiling the operating system itself. These achievements distinguished C as a unique language, one that could be used to write systems programs—previously the exclusive domain of assembly language—and one that could be used to write portable programs, a goal never achieved by the high-level languages that came before it.

For years, C existed mainly in Unix systems, and Unix remained an internal AT&T operating system. Eventually, AT&T made Unix available to universities at virtually no cost, and a generation of students was exposed to Unix and C. Those students left school and entered the field of programming with experience in and a love for Unix and C. This influence eventually found its way into corporate America, and C began to enjoy mainstream support in circles previously dominated by COBOL at the top and assembly language at the bottom.

Although C's origins are in the research labs of big business and academia, its widespread acceptance outside those walls was ensured when developers provided C compilers for the first personal computers. Early microcomputers ran on the 8080 and Z80 microprocessors under the CP/M operating system. At first, BASIC was the dominant programming language, with assembly language running a close second. Eventually, however, vendors published C compilers for those microcomputers, and programmers of the so-called home computers began making the switch. The IBM PC, introduced in 1981, and the clones that followed continued this trend. C rapidly became most programmers' favorite language for writing programs under MS-DOS. At one time more than a dozen C compilers were available for the PC. Most of the applications and systems software for the PC are written in C and C++. MS-DOS itself consists of C programs, as do most of its utility programs. The Windows 3.x graphical operating environment was written in C. Windows 95 and Windows NT are written mostly in C.

C was originally defined in 1981 in *The C Programming Language* (Prentice Hall), by Brian Kernighan and Dennis Ritchie. The book was not a formal language specification, but it described C the way Ritchie had implemented it. The book became known simply as K&R, for the initials of its authors, and the dialect of C that it described was, for many years, called K&R C. Some programmers now refer to K&R C as "Classic C." Over the years, compiler builders added features to C according to the requirements of their users. As the industry accepted the best of those extensions, a newer dialect came into being and a de facto standard evolved.

In 1983, the American National Standards Institute (ANSI) formed a committee whose task it was to define a standard definition of the C language based on the industry's de facto standard. It was joined by a committee of the International Standards Organization (ISO), which formed to define the language for the international programming community. Its charter was to codify the language as it existed without inventing new features. The combined committees published a standard document in 1990. The language that they defined is known as Standard C. A second edition of the K&R book describes Standard C, obscuring somewhat the identity of K&R C.

The C++ programming language was designed and developed by Bjarne Stroustrup, also at AT&T Bell Labs. He began this work in about 1980 to answer a need for a simulation language with the features of object-oriented programming, then a relatively new programming paradigm. Rather than design a language from the ground up, Dr. Stroustrup decided to build upon the C language.

C was already implemented on several architectures and supported portable program development, so Dr. Stroustrup made an historic decision: He elected to develop the C++ language system as a translator program that processes C++ source language into C source language. The translated C source language could then be compiled on any computer system that supports C. He called his translator program cfront, and many implementations of C++ have been ports of that same cfront program and its successors, the source code of which is available to language system developers under license from AT&T. The C++ language has been available outside AT&T since about 1985.

Over the years, C++ has continued through several versions. Dr. Stroustrup remains its staunchest advocate and is a strong contributing presence wherever C++ issues surface. A joint ANSI/ISO committee—designated X3J16 within ANSI and WG21 within ISO—was formed in 1989 to tackle the formidable task of defining a standard for C++. Eight years later that effort continues. In February 1994 the committee published its first working paper of a draft standard for informal public review. Several drafts have followed, and the work is almost complete.

C++, like C before it, has become the language of choice among programmers. Since the first edition of this book came out, C++ language systems have appeared in every environment and on most architectures where C once reigned supreme.

C's Continuing Role

You might wonder about C's future given the current popularity of C++ and object-oriented programming. Has C++ displaced C as the language of choice? For the most part, yes. Does that spell the demise of C as a viable programming language? Definitely not. Few good programming languages are ever completely killed off. There are almost always development circumstances in which they excel, and usually there are existing programs to maintain.

C is more suitable than C++ for solving some programming problems. Many staunch C++ advocates might not agree with this opinion, but it is widely held by others. C++ software development environments are typically big. They use lots of disk space and require large, fast computers. These requirements grow with each new version of the language and each new release of the compilers. Many C++ compilers are oriented toward development under graphical user interface environments such as Windows 95. Unless the development environment includes cross-platform targets, such compilers are not well suited for developing small programs to run on small systems. Object-oriented programs that use complex class hierarchies can compile large executable modules that do not run as efficiently as their C language procedural counterparts. C, which is a traditional procedural programming language, is sometimes a better choice for writing low-level device drivers and embedded applications.

The Windows 95 operating system is written almost entirely in C, even though its developer, Microsoft, also developed and aggressively markets a Visual C++ compiler product. I question, however, whether that apparent anomaly reflects an immature C++ mentality among Microsoft's operating system developers and the company's desire to leverage existing operating system code rather than the relative suitability of the two languages for writing operating systems. If one were to undertake the development from scratch of a new operating system today, the language of choice would probably be C++.

C VERSUS C++

C++ is a superset of C. We could say that C is a subset of C++, but C came first. As a general rule, a C++ compiler should be able to compile any C program. There are, however, small differences between C programs and C++ programs, differences that reveal subtle incompatibilities between the two languages.

For example, the C++ language adds keywords that are not reserved by the C language. Those keywords can legitimately be used in a C program as identifiers for functions and variables. Although C++ is said to include all of C, clearly no C++ compiler can compile such a C program.

C programmers can omit function prototypes. C++ programmers cannot. A C function prototype with no parameters must include the keyword *void* in the parameter list. A C++ prototype can use an empty parameter list. You learn about function prototypes in Chapter 3.

Many Standard C functions have counterparts in C++, and C++ programmers view them as improvements to the C language. Here are some examples:

- The C++ *new* and *delete* memory allocation operators (Chapter 5) replace Standard C's *malloc* and *free* functions.
- The Standard C++ *string* class (Chapter 16) replaces the character array processing functions declared in the Standard C library's **<cstring>** header file.
- The C++ *iostream* class library (Chapter 16) replaces Standard C's *stdio* function library for console input and output.
- C++'s try/catch/throw exception handling mechanism (Chapter 14) replaces Standard C's setjmp/longjmp functions.

The exercises in this book are C++ programs, and most of them can be compiled by any Standard C++ compiler. Except where it is necessary to make a particular point, I always use C++ idioms rather than their C counterparts. If you want a more comprehensive treatment of the C language without the C++ influence, I recommend *Al Stevens Teaches C* (MIS:Press, 1994).

A Brief Description of C++

This introduction describes C++ at the most elementary level, but don't expect to understand everything you read here right away. You will learn more about each of these concepts by studying the exercises in the chapters that follow. As you proceed through the lessons, return to this synopsis and see how it begins to fall into place.

C++ is a *procedural* programming language with *object-oriented* extensions. This means that you can design and code programs as procedural modules, and you can define and instantiate *objects*. The procedural modules in a C program are called *functions*. Object declarations are called *classes*.

Every C++ program begins execution in a function named *main* and terminates when the *main* function returns. The next section, "The *main* Function," explains the *main* function in more detail. The *main* function calls lower-level functions, which in turn call lower-level functions. A function starts execution at its first, topmost statement and continues until the last, bottommost statement executes or until the function executes a *return* statement from inside the function body. Each function, upon completion, returns to its caller. Execution then continues with the next program statement in the caller function.

You read a C++ program from the top to the bottom, but the functions do not have to be coded in that sequence. However, all declarations of functions and variables must be coded in the program above any statements that reference them. You can declare a function by providing a *function prototype* that describes its name, return value, and parameters to the compiler. You must provide a function's prototype ahead of any calls to the function; you can put the function itself anywhere in the program. The function's declaration and all calls to it must match the prototype with respect to its return type and the types of its parameters.

Functions may contain *parameters*. The caller of the function passes *arguments* that the function uses as the values for its parameters. The argument types must match or be compatible—with respect to type conversion—with the types of the parameters declared for the function.

Some functions return a value and others do not. The caller of a function that returns a value can code the function call on the right side of an *assignment* statement, assigning the returned value to a named data variable. You can also code a function call as the argument that provides the parameter value to another function call, as an *initializer* to a local data variable, or as an element in an *expression*.

Each function consists of one or more *blocks* of statements. The blocks are nested. Each block can have its own local variables, which remain in scope as long as statements in that block are executing. A C program can also have variables declared outside any function. Those variables are said to have *global* scope, because the statements in all the functions in the same source file can reference them.

Statements are one of the following: declarations, which declare *variables* and functions; definitions, which define instances of variables and functions; or procedural statements, which are executable code statements that reside inside a function's definition.

A variable *declaration* specifies the variable's storage class, data type, type qualifier, level of indirection (if it is a pointer), name, and dimensions (if it is an array). A function declaration, more frequently called its prototype, declares the function's return type, name, and the number and types of its arguments.

A variable *definition* includes the components of a declaration and may include an initializer if the variable has an initializing value. A definition defines the instance of the variable and reserves memory for it. A function definition contains the function's executable code.

Usually, a variable's declaration and definition are the same statement. A function's prototype and definition are usually in different places. If the function's definition appears in the source code file ahead of all calls to the function, however, the function's definition may also serve as its prototype.

Procedural statements are either assignments, expressions, or *program flow control* statements. An expression is a program statement that returns a value. An expression can stand on its own or be on the right side of an assignment statement. Expressions consist of variables, constants, operators, and function calls. Paradoxically, assignments are themselves expressions.

C++ uses the control structures of structured programming, which include *sequence* (one statement executing after another), *iteration* (*for* and *while* loops), and *selection* (*if-then-else* and *switch-case* control structures). C++ also permits unstructured programming with the *goto* statement.

Classes are aggregate definitions that consist of data members and member functions. A class encapsulates the *implementation* and *interface* of a user-defined data type and constitutes an *abstract data type.*

The class's implementation—its aggregate private members—is usually hidden from the class user (the programmer who instantiates objects of the class). The class's public interface is usually revealed to the class user in the form of *methods*: class member functions that operate on the data members of the class.

The class user instantiates objects of the class and invokes the class methods against that object by calling the class's member functions for the object.

A class is said to have *behavior*, which is another way of saying that an object of the class responds to its methods in ways that are understood by the class user at an abstract level without necessarily revealing the details of that behavior.

C++ supports *exception handling*, which permits a program to make an orderly jump to a defined location higher in the program's executing hierarchy.

C++ supports *parameterized types* or *genericity* through its *template* mechanism, a device that lets you define and instantiate objects of generic data types.

Like most contemporary compiled programming languages, C++ programs consist of multiple source code modules that are compiled into object code modules, which are then linked into a single executable program module. Much of the object code in a typical C++ program comes from packaged libraries of previously compiled, reusable software components implemented as classes or functions.

A C++ source-code module is a text file (usually ASCII) that you can read and modify with any text editor, such as Windows 95's Notepad applet. The Quincy compiler included on the CD-ROM that accompanies this book integrates a programmer's editor with the compiler. It also includes an integrated source-code debugger similar to those you see in larger C++ development platforms.

Unlike languages such as COBOL, BASIC, and FORTRAN, C++ has no built-in input/output statements. Instead, input and output are implemented by C++ classes in standard class libraries. Many such language features that are intrinsic parts of other languages are performed instead by classes in C++. Data conversions, string manipulations, and output formatting are three examples of operations that C++ supports with classes and functions taken from standard libraries rather than with intrinsic language features. C++ is a small language capable only of declaring and defining variables, assigning expressions to variables, and calling functions—only one of which, *main*, is defined as a part of the language proper. C++'s power comes in the way that it is extended with functions and classes. Standard C++ defines the format and behavior of a standard set of classes and functions in a standard suite of class and function libraries. User-defined classes and functions further extend the language to support specific problem domains.

THE *main* FUNCTION

Every C++ program has a function named *main*. It provides the entry and exit points of the program. Exercise 1.1 represents the minimum C++ program.

Exercise 1.1 *The minimum C++ program.*

```
int main()
{
    return 0;
}
```

This is a good time to turn to the Appendix and learn how to use Quincy to run the tutorial exercises. You can compile and run Exercise 1.1 if you want to, but it does nothing except return to the operating system.

N O T E

Exercise 1.1 declares and defines the *main* function. That's all the program does. The program begins executing with the first statement in *main* and terminates when the *main* function returns.

The minimum C++ program is also the minimum C program. Both languages require that a program have, at a minimum, a *main* function.

N O T E

The *main* function in Exercise 1.1 illustrates several things about C++ functions in general. The first line provides the function's return type and identifier. The *main* function returns an integer value and always has the identifier *main.* The *int* keyword specifies the function's integer return type. You learn about integers and other data types in Chapter 2.

The parentheses after the function's name contain the function's *parameter list.* In this case, *main* has no parameters, so the parameter list is empty. An empty parameter list is represented by the ( ) character sequence.

The *function body* follows the parameter list. The function body begins with a left brace character ({) and ends with a right brace character (}). In between are the function's statements, the lines of code that execute when the function is called. Exercise 1.1 has only one statement: the *return* statement that terminates the *main* function and, consequently, the program.

Observe the semicolon at the end of the *return* statement. Every C++ statement is terminated with a semicolon.

A brace-surrounded group of statements is called a statement block. Statement blocks may be nested. You see how this nesting contributes to program flow control in Chapter 4. Every function has at least one statement block; Exercise 1.1's *main* function has only one statement block.

A function finishes executing immediately after its last statement executes or when the *return* statement executes. Exercise 1.1's *main* function terminates when its *return* statement returns the integer constant 0. The *return* statement can be positioned anywhere inside the function.

The operating system calls *main,* and *main* returns to the operating system. Well, not really, but for beginning C++ programmers, that explanation suffices to describe *main*'s behavior. Later, when you study the execution of class constructor and destructor functions for external objects, you will learn how you can write code that executes before *main* starts and after it returns. But, for now, think of *main* as the entry and departure points of your program. Remember, too, that no other place in your program is allowed to call the *main* function.

SUMMARY

This chapter got you started toward your goal of teaching yourself the C++ programming language. You learned what you need in the way of hardware and prior knowledge to use this book. You gained an initial insight into the fundamentals of the C++ language. Finally, you saw what the minimum C++ program looks like. Chapter 2 continues this course by showing you how to get simple C++ programs compiled and running.

CHAPTER 2

Writing Simple C++ Programs

This chapter is your starting point for learning C++. We jump the first hurdle—writing the first real program. Then I introduce the data components of a C program: variables and constants. Use the exercises in this chapter to learn these basic lessons:

- Identifiers
- Keywords
- Comments
- Data types
- Expressions
- Assignments
- Initializers
- Console input and output

YOUR FIRST PROGRAM

Exercise 1.1 in Chapter 1 is a program, to be sure, but it does nothing except demonstrate the *main* function. For a program to have any consequence, it must do something meaningful from within that *main* function. That's our starting place in learning C++.

C++ programs consist of variables and functions. A function consists of variable declarations and executable statements organized into nested statement blocks. As Exercise 1.1 demonstrated, every C++ program begins with a function named *main*. The best way to get started is with a real program. Exercise 2.1 is your first C++ program, one that has a *main* function and several other fundamental C++ language constructs.

Exercise 2.1 Your first C++ program.

```
1: #include <iostream>
2: using namespace std;
3:
4: int main()
5: {
6:   cout << "My first C++ program"; // write to the screen
7:   return 0;
8: }
```

Exercise 2.1 is a tiny program that illustrates a lot of what a C++ programmer uses. It has some source-code comments, includes a standard library header file, and, from its *main* function, writes a message on the screen.

NOTE   If you are a C programmer and if, like most C programmers, you have read Kernighan and Ritchie's *The C Programming Language*, compare Exercise 2.1 to the famous "hello world" example, which is the first C program presented in that book.

Exercise 2.1 displays a message on the screen and returns to the operating system. It does all that with only eight lines of code in a source-code file. Let's examine Exercise 2.1 one line at a time.

The line numbers shown in Exercise 2.1's listing are to facilitate this discussion. They do not appear in the actual source code.

Line 1: The *#include* Directive

The first line of code in Exercise 2.1 is the *#include <iostream>* statement. This statement is a *preprocessing directive*. We'll discuss the preprocessor in more detail in Chapter 7. The *#include* directive tells the compiler to include a different source-code file in the program. Exercise 2.1 includes the file named **<iostream>**, a standard library header file that describes classes, functions, and global values used for console input and output. The exercise includes the header file so that it can use the *cout* object. Most exercises in this book include **<iostream>**, and that is why I mention it here. Do not worry about what else is in the header file just yet. It all becomes clear soon enough.

The file name in the *#include* directive is enclosed by *angle brackets*, another name for the combined use of the less-than and greater-than symbols. This usage identifies header files that the compiler system supplies. When you include your own header files, you surround those names with double quotes. Chapter 7 has more details about this usage.

Line 2: The *using namespace* Directive

The second line of code in Exercise 2.1 specifies that the program will be using identifiers that are declared to be part of the Standard C++ *std* namespace. (We'll discuss C++ identifiers later in this chapter.) The *cout* object, mentioned earlier, is declared in Standard C++ to be within the *std* namespace. By including the *using* directive at the top of the program, Exercise 2.1 avoids having to qualify every reference to every function and object that is declared within the *std* namespace with the *std* name. Without the *using* directive, the program would need to reference *cout* and any other identifiers declared in **<iostream>** and other standard library header files this way:

```
std::cout << "My first C++ program";
```

Most C++ programs have at least two namespaces: the *global* namespace, which has no name and requires no qualification; and the *std* namespace, which contains all the classes, objects, and functions from the Standard C and C++ libraries. By including the *using* directive in your programs as Exercise 2.1 does, you can ignore the namespace issue for now and treat all program components as if they are in the global namespace.

If all this seems confusing, don't worry. Chapter 15 discusses the C++ namespace feature in detail. For now, accept the usage shown in Exercise 2.1. Most of the examples will employ that usage.

NOTE

The GNU compiler that Quincy uses does not fully implement the Standard C++ namespace feature. That feature, an invention of the ANSI C++ X3J16 standardization committee, is relatively new to the language. The exercise programs would, in fact, compile and run correctly under Quincy without the *using* directive or the *std::* qualification, but that usage would not reflect Standard C++. Most commercial compilers have implemented the namespace feature by now, and I expect the next major release of the GNU compiler to support it, too. Wherever possible, this book strives to demonstrate how programs should look when Standard C++ is fully implemented.

Line 3: White Space

The third line in Exercise 2.1 is a blank line. The C++ language is a free-form language, and this means that white space characters—newlines, spaces, tabs, and blank lines—are extra. Except for the rare occasion when two keywords or identifiers are separated by a space (such as *else if*) or inside string constants (described later), a program needs no white space at all to compile. Without white space, however, most programs would be hard to read. Here is what Exercise 2.1 would look like without white space:

```
#include <iostream>using namespace std;int main(){
cout<<"My first C++ program";return 0;}
```

Programmers use white space to indent and separate code in various styles to make their programs legible. There are many styles for writing C++ code. I take no position with regard to style, although the exercises reflect my preferences. You will see other styles that use different conventions for indenting and the placement of brace characters, but there is no one right way. Choose a style that works for you, make it legible, and be consistent in its use.

Line 4: The *main* Function Declaration

Line 4 in Exercise 2.1 declares the *main* function as a function that returns an integer (*int*) value and that accepts no arguments. Chapter 3 discusses function declarations in more detail.

Line 5: The *main* Function's Statement Block

Line 5 consists of a single left brace ({) character to define the start of *main*'s outermost (and only, in this example) statement block. The statement block continues until the matching right brace (}) character is found (on line 8, in Exercise 2.1).

Line 6: Writing to the Console

Line 6 is the most complicated line in the program. Its cryptic code tells the compiler to display a string constant on the screen. I'll discuss all these things later in this and subsequent chapters.

Line 6: Source-Code Comments

Line 6 also contains a program *comment* in this format:

```
// write to the screen
```

Comments in a program's source-code document the meaning of the code. They have no effect on the executable program itself. C++ comments begin with the characters // and continue to the end of the source-code line.

C++ also supports the traditional C comment format. C comments begin with the /* character sequence and continue through the */ character sequence like this:

```
/* write to the screen */
```

C comments may span several source-code lines and may not be nested. They may occupy lines of their own, or they may appear on lines that have other code.

C++'s // comments may not span source-code lines, because there is no comment termination code like the C */ token. This book uses C++'s // comment format exclusively except in the rare C source-code module that contributes to a C++ program.

Use comments throughout your programs. Make them meaningful with respect to what they convey to programmers who might be reading your code. Do not make the two common mistakes that many programmers make: assuming that you will be the only programmer who reads your code and assuming that you will always remember why you wrote a program a certain way. Comments document your intentions. Use them.

Line 7: The *return* Statement

Line 7 is the statement that tells the *main* function to terminate processing and return a constant integer zero value to the operating system. Chapter 3 addresses the return statement in more detail. Constant expressions are discussed later in this chapter.

Line 8: Terminating the Statement Block

Line 8 contains the right brace (}) character that defines the end of the *main* function's statement block.

VARIATIONS ON *main*

Two alternative *main* declarations are widely used even though their propriety is questionable. I mention them here because you are bound to encounter them in programs and in other C++ books.

First, most C and C++ compilers permit you to declare *main* with a *void* return type. This means that the function returns nothing, and it allows you to either omit the *return* statement or provide a *return* statement with no return expression, such as this variation on Exercise 1.1 from Chapter 1. (Chapter 3 explains *void* functions in more detail.)

```
void main()
{
}
```

Apparently the ANSI standard permits this usage. It first states that *main*'s type is "implementation-defined" but then specifies that all implementations must support the declaration of a *main* function that returns an *int* value. This seeming contradiction is not contradictory after all. Compilers *must* support *main* returning int. Compilers *may* support any other return type for main.

Next, all compilers allow you to omit the function's return type. According to C++ language rules, this practice implies that the function returns an *int.* That usage by itself is acceptable, but some compilers allow you to return no value from such an implied *int main* as if it were *void,* as this variation shows:

```
main()
{
}
```

This usage, although widely supported, is clearly nonstandard. It allows a function declared as returning *int* to return without specifying a return value.

Neither of the usages described in the preceding two code fragments is portable in that compilers are not required to support them. The exercises in this book do not use them.

IDENTIFIERS

A C++ program consists of many things—variables, functions, classes, and so on—all of which have names. The name of a function, variable, or class is called its *identifier.* As the programmer, you assign identifiers to the parts of your program. Other identifiers are assigned in the Standard C and C++ libraries. Following are the rules for identifiers in the C++ language.

- An identifier consists of letters, digits, and the underscore character.
- An identifier must begin with a letter. (Underscores are allowed in the first character, but, by convention, leading underscores are reserved for identifiers that the compiler defines.)
- Identifiers are case-sensitive. For example, *MyFunc* and *myfunc* are different identifiers.

- An identifier may be any length, but only the first 32 characters are significant. Some early C implementations restricted the significance of external identifiers (ones with global scope) to six characters. This was because of limitations in the particular linker program and not because of any limitation in the C language.

- An identifier may not be one of the reserved C++ keywords, listed next.

KEYWORDS

A number of keywords are reserved by the C++ language. You must not use any of these keywords as identifiers in your program. I'll show you how to use each of them as the chapters and exercises progress.

Table 2.1 lists the Standard C++ keywords.

Table 2.1 Standard C++ Keywords

asm	do	inline	short	typeid
auto	double	int	signed	typename
bool	dynamic_cast	long	sizeof	union
break	else	mutable	static	unsigned
case	enum	namespace	static_cast	using
catch	explicit	new	struct	virtual
char	extern	operator	switch	void
class	false	private	template	volatile
const	float	protected	this	wchar_t
const_cast	for	public	throw	while
continue	friend	register	true	
default	goto	reinterpret_cast	try	
delete	if	return	typedef	

C++ includes other keywords that also cannot be used as identifiers. These keywords—alternatives to the Standard C trigraphs—are designed for international keyboards that do not have the special characters used in English to express some operators. The Committee added these keywords so that international programs would be more readable. This book does not use these keywords in any exercises. Table 2.2 lists them so that you know to avoid using them as identifiers.

Table 2.2 International C++ Keywords

and	bitor	or	xor_e
and_eq	compl	or_eq	not_eq
bitand	not	xor	

THE STANDARD OUTPUT STREAM

The *cout* variable, seen in Exercise 2.1, is the C++ standard output stream object, which writes to the console:

```
cout << "My first C++ program";
```

The string to be written is specified in the *string constant*, which is the character sequence between the double quotes. Just as a BASIC programmer knows that the PRINT statement writes data to the screen, a C++ programmer knows that the standard *cout* object does somewhat the same thing. The important difference is that PRINT is part of the BASIC language—an intrinsic operator—whereas *cout* happens to be the name that a programmer many years ago gave to the standard output stream object that displays data on the console. It could just as easily have been any other name.

The << operator is, in this context, the output operator. It is called the stream *insertion* operator, because you use it to insert data objects into the output stream. The operator points symbolically from what is being sent to where it is going.

You can think of *cout, cin,* and *cerr* (*cin* and *cerr* are described later in this chapter) as devices. In C++ stream input/output, *cout, cin,* and *cerr* are identifiers that name objects—instances—of classes. In this example, the string is being written to the *cout* object, which displays data on the console. Later in this chapter you will learn how to display other data types.

NOTE   This example is an early experience with C++ classes, the foundation of C++'s data abstraction and object-oriented programming support. A full understanding of the stream classes requires a thorough understanding of classes. For now, however, you need to understand only how a program uses objects of these classes so that you can manage basic console input/output. You learn more about classes beginning in Chapter 8.

VARIABLES

You saw in Exercise 2.1 how a C++ program declares a function—in this case, the *main* function. Programs declare data variables, too. A variable is a storage location that contains a data value. Every variable has a *type*. The type defines the format and behavior of the variable. C++ supports character, integer, and floating-point data types. C++ has six intrinsic data types, also called *built-in* types. They are *bool, char, wchar_t, int, float,* and *double.*

You can extend C++ and define your own types using the *class, struct* and *union* constructs. More about them later.

Each variable declaration in a program provides the variable's type and identifier. Variables can have other properties as well. Integer type specifiers can include *unsigned, long,* or *short* to further define the type. A *double* can also be a *long double,* increasing its precision. You can use the *static, extern, register,* and *auto* storage classes. There are *const* and *volatile* type qualifiers. I teach these things in this and later chapters.

The size of a variable depends on its type. The size of each type depends on the C++ implementation and is usually expressed as the number of bytes an object of the type occupies in memory. The examples in this book use data types with sizes typical of 32-bit C++ compilers for the PC.

Next, you will learn to declare variables of each of the types. Later you will learn how to put those declarations into their proper context in a program.

The *bool* Type

A *bool* variable is a two-state logical type that can contain one of two values: *true* and *false.* If you use a *bool* variable in an arithmetic expression, the *bool* variable contributes the integer value 0 or 1 to the expression depending on whether the variable is *false* or *true,* respectively. If you convert an integer to a *bool,* the *bool* variable becomes *false* if the integer is zero or *true* if the integer is nonzero. Variables of type *bool* are typically used for runtime Boolean indicators and can be used in logical tests to alter program flow. Exercise 2.2 is a small example of how the *bool* type is used.

Exercise 2.2 Using the bool *variable.*

```
#include <iostream>
using namespace std;

int main()
{

    bool senior;            // bool variable
    senior = true;          // set to true

    // --- test the senior variable
    if (senior)
        cout << "Senior citizen rates apply";
    return 0;
}
```

Exercise 2.2 begins by declaring a *bool* variable named *senior*. The program introduces the *assignment* statement, which I address in more detail later in this chapter. An assignment assigns the value of an expression to a variable. The value can be any complex expression that returns a value of a compatible type, but, until you get to that point, the exercises use simple constants; in this case, the constant is the reserved C++ keyword *true*, which, according to the rules of C++ semantics, can be assigned to a *bool* variable. The opposite of *true* is, of course, *false*.

Another new construct that you see in Exercise 2.2 is the C++ *if* statement, which tests the expression in parentheses to see whether it is true. In this case, it is, so the program executes the statement that follows, which displays a message on *cout*. You learn more about program flow control later in this chapter and in Chapter 4.

The *char* Type

A *char* variable contains one character from the computer's character set. Characters in PC implementations of the C++ language are contained in 8-bit bytes using the ASCII character set to represent character values. A program declares a character variable with the *char* type specification:

```
char ch;
```

The declaration just shown declares a variable of type *char* with the identifier *ch*. Once you declare a variable in this manner, the program can reference it in expressions, which are discussed in the next section.

Exercise 2.3 illustrates the use of the *char* variable.

Exercise 2.3 *Using the* char *variable.*

```cpp
#include <iostream>
using namespace std;

int main()
{
    char c;       // char variable
    c = 'b';      // assign 'b' to c
    cout << c;    // display 'b'
    c = 'y';      // assign 'y' to c
    cout << c;    // display 'y'
    c = 'e';      // assign 'e' to c
    cout << c;    // display 'e'
    return 0;
}
```

Exercise 2.3 employs three uses of the standard *cout* object to display a single character to display this message on the screen:

```
bye
```

Exercise 2.3 uses assignment statements to assign values to the *char* variable. The 'b', 'y', and 'e' values are ASCII character constant expressions in the C++ language.

N O T E   If you are guessing that there must be a better way to display the "bye" message, you are right. At the very least you could send a "bye" string constant to *cout* similar to what Exercise 2.1 did. Exercise 2.3, however, contrives to show you how the *char* data type is declared and used.

The *char* data type is, in fact, an integer 8-bit numerical type, and you can use it in numerical expressions just as you use any other integer type. As such, a *char* variable can be signed or unsigned. You declare an *unsigned char* variable this way:

```
unsigned char c;
```

Unless they are *unsigned, char* variables behave like 8-bit signed integers when you use them in arithmetic and comparison operations.

The *wchar_t* Type

C++ includes the *wchar_t* type to accommodate character sets that require more than eight bits. Many foreign language character sets have more than 256 characters and cannot be represented by the *char* data type. The *wchar_t* data type is typically 16 bits wide.

The Standard C++ *iostream* class library includes classes and objects to support wide characters. Exercise 2.4 repeats Exercise 2.3 but with the *wout* object, which is the wide character version of the *cout* object.

Exercise 2.4 Using the wchar_t *variable.*

```
#include <iostream>
using namespace std;

int main()
{
    wchar_t wc;     // wide char variable
    wc = 'b';       // assign 'b' to wc
    wout << wc;     // display 'b'
    wc = 'y';       // assign 'y' to wc
    wout << wc;     // display 'y'
    wc = 'e';       // assign 'e' to wc
    wout << wc;     // display 'e'
    return 0;
}
```

NOTE

The GNU compiler that Quincy uses does not implement *wchar_t* as an intrinsic data type but instead implements it as an integer alias, a convention introduced by Standard C. Consequently, Quincy does not support all the wide character operations that Standard C++ defines. I modified the GNU compiler's libraries to implement a simulation of the *wout* object to enable you to compile and run Exercise 2.4. Beyond this exercise, we won't concern ourselves with wide characters.

The *int* Type

Variables of integral types come in several varieties. The basic integer is a signed quantity, and you declare one with the *int* type specifier:

```
int Counter;
```

An integer can be *signed, unsigned, long, short*, or a plain signed integer such as the one just shown. These declarations show some of the different kinds of integers:

```
long int Amount;              // long integer
long Quantity;                // long integer
signed int Total;             // signed integer
signed Kellie;                // signed integer
unsigned int Offset;          // unsigned integer
unsigned Offset;              // unsigned integer
short SmallAmt;               // short integer
short int Tyler;              // short integer
unsigned short Landon;        // unsigned short integer
unsigned short int Woody;     // unsigned short integer
```

As the examples show, you can omit the *int* keyword when you specify *long, short, signed,* or *unsigned*. With some PC compilers, an *int* without a *long* or *short* type specification is typically 16 bits, although the increasing popularity of 32-bit compilers is changing that. A *long* integer is usually 32 bits. A *short* integer is usually 16 bits. Quincy uses a 16-bit *short* and 32-bit *ints* and *longs*.

The *signed* qualifier is redundant, because the integral types are signed unless you specify the *unsigned* qualifier. C++ includes the *signed* keyword mainly to preserve symmetry in the language specification.

Exercise 2.5 illustrates the use of the *int* data type.

Exercise 2.5 *The* int *data type.*

```
#include <iostream>
using namespace std;

int main()
{
    int Amount;       // an int variable
    Amount = 123;     // assign a value
    cout << Amount;   // display the int
    return 0;
}
```

Exercise 2.5 declares an *int* variable named *Amount*. Next, it assigns an integer constant value to the variable. Then it displays the variable on the console.

When a type has several properties, you can place the type keywords in any sequence. The following declarations are all the same.

```
// ---- 8 ways to declare an unsigned long integer
unsigned long Tyler1;
long unsigned Tyler2;
unsigned long int Tyler3;
unsigned int long Tyler4;
long unsigned int Tyler5;
long int unsigned Tyler6;
int unsigned long Tyler7;
int long unsigned Tyler8;
```

Floating-Point Numbers

C++ supports three kinds of floating-point numbers, which are distinguished by their precision. Following are declaration examples for all three.

```
float Amount;                // single precision
double BigAmount;            // double precision
long double ReallyBigAmount; // long double precision
```

Standard C++ does not specify the range of values that floating-point numbers can contain. These ranges depend on the particular implementation of the C++ language. The standard defines a header file, **<cfloat>**, with global symbols that identify the ranges.

NOTE

Now that you know about the ranges of floating-point numbers, you can forget about them for a while. This book has very little math, using only what we need in Chapter 6 to demonstrate some of the standard math functions. If you are mathematically inclined, you already know about precision, mantissas, exponents, scientific notation, and so on. If not, you can write C++ programs for the rest of your life without having to know any more about math than you do now.

Exercise 2.6 illustrates the declaration and use of the *float* data type.

Exercise 2.6 The float *data type.*

```
#include <iostream>
using namespace std;

int main()
{
    float realValue;      // a float variable
    realValue = 1.23;     // assign a value
    cout << realValue;    // display the float
    return 0;
}
```

Exercise 2.6 declares a *float* variable named *realValue*. Next, it assigns a constant value to the variable. Then it displays the value.

CONSTANTS

The next section explains C++ expressions, which consist of variables, operators, and constants. You have already learned about variables, and you have used some constants in the exercises. Now let's discuss constants in a C++ program.

    Constants, in this context, are what some languages call *literals* and others call *immediate* values. They are constant values that you use explicitly in expressions. A constant is distinguished from a variable in two ways. First, it has no apparent compiled place in memory except inside the statement in which it appears. Second, you cannot address the constant or change its value. Be aware that these constants are not the same as the *const* variable type qualifier discussed in Chapter 5.

Character Constants

Character constants specify values that a *char* variable can contain. Exercise 2.3 assigned character constants to a *char* variable. You can code a character constant with an ASCII expression—as shown in Exercise 2.3—or as an escape sequence surrounded by single quote characters (apostrophes). The following statements are assignments of character constants to *char* variables:

```
ch1 = 'A';    // ASCII char constant
ch3 = '\x2f'; // char constant expressed as hex value
ch3 = '\013'; // char constant expressed as octal value
```

Escape Sequences

The backslash in the second and third examples just shown is an *escape sequence*. It tells the compiler that something special is coming. In this case, \x means that the characters that follow are a hexadecimal number, and \0 (backslash-zero) means that the characters that follow are an octal number. Other escape sequences—consisting of a backslash and other characters that represent ASCII values—do not have a displayable character (one that you can type and print) in the character set. These escape sequences apply to character constants and string constants, described later. Table 2.3 shows all the escape sequences.

Table 2.3 Constant Escape Sequences

ESCAPE SEQUENCE	MEANING
\a	audible bell character
\b	backspace
\f	formfeed
\n	newline
\r	carriage return
\t	horizontal tab
\v	vertical tab
\\	backslash
\'	quote
\0	null (zero) character
\"	double quote
\0nnn	octal number (nnn) follows
\xhh	hexadecimal number (hh) follows

The backslash-backslash (\\) escape sequence allows you to code the backslash character itself into the constant so that the compiler does not translate it as an escape sequence. The quote (\') and double quote (\") escape sequences allow you to include those characters in character and string constants so that the compiler does not interpret them as the terminating character of the constant itself.

The newline (\n) escape sequence is probably the one you will use the most. When a screen output function finds a newline character in the output data, it resets the cursor to the leftmost column on the screen and moves the cursor down one line. It acts like a carriage return on a typewriter.

Integer Constants

An *integer constant* specifies a *long* or *short, signed* or *unsigned* integer value.

Quincy supports signed short integer values of -32768 to +32767, and unsigned short integer values of 0 to 65535. These are the ranges that you can represent in a 16-bit integer.

The *int* and the *long int* are both 32 bits in Quincy. Quincy supports signed long integer values of -2147483648 to +2147483647, and unsigned long integer values of 0 to 4294967295. These are the ranges that you can represent in a 32-bit integer.

You can specify an integer constant as a decimal, hexadecimal, or octal value, as shown in these statements:

```
Amount = -129;      // decimal integer constant
HexAmt = 0x12fe;    // hexadecimal integer constant
OctalAmt = 0177;    // octal integer constant
```

The leading 0x specifies that the constant is a hexadecimal expression. It can contain the digits 0–9 and the letters A–F in mixed uppercase or lowercase. A leading zero alone specifies that the constant is octal and may contain the digits 0–7.

You can specify that a constant is *long* or *unsigned* by adding the *L* or *U* suffix to the constant:

```
LongAmount = 52388L;    // long integer constant
LongHexAmt = 0x4fea2L   // long hex constant
UnsignedAmt = 40000U;   // unsigned integer constant
```

The suffixes can be uppercase or lowercase. On compiler systems in which *int* and *long* are the same length (Quincy, for example), the L suffix is unnecessary, but you should use it if you expect your program to be portable across compiler platforms that support other *int* lengths. Many MS-DOS compilers, for example, have 16-bit *int*s and 32-bit *long*s.

Floating Constants

A *floating constant* consists of integer and fractional parts separated by a decimal point. Some floating constants use *scientific*, or *exponential*, notation to represent numbers too big or too small to express with normal notation. Here are some examples:

```
Pi = 3.14159;           // regular decimal notation
SmallNumber = 1.234E-40; // 1.234 x 10 to the -40th power
BigNumber = 2.47E201    // 2.47 x 10 to the 201st power
```

Floating constants default to the *double* type unless you provide a suffix on the constant:

```
FloatNumber = 1.23E10F    // float constant
LongDoubleNumber = 3.45L  // long double constant
```

The suffixes can be uppercase or lowercase.

Address Constants

When you begin to use pointers in C++ programs, a subject that Chapter 5 covers, you will use *address constants*. Variables and functions have memory addresses, and C++ allows you to reference their addresses with address constants as shown here:

```
CounterPtr = &Counter;   // address of a variable
FunctPtr = &DoFunction;  // address of a function
```

Address expressions of array elements can be non-constant expressions, too, and Chapter 5 discusses them.

String Constants

Exercise 2.1 passed "My first C++ program," a string constant (also called a *string literal*), to the *cout* object. You code a string constant as a sequence of ASCII characters surrounded by double quote characters. Escape sequences inside the string constant work the same as they do in character constants. Here are some examples of string constants:

```
cp = "hello, dolly";
cout << "\nEnter selection: ";
cout << "\aError!";
```

The first statement apparently assigns a string constant to a variable. What it is really doing is assigning the *address* of the string constant to a pointer variable (Chapter 5). The compiler finds a place in memory for the string constant and compiles its address into the statement.

The same thing happens in the second and third statements in the example. The compiler passes the addresses of the string constants to the *cout* object.

The string constants in the second and third statements include escape sequences. The second statement's escape sequence is \n, the newline character. The third statement's escape sequence is \a, the audible alarm character. It makes a beeping sound from the computer's speaker.

Adjacent string constants concatenate to form a single string constant. This feature allows you to code long string constants on multiple source-code lines, as shown in Exercise 2.7.

Exercise 2.7 Concatenated string constants.

```
#include <iostream>
using namespace std;

int main()
{
    cout << "This is the beginning of a very long message\n"
            "that spans several lines of code.\n"
            "This format allows a program to build long\n"
            "string constants without going past the\n"
            "program editor's right margin.\n";
    return 0;
}
```

EXPRESSIONS

Statements in a function body consist of individual expressions terminated by the semicolon (;) character. All statements and declarations in C are terminated that way. The statement is not complete until the semicolon appears.

An expression is a combination of constants, variables, function calls, and operators that, when evaluated, returns a value. Following are some typical C++ expressions:

```
1+2;
Counter*3;
GrossPay-(FICA+GrossPay*WithHoldingRate);
```

By themselves, these expressions do nothing. They return values, but they have no effect because the program does nothing with the returned values. Expressions such as these take on meaning on the right side of assignment statements, discussed next, or as arguments in a function call (Chapter 3).

The numerical value that an expression returns has a type. The implicit type of an expression depends on the types of the variables and constants that contribute to the expression. Therefore, an expression might return an integer of any size, an address, or a floating-point number of any precision.

Each expression also has a logical property associated with its value. If the expression's value is nonzero, the expression is said to return a *true* value. If the value is zero, the expression returns a *false* value. These logical values can be used as *conditions* in program flow control statements, the subject of Chapter 4.

ASSIGNMENTS

An assignment statement assigns to a variable the value returned by an expression. The variable's contents are the value of the expression after the assignment statement. Here are the preceding expressions used in assignment statements:

```
Amount = 1+2;
Total = Counter*3;
NetPay = GrossPay-(FICA+GrossPay*WithHoldingRate);
```

Now the program does something meaningful with the expressions. Each of the assignment statements assigns an expression's returned value to a named variable. In this example, you can assume that the program declared the variables elsewhere.

A variable that receives an assigned value is called an *lvalue*, because its reference appears on the left side of the assignment. The expression that provides the assigned value is called an *rvalue*, because it is on the right side of the assignment. You will learn that this is an important distinction. Not all expressions can be used as *lvalues*. A constant, for example, is an *rvalue* but cannot be an *lvalue*. A variable can be an *lvalue* if it is not a *const* variable, which is discussed in Chapter 5.

The next exercise illustrates how a program would use assignments such as those just shown. To do that, the program declares variables to receive the values returned by the expressions. Declarations of local variables are made in a statement block at the beginning of the block before any statements. You learn more about local and global variables in Chapter 5. Exercise 2.8 declares three integer variables, assigns to those integers the values returned by the expressions, and displays the new values of the integer variables on the screen.

Exercise 2.8 *Assignments and expressions.*

```
#include <iostream>
using namespace std;

int main()
{
    // --- declare three integers
    int HourlyRate;
    int HoursWorked;
    int GrossPay;
    // --- assign values to the integers
    HourlyRate = 15;
    HoursWorked = 40;
    GrossPay = HourlyRate * HoursWorked;
```

Exercise 2.8 Assignments and expressions. (continued)

```
// --- display the variables on the screen
   cout << HourlyRate;
   cout << ' ';
   cout << HoursWorked;
   cout << ' ';
   cout << GrossPay;
   return 0;
}
```

NOTE   When you use Quincy's tutorial mode to run Exercise 2.8, observe that Quincy opens its Watch window at the bottom of the screen and displays the values of the three integer variables. As you step through the program, you can watch the values change when the assignment statements execute. Many of the exercises use this automatic variable Watch feature in Quincy to assist you with the lesson.

When you run Exercise 2.8, it displays these three values on the screen:

```
15 40 600
```

The first value in the display, 15, reflects the contents of the *HourlyRate* variable. The second value, 40, is *HoursWorked*. The third, 600, is *GrossPay*.

If you are a mathematician, assignments might look to you like algebraic equations. In some respects, the two concepts are almost the same thing, but at other times they are not. Consider this assignment:

```
AmountDue = Dues + Penalty;
```

Before the assignment statement executes, the two sides can be different, so the assignment statement is not an equation. After the execution, the two sides are the same, so the assignment statement appears to be an equation. Now consider this assignment statement:

```
AmountDue = AmountDue + 37.43;
```

This assignment statement is never an equation. The two sides can never be equal at any given time.

COMMA-SEPARATED DECLARATIONS

C++ permits you to use a comma-separated list of identifiers to declare multiple variables that have the same type. The three declarations in Exercise 2.8 could have been coded this way:

```
int HourlyRate, HoursWorked, GrossPay;
```

Some programmers use the comma-separated identifier notation but put each identifier on a separate line:

```
int HourlyRate,     // hourly rate
    HoursWorked,    // number of hours worked
    GrossPay;       // gross weekly pay
```

This style provides visual separation of the identifiers and allows you to add comments about each variable. There is another advantage to this style: You can use it to group all related variables. Later, if the requirements of the program call for you to change the type of a number of related variables, you need only make the change on the first line of code in the declaration. The types of all the others will then automatically be changed.

OPERATORS IN EXPRESSIONS

An expression consists of function calls, variables, constants, and operators. The previous exercises used some operators. Now you learn what they mean. Operators can be arithmetic, logical, bitwise logical, bitwise shift, relational, increment, decrement, or assignment operators. Most operators are *binary*, which means that you code the operator between two expressions. The addition operator is binary. Other operators are *unary*, which means that the operator is associated with one expression only. Unary plus and minus operators are examples.

Arithmetic Operators

The C++ language has two unary and five binary arithmetic operators, as shown in Table 2.4. The multiplication, division, and modulus operators have higher precedence than the binary addition and subtraction operators. The unary plus and minus operators are higher than the others. See "Precedence and Order of Evaluation" later in this chapter.

Table 2.4 Arithmetic Operators

SYMBOL	OPERATOR
+	unary plus
-	unary minus
*	multiplication
/	division
%	modulus
+	addition
-	subtraction

In the following are examples of assignment statements, where the expressions on the right side of the assignments use some of the arithmetic operators from Table 2.4:

```
Celsius = 5 * (Fahrenheit - 32) / 9;
Height = Top - Bottom + 1;
Area = Height * Width;
```

Exercise 2.9 uses the first expression to calculate and display Celsius temperatures from Fahrenheit values that you type in. This exercise is also your first use of the standard *cin* object, which reads keyboard data into program variables.

Exercise 2.9 Assigning an expression.

```cpp
#include <iostream>
using namespace std;

int main()
{
    int Celsius, Fahrenheit;
    // -- prompt for Fahrenheit temperature
    cout << "\nEnter temperature as degrees Fahrenheit: ";
    // -- read Fahrenheit temperature from keyboard
    cin >> Fahrenheit;
    // -- compute Celsius
    Celsius = 5 * (Fahrenheit - 32) / 9;
    // -- display the result
    cout << "Temperature is ";
    cout << Celsius;
    cout << " degrees Celsius";
    return 0;
}
```

Exercise 2.9 declares two integer variables and uses *cout* to prompt you to type in the temperature.

The *cin* object is the **<iostream>** input device. Observe that it uses the >> operator, which signifies that the data value flows from the device to the variable. The >> operator, in this context, is called the stream *extraction* operator because it extracts data values from the input stream.

When you run the program in Exercise 2.9, it displays the following messages. The value 75 in this example is what you type. The value 23 is the computed Celsius temperature. You can use other values to see their effects.

```
Enter temperature as degrees Fahrenheit: 75
Temperature is 23 degrees Celsius
```

The modulus % operator returns the remainder of a division when the first expression is divided by the second, as shown in the next example. The example uses a *BitNumber* variable, which contains a number from 0 to the highest bit in a bit array, to compute the *ByteOffset* and *BitOffset* variables.

```
ByteOffset = BitNumber / 8;   // offset to the byte
BitOffset = BitNumber % 8;    // bit offset within the byte
```

The unary minus operator returns the negative value of the numeric expression that follows it. If the value was already negative, the operator returns the positive value of the expression.

The unary plus operator is redundant and was added to Standard C++ for symmetry with unary minus. The unary plus operator doesn't change anything. It doesn't, for example, make a negative expression positive.

Logical Operators

Logical operators use the true/false properties of expressions to return a true or false value. In C++, the true result of an expression is nonzero. When a nonzero value is subjected to a logical operation, the value is converted to 1. False values are always zero. Table 2.5 lists the logical operators.

Table 2.5 Logical Operators

SYMBOL	OPERATOR
&&	logical AND
||	logical OR
!	unary NOT

Here are some expressions that use logical operators:

```
tf = flots && jets;   // 1 if flots and jets are nonzero
tf = flots || jets;   // 1 if flots or jets is nonzero
tf = !flots;          // 1 if flots is zero
```

Do not confuse the && and || operators with their bitwise & and | counterparts discussed in the next section.

The && and || logical operators can have more-complex expressions on either side than are shown in these examples. These operators are most often used to form conditional expressions in the C++ language's *if, for,* and *while* program flow control statements, which are discussed in Chapter 4.

Programs often use the unary NOT logical operator (!) to convert a variable's numeric value to its logical true/false property:

```
tf = !!blob; // 1 if blob is non-zero; 0 otherwise
```

The expression uses the unary NOT logical operator twice to compound the negation and return the desired 1 or zero, true or false value associated with the variable's numeric value.

Chapter 5 has exercises that use logical operators within program control flow statements.

Bitwise Logical Operators

The bitwise logical operators perform bit setting, clearing, inversion, and complement operations on the expressions and return the results. Table 2.6 lists the bitwise logical operators.

Table 2.6 Bitwise Logical Operators

SYMBOL	OPERATOR
&	bitwise AND
|	bitwise OR
^	bitwise exclusive OR
~	one's complement

All except the last of the operators in Table 2.6 are binary operators. The one's complement operator is a unary operator. You can use these operators with integer expressions only. Bitwise logical operators typically are used to set, clear, invert, and test selected bits in an integer variable. Programmers often use bits as on/off switches in programs. Low-level hardware device driver programs often must manipulate bits in the input/output device registers.

The first three operations in Table 2.6 perform bit mask operations as shown in these examples:

```
result = InputCh & 0x80; // clear all but most significant bit
newval = CtrlCh & ~0x80; // clear the most significant bit
mask = KeyChar | 0x80;   // set the most significant bit
newch = oldch ^ 1;       // invert the least significant bit
```

The second example also uses the ~ one's complement operator to convert the 0x80 constant to its one's complement, which is 0x7f. This usage emphasizes the bit that is cleared rather than the bits that are not cleared.

Let's get ahead of ourselves and anticipate Chapter 4 somewhat. Consider the following example, which shows a typical use for the bitwise AND operator—testing the setting of bits in a field:

```
if (Field & BITMASK)
    // at least one of the bits is set
```

The *if* statement tests the expression inside the parentheses that follow. If the expression returns a true value, the next statement or statement block executes. Otherwise, it is skipped. That's the part that I'll cover better in Chapter 4. For now, the usage demonstrates logical AND in a conditional expression. In this example, the program uses the operator to test whether any of the bits in the *BITMASK* variable match the contents of the *Field* variable.

Bitwise Shift Operators

The bitwise shift operators in Table 2.7 shift integer values right and left a specified number of bits. You can use these operators with integer expressions only.

Table 2.7 Bitwise Shift Operators

SYMBOL	OPERATOR
<<	left shift
>>	right shift

The shift operators return a value that is equal to the leftmost expression shifted a number of bits equal to the value of the rightmost expression, as shown here:

```
NewFld = OldFld << 3;   // Shift OldFld 3 bits to the left
MyData = YourData >> 2; // Shift YourData 2 bits to the right
```

In these statements, the field on the left of the assignment receives the shifted value. The variables on the right of the assignment are not themselves shifted. Instead, their values contribute to the expression, which returns a shifted value.

Shifting left inserts zero bits into the low order bits of the result. Shifting right propagates the most significant bit. This behavior preserves the signed property of an integer.

Programmers often use the shift left operator to multiply integers and the shift right operator to divide integers when the multiplier or divisor is known to be a power of two.

Relational Operators

Relational operators compare two expressions and return a true or false value depending on the relative values of the expressions and the operator. Table 2.8 shows the six relational operators.

Table 2.8 Relational Operators

Symbol	Operator
>	greater than
<	less than
>=	greater than or equal to
<=	less than or equal to
==	equal to
!=	not equal to

Relational operators typically are used in conditional expressions for program control flow statements as shown here:

```
while (Counter > 0)   {   // test Counter for zero
    // ...
}
```

Why do you suppose that C++ uses == for equality and = for assignment? Other languages, such as BASIC, use the same = operator for both. The reason is that an assignment statement is an expression that returns a value. The following code is valid:

```
if (Amount = 123)
    // ...
```

The code looks like a test for equality between *Amount* and the constant value 123, but it is not, because it uses the = assignment operator rather than the == equality operator. The assignment (*Amount = 123*) is an expression that returns the value 123. The *if* program flow statement tests the true/false condition of the expression. This statement would always return a true value, because 123, being nonzero, is always true. If the right side of the expression were a variable, then the true/false result of the test would depend on the value in the variable.

The syntax of the two operators and of conditional expressions invites coding errors. New C++ programmers often code the = operator when they mean to code the == operator. The previous statement is a valid statement, but because of the potential for confusion, most compilers issue a warning when they see such a statement. The warning says something like "Possibly incorrect assignment."

To eliminate warnings and to clarify the code's intentions, most programmers who want to test the result of an assignment for a true/false condition use one of two ways. The first is shown here:

```
Amount = NewAmount;
if (Amount != 0)
    // ...
```

This combination of statements is similar to the way you would code the assignment and test in programming languages that do not treat assignments as conditional expressions. It is clear and unambiguous. No one misunderstands what the code is doing. Once you are experienced and comfortable with C++, however, you might prefer this format:

```
if ((Amount = NewAmount) != 0)
    // ...
```

This format is more concise than the first one, and many C++ programmers prefer it. The parentheses are important. As you soon learn, the != operator has higher precedence than the = operator. If you omit the parentheses, *NewAmount != 0* is evaluated before the assignment, and *Amount* is assigned the true/false, one/zero result of that test. Without parentheses, the expression works like this one, which has parentheses added to emphasize the default precedence:

```
if (Amount = (NewAmount != 0))
    // ...
```

Chapter 5 has exercises that use relational operators within program control flow statements.

Increment and Decrement Operators

C++ includes several unique operators. Two of them, the ++ *increment* and— *decrement* operators, increment or decrement a variable by the value of 1. Table 2.9 shows these operators.

Table 2.9 Increment and Decrement Operators

SYMBOL	OPERATOR
++	increment operator
--	decrement operator

The increment and decrement operators can be placed before (prefix) or after (postfix) the variable that they change, as shown in these examples:

```
--Counter;    // decrement Counter, prefix notation
Quantity--;   // decrement Quantity, postfix notation
++Amount;     // increment Amount, prefix notation
Offset++;     // increment Offset, postfix notation
```

As used here, the prefix and postfix forms of the operators have the same effect. But when they are used as part of a larger expression, the two forms have a different meaning. The prefix operators change the variable before it contributes to the expression, and the postfix operators change it afterward. Exercise 2.10 demonstrates that behavior.

Exercise 2.10 Increment and decrement operators.

```
#include <iostream>
using namespace std;

int main()
{
    int Ctr, OldCtr, NewCtr;
    OldCtr = 123;           // OldCtr is 123
    NewCtr = ++OldCtr; // NewCtr is 124, OldCtr is 124
    Ctr = NewCtr--;    // Ctr is 124, NewCtr is 123
    // --- display the results
    cout << OldCtr;
    cout << ' ';
    cout << NewCtr;
    cout << ' ';
    cout << Ctr;
    return 0;
}
```

Exercise 2.10 declares three integer variables and assigns a value to one of them. Then it assigns that variable to one of the others but with a prefix increment operator. The variable is incremented, and the incremented value is assigned to the receiving variable. The third assignment uses a postfix decrement operator. The variable on the right side is decremented but not until after the assignment. The variable on the left side receives the value before the decrement. You can use Quincy's Watch window to observe these effects as they happen. Exercise 2.10 displays this value on the screen:

```
124 123 124
```

Assignment Operators

It might not be obvious, but the assignment statements you have been learning about in this chapter are themselves expressions that return values. C++ has a number of assignment statement formats, all of which are shown in Table 2.10.

Table 2.10 Assignment Operators

SYMBOL	OPERATOR
=	assignment
+=	addition assignment
-=	subtraction assignment
*=	multiplication assignment
/=	division assignment
%=	modulus assignment
<<=	shift left assignment
>>=	shift right assignment
&=	bitwise AND assignment
|=	bitwise OR assignment
^=	bitwise exclusive OR assignment

Consider first the garden-variety assignment operator that you have been using until now. Each assignment statement itself returns a value. The value that it returns is the value that is assigned to the variable on the left side of the assignment. That behavior makes possible a widely used C++ idiom that you do not see in other programming languages (except C, of course). This example shows that idiom:

```
FirstTotal = SecondTotal = 0;
```

The effect of this statement is to assign the value zero to both of the variables. Why is this? First, consider the order in which the assignment statements are evaluated. The assignment operator has *right to left associativity*, which means that the expressions are evaluated starting with the rightmost one. This means that *SecondTotal = 0* is evaluated first. That expression returns the result of the assignment, which is zero in this case. When the leftmost expression is evaluated, the zero return from the rightmost expression is assigned to the leftmost variable. It is as if you coded the expression this way:

```
FirstTotal = (SecondTotal = 0);
```

The parentheses are not needed to force the precedence of the rightmost expression over the leftmost expression, because the associativity of the operator takes care of that. Exercise 2.11 demonstrates this behavior.

Exercise 2.11 Assigning assignments.

```cpp
#include <iostream>
using namespace std;

int main()
{
    unsigned int This, That, Those;
    // --- assign the same value to three variables
    This = That = Those = 62440;
    // --- display three unsigned ints
    cout << This;
    cout << ' ';
    cout << That;
    cout << ' ';
    cout << Those;
    return 0;
}
```

The assignment statement in Exercise 2.11 assigns the same value to all three *unsigned int* variables. Exercise 2.11 displays this value on the screen:

```
62440 62440 62440
```

Can you see why the following multiple assignment expression does not work?

```
(FirstTotal = SecondTotal) = 0;
```

C++ compilers report an error if you try to code an expression such as this one. The reason is that the leftmost expression *(FirstTotal = SecondTotal)* is not an *lvalue*. It does not represent a variable that the program can modify. It is, instead, an *rvalue* expression—the value of an assignment—which would be whatever is in *SecondTotal* before the statement executes. You cannot assign a value to such an expression. An assignment expression is an *rvalue* and cannot appear on the left side of another assignment operator.

Compound Assignment Operators

The other assignment operators in Table 2.10 are unique to the C and C++ languages. Called *compound assignment* operators, they are a form of short-hand that provides a more concise way to modify a variable. Consider this simple assignment statement usage, which is common to most programming languages:

```
Total = Total + 3;
```

This statement assigns a value to a variable where the value is the result of an expression that includes the variable itself. C++ includes a set of compound assignment operators that do the same thing. The statement can be coded this way instead:

```
Total += 3;
```

Each of the other operand assignment operators in Table 2.10 has a similar effect on the variable but with the effects of the assignment's own operator. Exercise 2.12 demonstrates compound assignment.

Exercise 2.12 Compound assignment.

```
#include <iostream>
using namespace std;

int main()
{
    long Total, SubTotal, Detail;
    // --- initial values
    Total = 10000;
    SubTotal = 90;
    Detail = 5;
    SubTotal *= Detail;        // compute SubTotal
    Total += SubTotal;         // compute Total
    // ----- display all three
    cout << Total;
    cout << ' ';
    cout << SubTotal;
    cout << ' ';
    cout << Detail;
    return 0;
}
```

Exercise 2.12 displays this message on the screen:

```
10450 450 5
```

N O T E

There is one significant difference between simple and compound assignment. In a simple assignment, such as A = A + 1, the A expression is evaluated twice; in a compound assignment, such as A += 1, the A expression is evaluated once. Usually, this difference has no effect on the operation of the program, but if the expression dereferences an address returned from a function, the function would be called twice. Most C++ programmers intuitively avoid those kinds of side effects. It might not make sense just yet, but put a bookmark in this place. After you've learned about functions (Chapter 3) and pointers (Chapter 5), you might want to return here and reread this note.

Conditional Operator (?:)

The *conditional* operator tests an expression and returns the result of one of two other expressions depending on the true/false value of the first. The operator takes this form:

```
<expression1> ? <expression2> : <expression3>
```

The evaluation tests the first expression. If that value is true, the resulting value is that of the second expression. Otherwise, the resulting value is that of the third expression. Exercise 2.13 demonstrates the conditional operator with a simple algorithm that computes the penalty for overdue dues at 10%.

Exercise 2.13 *The conditional operator.*

```cpp
#include <iostream>
using namespace std;

int main()
{
    float Dues;        // dues amount
    // --- read the dues
    cout << "Enter dues amount: ";
    cin >> Dues;
    // --- are the dues paid on time?
    cout << "On time? (y/n) ";
    char yn;
    cin >> yn;
    bool Overdue;    // true if overdue, false if on time
    Overdue = yn != 'y';
    float AmountDue; // amount to be computed
    // --- use conditional operator to compute
    AmountDue = Overdue ? Dues * 1.10 : Dues;
```

Exercise 2.13 *The conditional operator. (continued)*

```
// --- display the dues amount
  cout << "Amount due: ";
  cout << AmountDue;
  return 0;
}
```

N O T E

Observe the declaration of the *char yn* variable in Exercise 2.13. If you are a C programmer, you might think there is an error in this code. In C, all declarations in a brace-surrounded statement block must appear before all executable statements in the block, yet there are several executable statements ahead of the *char yn* declaration. In C++, a declaration can appear anywhere in the block as long as the item is declared before any other statements refer to it.

When you run Exercise 2.13, it displays the following messages. The **35.50** is the amount you enter as dues. The **n** following the *On time? (y/n)* message is the response you type to the question. You can try the program with different dues amounts and different responses to the question.

```
Enter dues amount: 35.50
On time? (y/n) n
Amount due: 39.05
```

The conditional operator is a shorthand form of the traditional *if-then-else* program flow control operation. The expression just shown can be performed this way as well:

```
if (OverDue)
    AmountDue = Dues * 1.10;
else
    AmountDue = Dues;
```

It can also be performed this way:

```
AmountDue = Dues;
if (OverDue)
    AmountDue *= 1.10;
```

And this way, too:

```
AmountDue = Dues;
if (OverDue)
    AmountDue += AmountDue * 0.10;
```

And so on. As you can see, C++ is not only the language of choice but also a language of choices.

Comma Operator

Expressions can be separated by commas. Each comma-separated expression is evaluated, and the value returned from the group is the value of the right-most expression. Exercise 2.14 is an example of this behavior.

Exercise 2.14 Comma-separated expressions.

```
#include <iostream>
using namespace std;

int main()
{
    int Val, Amt, Tot, Cnt;
    Amt = 30;
    Tot = 12;
    Cnt = 46;
    // --- compute Val = rightmost expression
    Val = (Amt++, --Tot, Cnt+3);
    // --- display the result
    cout << Val;
    return 0;
}
```

Exercise 2.14 displays the value 49 on the screen, which is the value returned by the comma-separated expression.

NOTE Without the parentheses, *Val* would be assigned the value in *Amt* before the increment. This is because the assignment operator has higher precedence than the comma operator. I'll explain just what that means in the next section.

PRECEDENCE AND ASSOCIATIVITY

Operators have two important properties: their *precedence* and their *associativity* (also called *order of evaluation*). These properties affect the results of an expression that contains more than one operator or that might produce side effects. They determine when and if each inner expression in an outer expression is evaluated.

Table 2.11 shows the precedence and order of evaluation of the operators in the C++ language.

Table 2.11 Operator Precedence and Order of Evaluation

PRECEDENCE	OPERATORS	ASSOCIATIVITY
(Highest)	() []-> .	left-right
	! ~ ++-- +- * & (type) sizeof	right-left
	6* / %	left-right
	+ -	left-right
	<< >>	left-right
	< <= > >=	left-right
	== !=	left-right
	&	left-right
	^	left-right
	|	left-right
	&&	left-right
	||	left-right
	?:	right-left
	= += -= *= /= %= &= ^= |= <<= >>=	right-left
(Lowest)	,	left-right

The conditional operator (?:) behaves in a similar fashion, as shown in this example:

```
Amount = FirstTime ? InitialAmount++ : RunningAmount++;
```

Only one of the second two expressions is evaluated, depending on the true/false value of the first. This means that when *FirstTime* is true, only *InitialAmount* is incremented, and when *FirstTime* is false, only *RunningAmount* is incremented.

INITIALIZERS

Declaration of a variable does not put any data into the variable. The exercises so far have placed assignment statements after the declarations to provide initial data values. You can, however, initialize variables with data by providing an initializer as part of the declaration. Exercise 2.15 demonstrates three different variable initializers.

Exercise 2.15 Initializers.

```
include <iostream>
using namespace std;

int main()
{
    int Amount = 3;     // initialize an int
    char ch = 'A';      // initialize a char
    float Value = 1.23; // initialize a float

    // --- display the initialized variables
    cout << Amount;
    cout << ' ';
    cout << ch;
    cout << ' ';
    cout << Value;
    return 0;
}
```

Usually, a variable is initialized each time the declaration is executed. Exercise 2.15 initializes the three variables immediately after the *main* function begins execution. Variables that are declared inside other functions and statement blocks are initialized every time the function or statement block begins execution. An exception is the static local variable that is initialized the first time it is declared and never again. We'll discuss functions and statement blocks in Chapter 3 and static variables in Chapter 5.

Exercise 2.15 displays this message on the screen:

```
3 A 1.23
```

An initializer takes the form of an assignment statement, with the declaration on the left and an expression on the right. If the variable is global or static, the initializing expression must be a constant value; it cannot contain any function calls, references to other variables, or increment and decrement operators. It can contain multiple constants and operators, but that's all. Local variables—the kind you've been using until now—can contain any expression as their intializers.

There are two formats for coding initializers in C++. Exercise 2.15 demonstrates the format that C++ and C initializers use. The assignments in Exercise 2.15 could have been coded with the alternative C++ initializer syntax as shown here:

```
int Amount(3);      // initialize an int
char ch('A');       // initialize a char
float Value(1.23);  // initialize a float
```

The alternative initializer syntax reflects the syntax with which a class object declaration calls a class constructor function with initializer values. You learn about class constructors in Chapter 9.

TYPE CONVERSION

The various numeric types—characters, integers, long integers, and floating numbers—have different ranges of values because of their sizes and their signed and unsigned properties. What happens when you use them interchangeably? What happens if you assign a *long int* variable to a *char* variable, for example? Or vice versa?

C++ applies certain rules of *type conversion* in these cases. Numeric types are interchangeable within certain limits. If you assign a variable of a smaller type to one of a larger type, the value is *promoted* to that larger type, and no information is lost. If you assign a variable of a larger type to one of a smaller type, the value is *demoted*, and if the larger value is greater than the smaller type can contain, the demotion includes truncation of the excess data. Some compilers warn you when this can happen unless you use a typecast (Chapter 5) to tell the compiler that you know about it in advance.

Exercise 2.16 illustrates several type conversions in action.

Exercise 2.16 Type conversions.

```
#include <iostream>
using namespace std;

int main()
{
    // --- three uninitialized variables, different types
    char myChar;
    short int myInt;
    long myLong;
    // --- an initialized variable of yet another type
    float myFloat = 7e4;
    // --- assign and convert
    myChar = myInt = myLong = myFloat;
    // --- display the variables
    cout << myChar;
    cout << ' ';
    cout << myInt;
    cout << ' ';
    cout << myLong;
    cout << ' ';
    cout << myFloat;
    return 0;
}
```

When you compile Exercise 2.16, the compiler issues this warning message, which alerts you that some data could be lost in the conversion in the assignment statement on source-code line 13:

```
13: warning: assignment to 'long int' from 'float'
```

Exercise 2.16 displays this message on the screen:

```
p 4464 70000 70000
```

The *myInt* variable reflects the lost data when a *long int* variable with a value greater than can be held in 16 bits is assigned to a *short int* variable. The *long int* variable *MyLong* loses no data when the *float* variable is assigned to it, because a *long* can hold the value represented by 7e4, which is 7 times 10 raised to the 4th power, or 70000.

CONSOLE INPUT AND OUTPUT

You have been using *cin* and *cout* in the exercises in this chapter. They read the keyboard and write to the screen in Standard C++ programs. If you are writing a program that you intend to be portable, you will probably use *cin* and *cout* extensively, because they are the lowest common denominator for console input/output across all implementations of the C++ language on all computers.

Many commercial C++ programs never use *cin* and *cout*. They use screen and keyboard libraries associated with the user interfaces of the system on which the program is to be run: Windows 95, X-Windows, OS/2 Presentation Manager, Macintosh, and so on. You might rarely use *cin* and *cout* again after finishing this book, although many small utility programs run from the command line and do not use exotic user interfaces.

This section introduces console input/output because you need to know how to read the keyboard and write the screen in order to use the exercises in this book that teach other parts of the C++ language.

The Standard Output Stream

Our use of *cout* has been primitive until now. We used one statement for every item that we wanted to display. But *cout* is more powerful than that, providing shortcuts that allow us to achieve the same effect with fewer lines of code. Look back at Exercise 2.15. Observe how Exercise 2.17 gets the same result with less code.

Exercise 2.17 Improved cout *usage.*

```
#include <iostream>
using namespace std;

int main()
{
    int Amount = 3;        // initialize an int
    char ch = 'A';         // initialize a char
    float Value = 1.23;    // initialize a float

    // --- display the initialized variables
    cout << Amount << ' ' << ch << ' ' << Value;
    return 0;
}
```

Exercise 2.17 connects several data types with the << operator. The output is the same as that of Exercise 2.15. This behavior is a by-product of the C++ *this* pointer and the overloaded << operator for *ostream* objects. Both topics get full treatment later in the book. For now, don't worry about exactly how these things work; accept their behavior as this chapter describes it and forge ahead.

Formatted Output: Manipulators

Suppose you want to display the hexadecimal representation of an integer variable instead of its decimal value. The *iostream* class system associates a set of *manipulators* with the output stream. These manipulators change the displayed numerical base for integer arguments. You insert the manipulators into the stream to make the change. There are three such manipulators. Their symbolic values are *dec, oct,* and *hex.*

Exercise 2.18 uses manipulators to display an integer in three numerical base representations.

Exercise 2.18 Formatting numerical data.

```
#include <iostream>
using namespace std;

int main()
{
    int amount = 123;
    cout << dec << amount << ' ' << oct << amount << ' '
         << hex << amount;
    return 0;
}
```

The exercise inserts the manipulators *dec, oct,* and *hex* into the stream to convert the value that follows—*amount*—into different numerical base representations.

Exercise 2.18 displays the following result:

```
123 173 7b
```

Each of the values shown is the decimal value 123 in a different base representation.

The concept of sending so-called manipulators to a device might be alien to programmers who are more familiar with other languages. In BASIC, for example, all the data objects that you code after a PRINT statement get displayed. In C++, however, each console device is implemented as an object. The object reacts to the data you send it according to the data types. Manipulators are themselves data objects of a unique type defined within the *iostream* class system. When you send a manipulator to a stream object, the object uses the appearance of the manipulator to modify the console object's behavior for the next data object; in this case, the behavior to be modified is the format of the data to be displayed.

As you proceed through the exercises in later chapters, they use manipulators to control the display of their output. Whenever a new manipulator shows up, the discussion surrounding the exercise explains the manipulator.

The Standard Error Stream

The *cerr* object uses the same syntax as *cout*, except that *cerr*'s output goes to the standard error device. This technique allows you to display error messages on the console even when the program's user redirects the standard output device.

The Standard Input Stream

By using *cout* and *cerr* you can display all types of data on the screen. You must also be able to read data into your programs. The *iostream* version of standard input is implemented with the *cin* object, which you learned about earlier in this chapter. Let's revisit *cin* now.

Exercise 2.19 uses *cin* to read an integer from the keyboard.

Exercise 2.19 The standard input stream.

```
#include <iostream>
using namespace std;

int main()
{
    short int amount;
    cout << "Enter an amount...";
    cin >> amount;
    cout << "The amount you entered was " << amount;
    return 0;
}
```

Exercise 2.19 sends a string to *cout* to prompt you for input. The *cin* device writes the value into the *amount* integer variable. The exercise then displays the *amount* variable on *cout* to demonstrate that the *cin* operation worked.

Exercise 2.19 displays the following messages. (The first **123** is the value that you type into the program. It could be any integer value.)

```
Enter an amount...123
The amount you entered was 123
```

Suppose that you use this program in a system with a 16-bit short integer (Quincy, for example). If you enter the value **65535**, the program displays **-1**. If you enter **65536**, the program displays **0**. These displays occur because the *amount* variable is a signed integer. Change the *amount* variable's type to an unsigned integer and retry the program. For another experiment, see what happens when you enter a value with a decimal point and digits to the right of the decimal point.

Try entering alphabetic characters instead of numbers into Exercise 2.19. It doesn't work. The *cin* device is able to work with strings—character arrays, actually—as well as with numbers, but you must use the correct data type in the expression. To illustrate, Exercise 2.20 uses the *cin* device to read a string value from the keyboard into a character array.

Exercise 2.20 Reading a string.

```
#include <iostream>
using namespace std;

int main()
{
    char name[20];
    cout << "Enter a name...";
    cin >> name;
    cout << "The name you entered was " << name;
    return 0;
}
```

Exercise 2.20 displays the following messages. (The name **Tyler** is used here for the name that you type into the program.)

```
Enter a name...Tyler
The name you entered was Tyler
```

Exercise 2.20 has a flaw: The character array is only 20 characters long. If you type too many characters, whatever follows the *name* array in the computer's memory is overwritten, and peculiar things happen. An *iostream* function named *get* solves this problem; you learn about *get* in Chapter 16. For now, the exercises assume that you do not type more characters than the declared character array can accept.

The *cin, cout,* and *cerr* objects are not themselves a part of the compiled C++ language. They are defined by the ANSI Standard C++ specification, but they are not instrinsic language components. Binary plus (+) and minus (-) are examples of intrinsic operators. C++ has no instrinsic input/output operators that coincide with BASIC's PRINT statement or COBOL's WRITE verb. The stream classes are not built-in data types, and the << and >> operators are not, in this context, built-in C++ operators. Input and output streams are implemented as C++ classes, and *cin* and *cout* are global instances of those classes. This implementation exists outside the C++ language implementation. C++ allows you to define new data types and to associate custom operators with those data types, and that's what the designers of the *iostream* facility did to provide a standard console input/output system. This is a significant lesson. You learn how to do this for your own data types in later chapters.

SUMMARY

In this chapter, you learned that a C++ program consists of functions and variables. You learned about including header files and putting comments in your program. You learned the C++ data types, how to declare variables of those data types, and how to assign values to them. You learned about C++ constants, expressions, operators, and initializers. Finally, you learned how to display data on the screen by using *cout* and how to read data from the keyboard into memory variables by using *cin.*

CHAPTER 3

Functions

This chapter is about C++ functions, the building blocks of a C++ program. Functions hold the executable code of a program. The entry and exit points of every C++ program are in the *main* function. The *main* function calls other functions, each of which returns to the *main* function. Those other functions may—and probably do—call lower functions. Calling a function executes the function immediately. The calling function suspends operation until the called one returns. Functions can accept arguments, and they can return values.

The programmer learns to think of lower functions that are out of sight as trustworthy black box operations that do their jobs. All the standard library functions are in this category. Programmers also develop and acquire function libraries to serve in this capacity. You seldom see the majority of the source code that contributes to the whole of a particular program.

Read this chapter and use the exercises to learn about these subjects:

- Designing functions
- Function prototypes
- Calling functions
- Passing arguments
- Returning values
- Unnamed function parameters
- Default function arguments
- Inline functions
- Overloaded functions
- Type-safe linkages
- Linkage specifications

THE FUNCTION

A function has a function header and a statement body. The function header has three parts: a return type, a name, and a parameter list. The name is unique within the program. It obeys the rules for identifier naming that you learned in Chapter 2. The return value is a C++ data type. It is one of the data types from Chapter 2, a pointer to one of the types, a pointer to a structure, or a pointer to an array. (I teach about pointers, structures, and arrays in Chapter 5.) The parameter list consists of zero or more variables into which the caller's arguments are copied. The statement body holds the local variable declarations and executable code for the function.

All the exercises in Chapter 2 had *main* functions. None of them declared other functions, which is the subject of this chapter.

Remember the *main*

The *main* function is required in all C++ programs. The system declares it, and your program defines it. The *main* function returns an *int* data type and can accept two arguments. If you do not specify what the function returns, the function's definition defaults to a return of an *int* type.

In addition to its default return type, the *main* function has two default parameters—an *int* and a pointer to an array of *char* pointers—yet the *main* functions in Chapter 2 have empty parameter lists. You will learn about *main*'s default parameters in Chapter 5, but, for now, you should know that *main* can define no parameters when arguments are, in fact, passed to it. Other functions are required to adhere to their declarations, but *main* is exempt.

Your program never calls the *main* function. Doing so is illegal, according to the ANSI C++ Standard. The system's startup procedure calls *main* to begin running the program. When *main* returns, the system shutdown procedures take over. You do not have to worry about the startup and shutdown procedures. The compiler provides them when you compile and link the program. However, by convention, when the program terminates successfully, it should return an integer with a zero value. Other values are implementation-dependent, although the value -1 usually represents unsuccessful completion of the program. Operating systems often use shell programs that execute applications programs from a batch command file and include batch operators to respond to the return values from applications programs. The MS-DOS command-line processor is one such shell program, and Unix has several.

To get you into the habit of returning values from *main*, all exercise programs in this book declare *main* with an *int* return value and return something, usually zero, as shown here:

```
int main()
{
    // ...
    return 0;    // successful completion
}
```

You will learn other ways to use the *return* statement later in this chapter.

ARGUMENTS VERSUS PARAMETERS

The caller of a function passes expressions to the function as arguments. The apparently interchangeable terms *argument* and *parameter* appear frequently in discussions about the values passed. Here is the difference. A function has parameters, which are the variables into which the values passed are copied before the function begins executing. The function prototype declares the parameter types in its parameter list. The caller of a function passes arguments, which are the values returned from expressions to be copied into the function's parameter variables.

DECLARING FUNCTIONS BY USING PROTOTYPES

To call a function, you must declare the function first with respect to its return and parameter types. K&R C did not have that requirement. Functions could be declared implicitly by the first reference to them. They were assumed to expect whatever argument types the function call passed and, unless otherwise declared, were expected to return signed integers. Standard C++ has stronger type checking built into the language definition. Before you can call a function, you must tell the compiler the types of the function's parameters and return value. The declaration of a function is called its *prototype*. Here are examples of function prototypes:

```
unsigned int BuildRecord(char, int);
void GetRecord(char, int, int);
int isMonday(void);
void DoList(int, ...);
```

Unnamed Parameter Types

Observe that the parameter lists in the prototypes contain type specifications with no identifiers for the parameters. You can put parameter identifiers into prototypes, but the identifiers serve as documentation only. They need not correspond to the same identifiers in the function definition's parameter list. Some programmers prefer to omit the identifiers. Others prefer to assign meaningful parameter identifiers in the prototype to convey the meanings of the parameters to other programmers who read the prototype.

A Typical Prototype

Here is a typical prototype:

```
unsigned int BuildRecord(char, int);
```

This first prototype declares a function named *BuildRecord* with two parameters in its parameter list: a *char* argument and an *int* argument. The function returns an *unsigned int* value. You can see from this example why some programmers prefer to supply identifiers for prototype parameters. Nothing in the prototype just shown gives a clue as to the purpose of the parameters. A more descriptive (and less terse) prototype of the same function would look like this:

```
unsigned int BuildRecord(char RecordCode, int RecordNumber);
```

Functions Returning *void*

```
void GetRecord(char, int, int);
```

This prototype declares a function named *GetRecord* with three parameters of types *char, int,* and *int.* (This one is even more obscure than the previous one. Even if you remember the purposes of the parameters, you might easily forget which *int* comes first.) The *void* return type means that the function returns nothing. A *void* function cannot return a value, and you cannot call it in the context of an expression where it is expected to return a value. For example, you cannot call a *void* function from the right side of an assignment statement or as an argument in a function call.

N O T E

The concept of a *void* function appears to be a contradiction. Traditionally, a function is thought to be something that takes arguments, processes them, and returns a value. K&R C did not have *void* functions. Every function was assumed to return an *int* unless it was declared otherwise, even when the function itself returned nothing. That was one of the anomalies in the K&R C definition. Other languages, such as BASIC, Pascal, and PL/1, differentiate between functions—which return values—and *procedures* or *subroutines*, which do not. Standard C++ preserves the classic C tradition by using the *void* function to define a procedure that returns no value.

Functions with No Parameters

```
int isMonday();
```

This prototype defines a function with no parameters. The empty parameter list identifies it as such. You cannot pass arguments to a function with an empty parameter list. Functions that accept no arguments must be assumed to get the data that they work on from external sources instead of from arguments passed by the caller.

Functions with Variable Parameter Lists

```
void DoList(int, ...);
```

This prototype contains one integer parameter type and the *ellipse* (...) token. The ellipse identifies a function that accepts a variable number of arguments with unspecified types. The Standard C library *printf* and *scanf* functions are defined as accepting a variable number of arguments. That is how they can accept different numbers and types of arguments that match their formatting strings. There is a special procedure for writing functions with variable argument lists, and Chapter 6 describes it in the discussion about **<cstdarg>**.

Functions Returning Nothing and with No Parameters

```
void DoSomething();
```

What could be the purpose of a function that takes no arguments and returns no value? In fact, many functions do just that. They apparently have no input and no output. They perform some task, perhaps using data taken from external sources or maintained internally, and post their results externally. All functions have some effect; otherwise, there would be no reason to call them. The caller might invoke the function and not directly benefit from its execution, except when the caller uses an external data item that the called function modifies. An example is a *Beep()* function that sounds an audible alarm to alert the user. It needs no parameters and has nothing meaningful to return that a caller could use. Its purpose is singular, and its effect is unaltered by external influences. There are many similar examples.

Standard Library Prototypes

The prototypes for all the standard library classes and functions are in their respective header files. That is why you need to include **<iostream>**, for example, before you can use *cin, cout, cerr,* or any of the other standard input/output devices.

Functions without Prototypes

You need not code a prototype when the function definition itself appears in the code ahead of any call to it, in which case the function definition serves as its own prototype. To preserve the top-down representation of a program's execution, many programmers do not take advantage of this feature. They put prototypes at the beginning of the program and always make the *main* function the first function defined in the program.

DEFINING AND CALLING FUNCTIONS

You define a function when you write the code for its function header and statement body. All the exercises so far have defined one function, the *main* function. When a function has a prototype, the function definition must match the prototype exactly with respect to the types of its return value and parameters. Exercise 3.1 defines and calls a function that displays a message on the screen.

Exercise 3.1 Defining a function.

```
#include <iostream>
using namespace std;

void ErrorMsg();  // function prototype
int main()
{
    ErrorMsg();   // call the function
    return 0;
}
```

Exercise 3.1 Defining a function. (continued)

```
// ----- Display an error message
void ErrorMsg()
{
    cout << "\aError!";
}
```

Exercise 3.1 declares a function named *ErrorMsg* in a function prototype. The *ErrorMsg* function returns nothing and accepts no arguments. The *main* function calls the *ErrorMsg* function. The *ErrorMsg* function uses *cout* to sound the audible alarm and display the message "Error!" on the screen. (The \a escape sequence sounds the alarm.)

RETURNING FROM FUNCTIONS

A function stops executing in one of several ways. One way, to be discussed in Chapter 6, is by calling the standard *exit* function, which terminates both the calling function and the program. A function can terminate by falling through the bottom of its definition, as the *ErrorMsg* function in Exercise 3.1 does. A function that terminates that way must be declared as returning *void*, because falling through the bottom returns no value. A function can execute the *return* statement from within its body. The *main* function in Exercise 3.1 executes *return* with a value. A *void*-returning function can use the *return* statement with no value. The *ErrorMsg* function in Exercise 3.1 could have been coded this way:

```
void ErrorMsg()
{
    cout << "\aError!";
    return;              // return from the function
}
```

The *return* statement can appear anywhere in the function body, as illustrated by Exercise 3.2.

Exercise 3.2 *Returning with the* return *statement.*

```
#include <iostream>
using namespace std;

void DecideWhen();  // prototype
int main()
{
    DecideWhen();
    return 0;
}
// ----- Decide when to return
void DecideWhen()
{
    int when;
    cout << "When to return (0 = now, 1 = later): ";
    cin >> when;
    if (when == 0)  {
        cout << "Returning now";
        return;     // return from inside the function
    }
    cout << "Returning later";
    return;         // traditional return at the bottom
}
```

Exercise 3.2 prompts you to enter **0** or **1**. Depending on your entry, the program displays a message and returns. Observe that if you enter values other than 0 and 1, the program's behavior is unpredictable. This is a result of the way *cin* works. The exercise shows that you can return from anywhere in a function by using the *return* statement. Here are the messages that Exercise 3.2 returns when you enter **0** and then run the program again and enter **1**:

```
When to return (0 = now, 1 = later): 0
Returning now
When to return (0 = now, 1 = later): 1
Returning later
```

NOTE Some programming theorists contend that returning from anywhere except at the end of a function is one of several so-called improper programming practices. C++ permits the usage, and many programmers, including me, find it useful on occasion. There are, however, good reasons for this deprecation of what is a fairly common programming practice. If you always return from the last statement of a function, then you never need to search a function to see under what circumstances it returns. As with all choices in C++, use what works best for you.

Exercise 3.2 introduces a new construct: the nested, brace-enclosed statement block. The *if* statement's condition is followed by a left brace character, which starts a statement block. The matching right brace character three lines later closes the statement block. The block contains the statements that execute if the condition tested by the *if* statement is true. A program can return from inside a nested statement block, as the exercise demonstrates.

RETURNING VALUES FROM FUNCTIONS

Functions that return values do so in their return statement. Both exercises in this chapter have returned a zero value *int* from their *main* functions. Functions that you define in your programs can also return values. The prototype declares the return value, as Exercise 3.3 shows.

Exercise 3.3 Returning a value.

```
#include <iostream>
int WidthInInches();  // prototype
int main()
{
    int wd = WidthInInches(); // call a function that
                              // returns a value
    cout << "Width in inches = " << wd;
    return 0;
}
```

Exercise 3.3 *Returning a value. (continued)*

```
// ----- Compute width in inches
int WidthInInches()
{
    int feet;
    cout << "Enter width in feet: ";
    cin >> feet;
    return feet * 12;
}
```

Exercise 3.3 displays this prompt and then the following message. The value displayed is the value returned from the *WidthInInches* function.

```
Enter width in feet: 37
Width in inches = 444
```

Ignoring Return Values

What happens when you call a value-returning function in a context in which no value is expected—in which you do not use the return value, do not assign it to anything, nor use it as an argument to another function? Nothing unusual happens. The function executes, and it dutifully returns its value, but the caller can choose to ignore it.

PASSING AND USING ARGUMENTS

The *WidthInInches* function in Exercise 3.3 is not functionally strong. It has multiple purposes. Sound program design principles call for the definition of functions, each of which has one specific task. The *WidthInInches* function performs two related but independent tasks. First, it reads the width in feet from the keyboard, and then it uses that value to compute the width in inches. A stronger design would break these tasks into separate functions. Then other parts of the program could independently retrieve widths in feet and compute widths in inches without necessarily doing them both at the same time.

Strengthening Exercise 3.3 involves breaking the weak function into two stronger functions. One of the two illustrates how you pass arguments to functions, which is the point of this lesson. Exercise 3.4 is the program from Exercise 3.3, improved and strengthened.

Exercise 3.4 *Function arguments.*

```
#include <iostream>
using namespace std;

// --- prototypes
int WidthInFeet();
int WidthInInches(int feet);

int main()
    int feet = WidthInFeet();      // initialize variables
    int wd = WidthInInches(feet); // by calling functions
    cout << "Width in inches = " << wd;
    return 0;
}
// ----- Read width in feet
int WidthInFeet()
{
    int feet;
    cout << "Enter width in feet: ";
    cin >> feet;
    return feet;
}
// ----- Compute width in inches
int WidthInInches(int feet)
{
    return feet * 12;
}
```

Ignore everything else that Exercise 3.4 does for the moment, and observe that it declares the *WidthInInches* function differently than Exercise 3.3 did. The prototype specifies in the parameter list that the function expects an *int* argument.

The *main* function calls *WidthInInches* and passes an *int* variable argument named *feet*. The program defines *WidthInInches* to match the prototype with respect to the return type and parameter type, but the parameter list must assign an identifier to the parameter. This parameter, also named *feet*, is a local variable in the *WidthInInches* function. The function call copies the value of the argument into this variable. The *return* statement uses the *feet* variable in an expression to compute the return value. The declaration, call, and definition of functions that have parameters are the main lessons that Exercise 3.4 teaches. The program displays the same messages that Exercise 3.3 displays.

The Scope of Identifiers

Exercise 3.4 teaches other lessons in addition to the passing of arguments. First, observe that the *main, WidthInFeet*, and *WidthInInches* functions all have integer variables named *feet*. This is correct, because C++ supports variables with *local scope*. As long as an identifier is declared inside a statement block, that identifier is visible only to the statements in that and lower blocks. Identical identifiers in other blocks outside the function are distinct from the local one. Identical identifiers in higher blocks in the hierarchy are effectively overridden by the lower declaration until the identifier goes out of scope. You will learn more about the scope of identifiers in Chapter 5. The parameter variables declared in a function header are also local to the function, and that is why the *WidthInInches* function can name its parameter *feet*.

Initializing with Function Calls

The declarations of the *feet* and *wd* variables in *main* have initializers obtained from calls to the *WidthInFeet* and *WidthInInches* functions. Heretofore, you have seen initializers that contain constant expressions only. Initializers of *automatic* variables, such as these two variables, can contain any kind of expression that returns a value, including a call to a function. You will learn about automatic variables in Chapter 5.

The Sequence of Initializer Execution

There is another lesson in Exercise 3.4. The second initializer uses the first initialized variable as an argument to the function that the second initializer calls. This tells us that initializers are executed in the top-down order in which they occur in the program.

Passing Several Arguments

Some functions accept more than one argument. For example, a function to compute the volume of a brick-shaped object would need to know the height, width, and depth of the object. Exercise 3.5 is an example of a function with several parameters.

Exercise 3.5 *Functions with multiple parameters.*

```cpp
#include <iostream>
using namespace std;

// ---- prototype
double Volume(double, double, long);

int main()
{
    float ht, wd;
    long int dp;

    // ---- get the brick's dimensions
    cout << "Enter height (x.xx), width (x.xx), depth (x): ";
    cin >> ht >> wd >> dp;
    // ---- compute and display the volume
    //      calling a function with many arguments
    cout << "Volume = " << Volume(ht, wd, dp);
    return 0;
}
// ---- compute volume of a brick
double Volume(double height, double width, long depth)
{
    return height * width * depth;
}
```

Exercise 3.5 displays this message in response to your input:

```
Enter height (x.xx), width (x.xx), depth (x): 1.5 2.2 7
Volume = 23.1
```

Function Calls as Arguments

As with many exercises, I use Exercise 3.5 to teach another lesson in addition to its principal one. This time, the call to the *Volume* function is coded as an argument to *cout*'s << operator. It is perfectly acceptable to use a function call in the context of an expression that would return what the function returns. A more traditional programming language would require a temporary variable, an assignment, and the temporary variable passed as the argument. You can write C++ programs using that convention—as shown next—but most programmers prefer the more concise code used in Exercise 3.5.

```
double temp;    // temporary variable
temp = Volume(ht, wd, dp);
cout << "Volume = " << temp;
```

Pass by Value

C++ programs pass their arguments to functions *by value* as opposed to *by reference*. This means that a function gets a copy of the argument in its matching parameter. Sometimes, as in the case of large structures, passing by value is inefficient, and you would rather pass a *reference* to the argument than a copy of it. Other times, the function's purpose is to modify the caller's copy of the argument. In both cases, you can build functions that accept the addresses of arguments instead of the arguments themselves. The function declares the parameter to be a *pointer* to the type of the argument, and the caller passes the address of the argument. You are still passing by value, however, except that now you are passing the value of the address of the argument. You learn about pointers and addresses in Chapter 5.

C++ also supports *reference variables*, which are aliases for real variables. You can use reference variables for pass-by-reference, too. Chapter 5 discusses reference variables.

Type Conversions in Arguments and Return Values

Although the return and parameter types of the prototype and the function definition must match exactly, the caller of the function has a bit of leeway. The rules for type conversion that you learned in Chapter 2 apply to function return values and arguments. Just as it does in assignments, the compiler appropriately promotes or demotes numeric values to accommodate the expressions that your program provides.

UNNAMED FUNCTION PARAMETERS

You can declare a C++ function with one or more parameters that the function does not use. This circumstance often occurs when several functions are called through a generic function pointer. Some of the functions do not use all the parameters named in the function pointer declaration. Following is an example of such a function:

```
int func(int x, int y)
{
    return x * 2;
}
```

Although this usage is correct and common, most C and C++ compilers complain that you failed to use the parameter named y. C++, however, allows you to declare functions with unnamed parameters to indicate to the compiler that the parameter exists and that the callers pass an argument for the parameter, but that the called function does not use it. Following is the C++ function coded with an unnamed second parameter.

```
int func(int x, int)
{
    return x * 2;
}
```

DEFAULT FUNCTION ARGUMENTS

A C++ function prototype can declare that one or more of the function's parameters have default argument values. When a call to the function omits the corresponding arguments, the compiler inserts the default values where it expects to see the arguments.

You can declare default values for arguments in a C++ function prototype in the following way:

```
void myfunc(int = 5, double = 1.23);
```

The expressions declare default values for the arguments. The C++ compiler substitutes the default values if you omit the arguments when you call the function. You can call the function in any of the following ways:

```
myfunc(12, 3.45); // overrides both defaults
myfunc(3);        // effectively func(3, 1.23);
myfunc();         // effectively func(5, 1.23);
```

To omit the first argument in these examples, you must omit the second one; however, you can omit the second argument by itself. This rule applies to any number of arguments. You cannot omit an argument unless you omit the arguments to its right.

Exercise 3.6 shows the use of default arguments.

Exercise 3.6 *A function with default arguments.*

```
#include <iostream>
using namespace std;

void show(int = 1, float = 2.3, long = 4);
main()
{
    show();               // all three arguments default
    show(5);              // provide 1st argument
    show(6, 7.8);         // provide 1st two
    show(9, 10.11, 12L);  // provide all three arguments
}
void show(int first, float second, long third)
{
    cout << "  first = "  << first;
    cout << ", second = " << second;
    cout << ", third = "  << third << endl;
}
```

The first call to the *show* function in Exercise 3.6 allows the C++ compiler to provide the default values for the parameters just as the prototype specifies them. The second call provides the first parameter and allows the compiler to provide the other two. The third call provides the first two and allows the compiler to provide the last. The fourth call provides all three parameters, and none of the defaults is used.

inline Functions

You can tell the C++ compiler that a function is *inline*, which compiles a new copy of the function each time it is called. The *inline* function execution eliminates the function-call overhead of traditional functions. You should use *inline* functions only when the functions are small or when there are relatively few calls to them.

Exercise 3.7 uses the *inline* keyword to make a small function into an *inline* function.

Exercise 3.7 An inline *function.*

```
#include <iostream>
#include <cstdlib>
using namespace std;

inline void error_message(char* s)
{
    cout << '\a' << s;
    exit(1);
}
main()
{
    error_message("You called?");
}
```

Observe that Exercise 3.7 declares the *inline* function ahead of the call to it. The C++ draft standard does not define where an *inline* function must be declared as such and under what conditions the compiler may choose to ignore the *inline* declaration except to say that the compiler may do so. Because of this ambiguity in the language specification, compiler builders have leeway in how they interpret the requirements. You could declare an *inline* function (for performance reasons, perhaps) and have the compiler overrule you without saying so. To be safe, always declare *inline* functions ahead of all calls to them. If an *inline* function is to assume the appearance of an *extern* global function—if it is to be called by code in several source files, as Chapter 5 discusses—put its declaration in a header file.

Using *inline* supports two idioms. First, it offers an improved macro facility, which Chapter 7 discusses. Second, it permits you to break a large function with many nested levels of statement blocks into several smaller *inline* functions. This usage improves a program's readability without introducing unnecessary function-call overhead.

Chapter 7 compares *inline* functions to preprocessor *#define* macros.

RECURSION

All C++ functions are *recursive*, which means that a function can call itself, either directly or indirectly, by a lower function that is executing as the result of a call made by the recursive function.

Functions can be recursive because each execution of a function has private copies of its arguments and local data objects, and those copies are distinct from the copies owned by other executions of the same function.

Chapter 5 explains recursion in detail.

OVERLOADED FUNCTIONS

C++ allows you to assign the same function name to multiple functions but with different parameter types. All versions of the function are then available at the same time. This feature is called *function overloading*.

Overloading for Different Operations

Sometimes you overload a function because it performs a generic task but there are different permutations of what it does. The Standard C *strcpy* and *strncpy* functions (Chapter 6) are examples. Both functions copy strings but in slightly different ways. The *strcpy* function copies a string from the source to the destination. The *strncpy* function copies a string but stops copying when the source string terminates or after the function copies a specified number of characters.

Exercise 3.8 provides two functions named *string_copy* that copy strings two ways.

***Exercise 3.8** Overloading functions, example 1.*

```
#include <iostream>
using namespace std;

void string_copy(char *dest, const char* src)
{
    while((*dest++ = *src++) != '\0')
        ;
}

void string_copy(char* dest, const char* src, int len)
{
    while (len && (*dest++ = *src++) != '\0')
        --len;
    while (len--)
        *dest++ = '\0';
}

char misspiggy[20], kermit[20];

main()
{
    string_copy(misspiggy, "Miss Piggy");
    string_copy(kermit,
        "Kermit, the file transfer protocol", 6);
    cout << kermit << " and " << misspiggy;
}
```

There are two functions named *string_copy* in this program. What sets them apart is their different parameter lists. The first of the two *string_copy* functions has destination and source character pointers as parameters. The second function has the pointers as well as an integer length. The C++ compiler recognizes that these are two distinct functions by virtue of these differences in their parameter lists.

Overloading for Different Formats

Exercise 3.8 showed how to overload a function to get a different algorithm on similar data. Another reason to overload a function is to get the same result from data values that can be represented in different formats. Standard C++ has various ways of representing the date and time. You will find other ways in Unix, and still others in MS-DOS.

Exercise 3.9 shows how you can send two of the standard C formats to the overloaded *display_time* functions.

Exercise 3.9 *Overloading functions, example 2.*

```
#include <iostream>
#include <ctime>
using namespace std;

void display_time(const struct tm* tim)
{
    cout << "1. It is now " << asctime(tim);
}

void display_time(time_t* tim)
{
    cout << "2. It is now " << ctime(tim);
}

int main()
{
    time_t tim = time(0);
    struct tm* ltim = localtime(&tim);
    display_time(ltim);
    display_time(&tim);
    return 0;
}
```

Exercise 3.9 uses the Standard C data formats *time_t* and *struct tm*. It loads them with the value of the current date and time using the Standard C *time* and *localtime* functions. (Chapter 6 describes these data formats and functions.) Then the program calls its own overloaded *display_time* function for each of the formats.

Exercise 3.9 displays the following results:

```
1. It is now Mon Jan 27 12:05:20 1997
1. It is now Mon Jan 27 12:05:20 1997
```

Dates and times are good ways to experiment with overloaded functions. There are many ways to represent them internally, many ways that different systems report them to a program, and many ways to display them. In addition to all these formats, there are many common date and time algorithms. A comprehensive date and time package would be a solid addition to any programmer's tool collection.

TYPE-SAFE LINKAGES

If you can give several functions the same name, what reconciles the apparent conflicts between similarly named functions that are declared in different translation units (source code files)? It would seem that the linker would not know which function to use in resolving a reference to one of those functions. Function linkages would not be type-safe.

C++ solves this problem by applying a process called *name mangling* to the compiler's internal identifier of a function. The mangled name includes tokens that identify the function's return type and the types of its arguments. Calls to the function and the function definition itself are recorded in the relocatable object file as references to the mangled name, which is unique even though several functions might have the same unmangled name.

Mangled names also transcend the use of prototypes to ensure that the functions match their calls. Unlike C, the C++ type-checking system cannot be overridden simply by using different prototypes for the same function.

Algorithms for name mangling vary among compilers, but that is of no concern to programmers. You rarely see the mangled names. But you must understand the underlying principle, because it creates a problem—one that C++ linkage specifications, discussed next, solves.

LINKAGE SPECIFICATIONS

Although C++ mangles function names, other languages do not. In particular, C compilers and assembly language assemblers do not. This presents a problem, because a C++ program must be able to call functions that are compiled or assembled in other languages, and a C++ program must be able to provide functions that are called from other languages. If the C++ compiler always mangled function names internally, references to external functions in other languages would not be properly resolved.

All the Standard C functions are compiled by the C compiler component of any C++ development system. Consequently, their names are not internally mangled. Your project might employ other function libraries, too. Without some method for telling the C++ compiler not to mangle references to those functions, you could never call them from a C++ program.

C++ employs the *linkage-specification* to make functions that were compiled by compilers of other languages accessible to a C++ program. Unless you tell the C++ compiler otherwise, it assumes that external identifiers are subject to C++ name mangling. Therefore, you must tell the C++ compiler when a function has been (or must be) compiled with different linkage conventions.

The following code shows how a linkage-specification tells the C++ compiler that the functions in a header file were compiled by a C compiler.

```
extern "C"    {        // the linkage-specification
#include "mychdr.h"    // tells C++ that functions in the
}                      // library were compiled with C
int main()
{
    return foobar();   // call a C function
}
```

The *extern "C"* statement says that everything within the scope of the brace-surrounded block—in this case, everything in the **"mychdr.h"** header file—is compiled by a C compiler.

Language environments that support both languages manage the translation for you by hiding the linkage-specification in the Standard C library header files for the C functions. The GNU compiler uses the convention shown in the following code fragment:

```
/* --- typical Standard C Library header file --- */
#ifdef __cplusplus
extern "C" {
#endif

/* header file contents ... */
#ifdef __cplusplus
}
#endif
```

The compiler's front end (Quincy 97, in our case) defines with the #define preprocessing directive a global macro named _cplusplus_ when you compile a C++ source-code file. Other compilers might use other macro names. The compiler's preprocessor program uses the *#ifdef* and *#endif* directives to include or exclude the linkage-specification statements depending on whether _cplusplus_ is defined. Chapter 7 explains the preprocessor and its directives.

So with respect to Standard C library functions, you can ignore the name convention differences between C functions and C++ functions. There are times, however, when you need to use linkage-specifications. If you have a large library of custom C functions to include in your C++ system and if you do not want to take the time and trouble to port them to C++ (perhaps you do not have the source code), then you must use a linkage-specification. You can use the convention that the Standard C library uses, or you can code the linkage specifications directly into your C++ programs.

Exercise 3.10 is a C++ program that calls a function that is compiled with a C compiler and has C linkages. The C++ program also includes a function of its own that is called from the C program and, therefore, must be compiled with C linkages.

Exercise 3.10a *The C++ source.*

```
#include <iostream>
using namespace std;

// --------- array of string pointers to be sorted
static const char* brothers[] = {
"Frederick William",
"Joseph Jensen",
"Harry Alan",
"Walter Ellsworth",
"Julian Paul"
};
extern "C"
{
    // --- prototype of C function
    void SortCharArray(const char**);
    // --- C++ function to be called from the C program
    int SizeArray()
    {
        return sizeof brothers / sizeof (char*);
    }
}
int main()
{
    // --- sort the pointers
    SortCharArray(brothers);
    // --- display the brothers in sorted order
    int size = SizeArray();
    for (int i = 0; i < size; i++)
        cout << brothers[i] << endl;
    return 0;
}
```

Exercise 3.10b *The C source.*

```
#include <string.h>
#include <stdlib.h>

int SizeArray(void); /* prototype of the C++ function */
/* --- the compare function for qsort --- */
static int comp(const void *a, const void *b)
{
    return strcmp(*(char **)a, *(char **)b);
}
/* --- C function called from C++ program --- */
void SortCharArray(char **List)
{
    int sz = SizeArray();
    qsort(List, sz, sizeof(char *), comp);
}
```

Exercise 3.10 consists of two source files: a C++ source-code module (3.10a) and a C source-code module (3.10b). The C module has a *SortCharArray* function that sorts an array of character pointers but does not know the length of the array. It calls a function named *SizeArray*, which is provided by the C++ caller, to determine the length of the array. The C++ module declares two items within its *extern "C"* linkage-specification: the *SortCharArray* C function that the C++ program calls and its own *SizeArray* function that the C function calls.

Observe that the actual *SizeArray* function is defined within the *extern "C"* linkage-specification. The GNU compiler that Quincy uses allows such functions to call other functions without regard to whether they are compiled with *extern "C"* or *extern "C++"* linkage. The compiler figures it out at compile time. It is not clear whether this behavior is standard or merely idiomatic of the GNU compiler.

Without the linkage-specifications, the C++ compiler would mangle the names of the C++ function and the C++ program's call to the C function. The linker would not properly resolve the C++ program's call to the *SortCharArray* C function or the C function's call to the *SizeArray* C++ function.

NOTE

In the real world, you would take other measures to give the length of the array to the C function. You could null-terminate the array, and the C function could determine the array length on its own. You could pass the length of the array as an argument to the C function. You could pass the address of a function in the C++ program, which would then not need to be compiled with C linkages. Perhaps you are not in control of the C program, not having its source code, and you are stuck with whatever conventions the C programmer used. Perhaps the C function is already so widely used that you cannot change it.

Linkage-specifications can nest. For example, if you have C++ prototypes within a C linkage-specification, you can code a nested C++ linkage-specification.

Languages other than C and C++ can be supported by linkage-specifications, and their string values are implementation-dependent. The C++ compiler must know how to encode the names for those languages. The other language must support C++ compatible conventions for passing arguments and return values. If you are linking with assembly language or some other language that employs no name mangling, you can usually use *extern "C"* as the linkage-specification for those languages.

There are a few other things that Exercise 3.10 can show you, particularly with regard to the C source-code module shown in Exercise 3.10b. First, observe the #*include* directives. They specify **<string.h>** and **<stdlib.h>** whereas C++ source-code files specify **<cstring>** and **<cstdlib>**, as many of the exercises in this book do. The C specifications name the actual Standard C library header files. The C++ specifications name small header files that themselves include the C header files but within the *std* namespace. Chapter 2 introduced the *std* namespace. Chapter 15 discusses the C++ namespace feature in detail.

Next, observe the prototype for the *SizeArray* function. C prototypes for functions with empty parameter lists must include the *void* keyword. C++ prototypes may include that keyword, but it is not necessary. The C requirement is to allow the compiler to distinguish prototypes from old-style K&R function declarations, which Standard C continues to support but which C++ does not support.

Finally, the C module uses C-style comments only. Many contemporary C compilers permit you to use the C++ double-slash (//) comment format in C source code. Quincy's GNU compiler is one of them. However, that usage is nonstandard, and you should avoid it in C-only source-code files if you are concerned about portability.

Summary

In this chapter, you learned how to design and call functions. You learned that a function's prototype provides its declaration and that all uses of the function as well as the function definition itself must comply with the specification of the prototype. You learned how to define a function by providing a return type, function name, parameter list, and statement body. You learned some of the contexts in which function calls may be used: by themselves, in initializers of local variables, on the right side of expressions, and as arguments to other functions. You learned that function calls pass their arguments by value. You learned about default function arguments and inline functions as well as linkage-specifications and unnamed function parameters.

CHAPTER 4

Program Flow Control

This chapter is about C++ language statements that control the flow of a program's execution. C supports the sequence, selection, and iteration control structures of structured programming as well as the *goto* operation of unstructured programming. You will learn about the following subjects in this chapter:

- Statement blocks
- Selection: *if...else* and *switch*
- Iteration: *while*, *do...while*, and *for*
- Loop control: *break, continue*
- Jumping: *goto*

STATEMENT BLOCKS

Every C++ function has at least one brace-surrounded statement block: the one at the outer level just under the function header. Exercise 3.2 in Chapter 3 included a function with a statement block nested inside the outer statement block. A C++ function can have many nested levels of statement blocks. These nested blocks are important to C++'s ability to define groups of statements that execute under controlled conditions. They are also important to the management of local variable scope (Chapter 5).

Nesting Depth

As you develop your programs, be wary of constructs that have a great many nested levels of statement blocks. If you indent your statements properly, your code shifts farther to the right of the page as the nested levels increase. Go too far, and the code becomes difficult to read and understand. It is better to reorganize the function and put the more deeply nested blocks into their own functions.

Indentation Styles

There are several styles for indenting C++ code and for placement of the braces that define statement blocks. C++, being a free-form programming language, mandates no particular style for braces, indenting, and white space. The style of the exercises in this book reflects my personal preference. It is influenced by the style published in K&R. Here are examples of different styles for writing C++ code:

```
if (a == b)  {    // then ... endif
    // ...
}

if (a == b)       // begin ... end
{
    // ...
}
```

```
if (a == b)        // do ... doend
    {
    // ...
    }
```

The comments in these style examples show how C++ programmers use brace punctuation to express blocks in ways that other languages use keywords. No one style is right, and no one style is wrong. You should strive for consistency, using the same style throughout a program. Eventually, you will find one that you like. If you are modifying someone else's work, use the style that the program uses even if you don't like it. Consistency in code contributes to more readable and, therefore, more maintainable code.

SELECTION: TESTS

The power of the first digital computer was said to be in its ability to make decisions, and all its descendents inherited that ability. Programmers express decisions as tests of a *condition*, which is the true or false value of an expression. Almost every expression returns a value that can be tested for truth. Exceptions are the *void* function that returns nothing (Chapter 3) and the function that returns a *struct* (Chapter 5), which cannot by itself be tested for truth.

An expression is true if its value is not equal to zero; otherwise, it is false. As you learned in Chapter 2, an expression can consist of other expressions and operators and has a true/false condition based on the result of the evaluation of the full expression, which can include arithmetic, logical, relational, and bitwise operations. Any time an expression is used in a context in which the program is testing its true/false value, that use of the expression is said to be a condition.

The *if* Statement

C++ programs use the *if...else* program flow control statement to test conditions and execute one of two statements or statement blocks depending on the condition. Exercise 4.1 illustrates this usage.

Exercise 4.1 *Testing with* if *for zero.*

```
#include <iostream>
int main()
{

    int selection;
    cout << "Enter 0 to compute: ";
    cin >> selection;

    if (selection == 0)
        cout << "You chose to compute";

    return 0;

}
```

The expression tested by an *if* statement is always enclosed in parentheses. It can be a complex expression and can include function calls, operators, variables, and constants.

N O T E   By now you are accustomed to reading code and running exercises either with Quincy or your own C++ development system. Until now, this book has told you what to expect on the screen when you run the programs. You have reached the point where, in most cases, you can discern for yourself from the code what the programs will display, and you can certainly see it on the screen when you run them. Unless it is either not obvious or is critical to the point being made, the book won't belabor the output any further.

There is an important lesson in Exercise 4.1. The *if* statement tests to see whether the *selection* variable is equal to zero. This condition is true only if the variable is equal to zero. This might seem backwards. When the variable's value is zero, the expression is true. The explanation for this seeming anomaly is that the full expression includes a comparison with the constant 0. The condition returned by the expression depends on the value of the variable as compared with the constant 0 by the == equality operator; it does not depend on the value of the variable itself. Exercise 4.2 is the same program except that it tests for anything except zero in the variable.

Exercise 4.2 *Testing with* if *for nonzero.*

```
#include <iostream>
using namespace std;

int main()
{
    cout << "Enter any number but 0 to compute: ";
    int selection;
    cin >> selection;

    if (selection)
        cout << "You chose to compute";

    return 0;
}
```

The *if* statement in Exercise 4.2 uses the variable name alone in the condition. A nonzero value in the variable satisfies the test. Many programmers prefer to code such tests explicitly:

```
if (selection != 0)
```

There is no difference between that usage and the usage in Exercise 4.2.

Exercises 4.1 and 4.2 execute one statement if the condition being tested is true. Exercise 4.3 shows that a test executes the statement block that follows immediately when the condition is true.

Exercise 4.3 Conditionally executing a block.

```cpp
#include <iostream>
#include <cmath>
using namespace std;

int main()
{
    cout << "Enter a dimension to compute a cube: ";

    int dimension;
    cin >> dimension;

    if (dimension) {
        cout << dimension << " cubed = "
            << pow(dimension, 3);
        return 0;
    }
    cout << "You chose not to compute.";
    return 0;
}
```

Exercise 4.3 has several new lessons. First, it demonstrates that when the *if* statement finds a true condition—when you enter anything other than zero in response to the prompt—all the statements in the following brace-sur-rounded statement block execute. The indentation of that code emphasizes that relationship, but it has nothing to do with the effect. White space in a C++ program is for legibility and aesthetics only.

Also observe that Exercise 4.3 includes the **<cmath>** header file and uses the Standard C *pow* function to compute the third power of the *dimension* variable. Compiler header files (ones expressed between angle brackets) with names that begin with "c" and that have no file extension contain the declarations for the Standard C library functions. Standard C++ includes the complete Standard C library enclosed within the *std* namespace. Chapter 6 discusses the Standard C library in more detail. Chapter 15 discusses namespaces.

The *pow* function expects *double* types for its two parameters; yet Exercise 4.3 passes *int* arguments. This usage demonstrates a point made in Chapter 3 that function arguments are subject to the C++ language rules of type conversion. The compiler promotes the caller's arguments to the types expected by the *pow* function based on the function's prototype declaration in the **<cmath>** header file.

Finally, the program uses something that you learned in Chapter 3 may be considered improper programming: The *main* function returns from a place other than the bottom of the function. This book takes no position about the propriety of such code, but the next lesson, which is really about *else*, shows how to remove the so-called improper code.

The *if...else* Statements

In addition to allowing statements that execute when a condition is true, a test can specify that different statements execute when the condition is false. C++ uses the *else* statement for that purpose, and Exercise 4.4 modifies Exercise 4.3 to use it.

Exercise 4.4 Using else.

```
#include <iostream>
#include <cmath>
using namespace std;

int main()
{
    cout << "Enter a dimension to compute a cube: ";

    int dimension;
    cin >> dimension;

    if (dimension)
        cout << dimension << " cubed = "
             << pow(dimension, 3);
    else
        cout << "You chose not to compute.";
    return 0;
}
```

The *else* statement executes the statement or statement block that follows when the condition tested by the associated *if* statement is false. You can have an *else* statement only when it follows an *if* statement.

The *else if* Statements

Joining a sequence of *if* and *else* keywords produces the equivalent of the ELSEIF operator of other programming languages. It enables you to make a series of mutually exclusive tests. Exercise 4.5 demonstrates that usage by implementing a simple screen menu.

Exercise 4.5 Using else if *for a menu.*

```cpp
#include <iostream>
using namespace std;

// --- prototypes
void DisplayMenu();
int GetSelection();

int main()
{
    DisplayMenu();                  // display the menu
    int selection;
    selection = GetSelection();  // get menu selection
    // ---- select matching process
    if (selection == 1)
        cout << "Processing Receivables" << endl;
    else if (selection == 2)
        cout << "Processing Payables" << endl;
    else if (selection == 3)
        cout << "Quitting" << endl;
    else
        cout << "\aInvalid selection" << endl;
    return 0;
}
```

Exercise 4.5 Using else if *for a menu. (continued)*

```
// --- display a menu
void DisplayMenu()
{
    cout << "--- Menu ---" << endl;
    cout << "1=Receivables" << endl;
    cout << "2=Payables" << endl;
    cout << "3=Quit" << endl;
}
// --- read a menu selection from the keyboard
int GetSelection()
{
    int selection;
    cout << "Enter Selection: ";
    cin >> selection;
    return selection;
}
```

Exercise 4.5 displays a menu on the screen and reads the user's selection from the keyboard. Then the program uses the *else if* idiom to test the value of the selection and run an appropriate process, which in this case is simply a message on the screen to indicate which process the user selected.

Observe the *endl* identifier that the program sends to *cout* at the end of each message:

```
cout << "--- Menu ---" << endl;
```

The *endl* object is a newline character. It represents a portable way for a program to tell the console to position the display and input cursor at the beginning of the next line. The following statement does the same thing:

```
cout << "--- Menu ---\n";
```

The *switch...case* Statements

The *switch...case* statements provide a convenient notation for multiple *else if* tests when you test a single integral variable for multiple values. In Exercise 4.5, all the *if* statements test the value of the integer variable *selection*. The program could have been written with a *switch*. Exercise 4.6 illustrates how to do that.

Exercise 4.6 The switch...case *statement.*

```
int main()
{
    DisplayMenu();              // display the menu
    int selection;
    selection = GetSelection(); // get menu selection
    // ---- select matching process
    switch (selection)       {
        case 1:
            cout << "Processing Receivables" << endl;
            break;
        case 2:
            cout << "Processing Payables" << endl;
            break;
        case 3:
            cout << "Quitting" << endl;
            break;
        default:
            cout << "\aInvalid selection" << endl;
            break;
    }
    return 0;
}
```

NOTE For brevity, Exercise 4.6 shows only the *main* function, which is all that changes from Exercise 4.5. The rest of the code is in the program nonetheless and in the program on the Quincy CD-ROM. Subsequent exercises apply the same convention.

The condition tested by the *switch* statement must be an integral expression. This means that it can contain operators and function calls. The values tested by the *case* statements must be constant integral values. This means that they can have constant expressions and operators but cannot have variables, function calls, or side effects such as assignments and increment and decrement operators. When your tests use these things or when the series of tests involves different variables, use the *else if* idiom.

No two *case* values may evaluate to the same constant value.

The *default* statement is followed by code that executes if none of the *case* values is equal to the *switch* expression. You may omit the *default* statement, but if you include it, there may be only one in a *switch*.

The list of *cases* (including the *default*) is always enclosed by braces. The expression tested by the *switch* is always enclosed in parentheses.

The code executed for each *case* is followed by a *break* statement. If you omit the *break*, execution falls through to the code for the next case in the list. This is not always an error but often is exactly what you want. It allows you to assign the same statements to the same *case*, as shown here:

```
switch (keystroke)  {
    case 'a':
    case 'b':
    case 'c':
        doit("abc");  // executed for first three cases
        break;
    case 'd':
        // ...
    default:
        // ...
}
```

Declaration within an *if* Conditional Expression

You can declare a variable within the conditional expression of an *if* statement. This is a new C++ feature recently invented by the ANSI committee, and many compilers now implement the feature. The GNU compiler that Quincy supports does not implement the feature, so there are no exercises here to run. The following code fragment is an example:

```
if ((int selection = GetSelection()) != -1)  {
    // selection is in scope ...
}
// selection is not in scope ...
```

The program can reference the *selection* variable anywhere in the statement block that executes if the condition returns a true value. The program cannot reference the *selection* variable past that statement block. Chapter 5 explains the scope of variables in more detail.

ITERATIONS: LOOPING

In addition to making decisions, a program must be able to iterate: repeat sequences of instructions against successive data values. These iterating processes are called loops, and C++ has three looping statements: *while*, *do...while*, and *for*.

Most programs loop. They operate on a set of data values from a database, the keyboard, a text file, or any of a number of data sources that contain multiple records of similar data. Loop iterations proceed from the first of these records through subsequent ones until there are no more records to process.

Other loops occur within a program's main loop. The program might iterate through arrays once for each input record. Loops can have inner loops, too, such as an array that has multiple dimensions (Chapter 5).

The *while* Statement

The *while* statement tests a condition and, if the condition is true, executes the statement or statement block immediately following. When each iteration of the loop is finished, the program returns to the controlling *while* statement, which repeats its test. If the condition is false the first time, no iteration of the loop executes, and execution proceeds with the statement following the loop statements. If the test is true the first time, then something in the loop must, during the first or a subsequent iteration, cause the condition to become false. Otherwise, the loop would never terminate.

NOTE

In a typical mixed (or possibly, confused) programming metaphor, a loop that is never terminated is said to be a *dead* loop.

The program in Exercise 4.6 does not loop. It gets one menu selection from the user, processes it, and exits. More typically, programs process menu selections until the user chooses to exit. Exercise 4.7 uses the *while* statement to execute the program that way.

Exercise 4.7 Iterating with while.

```
int main()
{
    int selection = 0;
    while (selection != 3)    {
        DisplayMenu();                  // display the menu
        selection = GetSelection(); // get menu selection
        // ---- select matching process
        switch (selection)    {
            case 1:
                cout << "Processing Receivables" << endl;
                break;
            case 2:
                cout << "Processing Payables" << endl;
                break;
            case 3:
                cout << "Quitting" << endl;
                break;
            default:
                cout << "\aInvalid selection" << endl;
                break;
        }
    }
    return 0;
}
```

With one new line of code, Exercise 4.7 turns the earlier program into one that runs until the user says to stop. Note that because of the way the program is written, the first iteration of the loop always runs. The *selection* variable is initialized to zero, and the *while* statement tests it to be equal to 3. Often, a *while* statement does not execute its loop statements at all because the condition is false the first time it is tested.

N O T E   The *selection* variable's initializer is necessary in Exercise 4.7, because local variables are not guaranteed to be initialized to anything in particular, and the random value that *selection* could have on startup might just be a 3. Exercise 4.6 read data into the variable before it tested it, so the initializer was not necessary.

Can you see the potential in Exercise 4.7 for a so-called dead loop? If the user never enters a 3, the *while* loop goes on forever. This arrangement is not a problem in an interactive situation such as this one. The user can be expected to understand from the menu display what is required. Eventually, he or she will enter that 3 to get out of the program and on with other things. Dead loops in a program are usually bugs, often occurring in loops that involve no interaction with the user. Here's a simple one:

```
int x = 0, y = 0;
while (x < 3)
    y++;
```

The loop increments *y*, but the *while* statement tests *x*, which never changes. You'll know when you are in such a dead loop. The computer stops dead in its tracks. If you are running the program in Quincy, you can break out of the loop by choosing the **Stop** command on the Project menu. If you have compiled the program with a commercial compiler and are running it under an operating system, such as MS-DOS, in which preemptive interrupts of programs do not occur, you must reboot the computer.

The *do...while* Statement

Sometimes a loop iteration must execute at least once, regardless of the condition of the variable being tested. The *do...while* statement allows you to write such a loop. Exercise 4.8 demonstrates this behavior.

Exercise 4.8 *Iterating with* do…while.

```cpp
#include <iostream>
#include <cstdlib>
using namespace std;

int main()
{
    char ans;
    // --- loop until user is done
    do  {
        // --- choose a secret number
        int fav = rand() % 32;
        // --- loop until user guesses secret number
        int num;
        do  {
        cout << "Guess my secret number (0 - 32) ";
        cin >> num;
        // --- report the status of the guess
        cout << (num < fav ? "Too low"  :
                 num > fav ? "Too high" :
                             "Right") << endl;
        } while (num != fav);
        cout << "Go again? (y/n) ";
        cin >> ans;
    } while (ans == 'y');
    return 0;
}
```

Exercise 4.8 has two *do…while* constructs. Each *do* statement is followed by a statement block to be interated, which is followed by the *while* test. Observe that the conditions that follow the *while* keywords are in parentheses and are terminated with semicolons.

The difference between *while* and *do…while* is that the test in a *while* happens before each iteration, and the test in a *do…while* happens after each iteration. This behavior is reflected in the way you code the two loops. You code the *while* statement ahead of the loop statements in a *while* test, and after them for a *do...while* test.

The program in Exercise 4.8 computes a random number by calling the **<cstdlib>** Standard C *rand* function. This function returns a random integer between 0 and 32,768. The program reduces this number to one between 0 and 32 by computing the remainder of dividing the random number by 32. Then it goes into a *do...while* loop, letting you guess the number and telling you whether your guess is too high, too low, or right on. When you guess the number, the loop terminates. An outer *do...while* loop lets you exit or guess another number.

Observe the message displayed on *cout* after you enter a guess. It uses a compound conditional operator (?:) to determine which message to display. The first condition is *num < fav*. If that expression is true, the conditional operator passes the "Too low" message. If that expression is not true, the rightmost expression—which is evaluated and returned for the first conditional operator—is another conditional expression that tests *num > fav*. If that expression is true, the returned value is the "Too high" message. Otherwise, neither condition is true. This means that *num* is equal to *fav*, and the returned value is the "Right" message. This example demonstrates how you can use a series of conditional operators to make a compound test that evaluates to a single value.

The *for* Statement

The C++ *for* statement is similar to BASIC's FOR operator in that it can control a loop, modifying an initialized variable in each loop iteration. C++'s *for* statement is more general than BASIC's, however. It consists of three expressions separated by semicolons. The three expressions are surrounded by parentheses and are followed by the statement or statement block that constitutes the iteration. The first expression is evaluated once when the *for* statement executes. Then the second expression is evaluated. If it is true, the iteration executes, and the third expression is evaluated. The loop continues with another test of the second expression, and so on until the second expression is false. This is the format of the *for* statement:

```
for ( <expr1>; <expr2>; <expr3> )
    <iteration>
```

Although the three expressions can be anything you want, including comma-separated expressions, the *for* statement is a convenient notation for a common programming idiom that you could write by using *while* notation this way:

```
<expr1>;
while ( <expr2> )    {
    <iteration>
    <expr3>;
}
```

Consequently, a typical use of the *for* statement is to assign a value to a variable, test that variable for a maximum value, use the variable in the loop iteration, and increment the variable at the end of the iteration. Exercise 4.9 illustrates that usage.

Exercise 4.9 The for *statement.*

```
#include <iostream>
#include <cstdlib>
using namespace std;

int main()
{
    int counter;
    for (counter = 0; counter < 10; counter++) {
        srand(counter+1);
        cout << "Random number " << counter+1 << ": "
            << rand() << endl;
    }
    return 0;
}
```

The first expression in the *for* loop in Exercise 4.9 assigns a zero value to the *counter* variable. The second expression is a conditional expression that returns true if the *counter* variable is less than 10. The third expression increments the *counter* variable. That combination of expressions in a *for* statement iterates the loop 10 times, as long as nothing in the loop modifies the *counter* variable.

Each iteration uses the new value in the *counter* variable as an argument to the **<cstdlib>** Standard C function *srand*. This function *seeds* the standard random number generator. Then the program displays the *counter* variable and the next computed random number.

NOTE If you do not provide a seed value, the *rand* function always starts with a seed of 1, and the random number sequence is predictable. You might have observed that the program in Exercise 4.8 always computed the same progression of secret numbers for you to guess. In Chapter 6 you learn how to use values from the **<ctime>** functions to seed the random number generator to get less predictable results.

The *for* statement is convenient for iterating through the elements of arrays (Chapter 5). Exercise 4.10 introduces that concept.

Exercise 4.10 Iterating through an array.

```
#include <iostream>
using namespace std;

int main()
{
    int items[5] = {9, 43, 6, 22, 70};
    for (int i = 0; i < 5; i++)
        cout << "Item #" << i+1 << ": " << items[i] << endl;
    return 0;
}
```

The *items* declaration is a C++ array. The value inside the square brackets specifies the dimension—the number of elements—in the array. The *items* variable is an array of *int* objects that contains five elements.

The *for* statement iterates the *i* integer variable from zero through 4. Remember that the loop executes only when the second expression in the *for* statement is true; in this case, it is true only for the values zero through 4. When the integer is incremented at the end of the loop to the value 5, the second expression, *i* < 5, is false, and the loop is not executed again.

Array subscripts are relative to zero. Therefore, the elements of an array that has five elements can be accessed with subscripts zero through 4. The argument in the *cout* statement, *items[i]*, references the array element of *items* relative to the value in *i*. The expression *items[0]* returns the first element in the array, *items[1]* returns the second, and so on.

Declaration within a *for* Conditional Expression

Observe that the first expression in the *for* statement declares the *int i* variable that is used to iterate the loop. This variable is in scope for the *for* statement and for the statement(s) in the iteration. You learn more about variable scope in Chapter 5.

LOOP CONTROL

Often, a *while, do...while,* or *for* loop needs to break out of the loop abruptly regardless of the value of the conditional expression that keeps it going. Other times you need to terminate the current iteration and return to the top of the loop. C++ provides the *break* and *continue* loop control statements for these purposes.

break

The *break* statement terminates a loop and jumps out of it to the next statement following the iteration code. Be aware that this *break* statement is not the same one used in the *switch...case* selection statement. Exercise 4.11 illustrates the *break* statement from within a *while* loop.

Exercise 4.11 The break *statement.*

```
#include <iostream>
#include <cstdlib>
using namespace std;

int main()
{
    char selection = '\0';
    while (selection != 'q')     {
        cout << "S-how number, Q-uit: ";
        cin >> selection;
        if (selection != 's' && selection != 'q')     {
            cout << '\a';
            break;            // break out of while
        }
        if (selection == 's')
            cout << rand() << endl;
    }
    return 0;
}
```

Exercise 4.11 stays in a loop while the *selection* variable is not equal to the character constant *'q'*. The user can type any character. As long as that character is *'s'*, the program displays a new random number. If the user presses *'q'*, the loop terminates normally as the result of the *while* conditional expression. If the user presses any other key, the program sounds the audible alarm with the *cout* << *'\a'* statement and breaks out of the loop.

Similarly, the *break* statement is used to break out of *for* and *do...while* loops.

continue

Sometimes a program needs to return to the top of the loop iteration rather than break out. The program in Exercise 4.11 beeps and quits if the user enters an incorrect command code. A more hospitable program would give the user another chance. Exercise 4.12 uses the *continue* statement in place of *break*. This action terminates the current iteration and returns to the *while* statement to test for the next iteration.

Exercise 4.12 The continue *statement.*

```
#include <iostream>
#include <cstdlib>
using namespace std;

int main()
{
    char selection = '\0';
    while (selection != 'q')     {
        cout << "S-how number, Q-uit: ";
        cin >> selection;
        if (selection != 's' && selection != 'q')     {
            cout << '\a';
            continue;
        }
        if (selection == 's')
            cout << rand() << endl;
    }
    return 0;
}
```

By using the *continue* statement instead of *break*, the program continues to display the menu until the user presses *'q'*.

The *continue* statement works similarly with *for* and *do...while* loops. In a *for* loop, the *continue* statement jumps to evaluate the third expression in the *for* expression list and then to the evaluation of the second. This strategy continues the loop as you would expect it to be continued. In a *do...while* loop, the *continue* statement jumps to the *while* test at the bottom of the loop.

JUMPING: *GOTO*

The *goto* statement causes a program to immediately jump to an executable statement elsewhere in the function. The *goto* references an identifier that is declared as a statement label elsewhere in the same function. The label can be positioned ahead of any executable statement and is identified with a colon (:) suffix. You can jump in either direction, and you can jump into and out of loops.

Exercise 4.13 shows how you can use *goto* to jump out of an inner loop when a simple *break* would not work.

Exercise 4.13 The goto *statement.*

```
#include <iostream>
using namespace std;

int main()
{
    for (int dept = 1; dept < 10; dept++)     {
        cout << "Department " << dept << endl;
        int empl;
        do     {
            cout << "Enter Empl # "
                    "(0 to quit, 99 for next dept) ";
            cin >> empl;
            if (empl == 0)
                goto done;
            if (empl != 99)
                cout << "Dept: " << dept << ", "
                    << "Empl: " << empl << endl;
        } while (empl != 99);
    }
done:
    cout << "Entry complete" << endl;
    return 0;
}
```

Invalid Uses of *goto*

You cannot use a *goto* statement to jump around statements that declare variables that involve implicit or explicit initialization. C++ involves complicated initialization of class objects during construction, actions that must be undone when the object is destroyed. For example, class objects can allocate memory during initialization. If you were permitted to jump around the initialization of an object, its subsequent destruction—which is automatically invoked by the compiler and assumes that initialization of the object occurred—could have undesirable consequences. Furthermore, any use of such an uninitialized object could also be dangerous.

Consider, for example, this code:

```
int main()
{
    cout << "Compute a random number? (y/n) ";
    char ans;
    cin >> ans;
    if (ans == 'n')
        goto done;
    int ran = rand();
    cout << ran;
done:
    return 0;
}
```

The program will not compile, because the *goto* statement jumps around the initialization of the *ran* variable. The theory is that a variable that needs initialization must be guaranteed to have undergone that initialization as long as the variable is in scope.

C++ *goto* versus C *goto*

The restriction just described is unlike the C language *goto*, which permits such jumps, assuming that the programmer takes responsibility for the integrity of all variables under such circumstances. But C variables do not involve the kinds of construction and destruction often found in C++ class objects. You learn about class object construction and destruction in Chapter 9.

Fixing the Invalid *goto*

There are two ways to fix the program. The code in Exercise 4.14 is valid.

Exercise 4.14 The goto *program fixed.*

```
#include <iostream>
#include <cstdlib>
using namespace std;

int main()
{
    cout << "Compute a random number? (y/n) ";
    char ans;
    cin >> ans;
    if (ans == 'n')
        goto done;
    int ran;
    ran = rand();
    cout << ran;
done:
    return 0;
}
```

To fix the program wherein the *goto* jumps around an initialized variable, you can remove the initializer and replace it with an assignment. The compiler allows this usage, because the jump does not bypass an initialization. The variable is still in scope and has not been assigned a value, but the compiler leaves that problem for you to deal with.

The code in Exercise 4.15 is valid, too.

Exercise 4.15 The goto *program fixed again.*

```
#include <iostream>
#include <cstdlib>
using namespace std;

int main()
{
    cout << "Compute a random number? (y/n) ";
    char ans;
    cin >> ans;
    if (ans == 'n')
        goto done;
    else    {
        int ran = rand();
        cout << ran;
    }
done:
    return 0;
}
```

By enclosing the *ran* declaration in a brace-surrounded statement block, you fix the program in a different way. The compiler accepts this usage, because the *goto* jumps around the entire scope wherein the *ran* variable is declared and intialized.

 Exercises 4.14 and 4.15 are not particularly good examples of structured programming. See whether you can improve them by eliminating the *goto* statement and the label.

N O T E

Should You Use *goto*?

Everyone who writes about programming deprecates the *goto* statement and cautions you not to use it. Structured programming purists forbid its use. Yet most structured programming languages include some variant of the *goto* statement. Pascal, originally designed to be a language for teaching structured programming to university students, supports *goto*. Writers who caution against using *goto* often suggest programming idioms where *goto* might result in clearer, more efficient programs.

Take another look at how Exercise 4.13 uses *goto*. The program represents the way most people who write and teach about structured programming demonstrate *goto*, as if such an example justified the idiom's existence. Let's see whether it does.

As the theory goes, without the *goto* statement, the program in Exercise 4.13 would need extra measures to force its way out of both loops when the user enters zero into the employee number. In this particular program, that measure would not be a terrible burden, and it would preserve structure and correctness in the code. But I once encountered a programming problem in which propriety wouldn't do.

The program in question was a time-critical, real-time simulation (a game, actually). It had several nested loops that repeated many times during the rendering of a complex animated graphical scene. As in Exercise 4.13, the innermost loop always found a reason to exit so that the program could proceed with the next sequence. Without the *goto*, the extra measures that the program took to exit gracefully from the loop levied too severe a performance burden on the program, and the screen refreshed its images too slowly. The result was jerky, flickering animation. By abandoning structure in this one case and applying the less graceful but more efficient *goto*, I was able to achieve an acceptable refresh rate. Case closed.

Except for that one occasion, however, I have written and published a lot of C and C++ code without needing *goto*. It has been proven conclusively that any algorithm can be designed with the three control structures of structured programming (sequence, selection, and iteration) and without the *goto* statement. Nonetheless, *goto* is a part of the C++ language, and you should know how it works and decide for yourself—as I did that one time—whether you need to use it.

Summary

In this chapter you learned about C++ statements that manage program flow control. You learned about statement blocks and how they nest. You learned how to use the *if, if…else, switch…case, while, do…while,* and *for* flow control statements. You learned about testing and looping and how to use *break* and *continue* to manage loops. You also learned about jumping and the *goto* statement.

CHAPTER 5

More About C++ Data

This chapter adds substantially to what you already know about C++'s intrinsic data types and introduces user-defined data types. This chapter also explains the ways that a C++ program stores, references, and retrieves data objects in memory. You will learn about the following subjects:

- The scope of variables and functions
- Storage classes
- Type qualifiers
- Structures and unions
- Arrays
- Pointers and addresses
- Dynamic memory allocation
- Typecasts
- The *sizeof* operator
- Command-line arguments

- Recursion
- References

SCOPE

Identifiers in C++ programs are said to be in global, local, or file scope. An identifier's scope determines which statements in the program may reference it—that is, its visibility to other parts of the program. Scope is usually implied by position in the program. The exception is file scope, which must be declared. Variables in different scopes sometimes have the same identifiers.

Global Scope

Some variables and functions have global scope, which means that they can be referenced from anywhere in the program. When a variable is declared outside any function, it is called an *external* variable, and it has global scope by default. The declaration must occur before any references to the variable from within the same source-code file, but all functions past that point may reference it. Exercise 5.1 is an illustration of an external variable with global scope.

Exercise 5.1 *Global scope.*

```
#include <iostream>
using namespace std;

int Counter;         // --- variable with global scope

void AddCounter(int);

int main()
{
    AddCounter(53);
    // --- reference a global variable
    cout << "Counter = " << Counter;
    return 0;
}
```

Exercise 5.1 *Global scope. (continued)*

```
void AddCounter(int incr)
{
    // --- reference a global variable
    Counter += incr;
}
```

The *Counter* variable in Exercise 5.1 has global scope, because it is declared outside any function and is not *static* (explained later). Therefore, both the *main* and the *AddCounter* functions can reference *Counter*. All functions (except class member functions, which Chapters 8 and 9 explain) have global scope unless they are declared to be *static*.

A variable or function with global scope can be referenced from independently compiled source-code modules as long as each module that references the variable or function declares it to be *extern*. The *static* and *extern* storage classes are discussed later.

Local Scope

Most of the variables in the exercises of earlier chapters have local scope. They are declared inside functions and are not accessible to the code in other functions. Function parameter variables also have local scope. They are in the scope of—and, therefore, are accessible to—all the statement blocks in the function.

Variables declared in a statement block are in the scope of that block as well as all lower blocks in the declaring block. Exercise 5.2 illustrates variables with local scope.

Exercise 5.2 *Local scope.*

```
#include <iostream>
using namespace std;

int main()
{
    int i = 123;              // i is in scope from here down
    if (i > 0)    {
        int j = 456;          // j is in scope from here down
        if (j > 0)    {
            int k = 789;      // k is in scope from here down
            // --- all 3 are in scope
            cout << i << ' ' << j << ' ' << k;
        }
    }
    return 0;
}
```

Variables in different scopes can have the same identifiers. If a variable in a lower scope in a function uses the same name as a previously declared variable, the new declaration *hides* the earlier one from the program until the newer one goes out of scope. A local variable goes out of scope when the statement block in which it is declared completes executing. Exercise 5.3 demonstrates that behavior.

Exercise 5.3 *Variables hidden by scope.*

```
#include <iostream>
using namespace std;

int var = 1;    // this var is in global scope

int main()
{
```

Exercise 5.3　Variables hidden by scope. (continued)

```
    cout << var << ' ';
    if (var > 0)    {
        int var = 2;        // hides global var
        cout << var << ' ';
        if (var > 1)    {
            int var = 3;    // hides outer local var
            cout << var << ' ';
        }
        cout << var << ' ';
    }
    cout << var << ' ';
    return 0;
}
```

Exercise 5.3 has five *cout* statements, each one apparently displaying the value of the same variable. The first *cout* references the global *var*, because that is the only one that is in scope. The second *cout* references the local var that is initialized with the value 2 and that hides the global *var*. The third *cout* references the local *var* in an inner scope that is initialized with the value 3 and that hides both *var* objects in outer scopes.

When the innermost statement block completes executing, the next outer *var* comes back into scope. Similarly, when its statement block completes, the global *var* comes back into scope. Exercise 5.3 displays the following message on the screen:

```
1 2 3 2 1
```

The Global Scope Resolution Operator

As Exercise 5.3 showed, if a local variable and a global variable have the same name, all references to that name while the local variable is in scope refer to the local variable.

To tell the compiler that you want to refer to a global variable rather than the local one with the same name, use the :: global scope resolution operator. The global scope resolution operator—which is coded as a prefix to the variable's name (for example, *::varname*)—lets you explicitly reference a global variable from a scope in which a local variable has the same name.

Exercise 5.4 is an example of the scope resolution operator.

Exercise 5.4 *Global scope resolution operator.*

```
#include <iostream>
using namespace std;

int amount = 123;      // a global variable
int main()
{
    int amount = 456;    // a local variable

    cout << ::amount;    // display the global variable
    cout << ' ';
    cout << amount;      // display the local variable
    return 0;
}
```

The exercise has two variables named *amount*. The first is global and contains the value 123. The second is local to the *main* function.

The first *cout* statement displays **123**, the contents of the global *amount* variable, because that reference to the variable name uses the :: global scope resolution operator. The second *cout* statement displays **456**, the contents of the local *amount* variable, because that reference to the variable name has no global scope resolution operator and defaults to the local variable.

File Scope

File scope refers to external identifiers that are available only to functions declared in the same *translation unit,* which is the source-code file in which they are defined, including any source-code files specified by *#include* statements. The *static* storage class specifier declares identifiers with file scope. Exercise 5.5 illustrates the *static* storage class specifier.

Exercise 5.5 *File scope.*

```
#include <iostream>
using namespace std;

static int Counter;          // variable with file scope
static void AddCounter(int); // function with file scope

int main()
{
    // --- reference a file scope function
    AddCounter(1940);
    // --- reference a file scope variable
    cout << "Counter = " << Counter;
    return 0;
}
// ---- function with file scope
static void AddCounter(int incr)
{
    // --- reference a file scope variable
    Counter += incr;
}
```

The *Counter* variable and the *AddCounter* function are declared with the *static* storage class specifier. This gives them file scope, which makes them available only to the functions in the translation unit in which they are defined. Exercise 5.5 consists of only one translation unit.

NOTE Most of the exercises in this book have only one translation unit, because the programs are small examples. Larger C++ projects involve independent compilation of many source files, and the *static* storage class specifier hides the identifiers of functions and variables from other source-code files linked into the same program. However, as you will learn in later chapters, C++ classes and namespaces virtually eliminate the need for any program to use the *static* storage class for functions and for variables declared outside a function.

Scope vs. Lifetime

The term *scope* is often used to describe an identifier's *lifetime*: the period of time from when the program instantiates an object to when the object is destroyed. This usage is not altogether accurate and reflects a typical degree of ambiguity in the way we talk about programming.

A variable declared within a function's statement block exists from the point of the declaration until the program exits the statement block. As long as the program is executing in that statement block or in one nested inside the statement block, the variable is alive. That period of time is its lifetime. If, while the variable is still alive, the program calls another function, the variable effectively goes out of scope until the function returns. The variable is no longer in scope, because the executing function cannot reference the variable. Exercise 5.6 demonstrates this principle.

Exercise 5.6 Scope vs. lifetime.

```
#include <iostream>
using namespace std;

void DisplayTitle();

int main()
{
    auto int Amount = 500;   // auto storage class specifier
    DisplayTitle();
    cout << Amount;
    return 0;
}
// --- a function that executes during Amount's lifetime
void DisplayTitle()
{
    // --- main's Amount exists, but is not in scope here
    cout << "Amt = ";
}
```

The best way to grasp the lesson of Exercise 5.6 is to step through the program with a debugger while watching the *Amount* variable in a watch window. If you are running the exercises with Quincy, that environment is already set up for you. On the first step, the watch window displays **??** for the *Amount* variable's value; this means that the debugger cannot fetch the value from memory because the *Amount* identifier is out of scope. When you step into the *main* function, the **??** display changes to a random integer value that displays whatever the variable's memory location contains before the program initialized the variable. This tells you that the *Amount* identifier is alive and is in scope. After you step into the variable's initialized declaration, the value changes to 500, which is the initializer. When you step into the *DisplayTitle* function, however, the watched display reverts to **??**. The variable still exists but is temporarily out of scope. When you step through the *DisplayTitle* return and back into the *main* function, the watched variable displays the value 500 again, telling you that the *Amount* variable is back in scope.

Consequently, when you read that a variable is in scope from its definition until the program exits the statement block where the variable was declared, you will understand that that is not always the case. I'll try to avoid that confusion.

STORAGE CLASSES

Variables can be declared with *storage class* specifiers that tell the compiler how variables are to be treated. The storage classes are *auto, static, extern,* and *register.* For convenience, the *typedef* keyword is called a storage class, but it serves a different purpose. It is explained later in this chapter.

The *auto* Storage Class

The *auto* storage class specifier identifies a local variable as automatic, which means that each invocation of the statement block in which the variable is defined gets a fresh copy with its own memory space and with re-initialization each time. Local variables are implicitly declared *auto* unless the program declares them otherwise. Use of the *auto* keyword is optional. If you omit it and don't use any other storage class specifier on a local variable, that variable is automatically automatic, so to speak. The following code fragment illustrates the *auto* storage class specifier.

```
int main()
{
    // --- auto storage class specifier
    auto int Amount = 500;
    // ...
    return 0;
}
```

The code in the example works exactly the same whether or not you include the *auto* keyword in the declaration of the *Amount* variable.

Function parameters are, by default, *auto* unless you declare them to be in the *register* storage class, discussed later.

The *static* Storage Class

You learned the meaning of the *static* storage class when you applied it to function declarations and external variables in Exercise 5.5. The *static* storage class has a different meaning with local variables: It is the opposite of *auto*. Although the scope of a *static* local variable begins inside the statement block in which the variable is declared and ends when the block terminates, the variable itself retains its value between executions of the statement block. Initializers are effective only for the first time the statement block is executed. Subsequent executions find that the variable has the value it had when the previous execution ended. Exercise 5.7 shows how *static* local variables work.

Exercise 5.7 The static *storage class.*

```
#include <iostream>
using namespace std;

int Gather();  // prototype

int main()
{
    int gwool = 0;
    while (gwool < 60)    {
        gwool = Gather();
        cout << gwool <<endl;
    }
}

int Gather()
{
    static int wool = 50; // static local variable
    return ++wool;
}
```

The *wool* variable in the *Gather* function is a *static* local variable with an initial value of 50. The function increments the variable and returns the incremented value. When you run the program you can see from the output that the returned value is incremented each time, and the *wool* initializer does not have an effect after the first call of the function. If you were to remove the *static* storage class specifier from the declaration, the program would go into a dead loop, displaying the value 51. This is because the *wool* variable would be *auto* rather than *static*, and its intializer would execute every time the function was called, resetting it to 50. The *while* test in the *main* function would never find a true condition, and the program would stay in the loop until you interrupted it manually.

The *extern* Storage Class

The *extern* storage class declares external variables that haven't yet been defined but that the program needs to reference. Usually, an *extern* declaration refers to a variable defined in a different translation unit.

Exercise 5.8 demonstrates a program that uses an *extern* variable. This program involves two translation units: **Ex05008a.cpp** and **Ex05008b.cpp**.

Exercise 5.8 The extern *storage class.*

```
// ----- Ex05008a.cpp
#include <iostream>
using namespace std;

void AccumulateAmount(void);

int main()
{
    extern float Amount; // extern declaration
    AccumulateAmount();
    cout << Amount;
}
```

Exercise 5.8 *The extern storage class. (continued)*

```
// ----- Ex05008b.cpp
float Amount;              // definition of an extern

void AccumulateAmount()
{
    Amount = 5.72;
}
```

NOTE The two translation units—source-code files—are compiled independently and are linked into a single executable module. Quincy refers to such a program as a *project* and includes a project file that lists the source-code modules to be included.

The *Amount* variable that the *main* function refers to is actually declared in a different translation unit, the **Ex05007b.cpp** source-code file. Consequently, the compiler cannot compile an address for the variable when the compiler compiles **Ex05007a.cpp**. The *extern* declaration tells the compiler to compile all references to *Amount* as an as-yet unresolved reference and to delay resolving those references until the compiled object code modules are linked into an executable program module.

An *extern* variable declaration may be inside or outside the function that references the external variable. If the variable is outside, all functions in the translation unit following the declaration can reference the external variable. If the declaration is inside a function, only functions that contain the *extern* declaration of the variable can reference the variable.

A program can have several *extern* declarations of a variable but only one definition: a declaration without the *extern* storage class specifier. The definition must appear outside any functions. The declarations and definition may be scattered among many translation units, or all of them may be in the same one. Only one definition or declaration may have an initializer. The initializer may be in the definition or in any of the *extern* declarations, but it may not be in a declaration that is inside a function. If an *extern* declaration has an initializer, the variable does not need a definition elsewhere in the program, although it may have one. If there is no initializer, then there must be at least one definition.

N O T E   Remember from Chapter 1 that a declaration declares the format of a variable but does not reserve memory, and a definition defines the instance of a variable and reserves memory for it. Often, a variable's definition and declaration are the same C++ language statement.

Typically, a program declares all *extern* variables in project-specific header files that are included by all the translation units. Then it defines each external variable in the C++ source-code module where the variable logically originates.

The *register* Storage Class

A variable declared with the *register* storage class is the same as an *auto* variable except that the program cannot take the variable's address. You learn about variable addresses later in this chapter. Exercise 5.9 demonstrates a register variable.

Exercise 5.9 *The* register *storage class.*

```
#include <iostream>
using namespace std;

int main()
{
    register unsigned int Counter; // register declaration
    for (Counter = 100; Counter < 1000; Counter += 50)
        cout << "Counter: " << Counter << endl;
}
```

The *register* storage class is a relic. Its purpose was to allow the programmer to specify conditions under which the program's performance would be improved if certain local, automatic variables were maintained in one of the computer's hardware registers. It states the programmer's intention to use the variable in ways that might work best if the variable resided in a hardware register rather than in the computer's main memory. The *register* storage class is only a suggestion to the compiler that the variable occupy a register. The compiler can ignore the suggestion.

You cannot take the address of register variables, because hardware registers on most computers do not have memory addresses. The address restriction applies even when the compiler chooses to ignore the suggestion and puts the variable in addressable memory.

Effective application of the *register* storage class requires an assembly language programmer's understanding of the processor architecture with respect to the number and kinds of registers available to be used for variables and how the registers behave. That understanding would not necessarily apply to a different computer, so the *register* storage class does not contribute much to a portable program. In addition, contemporary optimizing compilers usually do a better job than the programmer of selecting which variables can be maintained in registers, although the *register* storage class could conceivably help an aggressive optimizer do its job.

INITIAL DEFAULT VALUES

Nonlocal and *static* local variables are guaranteed to be initialized with zeros if the program does not explicitly initialize them. Automatic variables are not guaranteed to have any particular initial value when they come into scope. You should either initialize them or assign an initial value to them before you use them. Parameters are always initialized with the values of the caller's arguments.

TYPE QUALIFIERS

C++ includes two *type qualifiers*—keywords *const* and *volatile*—that further define the nature and behavior of variables.

The *const* Type Qualifier

A *const* variable is one that the program may not modify except through initialization when the variable is declared. The phrase *const variable* seems to be an oxymoron. How can something be constant and variable at the same time? Nonetheless, the usage is common among programmers and writers about programming, and I won't try to change it.

Exercise 5.10 uses a *const* variable as the upper limit for a loop.

Exercise 5.10 *The* const *type qualifier.*

```
#include <iostream>
using namespace std;

int main()
{
    const int MaxCtr = 300; // const declaration

    for (int Ctr = 100; Ctr < MaxCtr; Ctr += 50)
        cout << "Ctr = " << Ctr << endl;
    return 0;
}
```

The *const* variable might or might not occupy memory, might have an address, and may be used in any context that does not or may not modify the contents of the variable. Whether it has an address depends on how you use it and on the C++ compiler implementation. If you take the address of a *const* variable, the compiler must give it a memory location. Otherwise, the compiler is free to treat a reference to the expression as if it were coded as a constant in an expression. When a variable is qualified as *const*, the compiler prevents the program from modifying the variable's contents. The discussion on pointers later in this chapter has more details about *const*.

The *volatile* Type Qualifier

A *volatile* variable is the opposite of a *const* variable. The *volatile* type qualifier tells the compiler that the program could be changing the variable in unseen ways. Those ways are implementation-dependent. One possibility is that a variable can be changed by an asynchronous interrupt service routine. The compiler must know about such a variable so that the compiler does not optimize its access in ways that would defeat the external changes. Exercise 5.11 shows how you declare a *volatile* variable.

Exercise 5.11 *The* volatile *type qualifier.*

```
#include <iostream>
using namespace std;

volatile int Value = 300; // volatile declaration

int main()
{
    int Counter;
    for (Counter = 100; Counter < Value; Counter += 50)
        cout << "Counter: " << Counter << endl;
    return 0;
}
```

Suppose that a program posts the address of a variable in an external pointer and that an interrupt service routine elsewhere in the program or in the system modifies the contents of the variable by dereferencing the pointer. If the compiler has optimized the function by using a register for the variable while the program uses its contents, the effects of the interrupt could be lost. The *volatile* type qualifier tells the compiler not to make such optimizations.

USER-DEFINED DATA TYPES

A C++ programmer can define collections of variables organized in a structure. A structure encapsulates related data into an aggregate. Programs can manipulate structures in ways similar to the manipulation of intrinsic data types. Another data aggregate, called a *union*, assigns one memory location to several variables, possibly of different types.

N O T E Structures have much more power than you will learn here. The C++ *struct* is a variant on the C++ *class*, and that discussion begins in Chapter 8. This discussion concentrates on the *struct* as it was used in C language programs, but with a few C++ improvements.

You can declare instances of unions and structures, initialize those instances, assign them to one another, pass them to functions, and return them from functions.

Declaring a *struct*

You declare a structure by using the *struct* keyword, giving the structure a name, and declaring the data types that are in the structure, as shown here:

```
struct Date {    // a struct named Date
    short int month;    // data members
    short int day;
    short int year;
};
```

A structure declaration begins with the *struct* keyword followed by the name of the structure. The structure consists of variables, which are called the structure's *members*. Their declarations are surrounded by braces. The structure declaration is terminated with a semicolon.

The *struct* declaration does not reserve memory. It merely defines the format of the structure for later use by the program. The structure members can be any valid C++ type, including other structures.

Defining a *struct* Variable

You define a variable of the *struct* type by providing, optionally, the *struct* keyword, the structure's name, and a name for the instance of the structure—the *struct* variable—as shown here:

```
struct Date birthday; // a Date structure named birthday
```

Because a *struct* declares a new data type, you can define a *struct* variable without including the *struct* keyword. This is one of the C++ improvements to the C *struct*.

```
Date date_hired; // a Date structure named date_hired
```

Referencing *struct* Members

You reference the members of a structure by providing the name of the structure variable, the dot (.) operator, and the name of the member, as shown here:

```
birthday.day = 24;    // assign a value to a structure member
```

Exercise 5.12 declares and uses a *struct* to show you how it all fits into a program.

Exercise 5.12 The struct *data type.*

```cpp
#include <iostream>
using namespace std;

// ---- declare a struct
struct Date {
    short int month, day, year;
};

int main()
{
    Date dt;        // a Date variable
    // --- assign values to the struct members
    dt.month = 6;
    dt.day = 24;
    dt.year = 1940;
    // --- display the struct
    cout << dt.month << '/' << dt.day << '/' << dt.year;
    return 0;
}
```

Initializing a Structure

Rather than assign values to each member of a structure variable, as Exercise 5.12 does, the program can initialize the variable when it is defined. Exercise 5.13 shows how to initialize a structure variable.

Exercise 5.13 *Initializing a* struct.

```
#include <iostream>
using namespace std;

// ---- declare a struct
struct Date {
    short int month, day, year;
};

int main()
{
    // an initialized Date variable
    Date dt = { 11, 17, 1941 };
    // --- display the struct
    cout << dt.month << '/' << dt.day << '/' << dt.year;
    return 0;
}
```

The brace-surrounded, comma-separated list of expressions is the structure's initialization list. Each expression initializes a member of the structure. The types of the expressions must be compatible with the types of the members. You may have fewer expressions than the number of structure members but not more. If you have fewer expressions, the compiler inserts zero values into the data members that are not initialized by your initialization list. An uninitialized automatic structure variable, however, is not filled with zeros. You need at least one initializing expression to pad the rest of the structure with zeros.

Structures within Structures

A structure can have other structures as members. Initialization of inner structures uses inner pairs of braces. References to the members of the inner structure include the names of both structure variables, as shown in Exercise 5.14.

Exercise 5.14 *Structures within structures.*

```
#include <iostream>
using namespace std;

// ---- Date struct
struct Date {
    int month, day, year;
};
// ---- Employee struct
struct Employee {
    int emplno;
    float salary;
    Date datehired;
};
int main()
{
    // --- an initialized Employee struct
    Employee joe = { 123, 35500, {5, 17, 82} };
    // --- display the Employee
    cout << "Empl #: " << joe.emplno << endl
         << "Salary: " << joe.salary << endl
         << "Date hired: "
         << joe.datehired.month << '/'
         << joe.datehired.day   << '/'
         << joe.datehired.year << endl;
    return 0;
}
```

Exercise 5.14 declares two structures. The second one has an instance of the first one as a member. When the program initializes an instance of the outer structure, it includes initializers for the inner structure by enclosing them in their own pair of braces.

Referencing the members of the inner structure involves naming both structure variables, each one followed by the dot (.) operator and the member name as the rightmost identifier in the expression.

Passing and Returning Structures to and from Functions

A function can accept a structure as a parameter, and a function can return a structure. For large structures, programmers usually pass structure pointers or reference variables (explained later) and let the calling and called functions share copies of the structures. This practice is more efficient, because it reduces the overhead of copying large memory segments. It is also somewhat safer. Arguments are passed on the stack, which can become exhausted if a program passes many large objects, particularly to recursive functions.

Nonetheless, sometimes you need to pass a private copy of a structure. Perhaps the called function changes the data and the calling function needs to preserve the original values of the data. Other times, a function returns a structure. Perhaps that function creates the structure as an automatic variable. The automatic structure goes out of scope when the function returns, so a returned copy is needed. Exercise 5.15 illustrates functions that pass and return structures.

Exercise 5.15 *Passing and returning structures.*

```cpp
#include <iostream>
using namespace std;

struct Date {
    int month, day, year;
};

Date GetToday(void);
void PrintDate(Date);

int main()
{
    Date dt = GetToday();
    PrintDate(dt);
    return 0;
}
```

Exercise 5.15 *Passing and returning structures. (continued)*

```
// ---- function that returns a struct
Date GetToday(void)
{
    Date dt;
    cout << "Enter date (mm dd yy): ";
    cin >> dt.month >> dt.day >> dt.year;
    return dt;
}
// ---- function that has a struct parameter
void PrintDate(Date dt)
{
    cout << dt.month << '/' << dt.day << '/' << dt.year;
}
```

The *union* Data Type

A union looks just like a structure except that it has the *union* keyword instead of *struct*. The difference between unions and structures is that a structure defines an aggregate of adjacent data members, and a union defines a memory address shared by all of its data members. A union can contain only one value at a time, and that value is of the type of one of its members. All its members occupy the same memory location. The size of a union is the size of its widest member. Exercise 5.16 illustrates the behavior of a union.

Exercise 5.16 *The* union *data type.*

```
#include <iostream>
using namespace std;

union Holder {
    char holdchar;
    short int holdint;
    long int holdlong;
    float holdfloat;
};
```

Exercise 5.16 The union *data type.* (*continued*)

```
void DisplayHolder(Holder, char*);

int main()
{
    Holder hld;
    hld.holdchar = 'X';          // assign to first member
    DisplayHolder(hld, "char");
    hld.holdint = 12345;         // assign to second member
    DisplayHolder(hld, "int");
    hld.holdlong = 7654321;      // assign to third member
    DisplayHolder(hld, "long");
    hld.holdfloat = 1.23;        // assign to fourth member
    DisplayHolder(hld, "float");
    return 0;
}

void DisplayHolder(Holder hld, char* tag)
{
    cout << "---Initialized " << tag << " ---" << endl;
    cout << "holdchar  " << hld.holdchar << endl;
    cout << "holdint   " << hld.holdint << endl;
    cout << "holdlong  " << hld.holdlong << endl;
    cout << "holdfloat " << hld.holdfloat << endl;
}
```

Running Exercise 5.16 demonstrates that changing one of a union's members changes the other members, too. When you assign a value to a particular member, the values of the other members have only coincidental meaning, because you are overlaying them with whatever bit configuration represents the assigned member's assigned value. You can observe this behavior by reading the output from the *DisplayHolder* function after each assignment or by using Quincy's Watch window to watch each of the members.

Initializing a Union

You can initialize only the first of a union's variables. The initializer is enclosed by braces, and there is only one data value. Its type must be compatible with the first member in the union, as shown here:

```
Holder hld = {'X'};   // initialize a union variable
```

If the first member of a union is a structure, the initialization may include the several expressions that initialize the structure. Exercise 5.17 demonstrates this usage.

Exercise 5.17 Initializing a struct-*containing* union.

```
#include <iostream>
using namespace std;

struct Date {
    int mo, da, yr;
};

union Holder {
    Date hdt;
    int hint;
};

int main()
{
int main()
{
    Holder hld = { {6, 24, 1940} };
    cout << hld.hdt.mo << '/' << hld.hdt.da << '/'
        << hld.hdt.yr;
    return 0;
}
```

Anonymous Unions

A C++ program can declare unnamed *unions*. You might use this feature to save space, or you might use it to intentionally redefine a variable.

Exercise 5.18 illustrates the use of the anonymous *union*.

Exercise 5.18 *Anonymous* unions.

```
#include <iostream>
int main()
{
    union    {
        int quantity_todate;
        int quantity_balance;
    };
    cout << "Enter quantity to date: ";
    cin >> quantity_todate;
    cout << "Enter quantity sold: ";
    int quantity_sold;
    cin >> quantity_sold;
    quantity_todate -= quantity_sold;
    cout << "Quantity balance = " << quantity_balance;
    return 0;
}
```

The program in Exercise 5.18 allows the two variables *quantity_todate* and *quantity_balance* to share the same space. After *quantity_sold* is subtracted from *quantity_todate, quantity_balance* contains the result shown by the program's output.

```
Enter quantity to date: 100
Enter quantity sold: 75
Quantity balance = 25
```

This feature eliminates many *union* name prefixes in places where the only purpose for the *union* name is to support the *union*.

You must declare a global anonymous *union* as *static*.

The *enum* Constant

You can define an enumerated constant by making an *enum* declaration, which defines an enumerated constant data type. An enumerated constant consists of a group of related identifiers, each with an integer value. For example:

```
enum Colors { Red, Green, Blue };
enum Bool { False, True };
```

In these enumerated constants, the first identifier in the brace-surrounded lists is equated with the numerical value zero, the second with 1, and so on. The names must be distinct, and they must not be keywords or any other identifier in the current scope.

You can specify an initializer value for a particular *enum* identifier within the declaration. Values that follow immediately are incremented starting from that point. For example:

```
enum WeekDay { Sun = 1, Mon, Tue, Wed, Thu, Fri, Sat };
```

In this example, *Sun* is equated to 1, *Mon* is 2, and so on.

You can declare variables of the enumerated type and use enumerated values wherever you can use integers. You can specify an enumerated type in a function's parameter list or anywhere else that you can use an integer constant.

Exercise 5.19 illustrates the use of an *enum* in a *switch* statement. C programmers should observe that the declaration of the *col* variable need not include the *enum* keyword. In C++, each *enum* type is a distinct new data type for the scope in which it is declared.

Exercise 5.19 The enum *data type.*

```
#include <iostream>
using namespace std;

enum Colors { red = 1, green, blue };

int main()
{
```

Exercise 5.19 The enum *data type. (continued)*

```
    Colors col;
    cout << "1=Red, 2=Green, 3=Blue. Select: ";
    int cl;
    cin >> cl;
    col = (Colors) cl;
    switch (col)    {
        case red:
            cout << "Red";
            break;
        case green:
            cout << "Green";
            break;
        case blue:
            cout << "Blue";
            break;
        default:
            cout << "??";
            break;
    }
    return 0;
}
```

ARRAYS

All of C++'s data types can be represented in arrays of one or more dimensions. The dimensions of an array are specified in its definition. An array consists of adjacent instances of variables of the same data type. The variables in an array are called its *elements*. You access the elements of an array by providing integer expression *subscripts*.

Declaring Arrays

You declare an array by adding its dimension or dimensions in bracketed expressions after its name. This lesson is about arrays having one dimension. Here is an example of an array of integers:

```
int Offsets[10];
```

This code defines 10 integer elements in an array named *Offsets*. The integers are adjacent in memory. The size of an array is the size of one of its elements multiplied by the number of elements in the array. The dimension expression within the brackets may have operators, but it must evaluate to a constant expression. The dimension is relative to 1.

Accessing Arrays with Subscripts

To access an element in an array, the program uses the array's identifier followed by a subscript expression in brackets:

```
Offsets[3] = 123;
```

The subscript expression is any expression that evaluates to an integer value. It does not have to be a constant expression unless the reference to the element is in a context that requires a constant expression. Subscripts are relative to zero, so the example just shown assigns 123 to the fourth element of the *Offsets* array of integers.

Initializing Arrays

You initialize an array by following its definition with a brace-enclosed initialization list. There may be as many initializers as there are elements in the array, as shown here:

```
int Zones[5] = {43, 77, 22, 35, 89};  // a 5-element array
```

If you code more initializers than there are elements in the dimension, a compile error occurs. If you code fewer, the remaining elements are initialized with zero values.

By using an empty dimension expression, you can implicitly specify the array's dimension from the number of initializers, as shown here:

```
int Zones[] = {43, 77, 22, 35, 89}; // 5 elements by default
```

Exercise 5.20 illustrates a simple array.

Exercise 5.20 *Array of integers.*

```
#include <iostream>
using namespace std;

int main()
{
    int Values[] = {1,2,3,5,8,13,21};
    for (int i = 0; i < 7; i++)
        cout << Values[i] << endl;
    return 0;
}
```

The program in Exercise 5.20 declares an array of seven integers. Then it accesses the array by using a *for* loop that iterates a subscript integer from 0 through 6. Figure 5.1 shows the *Values* array in memory with a subscripted expression that points to the fifth element.

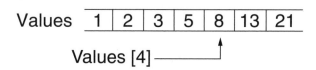

Figure 5.1 *An integer array.*

Arrays of Structures

You can build an array of structures and reference the members of each of the array's structure elements by using subscripts. Initialization of the structure uses inner brace-enclosed structure initializers within the brace-enclosed array initializer. Exercise 5.21 demonstrates an array of structures.

Exercise 5.21 *Array of structures.*

```
#include <iostream>
using namespace std;

// --- Employee record
struct Employee    {
    int emplno;
    float wage;
};
// --- array of Employee records
Employee emps[] = {
    { 1, 10.17 },          // #1 initialized
    { 2, 15.50 },          // #2 initialized
    { 3, 13.00 }           // #3 initialized
};

int main()
{
    int i;
    for (i = 0; i < 3; i++)
        cout << emps[i].emplno << ' '
             << emps[i].wage <<endl;
    return 0;
}
```

The *Employee* structure has two members. The *emps* array has three elements. The array initializer contains three inner initializers for the three structure elements in the array. The program iterates through the array with a *for* loop. Finally, the *cout* call dereferences the structure members with a bracketed subscript expression after the array identifier and before the structure member dot (.) operator.

Multidimensional Arrays

Sometimes an array must have more than one dimension. For example, a grid of numbers reflecting a quarter's monthly revenues by cost center could be implemented as an array with two dimensions. You define a two-dimensional array by adding a second bracketed dimension expression to the definition, as shown here:

```
float Revenues[3][8];  // 3 months, 8 cost centers
```

This array is, in effect, three adjacent integer arrays with eight elements each. It is organized in memory that way. The leftmost dimension's elements are adjacent. The first eight elements are followed by the second eight elements, which are followed by the third eight elements.

Exercise 5.22 uses the array just shown to demonstrate how multidimensional arrays work.

Exercise 5.22 *Two-dimensional array.*

```
#include <iostream>
using namespace std;

float Revenues[3][8] = {
 { 45.33, 55.55, 78.00, 37.26, 98.35, 23.55, 45.65, 22.00 },
 { 35.43, 45.45, 79.00, 30.26, 47.55, 34.65, 52.79, 32.50 },
 { 55.37, 75.05, 68.10, 31.27, 62.36, 53.56, 43.68, 24.06 }
};

int main()
{
    for (int mon = 0; mon < 3; mon++)     {
        cout << mon+1 << ':';
        for (int cc = 0; cc < 8; cc++)
            cout << ' ' << Revenues[mon][cc];
        cout << endl;
    }
    return 0;
}
```

Figure 5.2 shows how the two-dimensional array is organized in memory and how a subscripted reference accesses one of the array's elements.

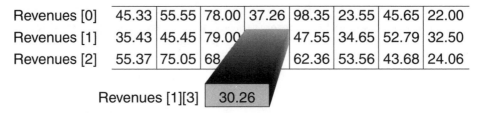

Revenues [0]	45.33	55.55	78.00	37.26	98.35	23.55	45.65	22.00
Revenues [1]	35.43	45.45	79.00		47.55	34.65	52.79	32.50
Revenues [2]	55.37	75.05	68		62.36	53.56	43.68	24.06

Revenues [1][3]   30.26

Figure 5.2 *Two-dimensional array.*

If any of the inner initializer lists has fewer initializers than there are elements in its corresponding array, the remaining elements are initialized to zero.

You can eliminate all but the outermost pair of braces in an array initialization as long as you provide enough intializers for all the elements in the inner arrays. The array in Exercise 5.22 could have been initialized like this:

```
float Revenues[3][8] = {
    45.33, 55.55, 78.00, 37.26, 98.35, 23.55, 45.65, 22.00,
    35.43, 45.45, 79.00, 30.26, 47.55, 34.65, 52.79, 32.50,
    55.37, 75.05, 68.10, 31.27, 62.36, 53.56, 43.68, 24.06
};
```

Arrays can have two, three, or more dimensions. Standard C++ imposes no limit on the number of dimensions an array can have, although a many-dimensioned array can become a confusing thing to work with.

Character Arrays: A Special Case

Character arrays get special treatment in C++. The C++ language has no intrinsic string data type like those of BASIC and other languages, although there is a standard string class that you will learn about in Chapter 16. Instead, C++ supports arrays of *char* variables in special ways. You have seen what appear to be string data types in the string constants in the excercises in Chapter 2. These string constants are actually null-terminated arrays of characters. Consider the string constant in this example:

```
cout << "Hello";
```

The compiler builds an internal unnamed character array. If you could see its declaration, the array would look like this:

```
char [] = { 'H', 'e', 'l', 'l', 'o', '\0' };
```

The compiler passes the address of the internal array to the *cout* object, which can recognize a pointer to type *char*. Pointers and addresses are discussed in detail in the next section of this chapter. No identifier is assigned to string literals, so the internal representation shown earlier has none. You cannot declare a *char* array that way yourself; only the compiler can do that. Observe the array's last character constant. It is initialized with the value zero. This is the standard null terminator for a C++ string constant.

You can initialize a character array with a string constant. Exercise 5.23 shows how that works.

Exercise 5.23 *Initializing a* char *array.*

```
#include <iostream>
using namespace std;

int main()
{
    char str[] = "Hello, Dolly";
    int i = 0;
    while (str[i] != '\0')
        cout << str[i++];
    return 0;
}
```

POINTERS AND ADDRESSES

Pointers are variables that contain the addresses of other variables and functions. A C++ program can declare a pointer to any data type, including structures and unions.

A program can use the address of any variable in an expression except variables declared with the *register* storage class.

A program can assign the address of a variable to a pointer variable. Furthermore, the program can pass the address of a variable as an argument to a function that has a pointer for a parameter.

A program can use the address of a function in an assignment or in an initializer, or as a function argument. A program can call a function through a pointer that has the function's address.

Pointers are an important part of the C++ language. All arguments are passed to functions by value; this means that a copy of the argument is written into the called function's parameter variable. Programs may not, however, pass arrays by value. Pointers simulate *passing by reference* in that you can pass the address of an array, structure, or intrinsic data type to be copied into the function's pointer variable parameter. The function's reference to the caller's data is the address of the data in the pointer.

Pointers, addresses, and the notational relationship between pointers and arrays are the source of much of the confusion that new C and C++ programmers experience. When I first started programming in C, I made a chart like the code in the following example, hung it on the wall over my desk, and left it there until pointers and addresses were second nature to me.

```
int i, j;  // int variables
int* ip;   // pointer to int variable
ip = &i;   // assign addr of int variable to pointer to int
j = *ip;   // retrieve int that int pointer points to
int** ipp; // pointer to int pointer
ipp = &ip  // assign address of pointer
j = **ipp; // retrieve int through pointer to int pointer
```

Pointers to Intrinsic Types

You declare a pointer by specifying the type of data that the pointer points to, one or more asterisks, and the name of the pointer itself. The *ip* pointer variable definition in the chart just shown is an example.

C programmers typically declare pointers by putting the asterisk immediately to the left of the identifier:

```
int *ip;   // pointer to int variable
```

C++ programmers often prefer to use an idiom in which the asterisk is adjacent to the type:

```
int* ip;   // pointer to int variable
```

Either way works. The following ways also work, because the white space is optional:

```
int*ip;      // pointer to int variable
int * ip;    // pointer to int variable
```

Remember that pointers are themselves variables. They are usually of uniform size regardless of what they point to, and you can coerce any value into one of them and dereference that value as if it were the address of a variable of the pointer's type. You must go out of your way, however, to get the C++ compiler to let you put into a pointer the address of something of a different type.

 When you are compiling programs for computers, such as the PC, that have segmented memory architecture, pointers to functions and pointers to data can have different sizes in programs compiled with different data and code

N O T E   memory models.

Exercise 5.24 demonstrates pointers to some of C++'s intrinsic types.

Exercise 5.24 *Pointers to intrinsic types.*

```
#include <iostream>
using namespace std;

int main()
{
    // --- intrinsic type variables
    char  c = 'A';
    int   i = 123;
    long  l = 54321;
    float f = 3.45;
```

Exercise 5.24 *Pointers to intrinsic types.* *(continued)*

```
// --- pointers
char*   cp;      // to char
int*    ip;      // to int
long*   lp;      // to long
float*  fp;      // to float
// --- assign variable addresses to pointers
cp = &c;
ip = &i;
lp = &l;
fp = &f;
// --- reference the variables through the pointers
cout <<  *cp << endl;
cout <<  *ip << endl;
cout <<  *lp << endl;
cout <<  *fp << endl;
return 0;
}
```

Recall that the *address-of* operator (&) returns the address of the identifier that follows. Assigning the address of a variable to a pointer points that pointer to the variable. Referencing the pointer with the * pointer operator notation dereferences the pointer by returning the value of the variable that the pointer points to.

Pointer Arithmetic

Pointers are integer-like variables. They contain numeric values that happen to be memory addresses. You can add integer values to and subtract them from a pointer. The difference between a pointer and a normal integer is that pointer arithmetic adds and subtracts the size of the type that the pointer points to. If you add 1 to or subtract 1 from a pointer, you really add or subtract the size of what the pointer points to. You can add integer values to or subtract them from pointers. The expression returns the new address. You can subtract pointers of the same type from one another. This subtraction returns an integer that represents the number of types between the two addresses. Those are the only arithmetic operations you can perform on pointers. Exercise 5.25 is a small example of pointer arithmetic.

Exercise 5.25 *Pointer arithmetic with the increment operator.*

```
#include <iostream>
using namespace std;

int CountDown[] = { 10,9,8,7,6,5,4,3,2,1,0 };

int main()
{
    int* cdp = &CountDown[0];
    do    {
        cout << *cdp << endl;
        cdp++;          // add 1 to the pointer
    } while (*cdp);
    cout << "blast-off";
    return 0;
}
```

The assignment in Exercise 5.25 assigns the address of the first element of the array to the *cdp* pointer. The next section explains a more convenient notation for taking the address of an array.

The statement that increments *cdp* does not add the integer value 1 to the address in the pointer. Because the pointer is declared with the *int* type, the increment adds the size of *int* variables, which in the Quincy implementation of C++ is 4. You could change the array and the pointer to a different integer type with a different size—*short int*, for example—and the program would work the same.

You can save some code in Exercise 5.25 by coding the *do* loop this way:

```
do
    cout << *cdp++ << endl;
while (*cdp);
```

The ++ auto-increment operator has a higher precedence than the * pointer operator, so the expression just shown retrieves what *cdp* points to and then increments *cdp*. To increment the pointer before you retrieve what it points to, you would code the statement this way:

```
cout << *++cdp;
```

Sometimes you want to increment what the pointer points to rather than the pointer. For a postfix increment, you would code the expression like this:

```
(*cdp)++
```

The parentheses override the default precedence and apply the increment operator to the variable that the pointer points to. The following notation applies the prefix increment operator to the variable that the pointer points to:

```
++*cdp;
```

Parentheses are not needed in this case, because the increment operator applies to the *lvalue* that follows it, which is the variable that the pointer points to.

The preceding rules apply equally to the auto-decrement operator.

You can use expressions to add values to and subtract values from pointers. Once again, the notation must take into consideration the precedence of the pointer operator and the arithmetic operators. Here are examples using a pointer to type *int*:

```
int ia[] = { 97, 32, 128 };
int i;
int* ip = &ia[0];
i = *ip+1;          // ip -> 97, returns 98
i = *(ip+1);        // ip -> 97, returns 32
```

The first assignment gets the *int* variable that *ip* points to, which is 97, and adds 1 to its value, returning 98.

The second assignment gets the *int* variable one past where the pointer points. The variable in that position has the value 32, which is what the expression returns.

Observe that neither expression changes the values that are stored in the pointer or in the array. The expressions compute values and use those values to form the assignments. The difference between this kind of pointer notation and using auto-increment and auto-decrement operators is that the latter two actually change the value of the pointer or what it points to. Which notation you use depends on what the program is supposed to do. Exercise 5.26 uses a variable to iterate through an array with a pointer.

Exercise 5.26 *Pointer arithmetic with expressions.*

```
#include <iostream>
using namespace std;

float dues[] = {
    30.00,        // paid quarterly
    55.00,        // paid semiannually
    100.00        // paid annually
};

int main()
{
    float* dp = &dues[0];
    for (int i = 0; i < 3; i++)
        cout << *(dp+i) << endl;
    return 0;
}
```

Pointers and Arrays

Pointers and arrays have a special and often confusing relationship. The confusion begins when you learn that there are two ways to get the address of an array or one of its elements. The exercises until now used the address-of operator (&) and took the address of the first element in the array. An alternative notation uses just the name of the array. Using the name of an array in an expression is the same as taking the address of the array's first element. The following example compares the notation in Exercise 5.26 with the alternative:

```
float* dp = &dues[0]; // address of 1st element
float* dp1 = dues;     // address of array (same address)
```

Carrying that notation further, if you use array address notation with the addition operator and an integer expression, it is the same as taking the address of the array's element subscripted by the expression. For example:

```
float* dp1 = &dues[2]; // address of 3rd element
float* dp2 = dues+2;   //    "     "   "     "
```

If the array has multiple dimensions, the same addressing notational conventions apply when you do not include subscripts for all the dimensions. Exercise 5.27 is an example.

Exercise 5.27 *Array address notation.*

```
#include <iostream>
using namespace std;

int calendar[5][7] = {          // a calendar array
    {  1, 2, 3, 4, 5, 6, 7 },
    {  8, 9,10,11,12,13,14 },
    { 15,16,17,18,19,20,21 },
    { 22,23,24,25,26,27,28 },
    { 29,30,31 }
};

int main()
{
    int* cp1 = &calendar[3][2]; // addr of 4th week, 3rd day
    int* cp2 = calendar[3]+2;   //   "    "   "    "    "    "
    int* cp3 = calendar[0];     // addr of array
    int* cp4 = calendar[2];     // addr of 3rd week, 1st day
    cout << *cp1 << ' '
         << *cp2 << ' '
         << *cp3 << ' '
         << *cp4;
    return 0;
}
```

To add to the confusion, you can dereference what a pointer points to by using array subscript notation. The following usages of a pointer are equivalent:

```
int* ip;      // a pointer (with address of array assumed)
x = *(ip+3);  // access 4th element of the array
x = ip[3];    // access 4th element with subscript notation
```

As the example shows, even though *ip* is a pointer, you can use it with array element notation when it points to an array.

If that weren't enough, you can access an element of an array by using pointer notation, as shown here:

```
int ia[10];   // an array
x = ia[3];    // access 4th element of the array
x = *(ia+3);  // access 4th element with pointer notation
```

No wonder arrays and pointers confuse new C and C++ programmers. You can reduce the level of confusion by sticking with a few basic usage conventions until you are comfortable with the interchangeable nature of pointers and arrays. Exercise 5.28 shows what you can do with pointers and arrays.

Exercise 5.28 *Pointers and arrays.*

```
#include <iostream>
using namespace std;

char msg[] = "Now is the time\n";

int main()
{
    char* cp;     // a pointer to char
    int i;        // an integer subscript

    // --- pointer access, pointer notation
    for (cp = msg; *cp; cp++)
        cout << *cp;
```

Exercise 5.28 *Pointers and arrays. (continued)*

```
    // --- subscript access, subscript notation
    for (i = 0; msg[i]; i++)
        cout << msg[i];
    // --- pointer access, subscript notation
    for (cp = msg; cp[0]; cp++)
        cout << cp[0];
    // --- subscript access, pointer notation
    for (i = 0; *(msg+i); i++)
        cout << *(msg+i);
    // --- pointer and subscript access, pointer notation
    for (i = 0, cp = msg; *(cp+i); i++)
        cout << *(cp+i);
    // --- pointer and subscript access, subscript notation
    for (i = 0, cp = msg; cp[i]; i++)
        cout << cp[i];
    return 0;
}
```

Exercise 5.28 demonstrates six ways that you can use combinations of pointers, subscripts, and notation to achieve the same result. All six loops display the same message on the console.

Another variation on this theme occurs when you change the array itself to a pointer to an array. Change the *msg* declaration in Exercise 5.28 to a character pointer like this:

```
char* msg = "Now is the time\n";
```

The program produces the same output that it did when *msg* was an array. As you can see, the notational conventions for pointers and arrays are virtually interchangeable, and that is where more confusion comes in. Until you are used to it, you are never sure what you are looking at when you see an expression that uses pointer or subscript notation (for both). It is best at first to use subscript notation with subscripts and pointer notation with pointers. The first two *for* loops in Exercise 5.28 reflect this convention.

The character pointer assignment just shown demonstrates that you can initialize a character pointer with a string constant. Recall that a string constant is a character array that the compiler builds internally; when you reference it, you are referencing its internal address. Therefore, assigning a string constant to a character pointer is really assigning the constant's address to the pointer.

Detractors of the C and C++ languages consider these pointer and array constructs to be convoluted. Proponents—who are usually experienced C/C++ programmers—consider them to be among the strengths of C and C++.

Pointers to Structures

Pointers to structures work in the same way as other pointers. A structure pointer points to an instance of its structure type. Incrementing and decrementing the pointer changes its address in multiples of the structure's size, which, you will recall, is the sum of the sizes of the structure's members. You access members in the structure through pointers by using the member pointer (->) operator. Exercise 5.29 modifies Exercise 5.21 to use a structure pointer rather than a subscript variable to iterate through the array of structures.

Exercise 5.29 Pointers to structures.

```
#include <iostream>
using namespace std;

// --- Employee record
struct Employee    {
    int emplno;
    float wage;
};
// --- array of Employee records
Employee emps[] = {
    { 1, 10.17 },        // #1 initialized
    { 2, 15.50 },        // #2 initialized
    { 3, 13.00 },        // #3 initialized
    {-1, 0     }         // terminal element
};
```

Exercise 5.29 *Pointers to structures. (continued)*

```
int main()
{
    Employee* ep = emps;    // addr of array in ptr

    while (ep->emplno != -1)    {
        cout << ep->emplno << ' '
             << ep->wage <<endl;
        ep++;
    }
    return 0;
}
```

Observe the two references to the structure members in the *cout* calls. Instead of the dot (.) structure member operator, they use the member pointer (->) operator. These operators differentiate direct member access to a named structure (.) from indirect member access made through a pointer to a structure (->).

We added the -1 terminal element to the array so that the while loop could sense when the *ep* pointer points to the end of the array.

Pointers as Function Arguments

When a function's prototype declares a pointer parameter, callers to the function are expected to pass an argument that is either a pointer variable or an address. There are two notational conventions for declaring a pointer parameter:

```
void ErrorMessage(char* msg);
void ErrorMessage(char msg[]);
```

The two prototypes are the same. Recall that you cannot pass an array as a function argument. The first notation implies that the parameter is a pointer to a character. The second notation implies that the parameter is a pointer to a character array. There is no difference except for the notation. They both work the same way.

If you declare a pointer parameter with array notation and a dimension, the compiler ignores the dimension. The following prototype is the same as the two just shown:

```
void ErrorMessage(char msg[25]);
```

All three prototypes tell the compiler that the parameter is a character pointer. Which form you use is up to you. Many programmers use the first usage, because it says exactly what the parameter is: a pointer to a character.

What you pass as an argument can be either a pointer variable or the address of a variable of the pointer's type. Exercise 5.30 demonstrates calls to such functions.

Exercise 5.30 Pointer arguments.

```
#include <iostream>
using namespace std;

inline void ErrorMessage(char* msg)
{
    cout << "\aError: " << msg << endl;
}
int main()
{
    char* ep = "Invalid Input";
    ErrorMessage(ep);           // pass a pointer variable
    char msg[] = "Disk Failure";
    ErrorMessage(msg);          // pass an array address
    ErrorMessage("Timeout");    // pass a constant address
}
```

Pointer arguments to multiple-dimension arrays must specify the outer dimensions if the function is going to be iterating through the array. The declaration tells the compiler the width of the outer arrays. Exercise 5.31 illustrates this usage.

Exercise 5.31 *Pointer arguments to multiple-dimension arrays.*

```cpp
#include <iostream>
#include <iomanip>
using namespace std;

void DisplayCalendar(int cal[][7]);

int main()
{
    static int calendar[5][7] = {
        {  1, 2, 3, 4, 5, 6, 7 },
        {  8, 9,10,11,12,13,14 },
        { 15,16,17,18,19,20,21 },
        { 22,23,24,25,26,27,28 },
        { 29,30,31 }
    };
    DisplayCalendar(calendar);
    return 0;
}
// -- cal argument points to 1st element
//    of an array of 7-element arrays
void DisplayCalendar(int cal[][7])
{
    cout << "Sun Mon Tue Wed Thu Fri Sat" << endl;
    for (int week = 0; week < 5; week++)    {
        for (int day = 0; day < 7; day++)    {
            int date = cal[week][day];
            if (date)
                cout << setw(3) << date << ' ';
        }
        cout << endl;
    }
}
```

Curiously, if you declare the *DisplayCalendar* function this way, the results are the same:

```
void DisplayCalendar(int* cal[7]) // ptr to 7-element array
```

Chapter 2 explained that a program can modify how the *cout* object displays objects by sending *dec, hex,* and *oct* manipulators to the stream. Exercise 5.31 includes a header file named **<iomanip>**. This file contains the declarations for other stream manipulators. The exercise uses one of them, the *setw* manipulator, to manage the format of the screen display. The *setw* manipulator includes an argument that specifies the minimum display width in character positions of the next object in the stream. By using *setw,* the program ensures that all the calendar's date displays line up properly:

```
Sun Mon Tue Wed Thu Fri Sat
  1   2   3   4   5   6   7
  8   9  10  11  12  13  14
 15  16  17  18  19  20  21
 22  23  24  25  26  27  28
 29  30  31
```

Chapter 16 discusses **<iomanip>** and manipulators in more detail.

Returning Addresses from Functions

When a function is declared to return a pointer, it actually returns an address that the calling function can use in an expression where a pointer or address is called for. Exercise 5.32 is an example of a function that returns an address.

Exercise 5.32 *Returning an address.*

```
#include <iostream>
using namespace std;

int* GetDate(int wk, int dy);

int main()
{
    int wk, dy;
    do {
        cout << "Enter week (1-5) day (1-7) ";
        cin >> wk >> dy;
    } while (wk < 1 || wk > 6 || dy < 1 || dy > 7);
    cout << *GetDate(wk, dy);
    return 0;
}

int* GetDate(int wk, int dy)
{
    static int calendar[5][7] = {
        {  1, 2, 3, 4, 5, 6, 7 },
        {  8, 9,10,11,12,13,14 },
        { 15,16,17,18,19,20,21 },
        { 22,23,24,25,26,27,28 },
        { 29,30,31,-1 }
    };
    // --- return the address of the date
    return &calendar[wk-1][dy-1];
}
```

Observe that the second *cout* call in the *main* function calls *GetDate* with a pointer (*) operator. This notation dereferences the address that the function returns and passes to *cout* the integer that the returned value points to. You can also assign the return value to a pointer variable and then use it to iterate through the array. Exercise 5.33 illustrates that usage.

Exercise 5.33 Iterating with a returned pointer.

```
#include <iostream>
using namespace std;

int* GetDate(int wk, int dy);

int main()
{
    int wk, dy;
    do {
        cout << "Enter week (1-5) day (1-7) ";
        cin >> wk >> dy;
    } while (wk < 1 || wk > 6 || dy < 1 || dy > 7);
    int* date = GetDate(wk, dy);
    while (*date != -1)
        cout << *date++ << ' ';
    return 0;
}
```

NOTE Exercise 5.33 has a bug. If you enter a week and day that subscripts past the -1 terminal element in the array, the loop displays whatever it finds at the effective address until it coincidentally finds the value 31. You would have to interrupt the running of the program to terminate the loop before that. Try to determine a way to prevent the program from going into such a loop.

Pointers to Functions

A pointer to a function contains the address of a function, and you can call the function through the pointer. You declare a function pointer using this format:

```
int (*fptr)();
```

The pointer's name is *fptr*. This particular pointer points to functions that return *int* and that accept no arguments. The pointer declaration must match those of the functions it points to.

The parentheses around the pointer name and its pointer operator (*) override the default operator precedence. Without them, the pointer definition would look like a prototype of a function that returns a pointer to *int*.

To assign the address of a function to a function pointer, use one of these two idioms:

```
fptr = &TheFunction;
fptr = TheFunction;
```

The & address-of operator is not required, because a function's identifier alone signifies its address rather than a call to the function, which would include an argument list in parentheses.

You call a function through its pointer using one of these formats:

```
x = (*fptr)();
x = fptr();
```

The second notation looks just like any other function call. Some programmers prefer to use the first notation, because it documents the fact that the function call is through a pointer rather than to a function of that name. Exercise 5.34 demonstrates how a function pointer works.

Exercise 5.34 Function pointers.

```
#include <iostream>
using namespace std;

void FileFunc(), EditFunc();

main()
{
    void (*funcp)();     // pointer to function

    funcp = FileFunc;    // put address in pointer
    (*funcp)();          // call the function
    funcp = EditFunc;    // put address in pointer
    (*funcp)();          // call the function
    return 0;

}
```

Exercise 5.34 Function pointers. (continued)

```
void FileFunc()
{
    cout << "File Function" << endl;
}

void EditFunc()
{
    cout << "Edit Function" << endl;
}
```

Exercise 5.34 demonstrates that a function pointer can have different function addresses at different times.

By using arrays of function pointers, you can build *finite state machines* in which the behavior of the program depends on the value of a *state variable* that determines which function executes next. One example of a finite state machine is a table-driven menu manager. Exercise 5.35 shows how such a program might be written. The four prototyped menu selection functions—which are not shown here but are in the program on the diskette—display messages just like the ones in Exercise 5.34. A production program would have custom menu structures and functions to do the work of the menu selections.

Exercise 5.35 A menu manager.

```
#include <iostream>
using namespace std;

// ---- a menu structure
struct Menu {
    char* name;
    void (*fn)();
};
// ---- menu selection functions
void FileFunc();
void EditFunc();
void ViewFunc();
void ExitFunc();
```

Exercise 5.35 A menu manager.

```
// ---- the menu
Menu menu[] = {
    { "File", FileFunc },
    { "Edit", EditFunc },
    { "View", ViewFunc },
    { "Exit", ExitFunc }
};
main()
{
    // ---- the menu manager
    unsigned sel = 0;
    while (sel != 4)    {
        for (int i = 0; i < 4; i++)
            cout << i+1 << ": " << menu[i].name << endl;
        cout << "Select: ";
        cin >> sel;
        if (sel < 5)
            // --- call through function pointer
            (*menu[sel-1].fn)();
    }
}
```

Pointers to Pointers

Pointers to pointers can be tricky. You declare them with two asterisks like this:

```
char** cpp;        // a pointer to a char pointer
```

It follows that three asterisks are used to declare a pointer to a pointer to a pointer, and four asterisks to declare a pointer to a pointer to a pointer to a pointer, and so on. You can deal with that level of complexity after you have familiarized yourself with the simplest case. This book addresses pointers to pointers and goes no deeper than that.

You initialize a pointer to a pointer using the address of a pointer:

```
char c = 'A';           // a char variable
char* cp = &c;          // a pointer to a char variable
char** cpp = &cp;       // a pointer to a pointer
```

You can use a pointer to a pointer to access either the pointer that it points to or the data item that the pointed-to pointer points to. Read that last sentence carefully. Here are examples using the pointers just defined:

```
char* cp1 = *cpp; // retrieve the pointer pointed to
char c1 = **cpp;  // retrieve the char pointed to indirectly
```

You might well wonder how you would use such constructs. Pointers to pointers can be used to allow a called function to modify a local pointer and to manage arrays of pointers. The latter usage is addressed in the next discussion. Exercise 5.36 demonstrates the former.

Exercise 5.36 *Pointers to pointers.*

```
#include <iostream>
using namespace std;

void FindCredit(float** fpp);

int main()
{
    float vals[] = {34.23, 67.33, 46.44, -99.22, 85.56, 0};
    float* fp = vals;
    FindCredit(&fp);
    cout << *fp;
    return 0;
}
```

Exercise 5.36 *Pointers to pointers. (continued)*

```
void FindCredit(float** fpp)
{
    while (**fpp != 0)
        if (**fpp < 0)
            break;
        else
            (*fpp)++;
}
```

Exercise 5.36 initializes the *fp* pointer with the address of an array and passes the address of the pointer to the *FindCredit* function, which is expecting a pointer to a pointer as an argument to its only parameter. *FindCredit* dereferences the array values indirectly with the ***fpp* expression. To iterate through the array in search of a negative value, *FindCredit* increments the caller's pointer to the array rather than its own local pointer to the caller's pointer. The *(*fpp)++* statement says to increment what the pointer parameter points to, which in this case is a pointer in the caller's scope. The parentheses are necessary because the * operator takes precedence over the ++ operator. Without the parentheses, the ++ operator would increment the pointer rather than what it points to, which, in this case, is also a pointer. When *FindCredit* returns, the *fp* pointer in *main*—the caller— points to the negative value in the table.

Pointers to Arrays of Pointers

Another use of pointers to pointers is to manage arrays of pointers. Some programmers prefer to use arrays of pointers rather than multiple-dimension arrays. One common use is to point to a table of strings, as shown in Exercise 5.37.

Exercise 5.37 *Pointers to arrays of pointers.*

```
#include <iostream>
using namespace std;

char* Names[] = {   // array of char pointers
    "Bill",         // initialized with names
    "Sam",
    "Jim",
    "Paul",
    "Charles",
    "Donald",
    0               // null pointer to terminate array
};

int main()
{
    char** nm = Names;          // pointer to pointer
    while (*nm != 0)
        cout << *nm++ << endl; // point to next pointer
    return 0;
}
```

Exercise 5.37 initializes the *nm* pointer to the address of the *Names* array, which is an array of character pointers. Each *cout* call passes the character pointer that the *nm* pointer points to and then increments the pointer to the next element (pointer) in the array. Observe that the syntax for doing that is *nm++*, which retrieves what the pointer points to and then increments the pointer itself.

Observe the zero initializer assigned to the last element of the array and tested for in the *while* loop. A zero value pointer is frequently used as a terminal symbol in arrays of pointers. Programmers call a pointer with a zero value a *null pointer*. By using a null pointer this way, you can add elements to and remove elements from the array without having to change the code that searches the array. The code adjusts to the new array, because it iterates through the array until it finds the null value pointer.

Pointers to *const* Variables

When you declare a pointer that points to a *const* variable, you are saying that the program cannot modify the variable through the pointer. The declaration looks like this:

```
const char* str;
```

Any reference to the character data that *str* points to must be read-only. This usage has a number of implications. First, you may not assign the address of a *const* variable to a pointer unless the pointer is declared as just shown. Furthermore, you may not pass the address of a *const* variable as an argument to a function in which the matching parameter is declared to be a pointer to a non-*const* variable. The following code illustrates this usage:

```
const char s1[] = "abcde"; // const variable, cannot change
char* cp1 = s1;            // error, pointer is not to const
const char* cp2 = s1;      // ok, pointer is to const
void foo(char* ps);
void bar(const char* ps);
foo(s1);                   // error, parameter is not const
bar(s1);                   // ok, parameter is const
```

Typical uses of a pointer to *const* are to qualify a function parameter so that the compiler prevents the function from trying to change the caller's copy of the variable and to allow callers to pass addresses of *const* variables. Exercise 5.38 implements the Standard C *strcpy* function to demonstrate how this works.

Exercise 5.38 const *pointer arguments.*

```
#include <iostream>
#include <cstring>
using namespace std;

char* strcpy(char* s1, const char* s2)  // const argument
{
    char* s = s1;
    while ((*s1++ = *s2++) != '\0')
        ;
    return s;
}
```

Exercise 5.38 const *pointer arguments. (continued)*

```
int main()
{
    char rcv[25];
    const char snd[] = "Hello, Dolly";
    strcpy(rcv, snd);
    cout << rcv;
    return 0;
}
```

The call to *strcpy* works because the first parameter is non-*const,* the second parameter is *const,* and the arguments match. The function modifies what the first argument points to by reading the second argument. The function would still work if both arguments were non-*const,* but it is a compile-time error to pass a *const* argument for the first parameter. The non-*const* property of the parameter indicates that the function could modify what the pointer points to, so the compiler does not permit it to point to a *const* variable.

As a rule, declare pointer function parameters as pointing to *const* when the function needs read-only access to the argument. This arrangement permits you to call the function by passing the address of *const* variables.

N O T E

Exercise 5.38 defines the Standard C *strcpy* function, which is declared in <**cstring**> (Chapter 6). You would not usually redefine a standard function unless you wanted to change its definition. That is legitimate C++ usage, as Exercise 5.38 demonstrates, but it is not usually a good idea to rewrite standard library functions. Exercise 5.38 uses the function to illustrate a valid usage for argument pointers to *const* variables.

const Pointer Variables

You can define pointers that cannot themselves change after they have been initialized. This practice allows you to build a small amount of safety into your code. If a pointer should never be used to iterate—if it should always retain its original value—declare it as *const* in this way:

```
char* const ptr = buf;
```

This declaration builds a char pointer that is itself *const.* You can also have a *const* pointer as a function parameter. The function cannot modify the pointer itself. These measures let the compiler catch your errors. Exercise 5.39 shows *const* pointers.

Exercise 5.39 const *pointers.*

```
#include <iostream>
#include <cctype>
using namespace std;

void ShowAllUppers(char* const str);

int main()
{
    char hb[] = "happy birthday";
    ShowAllUppers(hb);
    return 0;
}

void ShowAllUppers(char* const str)
{
    int i = 0;
    while (*(str+i))    {
        *(str+i) = toupper(*(str+i));
        i++;
    }
    cout << str;
}
```

Exercise 5.39 calls a function that converts a string constant to uppercase and then displays it. It uses the Standard C *toupper* function, which is declared in **<cctype>** (Chapter 6).

The function argument is a *const* pointer, which means that the function cannot change the value of the pointer. The reason, in this contrived example, is that the function needs the pointer's original value for the *cout* call after the conversion is done. The program would work the same way if you removed the *const* qualification from the argument's declaration. If, however, you later modified the function to change the pointer, the compiler would not catch the error, and the *cout* call would be using the wrong value.

You declare a pointer that itself is *const* and that points to a *const* variable using this format:

```
const char* const ptr = buf;
```

void Pointers

A *void* pointer can point to any kind of variable. It is declared like this:

```
void* vptr;
```

You can assign any address to a *void* pointer. You cannot use a *void* pointer to dereference a variable unless you provide a *cast*, described in a later section. You cannot perform pointer arithmetic on a *void* pointer without a cast. You use *void* pointers as parameters to functions that can operate on any kind of memory. You return *void* pointers from functions to assign to any of several different kinds of pointers. Typical examples are the Standard C memory allocation functions declared in **<cstdlib>** (Chapter 6). Exercise 5.40 declares the *malloc* and *free* function prototypes locally to show you how the *void* pointer mechanism works.

***Exercise 5.40** The* void *pointer.*

```
#include <iostream>
#include <cstdlib>
using namespace std;

void* malloc(size_t sz); // function returning void*
void free(void* bf);     // function accepting void* argument

struct Employee {         // Employee record structure
    short int emplno;
    char* name;
    float salary;
};
```

Exercise 5.40 *The* void *pointer. (continued)*

```
void ShowEmployee(const Employee* emp);

int main()
{
    Employee* emp;
    emp = (Employee*) malloc(sizeof(Employee)); // allocate
    if (emp != 0)    {
        // --- build an Employee record
        emp->emplno = 123;
        emp->name = "Jones";
        emp->salary = 37500;
        ShowEmployee(emp);
        free(emp);                       // free allocated memory
    }
    return 0;
}
// ---- display an Employee record
void ShowEmployee(const Employee* emp)
{
    cout << "Empl#:  " << emp->emplno << endl;
    cout << "Name:   " << emp->name   << endl;
    cout << "Salary: " << emp->salary << endl;
}
```

Exercise 5.40 calls *malloc* to allocate a block of memory big enough to hold an instance of an *Employee* structure. That call returns the address of a user-defined structure from a general-purpose memory allocation function. The function itself returns a *void* pointer, which is assigned to a pointer to the structure type. The function is declared to return a *void* pointer because you use the same memory allocation library functions to allocate memory for all types. C++ does not allow implicit conversion from a void pointer to another pointer type (although C does), so the *(Employee*)* expression, which is a *type-cast*, casts the return value to the desired pointer type, in this case a pointer to an *Employee* structure.

A typecast tells the compiler to ignore what it knows about the type and assume instead what the cast specifies. We discuss C-style casting in more detail elsewhere in this chapter and C++ casting in Chapter 15.

The program assigns some values to the structure members and calls a function to display the employee data. Then it calls the Standard C *free* function to release the memory that was allocated. The *free* function expects a *void* pointer to identify the memory to be freed. C++ allows a pointer of any type to be automatically converted to a *void* pointer, so the program may use the *emp* pointer without a typecast. The *free* function declares a *void* pointer, because it frees memory that was allocated for all types.

 C++ provides an improved typecasting mechanism discussed in Chapter 15.

N O T E

Although Exercise 5.40's purpose is to explain *void* pointers, it also introduces dynamic memory allocation, one of the cornerstones of C and C++ programming. Programs allocate dynamic memory from a memory pool called the *heap*, which is discussed later in this chapter under "Program Memory Architecture."

THE *sizeof* OPERATOR

Exercise 5.40 teaches another lesson. The program allocates 12 bytes of memory for the *Employee* structure by using the *sizeof* operator. This number works out to be 12 with Quincy, because short integers are two bytes long, pointers are four bytes, and a float is four. Instead of using the *sizeof* expression, the program could have used the constant 12. There are three problems associated with this approach.

First, you must count the bytes in a structure to know its size, and you could make a mistake. The *malloc* function wouldn't care; it allocates whatever you ask for. The assignment accepts whatever address *malloc* returns and assumes that there are enough bytes there to hold the structure.

The second problem arises when you change the size of the structure later during the program's development. Using an explicit constant size for the structure, you would have to find such references and change them.

The last problem is one of portability. The program would work only when the sizes of the intrinsic data types add up to 12. If you compiled the program with a different compiler or a different memory model or on a different computer, the sizes would probably be different, and the value 12 would be incorrect. The *sizeof* operator avoids all three of these problems.

The *sizeof* operator returns the size in characters of a variable or a type. The variable or type can be an array, structure, pointer, or one of the intrinsic types. When the operand is a type, such as the one in Exercise 5.40, the operand must be surrounded by parentheses. When the operand is a variable identifier, the parentheses are optional. Here are examples:

```
// ----- some things to take the size of
int w;
int* x;
int y[5];
struct z { int a,b,c; };
struct z zs;
struct z* zp;
// ----- some sizeof expressions
sizeof w;           // the size of an int
sizeof(int);        // the size of an int
sizeof x;           // the size of a pointer
sizeof &w;          // the size of an address constant
sizeof *x;          // the size of an int
sizeof y;           // the size of the array
sizeof(struct z);   // the size of the structure
sizeof zs;          // the size of the structure
sizeof zp;          // the size of a pointer
```

Programs use *sizeof* as a portable way to express structure sizes and the sizes of input/output buffers.

You can also use *sizeof* to dynamically compute the number of elements in an array. Refer to the menu manager in Exercise 5.35. It uses three constants that you must modify when you add or delete selections in the menu. One constant identifies the last selection, which is always the Exit command. The next iterates through the menu. The third constant ensures that the user enters a valid menu selection. All three constants reflect the number of structure elements in the menu-defining array. By using *sizeof* to dynamically compute the number of elements, the program can automatically adjust to changes that you make to the menus. Exercise 5.41 shows how this works.

Exercise 5.41 Using sizeof *to compute array elements.*

```
const int Selections = sizeof menu / sizeof(Menu);

main()
{
    // ---- the menu manager
    unsigned i, sel = 0;
    while (sel != Selections)    {
        for (i = 0; i < Selections; i++)
            cout << i+1 << ": " << menu[i].name << endl;
        cout << "Select: ";
        cin >> sel;
        if (sel < Selections+1)
            // --- call through function pointer
            (*menu[sel-1].fn)();
    }
}
```

(The listing in Exercise 5.41 repeats only the changed parts of Exercise 5.35.) Exercise 5.41 defines a *const int* variable with an initialized value computed by dividing the size of the *menu* array by the size of one element—the *Menu* type—in the array. The exercise uses a variable, *Selections*, instead of the constant expressions in Exercise 5.35. If you change the program later by adding or removing menu items or if you add members to the structure, the program adjusts to the new size, and the menu management code does not need to be modified.

C-STYLE TYPECASTS

Sometimes you need to coerce the compiler into thinking that a variable or constant is a different type from the one that you declared it to be or, as in the case of an expression, a different type from the one implied by its context. For that, you use a traditional typecast, which has this format:

```
int* iptr = (int*) &table;
```

The *(int*)* prefix to the expression is a traditional C-style typecast, also called a *cast*. The cast tells the compiler to convert the value of the expression to the type in the cast. Some casts are not permitted. You cannot cast a structure of one type to something else. You can cast any numerical type to any other numerical type and any pointer to any other pointer. You can cast numerical values to pointers and vice versa, although such practices are generally considered unsafe and unnecessary.

Casts can be used to suppress compiler warnings. Some compilers warn you when an implicit type conversion could result in the loss of information. For example:

```
long el = 123;
short i = (int) el;  // compiler warning without the cast
```

Many compilers alert you that the assignment of a *long* to an *short* could lose data. There are times when you know better, as in the example. The value 123 is well within the range of a *short*. Other times you don't care, such as when you need the integral part of a real number:

```
float rn = 34.56;
int i = (int) rn;    // i = 34
```

These are the best uses of the cast: to suppress compiler warnings about things that you do intentionally. Using the cast to override the compiler's type-checking facilities is a bad practice.

Casts are usually deprecated by the knowledgeable, but there are times when they are unavoidable, such as the cast from a void pointer to a specific pointer type when you call *malloc*, as Exercise 5.40 showed. Chapter 14 discusses an improved C++ typecasting mechanism introduced by the ANSI C++ committee to solve some of the problems associated with C-style typecasts described here.

typedef

The C++ *typedef* storage class specifier does not really specify a storage class. It is grouped with the *static, extern, register,* and *auto* storage classes, because all five appear syntactically in the same place in a declaration and because they are mutually exclusive. Therefore, *typedef* is called a storage class specifier. However, *typedef* has a much different role: It allows you to assign your own names to types. These names are aliases of existing types. Exercise 5.42 is an example of *typedef*.

Exercise 5.42 The typedef *storage class.*

```
#include <iostream>
using namespace std;

typedef int RcdCounter;

int main()
{
    RcdCounter rc = 123;
    cout << rc << " records";
    return 0;
}
```

Exercise 5.42 uses *typedef* to declare an integer type for a record counter. If you decide, later in the program's development, that a record counter needs to be a different integral type—*long,* perhaps, or *unsigned*—you can change the *typedef* declaration and the program adjusts all uses of it. Here are some of the ways that the *typedef* in Exercise 5.42 could be changed:

```
typedef long RcdCounter;
typedef unsigned RcdCounter;
typedef unsigned char RcdCounter;
```

The *typedef* storage class works with pointers and structures, too. Here is an example:

```
typedef struct window  {
    char *title;
    int x,y;
    int ht, wd;
} * WINDOW;
```

Pointers to the *window* structure can be declared with the *WINDOW* identifier. Perhaps the structure and *typedef* declarations are in a header file and the code that supports windows is in a library. Programmers don't need to know that a *WINDOW* is a pointer or what it points to. The identifier might be a *handle* used to communicate between the applications program and the screen manager library software, as in this example:

```
#include "windows.h"

void foo()
{
    WINDOW wnd = CreateWindow("hi", 3, 5, 10, 60);
    DisplayWindow(wnd);
    // etc...
}
```

The underlying structure of screen windows in this example is unimportant to the programmer who uses the *WINDOW* handle. This practice, called *information hiding*, is a basic concept in structured programming.

COMMAND-LINE ARGUMENTS: *argc* AND *argv*

Every C++ program has a *main* function, a fact that you have been using in all the exercises in this book. The *main* function has two parameters that you have not yet seen, because none of the programs have defined them. In fact, *main* is the only function that can get by without defining its parameters. The two parameters are an *int* and a pointer to an array of *char* pointers. The *int* parameter contains the number of command-line arguments that the user typed on the command-line to run the program. The *char*[]* argument points to an array of character pointers, which themselves point to the command-line arguments. Although you may name these two parameters anything you like, the convention is to name them *argc* and *argv* and to declare them in the *main* function header:

```
int main(int argc, char* argv[])
{
    // ...
}
```

The *argc* parameter has a count of at least 1 and has a higher count if the user typed arguments on the command-line. There is always at least one *char* pointer in the array pointed to by *argv*, and it, *argv[0]*, usually points to the name of the program's executable file. Some implementations include the path that the program is run from. Most MS-DOS implementations work that way.

NOTE   Quincy is a Windows 95-hosted integrated development environment that acts as a front end to the GNU compiler and that provides integrated program editing, compiling, and debugging. Although you could run Quincy from the command-line, you do not run your C++ programs from the command-line. Instead, you run them from within Quincy's integrated development environment. Quincy emulates command-line entries, however, and some of the exercises take advantage of that. Before proceeding, you should refer again to the Appendix and refresh your knowledge of how to set command-line arguments into Quincy's operating environment.

Exercise 5.43 shows how a program uses command-line arguments.

Exercise 5.43 Command-line arguments.

```
#include <iostream>
using namespace std;

int main(int argc, char* argv[])
{
    cout << "This program is " << argv[0] << endl;
    for (int arg = 1; arg < argc; arg++)
        cout << "Argument " << arg << ": "
             << argv[arg] << endl;
}
```

PROGRAM MEMORY ARCHITECTURE

Programs load into and execute from the computer's core or semiconductor memory. That concept—the stored program—is the basis for all contemporary digital computers. The program's machine language instructions and its data are stored in the same logical memory space. The program is organized into four logical segments: executable code, statically allocated data, dynamically allocated data (the heap), and the stack.

Executable code and statically allocated data are stored in fixed memory locations.

Program-requested, dynamically allocated memory is drawn from a memory pool called the *heap*.

Local data objects, function arguments, and the linkage from a calling function to a called function are maintained in a memory pool called the *stack*.

Depending on the operating platform and the compiler, the heap and stack could be operating system resources that are shared by all concurrently running programs, or they could be local resources owned exclusively by the programs that use them.

The Heap

A C++ program allocates and deallocates dynamic blocks of memory from a global store of memory sometimes called the *free store*, more commonly called the *heap*.

Exercise 5.40 showed how a program uses the Standard C *malloc* and *free* functions to allocate and deallocate memory on the heap. As a C++ programmer, you can forget about *malloc* and *free*. C++ provides the *new* and *delete* operators for memory allocation.

new and delete Operators

The *new* operator, when used with the name of a pointer to a data type, structure, or array, allocates memory for the item and assigns the address of that memory to the pointer.

The *delete* operator returns to the heap the memory specified by the operand, which must be the address of previously allocated memory.

Exercise 5.44 demonstrates the *new* and *delete* operators.

Exercise 5.44 *The* new *and* delete *operators.*

```
#include <iostream>
using namespace std;

struct Date {    // a date structure
    int month;
    int day;
    int year;
};

int main()
{
    Date* birthday = new Date; // get memory for a date
    birthday->month = 6;       // assign a value to the date
    birthday->day = 24;
    birthday->year = 1940;
    cout << "I was born on "   // display the date
        << birthday->month << '/'
        << birthday->day   << '/'
        << birthday->year;
    delete birthday;           // return memory to the heap
    return 0;
}
```

The structure in this exercise defines a date. The program uses the *new* operator to allocate memory for an instance of the structure. Then the program initializes the new *Date* object with date values. After displaying the contents of the object, the program disposes of it with the *delete* operator.

Allocating a Fixed-Dimension Array

The advantages of *new* and *delete* over the Standard C functions *malloc* and *free* are not obvious in Exercise 5.44. The two approaches appear to be roughly the same. However, in addition to providing a more readable syntax for memory allocation, *new* and *delete* have other advantages, some of which become evident when you learn about classes and their constructor and destructor functions in Chapter 9.

Exercise 5.45 shows how you can use *new* and *delete* to acquire and dispose of memory for an array.

Exercise 5.45 new *and* delete *with an array.*

```
#include <iostream>
using namespace std;

int main()
{
    int* birthday = new int[3];    // get memory for an array
    birthday[0] = 6;               // assign values to array
    birthday[1] = 24;
    birthday[2] = 1940;
    cout << "I was born on "       // display the date
        << birthday[0] << '/'
        << birthday[1] << '/'
        << birthday[2];
    delete [] birthday;        // return memory to the heap
    return 0;
}
```

Observe that the *delete* operator in Exercise 5.45 is followed by a pair of brackets. This notation tells the compiler that the memory being deleted is an array. In this example, the notation probably has no effect, depending on the compiler. By convention, programmers use the notation for all deletions of dynamically allocated arrays. The notation has consequences when the array contains objects of user-defined class types. You learn about them in Chapter 9.

Allocating Dynamic Arrays

Exercise 5.45 showed how the *new* operator accepts a data type with an array dimension. The dimension in the exercise is a constant 3, representing the number of integers in the date. You can, however, supply a variable dimension, and the *new* operator allocates the correct amount of memory.

Exercise 5.46 shows the use of a variably dimensioned array as allocated by the *new* operator.

Exercise 5.46 *The* new *operator and dynamic arrays.*

```
#include <iostream>
#include <cstdlib>
using namespace std;

int main()
{
    cout << "Enter the array size: ";
    int size;
    cin >> size;                  // get the array size
    int* array = new int[size];   // allocate an array
    for (int i = 0; i < size; i++) // load the array
        array[i] = rand();        // with random numbers
    for (int i = 0; i < size; i++) // display the array
        cout << '\n' << array[i];
    delete [] array; // return the array to the heap
    return 0;
}
```

When running this exercise, you type in the size of the array. The *new* operator uses that value to establish the size of the memory buffer to be allocated. It multiplies the *size* value by the size of the array type, which is *int* in this example. The program builds the array by using the *new* operator, fills it with random numbers, displays each of the elements in the array, and deletes the array by using the *delete* operator.

When the Heap Is Exhausted

So far these exercises have not considered the question of what to do if the heap is out of memory when you use the *new* operator. Instead, they assume that the heap is never exhausted. Clearly, this is not a realistic approach. The Standard C *malloc* function returns a null pointer under that condition, and C programs that call *malloc* usually test for the null return and do something meaningful about it. The C++ *new* operator, on the other hand, throws a runtime exception if you request memory that the system cannot supply. Chapter 14 deals with C++ exception handling.

The Stack

Programs do not explicitly allocate memory on the stack as they do on the heap. The system allocates memory automatically when the program calls functions and declares local variables.

A stack is a push-down, pop-up data structure. The runtime system pushes objects on the stack one at a time, and the stack pointer moves down one entry. When the system pops an object from the stack, the most recently pushed object—the one just above the current stack pointer—is popped, and the stack pointer moves up one entry. When the pointer is at the top, the stack is empty. When the pointer is one past the bottommost entry, the stack is full.

Programmers often use stack data structures to solve programming problems that are best addressed with push-down, pop-up logic. The program's stack that we are discussing here exists in every program. It is maintained, not by the part of the program that you write, but by the runtime system. The runtime system maintenance is actually code that the compiler generates in the program. You do not see this code in your program, but it is there, and you should understand what it does. This behavior and the push-down, pop-up nature of a stack are what distinguishes the stack from the heap.

Here is how the program stack works. When one function (the caller) calls another function (the callee), the runtime system (the system) pushes all the caller's arguments and the caller's return address onto the stack. The stack pointer moves down as many places as necessary to accommodate these pushes. The last object pushed is the caller's return address.

When the callee starts executing, the system pushes the callee's automatic variables on the stack, moving the stack pointer down enough entries to make room for all the automatic variables that the callee declares.

The callee addresses its parameters on the stack as automatic variables created when the caller pushed its arguments. The callee address its own automatic variables on the stack, too. The stack pointer is, however, below all these local variables because of the pushes, but the callee uses negative and positive offsets from the stack pointer's original value when the callee started executing.

When the callee is ready to return, the system pops the callee's automatic variables from the stack. The stack pointer now points to where it pointed when the callee first started. When the callee returns, the system pops the return address from the stack, and the caller resumes executing just past the call to the callee.

When the caller resumes executing, the system pops the caller's arguments from the stack, and the stack pointer is now positioned where it was before the caller called the callee.

RECURSION

Let's review what Chapter 3 says about recursion: Any C++ function can call itself, either directly or by a lower function that is executing as the result of a call made by the recursive function. We delayed the detailed discussion of recursion until you learned what this chapter teaches about pointers, arrays, and the stack. Recursion is relevant in this chapter because of the way recursion works in the C++ language.

Recursion works because every function execution gets private copies of its parameters and local variables on the stack, and because those copies are distinct from the copies owned by other executions of the same function.

This mechanism, which is the foundation of subroutine architecture in most contemporary programming languages, is what enables recursion. Suppose a caller function calls a callee function. Suppose then that the callee turns around and calls the caller. That call would be a recursive execution of the caller, and it would happen before the current execution of the caller has completed. It works, however, because the then-caller, now-callee function starts with a separate set of parameter arguments and automatic variables in a lower position on the stack. Its original parameters and variables are not disturbed during this recursive execution. The program is executing what is called a *recursive descent* through its functions.

It is the programmer's responsibility to ensure that a function that is to be used recursively does not change the values of static or global variables in ways that could inappropriately alter some other invocation of itself higher in the recursive descent through the program's functions. It is also the programmer's responsibility to ensure that some condition enables a recursive descent to stop descending and find its way back to the top.

There are no exercises that demonstrate the stack. It just works.

A Simple Recursive Example

Exercise 5.47 is a simple program that uses a recursive function. The contrived problem that the program solves is this: There is a list of names in a specific order. You want the names displayed in the reverse order in which they are listed.

Exercise 5.47 *Recursion.*

```cpp
#include <iostream>
using namespace std;

char* Names[] = {  // array of char pointers
    "Bill",         // initialized with names
    "Sam",
    "Jim",
    "Paul",
    "Charles",
    "Donald",
    0            // null pointer to terminate array
};
// --- a recursive function
void DisplayNames(char** nm)
{
    if (*nm != 0)    {
        DisplayNames(nm + 1);     // recursive call
        cout << *nm << endl;
    }
}
int main()
{
    DisplayNames(Names);
    return 0;
}
```

The *main* function in Exercise 5.47 calls the program's *DisplayNames* function, passing the address of the first element of the array of pointers to name strings, which is terminated with a null pointer. The *DisplayNames* function examines its parameter to see whether it points to a null pointer. If it does not, *DisplayNames* calls itself and passes the address of the next element in the array. Those calls continue until *DisplayNames* finds that its parameter points to the null terminator pointer, whereupon the function returns.

Here's where it gets tricky. The first time the function returns, it returns to itself in its next-to-the-last execution, which has an argument that points to the last non-null pointer in the array. The function displays that name and returns to—guess where—the invocation of the function that points to the name immediately preceding the one that the function just displayed. And so on, until the function returns to the iteration of itself that points to the first element in the array. It displays that name and returns to the *main* function. Recursive descent.

A Recursive Calculator

Recursion is used in sorting and parsing algorithms. As a programmer, you use recursive descent algorithms every time you compile source-code. You didn't write them, of course; the programmer who wrote the compiler wrote the algorithms. The algorithms parse the source-code for correct syntax and evaluate expressions. Perhaps you have wondered how that works.

Exercise 5.48 is a calculator program that evaluates numeric expressions similar to but simpler than those that you code with the C++ language. The small calculator implements only addition, subtraction, multiplication, division, and parentheses in an expression. You type the expression into the program with no white space. The program evaluates the expression and displays either the result or, if you typed an error, an error message.

Exercise 5.48 *A recursive calculator.*

```cpp
#include <iostream>
#include <cstdlib>
#include <cctype>
using namespace std;

// ---- prototypes
int addsubt();
int multdiv();
int number();
void error();

// --- global expression buffer
static char expr[81];
static int pos;

int main()
{
    int ans;
    do   {
        pos = 0;  // initialize string subscript
        // ---- read an expression
        cout << "Enter expression (0 to quit):" << endl;
        cin >> expr;
        // --- evaluate the expression
        ans = addsubt();
        if (expr[pos] != '\0')
            error();
        if (ans != 0)
            cout << ans << endl;
    } while (ans != 0);
    return 0;
}
```

Exercise 5.48 *A recursive calculator.* *(continued)*

```
// ---- top of recursive descent: add/subtract
int addsubt()
{
    int rtn = multdiv();
    while (expr[pos] == '+' || expr[pos] == '-') {
        int op = expr[pos++];
        int opr2 = multdiv();
        if (op == '+')
            rtn += opr2;
        else
            rtn -= opr2;
    }
    return rtn;
}
// ---- highest precedence: multiply/divide
int multdiv()
{
    int rtn = number();
    while (expr[pos] == '*' || expr[pos] == '/') {
        int op = expr[pos++];
        int opr2 = number();
        if (op == '*')
            rtn *= opr2;
        else
            rtn /= opr2;
    }
    return rtn;
}
```

Exercise 5.48 *A recursive calculator. (continued)*

```
// ---- extract a number
int number()
{
    int rtn;
    if (expr[pos] == '(')   {
        // --- parenthetical expression
        pos++;
        rtn = addsubt();          // back to top
        if (expr[pos++] != ')') // must have ')'
            error();
         return rtn;
    }
    // --- extract the number
    if (!isdigit(expr[pos]))
        error();
    rtn = atoi(expr+pos);
    while (isdigit(expr[pos]))
        pos++;
    return rtn;
}
// ---- syntax error
void error()
{
    cout << '\r';
    while (pos--)       // position error pointer
        cout << ' ';
    cout << "^ syntax error" << endl << '\a';
    exit(-1);
}
```

The program in Exercise 5.48 scans the expression by subscripting through an array of characters that it reads with the standard *cin* object.

When you type the expression, the program sets the *pos* subscript to zero and calls the *addsubt* function. Addition and subtraction have the same precedence and, in this calculator, the lowest precedence. The first thing the *addsubt* function does is to call the *multdiv* function. Multiplication and division have the same precedence and the highest precedence of the operators.

Before doing anything else, the *multdiv* function calls the *number* function to extract the first operand from the expression. That function checks first for a left parenthesis. If it doesn't find one, a number must be next. The program uses the Standard C *atoi* function, which converts a string of ASCII digits into an integer. The *atoi* function is declared in the **<cstdlib>** header file. The *number* function returns the integer to the *multdiv* function, but first the function uses the Standard C *isdigit* function, declared in the **<cctype>** header file, to bypass the digits in the number so that the scan proceeds with the next element in the expression.

If the *number* function finds a left parenthesis instead of a number, precedence is being overridden, and the function calls *addsubt* to evaluate the parenthetical expression. This is where recursion comes in. The *number* function is executed indirectly by the *addsubt* function, and yet the *number* function itself calls the *addsubt* function.

The recursive call to *addsubt* can initiate other recursive sequences depending on what is in the expression. Eventually they all return to *number*, which returns the value that *addsubt* returned.

The *multdiv* function stores the result from the *number* function. Then it looks for the multiplication and division operators. As long as it finds one of them, it calls the *number* function to get the second operand and computes its result by multiplying or dividing the two values returned by *number*. When it sees no more multiplication or division operators, the *multdiv* function returns its computed value. The *addsubt* function processes the values returned by *multdiv* in a similar way but with the addition and subtraction operators.

When the first execution of *addsubt* returns to the *main* function, the expression evaluation is complete, and the value that it returns is the result of the evaluation.

The program continues to run, getting new expressions from the user until one of them evaluates to zero, telling the program to terminate.

If the evaluation scan finds an error, it calls the *error* function, which displays an error message and terminates the program. It can't simply return, because the error might have occurred at any depth in the recursive descent.

A return would cause the expression evaluation to continue from an illogical data position.

One way to deal with such errors so that the program keeps running and gets another expression is to set a global error flag and have each function simply return if the flag is set. Eventually, the program would get back to the top of the algorithm. That would work, but there are better ways. You will learn about them in Chapter 6 when you read about the Standard C *setjmp* and *longjmp* functions and in Chapter 14 when you read about C++ exception handling.

Observe that the *expr* character array and the *pos* subscript variable are declared outside any function. This positioning makes the variables accessible to all the functions in the program. Because of their *static* storage class, they are in file scope. You learned about storage classes and the scope of variables earlier in this chapter.

The calculator program has a small bug. The *expr* array is only 81 characters long, and the program uses *cin* to read the string. If you typed an expression more than 80 characters, the input stream would overrun the buffer, and the program would behave unpredictably. Also, because we use *cin*'s >> operator, you cannot type any white space into the expression. We will fix these problems in Chapter 16.

REFERENCE VARIABLES

A *reference* variable is an alias, or synonym, for another variable. It is often used for passing parameters and returning values by reference rather than by value. Like pointers, the reference lets you pass and return large data structures without the overhead of copying them.

If you are a C programmer, you probably found pointers most troubling when you first learned C. You are not alone. Even veteran C programmers get bogged down trying to comprehend some of the complex operations allowed by C pointers, pointers to pointers, pointers to arrays, arrays of pointers, and so on. The C++ reference variable can give you the same kind of trouble until you understand it. Its syntax and usage, however, prevent many of the pointer pitfalls that trap C programmers.

References are very much like pointers. As you will see later, anything you can do with a reference you can do with a pointer, but references offer certain advantages. For example, the reference lets you refer to a referenced object as if the reference were a real object, eliminating the pointer dereferencing (*) operator for simple objects and the pointer-to-member operator for members of referenced structures. A reference can also simplify notation when you dereference complex objects that are found inside arrays, structures, arrays of structures, arrays inside structures, structures inside structures, and so on.

Following is a list of attributes shared by references and pointers:

- You can pass and return references and pointers to and from functions.
- A call to a function that returns a reference or an address (a pointer) can appear on either side of an assignment.

Following is a list of attributes in which references are unlike pointers:

- A reference is a logical alias for an actual variable.
- You must initialize a reference to refer to a real object when it is declared.
- You may not change the value of a reference after it has been initialized.
- There is no such thing as a null reference.

The Reference Is an Alias

A C++ reference is an alias for another variable. When you declare a reference variable, you give it a value that you cannot change for the life of the reference. The & operator identifies a reference variable as in the following example:

```
int actualint;
int& otherint = actualint;
```

These statements declare an integer, named *actualint,* that has another name, *otherint.* Now all references to either name have the same effect. Exercise 5.49 demonstrates a simple reference variable.

Exercise 5.49 *Reference variable.*

```
#include <iostream>
using namespace std;

int main()
{
    int actualint = 123;
    int& otherint = actualint;

    cout << actualint << endl;
    cout << otherint  << endl;
    otherint++;
    cout << actualint << endl;
    cout << otherint  << endl;
    actualint++;
    cout << actualint << endl;
    cout << otherint  << endl;
    return 0;
}
```

Exercise 5.49 shows that all operations on the reference variable *otherint* act upon the actual variable *actualint*. The exercise demonstrates that whatever you do to *otherint*, you do to *actualint*, and vice versa.

A reference is neither a copy of nor a pointer to the thing to which it refers. Instead, it behaves like another name that the compiler recognizes for the thing to which it refers. The reference variable is not, however, implemented like a #define macro (Chapter 7). Its internal implementation is more like that of a pointer but with restrictions, mainly involving initialization and modification of the reference variable. But in the programmer's view, the reference variable is more like an alias than a pointer.

Exercise 5.50 demonstrates the alias metaphor by displaying the values returned when you compare the address of an actual variable to the address of a reference to that variable.

Exercise 5.50 *Addresses of references.*

```
#include <iostream>
using namespace std;

int main()
{
    int actualint = 123;
    int& otherint = actualint;

    cout << &actualint << ' ' << &otherint;
    return 0;
}
```

Exercise 5.50 displays something similar to the following message.

```
0x64fdac 0x64fdac
```

The format and values of these addresses depend on where your runtime system locates the variables and the format of the hexadecimal address in your compiler. The point here is not what the two addresses are. The point is that they are the same.

Initializing a Reference

Unlike a pointer, a reference cannot be manipulated. It is, as you learned in the first two exercises in this chapter, an alias for something else, something real. It follows that you must initialize a reference (explicitly give the reference something to refer to) when you declare it unless one of the following statements is true:

- The reference variable is declared with *extern*, in which case it would have been initialized elsewhere.
- The reference variable is a member of a class, in which case the class's constructor function initializes the reference (Chapter 9).

- The reference variable is a parameter in a function declaration, in which case the reference parameter variable is initialized by the caller's argument when the function is called.

As you work through the exercises in this and later chapters, observe all uses of references to see that each one matches one of these criteria.

References to Reduce Complex Notation

You can use a reference to reduce the complex notation that some expressions use to dereference members of structures and elements of arrays. This idiom is useful when there are many such expressions after a particular element has been located. Exercise 5.51 demonstrates this principle.

Exercise 5.51 References to reduce complex notation.

```
#include <iostream>
using namespace std;

// --- a Date structure
struct Date {
    int month, day, year;
};

// --- an Employee structure
struct Employee    {
    int empno;
    char name[35];
    Date dates[3];    // hired, last review, terminated
    float salary;
};
```

Exercise 5.51 *References to reduce complex notation. (continued)*

```
Employee staff[] = {
    { 1, "Bill", {{12,1,88},{2,24,92},{5,5,95}}, 35000 },
    { 1, "Paul", {{10,3,87},{5,17,94},{3,7,96}}, 25000 },
    { 1, "Jim",  {{ 9,5,80},{9,11,96},{0,0, 0}}, 42000 },
    { 0 }
};

int main()
{
    Employee* pEmpl = staff;
    while (pEmpl->empno != 0)    {
        for (int i = 0; i < 3; i++)    {
            Date& rd = pEmpl->dates[i];
            cout << rd.month << '/'
                 << rd.day   << '/'
                 << rd.year  << " ";
        }
        cout << endl;
        pEmpl++;
    }
    return 0;
}
```

Exercise 5.51 contains an array of employee records. Each record is an element in the array and consists of an object of a structure. This structure includes as one of its members an array of date structures, presumably to record an employee's date of hire, date of last review, and termination date. This example, although seemingly complex on the surface, is much less so than many typical data structures that C++ programmers deal with routinely.

The program assigns the address of the *Employee* array to a pointer and iterates through the array by incrementing the pointer until it points to the terminal entry. For each element in the array, the program iterates through the array of dates to display them on the console. By now, the members of the Date structure are pointed to by a pointer and are subscripted by a subscript value. To simplify the dereferencing notation of these Date structure members, the program declares a reference to a Date object and initializes the reference to refer to the object currently referred to. Then the program displays the Date object's members by dereferencing the reference's members to send to the *cout* object.

Without the reference variable, the program would have to use the following notation to address the members of the Date structure:

```
cout << staff[i].dates[1].month << '/'
     << staff[i].dates[1].day   << '/'
     << staff[i].dates[1].year  << endl;
```

References as Function Parameters

References are often used as function parameters. There is little need to build a reference that exists only in the scope of the variable that the reference variable refers to. You might as well use the original name of the variable. Exercises 5.49 and 5.50 used references in that way, but the purpose of those exercises was to show you the behavior of references and not necessarily to show the best way to use them. Following are some advantages of using references as function parameters rather than using copies of the caller's arguments:

- References eliminate the overhead associated with passing large data structures as parameters and with returning large data structures from functions.

- References eliminate the pointer dereferencing notation used in functions to which you pass references as arguments.

Exercise 5.52 demonstrates these advantages.

Exercise 5.52 References as function parameters.

```
#include <iostream>
using namespace std;

// ---------- a big structure
struct bigone     {
    int serno;
    char text[1000];     // a lot of chars
};

// -- two functions with a structure parameter
void slowfunc(bigone p1);         // call by value
void fastfunc(bigone& p1);        // call by reference

int main()
{
    static bigone bo = { 123, "This is a BIG structure"};
    slowfunc(bo);      // this will take a while
    fastfunc(bo);      // this will be faster
    return 0;
}

// ---- a call-by-value function
void slowfunc(bigone p1)
{
    cout << p1.serno << endl;
    cout << p1.text << endl;
}

// ---- a call by reference function
void fastfunc(bigone& p1)
{
    cout << p1.serno << endl;
    cout << p1.text << endl;
}
```

Observe that the calls to both functions in Exercise 5.52 specify the name of the structure object. Observe also that both functions refer to the structure members by using the structure member dot (.) operator.

Unfortunately, nothing in the exercise jumps out at you to demonstrate the advantage of using a reference parameter. The only apparent difference is the use of the reference (&) operator in the function's prototype and parameter declaration. But the differences are real, and you can see them if you use Quincy to step through the program. It takes a measurably longer time to call *slowfunc* than it does to call *fastfunc*. This difference is due to the overhead added by Quincy's debugger as it watches for the call statement to proceed, combined with the code that the compiler generates to copy the large structure. The difference would not be as dramatic without the debugger overhead, but it would be there.

This example implies another performance consequence. Remember the discussions about the stack and recursion earlier in this chapter. If a program recursively calls a function such as the *bigone* function, the stack pointer goes deeper and deeper with each recursive call. If the recursive descent goes deep enough, the program stack becomes exhausted, and the program probably crashes. This problem alone justifies the use of references as function parameters.

Call by Reference

When one function passes a reference as an argument to another function, the called function is working on the caller's copy of the parameter and not on a local copy (as it does when you pass the variable itself). This behavior is known as *call by reference*. Passing the parameter's value to a private copy in the called function is known as *call by value*. Exercise 5.53 demonstrates call by reference.

Exercise 5.53 *Call by reference.*

```cpp
#include <iostream>
using namespace std;

// ------ date structure
struct Date {
    int month, day, year;
};

void display(const Date&, const char*);
void swapper(Date&, Date&);

int main()
{
    static Date now  = {2,23,90}; // two dates
    static Date then = {9,10,60};

    display(now, "Now:  ");      // display the dates
    display(then, "Then: ");

    swapper(now, then);          // swap them

    display(now, "Now:  ");      // display dates swapped
    display(then, "Then: ");
    return 0;
}
// ----- swap the caller's dates
void swapper(Date& dt1, Date& dt2)
{
    Date save;
    save = dt1;
    dt1 = dt2;
    dt2 = save;
}
```

Exercise 5.53 *Call by reference. (continued)*

```
// ------ display a Date object
void display(const Date& dt, const char* ttl)
{
    cout << ttl;
    cout << dt.month << '/'
         << dt.day   << '/'
         << dt.year  << endl;
}
```

In Exercise 5.53, the first two dates are initialized with different values as local variables in the *main* function. The *swapper* function swaps those two dates. It accepts two *Date* references and swaps them by using simple assignment statements. Because the parameters are references, the swapping occurs to the *main* function's copy of the structures.

const Reference Parameters

The *swapper* function in Exercise 5.53 is permitted to modify the caller's variables, because the parameters are references to those variables. But suppose that you want to prevent a function from being able to modify its caller's referenced variables. For example, the *display* function in Exercise 5.53 accepts two referenced arguments but does not modify them. By declaring those arguments as *const*, the program ensures to the caller that the called function will view but not disturb the values in the referenced arguments.

Returning a Reference

You have seen how you can pass a reference to a function as a parameter. You can also return a reference from a function. When a function returns a reference, the function call can exist in any context in which a reference can exist, including being on the receiving side of an assignment. Exercise 5.54 demonstrates this principle.

Exercise 5.54 *Returning references.*

```
#include <iostream>
using namespace std;

// ---------- a date structure
struct Date {
    int month, day, year;
};
// -------- an array of dates
Date birthdays[] = {
    {12, 17, 37},
    {10, 31, 38},
    { 6, 24, 40},
    {11, 23, 42},
    { 8,  5, 44},
};
// ----- a function to retrieve a date
const Date& getdate(int n)
{
    return birthdays[n-1];
}
int main()
{
    int dt = 99;
    while (dt != 0)    {
        cout << endl << "Enter date # (1-5, 0 to quit): ";
        cin >> dt;
        if (dt > 0 && dt < 6)    {
            const Date& bd = getdate(dt);
            cout << bd.month << '/'
                 << bd.day   << '/'
                 << bd.year  << endl;
        }
    }
    return 0;
}
```

Exercise 5.54 displays a different date depending on your response to the prompt, which must be 1–5 or 0 to quit displaying. Observe that the program declares a Date reference named *bd* and initializes the reference with the reference returned by the *getdate* function.

const *Return References*

Observe that Exercise 5.54 declares the *getdate* function as returning a *const* reference. This usage prevents the caller from using the returned reference to modify the callee's returned variable. The *bd* reference must, therefore, also be *const*. If you remove the *const* qualifier from the *bd* declaration, some compilers (Quincy's GNU compiler, for example) issue a warning message. Others issue an error message and refuse to compile the program.

Returning a Reference to an Automatic Variable

You must not return a reference to an automatic variable. The code in the following example is incorrect:

```
Date& getdate(void)
{
    Date dt = {6, 24, 40};
    return dt;    // bad-reference to auto variable
}
```

The problem is that the *dt* variable goes out of scope when the function returns. You would, therefore, be returning a reference to a variable that no longer exists, and the calling program would be referring to a *Date* object that does not exist. Many C++ compilers (Quincy's GNU compiler, for example) issue a warning when they see code that returns references to automatic variables. If you ignore the warning you will get unpredictable results. Sometimes the program appears to work, because the stack location where the automatic variable existed is intact when the reference is used. A program that appears to work in some cases can fail in others because of device or multitasking interrupts that use the stack.

Pointers vs. References

When should you use a pointer and when should you use a reference? Here some guidelines.

If the referenced variable *might not* exist, use a pointer. You can use a null address in a pointer parameter to indicate that the variable does not exist. There is no such thing as a null reference. If the variable *must* exist, use a reference.

If the program must iterate through an array of referenced objects, consider using a pointer. Pointer arithmetic is often more efficient than using subscript notation on a reference. The program needs to dereference two variables—the reference and the subscript—for the latter, but only one—the pointer—for the former.

Anything you can do with a reference, you can do with a pointer. The reference variable is an improvement over the pointer in one respect. You cannot modify the reference variable or derive a new object address by applying pointer arithmetic, and that eliminates much of the trouble that C programmers get into with pointers. Assuming that a reference is properly initialized to refer to an object of the referenced type, you cannot coerce the reference to refer elsewhere, perhaps where it should not refer. There are no guarantees, of course. Nothing in the language or in any C++ compiler prevents you from using this idiom or an equally troublesome variation:

```
Object* pObject = 0;          // null pointer
// ... later
Object& rObject = *pObject;   // refers to invalid object
```

Also, if the reference refers to an array, you can unintentionally use an invalid subscript and exceed the bounds of the array just as you can with the actual array.

The only other advantage of the reference over the pointer is that the program can avoid using pointer dereferencing notation to refer to the referenced object. This advantage is one of perception and preference. Not all programmers agree on this issue.

SUMMARY

With the exercises and lessons in this chapter, you learned about the scope of identifiers, storage classes, type qualifiers, structures, unions, enumerated data types, arrays, pointers, addresses, the *sizeof* operator, casts, *typedefs*, command-line arguments, the heap, the stack, recursion, and reference variables.

CHAPTER 6

Library Functions

Standard C includes a full library of portable, general-purpose functions. Inasmuch as Standard C is included in Standard C++, the complete Standard C library is a part of Standard C++. You used a few of the Standard C functions in the exercises in earlier chapters. This book does not attempt to teach the complete Standard C library. Instead we discuss selected ones that are the most useful to C++ programmers and that best teach the language and its software development environment. Some Standard C functions support features that Standard C++ supports in improved ways. Others are not supported by Standard C++ except through its inclusion of the Standard C library.

This chapter is organized alphabetically by the header files where library functions are declared. To use a function from the standard library, you must include its header file in your program ahead of any references to the function. Some of the standard header files define global values, macros, functions, and data structures that support the library and your use of it.

A *macro* looks like a function; in some cases, a macro assigns an identifier to a value. You learn how to build your own macros by using the *#define* preprocessor directive discussed in Chapter 7.

This chapter describes many of the functions and macros without including detailed examples. You have already used some of them, and many of them are similar enough that you do not need anything more than a description. However, where examples provide better explanations, this chapter includes exercises. You will learn about the functions in the following header files:

- **<cassert>**
- **<cctype>**
- **<cerrno>**
- **<cmath>**
- **<csetjmp>**
- **<cstdarg>**
- **<cstdio>**
- **<cstdlib>**
- **<cstring>**
- **<ctime>**

<cassert>

The **<cassert>** header is used for debugging. It defines the *assert* macro, which lets the compiler help you debug the program with defensive code.

There are certain program conditions that you assume to be just so. You intend for them to be so and expect the code to run as if they are so. If the conditions are not as you assume them to be, a program bug results. You could put tests throughout your program for these conditions, but, because you fully intend for them to be a certain way, you do not want the distributed program to bear the burden of code that serves only to ensure that the program works the way you intended.

By using the *assert* macro, you can have your validation code during testing and remove it for the production program without much fuss. The *assert* macro asserts that a condition is true. If it is not, the macro displays the condition, indicates where in the program the test failed, and aborts the program. The macro is effectively disabled when you compile with the *NDEBUG* macro.

When the program is completely checked out and none of the assertions fail, you disable the *assert* macro by defining the *NDEBUG* macro and doing a final compile. The *NDEBUG* macro changes all *assert* macro calls to null expressions. Exercise 6.1 demonstrates the use of the *assert* macro.

Exercise 6.1 The assert *macro.*

```
#include <iostream>
#include <cassert>
using namespace std;

void DisplayMsg(char* msg);

int main()
{
    char* cp = 0;
    DisplayMsg(cp);
    return 0;
}


void DisplayMsg(char *msg)
{
    assert(msg != 0);
    cout << msg;

}
```

Exercise 6.1 has a bug, which the *assert* macro catches. The *main* function calls the *DisplayMsg* function with a null (zero-value) pointer argument. When you run this program, the *assert* macro displays the following message and aborts the program:

```
assertion "msg != 0" failed: file: "EX06001.cpp", line: 16
```

The message tells you that the *assert* call on line 16 of the translation unit **EX06001.cpp** failed. It even displays the condition that was false and that caused the abort.

When you use the *assert* macro, you are asserting that a condition must be true. It is a good practice to use *assert* in places where your program makes assumptions about values and other conditions.

You can correct the program by passing a valid pointer to *DisplayMsg*. Then you can insert this line of code ahead of the code that includes **<cassert>**:

```
#define NDEBUG
```

It is better to use this technique than to take out all the *assert* calls. Leave them in. They'll be there to help you debug the program when you make modifications to it later.

<cctype>

The functions in **<cctype>** convert *char* variables and test them for defined ranges. You used the *toupper* function in Exercise 5.39 in Chapter 5.

Some C++ implementations implement the **<cctype>** functions as macros. Table 6.1 summarizes the **<cctype>** functions.

Table 6.1 <cctype> Functions and Macros.

<CCTYPE> FUNCTION/MACRO	RETURNS:
int isdigit(int c);	true if c is a digit (0–9)
int isupper(int c);	true if c is an uppercase letter (A–Z)
int islower(int c);	true if c is a lowercase letter (a–z)
int isalpha(int c);	true if c is an alphabetic character (A–Z,a–z)
int isalnum(int c);	true if isalpha(c) or isdigit(c)
int isprint(int c);	true if c is a displayable ASCII character
int isspace(int c);	true if c is a white space character
int toupper(int c);	the uppercase equivalent of c
int tolower(int c);	the lowercase equivalent of c

Do not use expressions that could have side effects when you call macros in **<cctype>**. Depending on how the macro is implemented, the side effects could produce incorrect results. This statement, for example, has potential side effects:

```
a = toupper(c++);
```

A side effect is an action that changes the value of a variable in an argument or an argument that uses a function call in its expression. The auto-increment operator changes the variable argument. The expansion of the macro could cause the argument expression to be evaluated more than once. The variable would be incremented more than once, and that is a hidden side effect of the macro.

You will learn about macro side effects in Chapter 7.

<cerrno>

The **<cerrno>** header defines a global modifiable *lvalue* named *errno* and global symbols named *EDOM* and *ERANGE*.

Some library functions set a value into *errno* to indicate that an error occurred in a function call. The ANSI C Standard defines only the two error values *EDOM* (which means that an error occurred in an argument to a math function) and *ERANGE* (which means that a floating-point number is too big).

The value of *errno* is zero when the program starts. If a library function sets it to some value, it retains that value until something changes it. Therefore, if you are going to use *errno* after a function call, set it to zero before the function call. Exercise 6.2 demonstrates the use of *errno*.

Exercise 6.2 Using errno.

```
#include <iostream>
#include <cmath>
#include <cerrno>
using namespace std;

int main()
{
    double f;
    do    {
        errno = 0;
        cout << "Enter positive float (0 to quit) ";
        cin >> f;
        if (f != 0)     {
            double sq = sqrt(f);
            if (errno == 0)
                cout << "Square root of " << f
                    << " is " << sq << endl;
            else
                cout << "Invalid entry" << endl;
        }
    } while (f != 0);
}
```

Exercise 6.2 uses the *sqrt* function from **<cmath>**, discussed next, to compute the square root of a number entered by the user. If, for example, you enter a negative number or a number that's too big to be held in a *double*, the function sets *errno* to a nonzero value. The program displays the square root only if there is no error indicated by *errno*.

<cmath>

The **<cmath>** header declares the standard math functions. You just used one of them, *sqrt*, in Exercise 6.2. Table 6.2 summarizes the math functions.

Table 6.2 <cmath> Functions

<CMATH> FUNCTION	RETURNS
double acos(double x);	arc cosine of x
double asin(double x);	arc sine of x
double atan(double x);	arc tangent of x
double atan2(double y,double x);	arc tangent of y/x
double ceil(double x);	smallest integer not < x
double cos(double x);	cosine of x
double cosh(double x);	hyperbolic cosine of x
double exp(double x);	exponential value of x
double fabs(double x);	absolute value of x
double floor(double x);	largest integer not > x
double log(double x);	natural logarithm of x
double log10(double x);	base-10 logarithm of x
double pow(double x,double y);	x raised to the power y
double sin(double x);	sin of x
double sinh(double x);	hyberbolic sine of x
double sqrt(double x);	square root of x
double tan(double x);	tangent of x
double tanh(double x);	hyperbolic tangent of x

<csetjmp>

The **<csetjmp>** header defines two functions—*setjmp* and *longjmp*—and a data type, the *jmp_buf* structure.

The functions in **<csetjmp>** are used to jump from somewhere in the depths of the called functions to a defined place higher in the program. Why would you want to do that? One example is a program that validates records in an input stream. The program might detect an error in a function that is deep inside the function calling stack. This is particularly true if the program uses recursive descent parsing logic. The program needs to reject the data in question and return to the top of the program to read the next record.

One approach is to set an error variable and return. Every function tests the error variable upon return from every lower function call and returns to its caller rather than proceeding with the current input record. This approach is error-prone and uses additional code to manage and test the error variable.

Standard C provides *setjmp* and *longjmp* to serve this purpose. The *setjmp* function records the program's operating state in a *jmp_buf* structure. A *longjmp* call from a lower function can reference the *jmp_buf* structure and cause an immediate jump to the place where the matching *setjmp* occurred.

Remember the calculator program in Exercise 5.48. When it found an input error, it aborted the program. Exercise 6.3 modifies that program to use *setjmp* and *longjmp* to keep the program running after an error is found.

The listings shown here include the modified *main* and *error* functions, the *#include <csetjmp>* statement, and the definition of the *jmp_buf* variable. The rest of the program is the same as Exercise 5.48.

Exercise 6.3 setjmp *and* longjmp.

```cpp
#include <csetjmp>

// --- error jmp_buf buffer
static jmp_buf errjb;

int main()
{
    int ans;
    do    {
        // --- mark the top of the parsing descent
        if (setjmp(errjb) == 0) {
            pos = 0;    // initialize string subscript
            // ---- read an expression
            cout << "Enter expression (0 to quit):" << endl;
            cin >> expr;
            // --- evaluate the expression
            ans = addsubt();
            if (expr[pos] != '\0')
                error();
            if (ans != 0)
                cout << ans << endl;
        }
```

Exercise 6.3 setjmp *and* longjmp. *(continued)*

```
        else    {
            // --- an error occurred
            cout << "Try again" << endl;
            ans = 1;
        }
    } while (ans != 0);
    return 0;
}
// ---- syntax error
void error()
{
    cout << '\r';
    while (pos--)          // position error pointer
        cout << ' ';
    cout << "^ syntax error" << endl << '\a';
    longjmp(errjb, 1);  // return to top of program
}
```

The *setjmp* function marks the program's position and context and stores that information in its *jmp_buf* argument. Then *setjmp* returns zero. The *longjmp* function restores the program's context from its *jmp_buf* argument and jumps to the associated *setjmp* expression, causing the *setjmp* call to return the value of the *longjmp* call's second argument. If Exercise 6.3 senses an error in the user's expression entry, it jumps to the *main* function at the point of the *setjmp* call, returning the value 1. The *error* function invocation that reports the error could be several levels down in the recursive descent parsing algorithm, but the *longjmp* call restores the program's function depth context to the top of the program.

The *setjmp* and *longjmp* functions are C idioms. They work well in the calculator program, because the program declares no C++ class objects that require destruction between the top of the program and the detection of any error. Standard C++ offers a much improved mechanism, C++ exception handling, which you learn about in Chapter 14.

<cstdarg>

Recall from Chapter 3 that functions with variable parameter lists are declared with ellipses such as this:

```
void DoList(int, ...);
```

Several of the functions declared in **<cstdio>**, discussed next, use ellipses. It is the mechanism by which calls to the Standard C *printf* function, for example, can pass any kind and number of arguments after a formatting string. The ellipses tell the compiler not to check parameter types in calls to the function. In this example, the compiler ensures that the first argument is an *int*; it ignores the rest of the arguments.

You write a function that has variable arguments by including **<cstdarg>** and using a *typedef* and the three macros defined there. The *typedef* defines the *va_list* type. The macros are *va_start*, *va_arg*, and *va_end*. Exercise 6.4 shows how these macros are used.

Exercise 6.4 Variable argument lists.

```
#include <iostream>
#include <cstdarg>
using namespace std;

void Presidents(int n, ...)
{
    va_list ap;
    va_start(ap, n);
    while (n--)     {
        char* nm = va_arg(ap, char*);    // char* argument
        int year = va_arg(ap, int);      // int argument
        cout << year << ' ' << nm << endl;
    }
    va_end(ap);
}
```

Exercise 6.4 *Variable argument lists. (continued)*

```
int main()
{
    Presidents(5, "Carter", 1976, "Reagan",  1980,
                   "Bush",   1988, "Clinton", 1992,
                    "??",    2000);
    return 0;
}
```

A function with variable arguments usually needs at least one fixed argument that it can use to determine the number and types of the other arguments. Exercise 6.4 takes an integer first argument as a count of the pairs of arguments that follow. Then it assumes that the list has that many argument pairs of one character pointer and one integer.

va_list

The macros use the *va_list* variable as a point of reference.

va_start

Scanning the variable argument list starts with the *va_start* macro call, which takes the names of the *va_list* variable and of the function's fixed argument as macro arguments. The *va_start* macro establishes the starting point for the variable argument scan and stores that information in the *va_list* variable. If the function had more than one fixed argument, the *va_start* macro would use the identifier of the last one immediately before the ellipse.

va_arg

The function uses the *va_arg* macro to extract arguments from the variable argument list. The *va_arg* macro's arguments are the *va_list* variable and the type of the next expected argument. Observe that the two *va_arg* macro calls have *int* and *char** as their second argument. The function knows what types of arguments to expect. It knows the number of arguments based on the value stored in the fixed argument.

va_end

The *va_end* macro takes the *va_list* variable as an argument. In many C++ language implementations, this macro does nothing. You should always include it, though, so that your programs are portable to other compilers and other computers.

Because the compiler does no type checking of arguments represented by the ellipse in function declarations, you can pass anything at all to a variable argument function. Naturally, if you pass something other than what the function expects, the results are unpredictable.

<cstdio>

The **<cstdio>** header declares functions and global symbols that support standard input and output. C programs use standard devices for all input and output. Unless you redirect them, the standard input device is the keyboard, and the standard output device is the screen. There are also standard error and auxiliary devices. The functions in **<cstdio>** support C programming idioms for console and file input/output. We will not dwell on those functions here because C++ employs improved techniques implemented in the **<iostream>** class library, which Chapter 16 discusses.

Global Symbols

<cstdio> declares several global symbols with *typedef* statements and *#define* (Chapter 7) macros. Most of these symbols have to do with Standard C functions for working with disk files. Curiously, **<cstdio>** also defines *NULL*, a global symbol that represents a null pointer. *NULL* has nothing to do with standard input/output except that some of the functions return a null pointer. **<cstdio>** defines it by tradition. C++ programmers by tradition do not use the *NULL* global symbol, preferring to address zero pointer values with the constant integer value, 0.

<cstdlib>

<cstdlib> declares a number of standard library functions and macros in four categories: numerical functions, memory allocation functions, system functions, and random number generation.

Numerical Functions

Table 6.3 lists the **<cstdlib>** numerical functions and describes what each one returns.

Table 6.3 <cstdlib> Numerical Functions.

NUMERICAL FUNCTION	RETURNS
int abs(int i);	the absolute value of i
int atoi(const char *s);	the integer value of the string
long atol(const char *s);	the long integer value of the string
float atof(const char *s);	the float value of the string

Memory Allocation Functions

C and C++ programs have a store of memory available for dynamic allocations. That store is called the *heap*. A program can allocate memory from the heap and return the memory to the heap when the program is finished using it. Dynamic memory allocation allows a program to use memory buffers only when they are needed. In that way, a program can operate in a system with an amount of available memory smaller than the program's total requirement. Table 6.4 lists the Standard C memory allocation functions.

Table 6.4 <cstdlib> Memory Allocation Functions.

MEMORY ALLOCATION FUNCTION	RETURNS
void *calloc(int sz, int n);	address of buffer or 0
void *malloc(int sz);	address of buffer or 0
void free(void *buf);	nothing

You used *malloc* and *free* in Exercise 5.40. The *calloc* function is similar to *malloc* with these exceptions: First, instead of specifying a character count for the memory allocation, you specify an item size and the number of items. Second, *calloc* initializes the allocated memory to zeros, whereas *malloc* does not.

If there is not enough memory available for either *malloc* or *calloc*, they return a zero-value null pointer. Programs should always check for a zero return and do something appropriate when that happens. Ignoring a zero return could crash the system when the program tries to assign values through a zero-value pointer.

C++ employs a much-improved memory allocation mechanism implemented with the *new* and *delete* operators, which Chapter 5 explains.

System Functions

<cstdlib> declares functions related to the operation of the program as shown in Table 6.5.

Table 6.5 <cstdlib> system functions.

```
void abort(void);

void exit(int n);

int system(const char *cmd);
```

The *abort* and *exit* functions terminate the program. The *abort* function is used for an abnormal termination. Standard C does not define a value for *abort* to return except to specify that it returns an implementation-dependent *unsuccessful termination* value. The *exit* function is for normal termination. It closes all open stream files and returns to the operating system whatever value you pass as an argument.

The *system* function calls the operating system to execute an operating system command. In MS-DOS, the commands executed are the same as commands you would type on the DOS command line. The following code shows the *system* function executing the DOS *dir* command to view a list of document files:

```
#include <cstdlib>

int main()
{
    system("dir *.doc");
    return 0;
}
```

Random Number Generation Functions

Exercises 4.8, 4.9, 4.11, and 4.12 used the *rand* and *srand* functions (shown in Table 6.6) to compute random numbers.

Table 6.6 <cstdlib> Random Number Functions

....

int rand(void);

void srand(unsigned int seed);

Recall that Exercise 4.8 is a guessing game. The program computes a random number and you guess what it is. The problem with that program is that the random number generator is predictable. It always starts with the same number and progresses through an identical sequence of numbers, and that process isn't random at all. Exercise 6.5 adds one line of code to the program to make the first random number less predictable. It calls *srand* to seed the generator with a value based on the current date and time. The *time* function, described later in this chapter, returns an integer value based on the system clock. That value is the seed in Exercise 6.5.

Exercise 6.5   *Seeding the random number generator.*

```
##include <iostream>
#include <cstdlib>
#include <ctime>
using namespace std;

int main()
{
    srand(time(0));
    char ans;
    // --- loop until user is done
    do    {
        // --- choose a secret number
        int fav = rand() % 32;
        // --- loop until user guesses secret number
        int num;
        do    {
            cout << "Guess my secret number (0 - 32) ";
            cin >> num;
```

Exercise 6.5 *Seeding the random number generator. (continued)*

```
        // --- report the status of the guess
        cout << (num < fav ? "Too low"  :
                 num > fav ? "Too high" :
                             "Right") << endl;
      } while (num != fav);
      cout << "Go again? (y/n) ";
      cin >> ans;
    } while (ans == 'y');
    return 0;
}
```

<cstring>

The **<cstring>** header declares functions that work with null-terminated character arrays. There are two comparison functions, two copy functions, two concatenation functions, one function to return the length of a string, and one function to fill an area of memory with a specified character value. Table 6.7 lists the **<cstring>** functions.

Table 6.7 <cstring> Functions

int strcmp(const char *s1, const char *s2);

int strncmp(const char *s1, const char *s2, int n);

char *strcpy(char *s1, const char *s2);

char *strncpy(char *s1, const char *s2, int n);

int strlen(const char *s);

char *strcat(char *s1, const char *s2);

char *strncat(char *s1, const char *s2, int n);

char *memset(void *s, int c, int n)

Exercise 6.6 demonstrates the *strcmp*, *strcpy*, and *strlen* functions.

Exercise 6.6 strcmp, strcpy, *and* strlen.

```
#include <iostream>
#include <cstring>
using namespace std;

int main()
{
    int len;
    char msg[] = "Wrong.";

    cout << "Password? ";
    char pwd[40];
    cin >> pwd;
    // --- find string length
    len = strlen(pwd);
    // --- compare string with string constant
    if (strcmp(pwd, "boobah") == 0)
        // --- copy constant to message
        strcpy(msg, "OK.");
    cout << msg << " You typed " << len << " characters";
    return 0;
}
```

You run the program in Exercise 6.6 and enter a password in response to the prompt. Do not enter more than 39 characters, or you will overwrite the 40-character *pwd* array.

strlen

The program passes the address of the password to *strlen* to get the length of the input string, which counts all the characters except the null terminator.

strcmp

The *strcmp* function compares two strings. It returns zero if the two strings are equal, less than zero if the first string is less than the second string, and greater than zero if the first string is greater than the second string. Comparisons proceed from the first character in both strings and iterate forward until null terminators are found or different character values are found in the strings. If one string is shorter than the other and if all the character values are equal up to the end of the shorter string, the longer string compares greater than the shorter one.

strcpy

If the password you typed is equal to the constant password, the program calls *strcpy* to copy the string constant "OK." to the *msg* string. This operation overwrites the *msg* string's initialized value of "Wrong.". The *msg* array has six elements based on the default dimension declared by its initializer. The *strcpy* function copies only four characters: 'O', 'K', '.', and a null terminator. The resulting *msg* array looks like this in memory:

```
'O', 'K', '.', '\0', 'g', '.', '\0'
```

If the second string argument to *strcpy* is longer than five characters plus a null terminator, the results are unpredictable. Usually, the program fails immediately or soon afterward, because it has overwritten whatever coincidentally follows the receiving array in memory.

strcat

The *strcat* function appends the string value of its second argument to the string in its first argument. There must be enough space past the significant characters (up to the null terminator) of the first argument for the second argument and its null terminator. For example:

```
char s[13] = "Hello";  // must be at least 13 chars
strcat(s, ", Dolly");  // s1 = "Hello, Dolly"
```

strncmp, strncpy, and strncat

These three functions are similar to the preceding three functions except that each has a third integer parameter that specifies the maximum number of characters to compare, copy, or concatenate. If the second argument to *strncpy* has fewer characters to copy than the integer argument specifies, the function pads the remaining characters in the first argument with zeros.

memset

The *memset* function is not just a string function. It fills a block of memory with a specified character. Its first argument is a *void* pointer to the block of memory. By using a *void* pointer in its declaration, the function allows you to use it to initialize any buffer. The second argument specifies the fill character value. The third argument specifies the length of the memory area to be filled. The *memset* function is used most often to zero-fill uninitialized memory for data aggregates such as structures and arrays.

<ctime>

<ctime> declares several functions, a structure, and a data type related to time and date. The structure is shown here:

```
struct tm
{
  int    tm_sec;    // seconds (0-61)
  int    tm_min;    // minutes (0-59)
  int    tm_hour;   // hours   (0-23)
  int    tm_mday;   // day of the month (1-31)
  int    tm_mon;    // months since January (0-11)
  int    tm_year;   // years since 1900
  int    tm_wday;   // days since Sunday (0-6)
  int    tm_yday;   // days since January 1 (0-365)
  int    tm_isdst;  // Daylight Saving Time flag
};
```

The data type is *typedef long time_t*. It is an integer value that represents the date and time as the number of clock ticks since a defined time in the past. Applications programs do not deal with the actual integral representation of the time. Instead, they accept and pass *time_t* values between functions declared in **<ctime>**.

Table 6.8 lists the time and date functions.

Table 6.8 <ctime> Functions

```
char *asctime(const struct tm *tim);
char *ctime(const time_t *t);
double difftime(time_t t1, time_t t2);
struct tm *gmtime(const time_t *t);
struct tm *localtime(const time_t *t);
time_t mktime(struct tm *tim);
time_t time(time_t *t);
```

asctime

This function converts the *struct tm* structure pointed to by its argument into a null-terminated string suitable for displaying. The string is in this format:

```
"Mon Apr 25 14:41:22 1994\n"
```

ctime

This function converts the *time_t* variable pointed to by its argument into a string in the same format as the string produced by *asctime*.

difftime

This function returns a *double* value representing the difference in seconds between its two *time_t* arguments by subtracting the second argument from the first.

gmtime

This function converts the *time_t* variable pointed to by its argument into a *struct tm* variable representing Coordinated Universal Time, also called Greenwich mean time. The *gmtime* function returns a pointer to the structure that it builds.

localtime

This function converts the *time_t* variable pointed to by its argument into a *struct tm* variable representing local time. It returns a pointer to the structure that it builds.

mktime

This function converts the *struct tm* variable pointed to by its argument into a *time_t* variable, which *mktime* returns.

time

This function returns the current time as a *time_t* variable. If its argument is not NULL, the function also copies the *time_t* variable into the variable pointed to by the argument.

Exercise 6.7 uses some of the functions here to display the current Greenwich mean time.

Exercise 6.7 <ctime> *functions.*

```
#include <iostream>
#include <ctime>
using namespace std;

int main()
{
    time_t now = time(0);
    cout << asctime(gmtime(&now));
    return 0;
}
```

Summary

This chapter discussed some of the Standard C library functions. When you begin using other compiler systems, you will find that they offer not only the Standard C library but also many other compiler-dependent libraries. You can also use third-party libraries that support various functional applications and operating environments. There are libraries for graphics, user interfaces, database management, communications, mathematics, direct access to DOS functions, and many more.

The Preprocessor

The term *preprocessor* designates a process that reads source code, performs some preliminary translation of that code, and writes new source code to be read by the compiler. The preprocessor processes source code before the compiler does.

The C and C++ languages have no built-in facilities for including other source files during the compile, for defining macros, or for compile-time directives that include some lines of code and exclude others based on conditions. Those capabilities are provided by the preprocessor. Although it is integrated with most contemporary compilers, the preprocessor is regarded as a process independent of the compiler. The preprocessor reads source code, looks for preprocessing directive statements and macro invocations, and translates the source code accordingly. It also eliminates program comments and excess white space. This chapter describes how to use preprocessing directives in a program. You will learn about:

- Including files
- Writing macros
- Compile-time conditional directives

PREPROCESSING DIRECTIVES

Preprocessing directives are lines of code that begin with a pound sign (#). The pound sign must be the first character on a line of code after any optional white space. The directive keyword follows, with optional white space between it and the pound sign. The entire line is devoted to the directive, which affects the translation of the source code to be passed to the compiler. Table 7.1 lists the preprocessing directives.

Table 7.1 Preprocessing Directives

DIRECTIVE	MEANING
#	Null directive, no action
#include	Include a source code file
#define	Define a macro
#undef	Remove the definition of a macro
#if	Compile code if condition is true
#ifdef	Compile code if macro is defined
#ifndef	Compile code if macro is not defined
#else	Compile code if previous #if... condition is not true
#elif	Compile code if previous #if... condition is not true and current condition is true
#endif	Terminate #if...#else conditional block
#error	Stop compiling and display error message

Preprocessing directives are effective beginning with their position in the translation unit and continuing until another directive changes their meaning.

INCLUDING FILES

A translation unit is an independently compiled program module consisting of the C++ source-code file and any other source-code files that the program includes.

By convention, C++ source-code files have a **.cpp** file name extension and include header source-code files, which, for standard libraries, have no file extension and which, for header files related to your program, have a file name extension of **.h**. All the function definitions are in the C source-code file. Header files contain declarations that are shared among translation units. Header files typically declare external variables, structure and union formats, macros, and function prototypes. Header files do not contain any function or variable definitions. In other words, header files, which can be included in multiple translation units that are linked into a single program, do not define anything that reserves memory.

#include

The #include preprocessing directive includes the named file in the translation unit, replacing the directive. You can have multiple levels of includes; an included file can include other files. Standard C++ requires that a conforming compiler supports nesting of at least eight levels of included header files.

The preprocessor does not detect and suppress inclusion of a file that has already been included in a translation unit. This arrangement allows compile-time conditionals to modify subsequent inclusions of header files:

```
#define MODHEADER
#include "table.c"
#undef MODHEADER
#include "table.c"
```

To avoid the problems associated with multiple inclusions of a header file that should be included only once, you can use these compile-time conditional controls in a header file:

```
// --- myhdr.h
#ifndef MYHDR_H
#define MYHDR_H

// the header file information ...

#endif
```

There are two ways to include header files in a program:

```
#include <iostream>
#include "menus.h"
```

The first usage surrounds the file name with "less-than" and "greater-than" symbols. This notation tells the preprocessor to search for the header file among the header files that came with the compiler or with an external library. The second usage surrounds the file name with double quotes. This notation tells the preprocessor to search for the header file among the source code of the application being compiled; if the preprocessor does not find the header file there, the preprocessor is to search the compiler's header files.

The theory is that a compiler, which is installed in a public subdirectory, compiles applications that are installed in their own private subdirectories. An application includes the compiler's public header files and the application's own private header files. The two notations allow the compiler to discern the one common set of header files from the many other sets.

MACROS

A macro defines a meaning for an identifier. The preprocessor replaces macro invocations in the source code with values derived from the macro definition. The most common usage for macros defines a global symbol that represents a value. A second usage defines macros with parameters that, when invoked, resemble function calls but that generate in-line substitution of the invoking statement's arguments with the macro definition's parameters.

#define

The *#define* preprocessing directive defines a macro. In its simplest format, the directive declares an identifier and adds code that replaces the identifier wherever it appears in subsequent source code. Such macros isolate global value definitions, assigning mnemonic identifiers, as this example illustrates:

```
#define MAXNBRS 10
int narray[MAXNBRS];
for (int i = 0; i < MAXNBRS; i++)
    // ...
```

In this example, the MAXNBRS symbol has meaning to the programmer who reads the code. It is a mnemonic value associated with the maximum number of entries in that particular array. You might use the value many places in the

Chapter 7: The Preprocessor

program. By convention, some programmers use all uppercase letters to identify these macros. It tells them that they are looking at a macro invocation rather than a variable identifier when they see the identifier used in code.

If you decide later that the array needs to be a different size, you can change the macro and recompile the program. If the macro is used in more than one translation unit, you code the macro into a header file and include the header in all the source-code files that use the macro. Then, to change the value, you change the macro in the header file, recompile all the translation units, and relink the executable program. The idea is to isolate potential global changes in one source-code location and to assign meaningful mnemonic symbols to what might otherwise be meaningless numerical values.

The substituted value can be a constant expression, and it can include identifiers that are declared in previous macros, as shown in this example:

```
#define SCREENHEIGHT 25
#define SCREENWIDTH 80
#define SCREENBUFFER (SCREENHEIGHT*SCREENWIDTH)
```

Observe the parentheses around the macro definition's expression. They are not necessary, but their use is prudent. Consider this example:

```
#define HEIGHT bottom-top+1
area=width*HEIGHT;
```

The preprocessor would emit this code for the statement:

```
area=width*bottom-top+1;
```

Because of the rules of precedence, the result would probably be wrong. Here is how you should define the macro and how it would be expanded:

```
#define HEIGHT (bottom-top+1)
area=width*HEIGHT;           // as coded
area=width*(bottom-top+1);  // as expanded
```

You can define a macro that expands to a string constant, as shown here:

```
#define VERSION "Version 4.1\nCopyright (c) 1994"
cout << VERSION;
```

#define with Arguments

Macros with parameters resemble functions that are expanded in-line, but they do not work exactly like function calls. Consider this example:

```
#define Cube(x) ((x)*(x)*(x))
```

The *x* parameter can be replaced by any numerical expression, including one with a function call. Observe again the parentheses. The complete expansion is enclosed in parentheses to preserve the integrity of its argument in the context of an enclosing expression. So are the macro parameters, for the same reason. Here is a typical, safe use of the *Cube* macro:

```
int height = 123;
int volume = Cube(height);
```

Here are some unsafe uses of *Cube*:

```
int volume = Cube(height++);
int randomvolume = Cube(rand());
```

If *Cube* were a function, these statements would be correct. However, because *Cube* is a macro, these usages have side effects. Their arguments are more than simple expressions; they do other things. The first usage auto-increments the argument and would be expanded this way:

```
int volume = ((height++)*(height++)*(height++));
```

If *height* starts with a value of 123, the effective expression would be this:

```
int volume = 123*124*125;
```

The second unsafe usage involves a function call. The preprocessor would expand it to this code:

```
int randomvolume = ((rand())*(rand())*(rand()))
```

At best, this code is less efficient than it needs to be because it calls the *rand* function three times. This example is a worst case, however, because the code produces the wrong result. The *rand* function returns a different value for each call, and the result is not the volume of anything meaningful.

How would you use the *Cube* macro safely to produce the correct results? You must remove the side effects by moving their actions outside the macro calls:

```
int volume = Cube(height);
height++;
int randomheight = rand();
int randomvolume = Cube(randomheight);
```

A macro's parameters can include expressions and references to previously defined macros, making for some exotic macro definitions. Consider Exercise 7.1, which follows.

Exercise 7.1 #define *macros.*

```
#include <iostream>
#include <iomanip>
using namespace std;


#define OVERTIME        1.5
#define TAXRATE         0.15
#define WKWEEK          40
#define REG(h)          ((h) < WKWEEK ? (h) : WKWEEK)
#define OTIME(h)        ((h) < WKWEEK ? 0 : h - WKWEEK)
#define OTIMEPAY(h,r)   ((r) * OTIME(h) * OVERTIME)
#define REGPAY(h,r)     ((r) * REG(h))
#define GROSSPAY(h,r)   (OTIMEPAY(h,r) + REGPAY(h,r))
#define WHOLDING(h,r)   (GROSSPAY(h,r) * TAXRATE)
#define NETPAY(h,r)     (GROSSPAY(h,r) - WHOLDING(h,r))


void setformat();
```

Exercise 7.1 #define *macros. (continued)*

```
int main()
{
    cout << "Enter hours (xx) rate (x.xx): ";
    int hours;
    float rate;
    cin >> hours >> rate;
    cout << "Regular:    ";
    setformat();
    cout << REGPAY(hours, rate)   << endl;
    cout << "Overtime:   ";
    setformat();
    cout << OTIMEPAY(hours, rate) << endl;
    cout << "Gross:      ";
    setformat();
    cout << GROSSPAY(hours, rate) << endl;
    cout << "Witholding: ";
    setformat();
    cout << WHOLDING(hours, rate) << endl;
    cout << "Net Pay:    ";
    setformat();
    cout << NETPAY(hours, rate)   << endl;
    return 0;
}


void setformat()
{
    cout << setw(10)
        << setiosflags(ios::fixed)
        << setiosflags(ios::right)
        << setprecision(2);
}
```

The macros in Exercise 7.1 cooperate to compute values for a payroll. Read the macros carefully as you follow this explanation. The first three macros define constant global values, assigning identifiers to the values for the overtime rate (*OVERTIME*), tax withholding rate (*TAXRATE*), and the number of regular hours in a work week (*WKWEEK*).

The *REG* macro computes the number of regular (non-overtime) hours from the total number of hours worked that week. The expression returns the actual number of hours if it is less than a work week. Otherwise, it returns the number of hours in a work week.

The *OTIME* macro computes the number of overtime hours from the total hours worked. If the number of hours worked is less than a work week, the value returned is zero; otherwise, it is the difference between the number of hours worked and a work week.

The *OTIMEPAY* macro computes the amount of overtime pay from the hours worked and the hourly wage. It multiplies the wage times the overtime hours times the overtime rate.

The *REGPAY* macro computes the amount of regular pay from the hours worked and the hourly wage. It multiplies the wage times the regular hours.

Observe that these macros call previously defined macros.

The *GROSSPAY* macro computes the sum of the overtime and regular pay from the hours worked and the hourly wage.

The *WHOLDING* macro computes the amount of taxes to withhold from the hours worked and the hourly wage. It multiplies the gross pay times the tax withholding rate.

The *NETPAY* macro computes the net pay from the hours worked and the hourly wage. It computes the difference between gross pay and withholding.

The program reads the number of hours worked and the hourly wage from standard input and displays the results on standard output. Following is a typical session:

```
Enter hours (xx) rate (x.xx): 45 18.50
Regular:        740.00
Overtime:       138.75
Gross:          878.75
Witholding:     131.81
Net Pay:        746.94
```

You can modify the algorithm by changing any of the first three constants and recompiling the program. In a real payroll program, tax rates are based on the employee's salary, number of dependents, and whatever tables the IRS has in effect for the current year.

All the macros with parameters could have been functions. What is the advantage of using macros? First, a macro expands to inline code. No function call overhead is involved when you call a macro. Macros that are used often should not expand to a lot of code, because every call to them is an individual expansion.

The macros without functions could have been coded as *const* variables (Chapter 5) with no loss of efficiency. C++'s in-line function feature (Chapter 3) provides an improved facility for writing macros.

Functions declared *inline* are similar to #*define* macros with these exceptions: An *inline* function is subject to the same C++ type checking as normal functions; *inline* functions are not subject to macro side effects. For example, consider this macro:

```
#define min(a,b) (a < b ? a : b)
```

As discussed earlier in this chapter, the *min* macro has potential side effects. Suppose you called it this way:

```
int c = min(a++,b++);
```

The macro expansion, shown next, invokes undesirable side effects in that the lesser of the *a* and *b* variables is incremented twice.

```
int c = a++ < b++ ? a++ : b++;
```

inline function calls, which the compiler treats as normal function calls, do not have such side effects.

Exercise 7.2 improves Exercise 7.1 by using preferred C++ idioms and avoiding the use of preprocessing directive macros.

Exercise 7.2 *No macros.*

```
#include <iostream>
#include <iomanip>
using namespace std;

const float overtime = 1.5;
const float taxrate = 0.15;
const int wkweek = 40;
inline int reg(int h)
{
    return h < wkweek ? h : wkweek;
}
inline int otime(int h)
{
    return h < wkweek ? 0 : h - wkweek;
}
inline float otimepay(int h,float r)
{
    return r * otime(h) * overtime;
}
inline float regpay(int h,float r)
{
    return r * reg(h);
}
inline float grosspay(int h,float r)
{
    return otimepay(h,r) + regpay(h,r);
}
inline float wholding(int h,float r)
{
    return grosspay(h,r) * taxrate;
}
inline float netpay(int h,float r)
{
    return grosspay(h,r) - wholding(h,r);
}
```

Exercise 7.2 No macros. (continued)

```
void setformat();

int main()
{
    cout << "Enter hours (xx) rate (x.xx): ";
    int hours;
    float rate;
    cin >> hours >> rate;
    cout << "Regular:    ";
    setformat();
    cout << regpay(hours, rate)   << endl;
    cout << "Overtime:   ";
    setformat();
    cout << otimepay(hours, rate) << endl;
    cout << "Gross:      ";
    setformat();
    cout << grosspay(hours, rate) << endl;
    cout << "Withholding: ";
    setformat();
    cout << wholding(hours, rate) << endl;
    cout << "Net Pay:    ";
    setformat();
    cout << netpay(hours, rate)   << endl;
    return 0;
}
void setformat()
{
    cout << setw(10)
         << setiosflags(ios::fixed)
         << setiosflags(ios::right)
         << setprecision(2);
}
```

Inline functions are not always as efficient as macros, because the compiled code includes the overhead of maintaining function parameters as variables on the stack.

Notation and Justification

Chapter 5 introduced the **<iomanip>** header file, which declares stream manipulators that you send to a stream to control how the stream displays objects. You learned that the *setw* manipulator's argument specifies the minimum display width in character positions of the next object in the stream. Exercises 7.1 and 7.2 use two additional manipulators. Before each display of one of the *float* objects, the programs call their *setformat* function. That function uses *setw* to set the width of the numerical display. The two uses of *setiosflags* tell the stream to display the *float* value in fixed rather than scientific notation and to display the value right-justified. Chapter 16 discusses manipulators in more detail.

The *#* *"Stringizing"* Operator

The # operator within a macro definition converts into a string the argument for the parameter that follows. Consider an *Error* macro that displays the error code on standard output. Without the # operator, you could write the macro as shown here:

```
#define Error(n) cout << "Error " << n
```

You can get the same effect by using the # operator, sometimes called the *stringizing* operator. Exercise 7.3 demonstrates that usage.

Exercise 7.3 *The # stringizing operator.*

```
#include <iostream>
using namespace std;


#define Error(n) cout << "Error " #n


int main()
{
    Error(53);
    return 0;
}
```

The *#n* sequence in the macro definition tells the preprocessor to convert into a string whatever is passed as an argument. The macro call has 53 as the argument, so the macro is expanded this way:

```
cout << "Error " "53");
```

The adjacent strings are concatenated (pasted together) according to the syntax for string constants, and the effective statement is this:

```
cout << "Error 53";
```

The ## Operator

The ## operator concatenates arguments. The preprocessor takes the arguments that match the parameter references on either side of the ## operator and turns them into a single token. Exercise 7.4 is an example.

Exercise 7.4 The ## token pasting operator.

```
#include <iostream>
using namespace std;


#define BookChapterVerse(b,c,v) b ## c ## v


int main()
{
    unsigned bcv = BookChapterVerse(5,12,43);
    cout << bcv;
    return 0;
}
```

The program displays the value **51243**, which is the constant long integer that results when you paste the three arguments 5, 12, and 43.

Understand that you don't get the same results by passing variables with those values to the macro. The macro is expanded by the preprocessor, which would paste the names of the variables rather than some future values that they might contain.

After the concatenation, the resulting value is scanned again by the preprocessor, so you can use the facility to build some complex—if not bizarre—macros. Exercise 7.5 is a demonstration.

Exercise 7.5 More ## pasting.

```
#include <iostream>
using namespace std;


#define AbleBaker "alpha bravo"
#define cat(a,b)    a ## b


int main()
{
    cout << cat(Able, Baker);
    return 0;
}
```

The *AbleBaker* macro defines a string value. The *cat* macro is a general-purpose, two-argument concatenation macro. The *cout* call invokes the *cat* macro with the arguments *Able* and *Baker*. Those arguments concatenate to form the single identifier *AbleBaker*, which is then expanded into the string constant "alpha bravo," which gets passed to *cout*.

Do not be concerned if you are confused by all this. Few programmers understand ## until they need it or see it used meaningfully in a way that is relevant to a problem at hand. Most programmers never need it.

#undef

The *#undef* preprocessor directive removes the definition of a macro for the ensuing source-code lines in the translation unit. You use this directive when you want the meaning of the identifier to return to its default meaning or when you want to change the meaning. You cannot have multiple definitions of a macro in effect at the same time.

COMPILE-TIME CONDITIONAL DIRECTIVES

Compile-time conditional directives control which lines of code get compiled and which ones do not. You can control code compilation based on the value of an expression or on whether a particular macro has been defined.

#if

The *#if* directive tests the constant expression that follows the directive keyword. If the expression evaluates to true, the ensuing source-code group, up to the next *#else*, *#elif*, or *#endif*, is passed to the compiler. Otherwise, it is not.

#endif

This directive is the terminator for all *#if...* preprocessing directives. Exercise 7.6 demonstrates *#if* and *#endif*.

Exercise 7.6 The #if *and* #endif *preprocessing directives.*

```
#include <iostream>
using namespace std;


#define DEBUG 1


int main()
{
#if DEBUG
    cout << "Debugging" << endl;
#endif
    cout << "Running" << endl;
    return 0;
}
```

The line of code between the *#if* and the *#endif* compiles only if the expression *DEBUG* evaluates to a true value. In this case it does, because *DEBUG* is defined as a global integer constant with a value of 1. Use the Quincy editor to change the definition to this:

```
#define DEBUG 0
```

Now when you compile and run the program, the line of code under control of the *#if, #endif* pair does not compile. The same thing happens if you remove the *#define* statement.

#if defined

You can test to see whether a macro is defined rather than test its value, as shown in Exercise 7.7.

Exercise 7.7 #if *defined preprocessing directive.*

```
#include <iostream>
using namespace std;


#define DEBUG


int main()
{
#if defined DEBUG
    cout << "Debugging" << endl;
#endif
    cout << "Running" << endl;
    return 0;
}
```

To test that a macro is not defined, use this notation:

```
#if !defined DEBUG
```

#ifdef and #ifndef

The *#ifdef* and *#ifndef* directives are variations on *#if defined* and *#if !defined,* respectively. They work the same way.

#else

You can code the *#else* directive after the statement group that is controlled by one of the *#if...* directives. The statement group that follows the *#else* compiles if the condition tested by the *#if...* is not true. One *#endif* directive terminates the two groups, as shown in Exercise 7.8.

Exercise 7.8 The #else *preprocessing directive.*

```
#include <iostream>
using namespace std;


#define DEBUG


int main()
{
#if defined DEBUG
    cout << "Debugging" << endl;
#else
    cout << "Not debugging" << endl;
#endif
    cout << "Running" << endl;
    return 0;
}
```

#elif

The *elif* preprocessing directive combines the effects of the *#else* and *#if* directives, as shown in Exercise 7.9.

Exercise 7.9 The #elif *preprocessing directive.*

```
#include <iostream>
using namespace std;


#define DEBUG


int main()
{
#if defined DEBUG
    cout << "Debugging" << endl;
```

Exercise 7.9 The #elif preprocessing directive. (continued)

```
#elif defined TESTING
    cout << "Testing" << endl;
#elif defined EXPERIMENTAL
    cout << "Experimental" << endl;
#else
    cout << "None of the above" << endl;
#endif
    cout << "Running" << endl;
    return 0;
}
```

#error

This directive causes the compiler to display an error message that includes whatever information you provide on the line past the directive keyword. It stops the compilation. It is typically used within the control of a compile-time conditional statement to alert the programmer that something is wrong in the way the compile has been set up. You can construct complex compile-time conditions with nested and mutually exclusive tests. The *#error* directive allows you to assert a compile-time error if the conditions are not logically organized. Exercise 7.10 is an example.

Exercise 7.10 The #error preprocessing directive.

```
#include <iostream>
using namespace std;


#define DEBUG   1
#define TESTING 1


#if DEBUG & TESTING
  #error DEBUG & TESTING both have values
#endif
```

Exercise 7.10 The #error *preprocessing directive. (continued)*

```
int main()
{
#if DEBUG
    cout << "Debugging" << endl;
#elif TESTING
    cout << "Testing" << endl;
#else
    cout << "Not debugging" << endl;
#endif
    cout << "Running" << endl;
    return 0;
}
```

An alternative notation can be used when you are testing for the definition of macros rather than their values, as shown here:

```
#define DEBUG
#define TESTING


#ifdef DEBUG
  #ifdef TESTING
    #error DEBUG & TESTING both defined
  #endif
#endif
```

OTHER STANDARD DIRECTIVES

Standard C++ defines two other preprocessing directives.

#line

This directive lets you change the file name and line number that the compiler uses to report subsequent warning and error messages.

#pragma

This directive has no formal definition. Compilers may use it in ways that the compiler vendor sees fit. Typical uses are to suppress and enable certain annoying warning messages. You could use the compiler's custom *#pragma* to suppress the warning messages.

SUMMARY

In this chapter, you learned how to include system and application header files, define macros, and use compile-time conditional directives.

CHAPTER 8

Structures and Classes

Before coming up with its present name, Dr. Stroustrup called C++ "C with classes." This version represented his first effort to extend the C language by using classes to implement an object-oriented programming model. Classes support *data abstraction*, wherein you extend the C++ language by designing *user-defined data types*. Classes also support the construction of full-blown object-oriented class hierarchies. This chapter introduces classes and explains data abstraction. You will learn about:

- The attributes of data types
- Intrinsic and user-defined data types
- Data members and member functions
- Access specifiers
- Structures versus classes

The C++ Class

The *class* is the C++ mechanism by which a programmer expresses the design of custom data types. Classes are similar to the structure that you learned about in Chapter 5. In fact, they are almost the same. The structure Chapter 5 describes is really the structure that C++ inherited from the C language. C++ adds substantially to the C structure and gives it a second identity with another name—class.

In its implementation of classes and structures, C++ significantly extends the support found in C of both elements. In C++, the class differs from the structure in the defaults that each assumes with respect to access specifiers, which are explained later in this chapter. Everything you learned about structures in Chapter 5 applies to classes. Everything that you learn about classes in this chapter and subsequent chapters also applies to structures and adds to what you learned about structures in Chapter 5.

We will use structures until you learn about access specifiers, whereupon we will revisit the subject of the class versus the structure. Chapter 9 shifts focus to the C++ class.

The Characteristics of Data Types

Before you can design your own custom data types, you must learn about data types in general. Consider the intrinsic numerical C++ data types that you learned about in Chapter 2. Each instrinsic data type has a *data representation* and exhibits predictable *behavior* when addressed in certain ways by the program. Each intrinsic data type has its own *implementation*—how the compiler implements the behavior—and its own *interface*—how a program invokes the behavior of an object of the data type. We'll use a well understood instrinsic data type, the signed integer, as an example.

Data Representation

A *signed int* typically contains 32 bits, although that is not a standard. The GNU C++ compiler used by Quincy supports a 32-bit *signed int,* so we use that example in this discussion. A 32-bit signed integer can contain values ranging from - 2147483648 to 2147483647. That format is the *signed int* data type's data representation.

Implementation

The internal twos-complement arithmetic of the *int* data type is the *signed int*s implementation. The C++ compiler provides that implementation, usually based on the underlying architecture of the target computer's arithmetic registers.

Behavior

When you apply the increment (++) operator (Chapter 2) to an object of type *signed int*, the object increments its value by 1. That reaction is a part of the *signed int* data type's behavior. Other behaviors are defined for other operators.

Interface

The source code program's expression that applies the auto-increment operator to a signed *int* variable is part of the *signed int* data type's interface.

USER-DEFINED DATA TYPES

The intrinsic numerical types suffice for most of a program's numerical needs, but there are times when the language needs to be extended (e.g., when your program requires user-defined data types, each with its own unique data representation, behavior, implementation and interface).

Abstraction

In object-oriented programming, *abstraction* is the name given to the process by which you design a new data type that you and other programmers can then view from a higher level of abstraction, concerning yourselves only with the interface and disregarding the details of the implementation.

A programmer must understand each data type's interface and behavior. Clearly, you need to know what happens when you add a constant value to an integer variable, for example. That understanding is the level of abstraction with which a programmer views an *int*. You might also understand the underlying data representation and implementation—often you must—but the essence of object-oriented programming is that a programmer who uses objects of any data type views that type from a higher level of abstraction and pays little attention to the details of the data type's implementation.

What Are the Objects?

When do you need to use data abstraction in your design? How can you leverage what you already know about programming to help you understand this different view of a program, this so-called object-oriented view?

What kinds of data cannot be represented by the compiler's intrinsic types? In procedural programming languages (e.g., C, Pascal, COBOL, FORTRAN, PL/1, BASIC), you commonly group data elements into record formats to gather related data items into a logical aggregate that the program can work with. An employee record in a personnel system is one example. The department record is another. These aggregates may include among their members other data items that are themselves aggregates of data types. Date hired is an example.

No matter what language you programmed in before you came to C++, you used data aggregates of one form or another. As a general rule, whenever you would have built a C structure, a BASIC TYPE, or a COBOL record definition, you will now use data abstraction to build the same thing as a user-defined data type described by a class or structure in C++. Let's examine that process in more detail.

Data Abstraction and Procedural Programming

To design a new data type with traditional procedural programming, you organized the basic types into a logical structure and wrote functions to process that structure. The functions were reusable throughout the program for other objects of the same structure, because you passed to the functions a reference to the affected object. Exercise 8.1 illustrates that principle.

Exercise 8.1 *Data abstraction and procedural programming.*

```
#include <iostream>
using namespace std;

// ------ date structure
struct Date {
    int month, day, year;
};

void display(Date& dt)
{
    static char *mon[] = {
        "January","February","March","April","May","June",
        "July","August","September","October","November",
        "December"};
    cout << mon[dt.month-1] << ' '
        << dt.day << ", " << dt.year;
}

int main()
{
    Date birthday = {4, 6, 1961};
    cout << "Alan's date of birth is ";
    display(birthday);
    return 0;
}
```

Exercise 8.1 is a good example of procedural programming, and except for the use of the *cout* object and the reference parameter, it is what you would expect to see in a C program that displays a date on the console. C is a procedural programming language.

The *Date* structure defines a data format. The format of the structure constitutes the data representation of the user-defined data type, in this case, a calendar date.

The *display* function takes a reference to an object of the *Date* structure and displays the object's values on the console, constituting the behavior of the data type.

The *Date* data type's implementation of the *display* behavior sends to the *cout* object the three integers that represent the month, day, and year.

The type's interface is the *display* function's identifier and parameter list.

Although Exercise 8.1 demonstrates data abstraction with procedural programming, it is a better example of why data abstraction with object-oriented programming is a superior programming model. The *display* function is loosely bound to the *Date* structure, because the function refers to the structure's members, dereferencing them through the address passed by the caller as an argument to the *dt* parameter. The *display* function and all calls to it must be declared in the same scope as the *Date* structure.

However, the *Date* structure's design is not perfect. The implementation and data representation are an open architecture. A program can readily instantiate an invalid *Date* object by initializing it with values that are out of the prescribed range of a calendar date. The program can also instantiate an uninitialized *Date* object with random invalid values in its data members. The program can similarly modify any of the data members of an existing *Date* object with invalid values. The design offers no protection from careless programming. Furthermore, the design permits unrelated functions that implement the *Date*'s behavior to be scattered helter-skelter throughout the program.

The program distributes its dependency on the *Date* structure's implementation throughout all modules of the program's code that address *Date* objects. The details of the structure's data representation are public, and the program depends on those details.

The *Date* structure and the *display* function described earlier are loosely bound by the *display* function's use of a *Date* object reference. Anywhere the *Date* declaration is in scope, you can write such a function and alter the behavior of all *Date* objects for which the program calls that function. The *Date* data type's interface and behavior are logically distanced from its implementation and data representation.

The consequence of such a procedural design approach is that any modification to the *Date* structure's data representation levies a potential impact on widely distributed software modules, all of which are intimate with the details of the data type's implementation:

This consequence is one of the principal reasons that complex procedural programs are often difficult to maintain.

Data Abstraction and Encapsulation

Although the *Date* structure and the *display* function described earlier are loosely bound, they are not encapsulated. *Encapsulation* is an object-oriented design approach that closely binds the implementation of a class to its data representation, logically hides the details of the implementation from users of the data type, and provides a public interface to the data type's behavior.

Encapsulation is exactly what a compiler of any high-level programming language—object oriented or otherwise—does with intrinsic data types. An object-oriented programming language permits encapsulation of user-defined data types, too.

C++ uses features of the class mechanism to support encapsulation of user-defined data types. In the next section, we will improve the procedural *Date* design by applying encapsulation.

You can circumvent these improved design methods by using clever or careless C++ programming idioms, but C++'s support of encapsulation encourages you to write better programs.

STRUCTURES WITH FUNCTIONS

A structure is an aggregate of data types forming a user-defined data type. The structure can contain *chars, integers, enums, floats, doubles, arrays, pointers, typedefs, unions,* and other structures. In other words, any valid data type can be a member of a structure. This convention is consistent with the traditional C definition of a structure. C++ adds another type of member to the structure. In C++, structures can include functions.

Take a moment to consider the implications of what you just read. By adding functions to structures, you add the ability for a structure to include algorithms that are bound to and work with the other structure members. You closely associate the algorithms with the data they process; this association is how C++ supports encapsulation.

Adding Functions to Structures

Exercise 8.2 adds a function to the *Date* structure described earlier. The function's name is *display*, and its purpose is to display the contents of an instance of the *Date* structure. This new function is a member of the structure and is called a *member function*. It eliminates the nonmember *display* function from the code fragment.

Exercise 8.2 Structures with functions.

```
#include <iostream>
using namespace std;

// ------  structure with a function
struct Date {
    int month, day, year;
    void display();          // a function to display the date
};

void Date::display()
{
    static char *mon[] = {
        "January","February","March","April","May","June",
        "July","August","September","October","November",
        "December"};
    cout << mon[month-1] << ' ' << day << ", " << year;
}

int main()
{
    Date birthday = {4, 6, 1961};
    cout << "Alan's date of birth is ";
    birthday.display();
    return 0;
}
```

Exercise 8.2 codes the display function's declaration outside the class declaration as *Date::display*. This notation tells the C++ compiler that the *display* member function exists to support instances of the *Date* structure. In fact, the only way to call this *display* function is as a member of a declared *Date*.

The *main* function declares a *Date* named *birthday* and initializes it with a value. Then the main function calls the *Date::display* function by identifying it as a member of the *birthday* structure with the following notation:

```
birthday.display();
```

The *Date::display* function can reference members of the structure with which it is associated directly without naming an instance of the structure, because the function itself is a member of the structure.

Multiple Instances of the Same Structure

You can declare more than one instance of the same structure, and the member function associates itself with the data in the particular structure object for which you call the function. Exercise 8.3 adds two objects to the preceding exercise to demonstrate this behavior.

Exercise 8.3 Multiple instances of a structure.

```
#include <iostream>
using namespace std;

// ------ structure with a function
struct Date {
    int month, day, year;
    void display();   // a function to display the date
};
```

Exercise 8.3 *Multiple instances of a structure. (continued)*

```
void Date::display()
{
    static char *mon[] = {
        "January","February","March","April","May","June",
        "July","August","September","October","November",
        "December"};
    cout << mon[month-1] << ' ' << day << ", " << year;
}


int main()
{
    Date alans_birthday = {4, 6, 1961};
    cout << "Alan's date of birth is ";
    alans_birthday.display();
    cout << endl;

    Date sharons_birthday = {10, 12, 1962};
    cout << "Sharon's date of birth is ";
    sharons_birthday.display();
    cout << endl;

    Date wendys_birthday = {4, 28, 1965};
    cout << "Wendy's date of birth is ";
    wendys_birthday.display();
    cout << endl;
    return 0;
}
```

The program in Exercise 8.3 declares three *Date* structures and uses the *display* function to display the dates for all three.

Different Structures, Same Function Names

You can have different structures that use the same function name. Exercise 8.4 is an example of two different structures, each of which uses a function named *display*.

Exercise 8.4 *Two structures with the same function name.*

```
#include <iostream>
#include <iomanip>
#include <ctime>
using namespace std;

// ------  date structure with a function
struct Date {
    int month, day, year;
    void display();    // a function to display the date
};
void Date::display()
{
    static char *mon[] = {
        "January","February","March","April","May","June",
        "July","August","September","October","November",
        "December"};
    cout << mon[month] << ' ' << day << ", " << year;
}
// ------  time structure with a function
struct Time {
    int hour, minute, second;
    void display();    // a function to display the time
};
void Time::display()
{
    cout.fill('0');
    cout << (hour>12?hour-12:(hour==0?12:hour)) << ':'
        << setw(2) << minute << ':'
        << setw(2) << second
        << (hour < 12 ? "am" : "pm");
}
```

Exercise 8.4 *Two structures with the same function name. (continued)*

```
int main()
{
    // -------- get the current time from the OS
    time_t curtime = time(0);
    struct tm tim = *localtime(&curtime);
    // --------- time and date structures
    Time now;
    Date today;
    // --------- initialize the structures
    now.hour = tim.tm_hour;
    now.minute = tim.tm_min;
    now.second = tim.tm_sec;
    today.month = tim.tm_mon;
    today.day = tim.tm_mday;
    today.year = tim.tm_year+1900;
    // ---------- display the current date and time
    cout << "At the tone it will be ";
    now.display();
    cout << " on ";
    today.display();
    cout << '\a' << endl;
    return 0;
}
```

The program in Exercise 8.4 has a *Date* structure and a *Time* structure. Both structures have functions named *display*. The *display* function associated with the *Date* structure displays the date; the *display* function associated with the *Time* structure displays the time.

N O T E   Observe the use of the call to the *fill* function for the *cout* object. The *fill* function is a member function of the *ostream* class, of which *cout* is an object. The function tells *cout* to fill any displayed items that are shorter than the space allotted for them (by the *setw* manipulator) with the argument character, which, in this example, is a zero.

Observe also that the Standard C *localtime* function returns a year value in the *tm.tm_year* data member. When added to the integer constant 1900, this value produces the correct year, even during and after the year 2000. Be ever mindful of the dreaded Year 2K issue, and follow the example set by this book: Do not write programs that have that bug built into them.

NOTE

ACCESS SPECIFIERS

By default, the members of a structure are visible to all the functions within the scope of the structure object. This visibility permits a program to directly modify the values of data members. Such access promotes weak programming idioms wherein unrelated parts of a program come to depend on the details of a data type's implementation. An objective of data abstraction is to hide those details from the user of the class, providing instead a public interface that translates the implementation for the user of the class.

You can limit this free access to a data type's data members by placing *access specifiers* in the structure's definition. The *Date* structure in Exercise 8.4 can be modified with the *private* and *public* access specifiers, as shown here:

```
struct Date {
private:
    int month, day, year;
public:
    void display(void);
};
```

All members following the *private* access specifier are accessible only to the member functions within the structure definition. All members following the *public* access specifier are accessible to any function that is within the scope of the structure. If you omit the access specifiers, everything is *public*. You can use an access specifier more than once in the same structure definition.

A third access specifier, *protected*, is the same as the private access specifier unless the structure is a part of a class hierarchy, a subject that Chapter 11 addresses.

NOTE

The structure just shown is unusable. Here's why. You cannot initialize an instance of that structure with a brace-separated list of integers, because the data members are private to the member functions and are not accessible to the rest of the program. The *Date* structure is useless, because it has no way for a program to put data values into the data members. You need to define and call a member function that initializes the data members before you use an object of this structure.

C++ structures and classes can have *constructor* and *destructor* member functions that are automatically called to handle initialization and destruction when objects of the classes enter and depart scope. We'll solve the problem of the unusable class in Chapter 9, which, among other things, explains constructors and destructors.

SHOULD YOU USE PROCEDURAL PROGRAMMING?

Nothing in C++ prevents you from using the procedural programming model of Exercise 8.1. Encapsulation of the *Date* structure's data representation and behavior occurs when member functions are declared as part of the structure declaration.

You could add to Exercises 8.2, 8.3, and 8.4 a procedural *display* non-member function similar to the one in Exercise 8.1, and the program would work. However, by using access specifiers to make the data members private, you prevent functions that are not members of the structure from accessing the data members of an object of the structure. When you do that and when the class fully serves its purpose, data abstraction and encapsulation of that user-defined data type are complete.

THE CLASS VERSUS THE STRUCTURE

C++ defines structures and classes almost identically. To declare a class, you use the *class* keyword in place of the *struct* keyword. The only other differences are related to the default access specifiers. The members of a structure have public access by default. The members of a class have private access by default.

NOTE

There are similar differences when you declare classes and structures in hierarchies using class inheritance, the subject of Chapter 11.

The *Date* structure shown earlier is exactly the same as the *Date* class shown here:

```
class Date {
    int month, day, year;
public:
    void display(void);
};
```

So why have two different constructs when the differences are so small? The answer goes back to the early days of C++ when the class was evolving from the C *struct*. There is no technical reason that the C++ *struct* should include all the properties of the class. C++ cannot eliminate the *struct* altogether; it must, however, support the C *struct* to preserve compatibility between the languages, according to the original objectives of the C++ language. But without the explanation provided by Bjarne Stroustrup, the creator of C++, it is not clear why the structure needs member functions, access specifiers, and the ability to participate in class hierarchies. In *The Design and Evolution of C++* (Addison-Wesley, 1994) Dr. Stroustrup says:

> My intent was to have a single concept: a single set of layout rules, a single set of lookup rules, a single set of resolution rules, etc.... Only a single concept would support my ideas of a smooth and gradual transition from "traditional C-style programming," through data abstraction, to object-oriented programming.

So the reason is cultural rather than technical. Dr. Stroustrup goes on to explain that keeping the class and *struct* the same forestalled an otherwise unavoidable tendency on the part of language standardizers and specifiers to overwhelm the class specification with excess features while leaving the *struct* to implement only those features that involve low overhead and simplicity.

Given all that, when should you use a *struct* instead of a class? Many programmers adopt this rule:

> When the data structure's implementation is the same as its interface, use a *struct*. Otherwise, use a class.

What are the implications of this rule? What does it mean when you say that the implementation is the interface? It means simply that you have a typical C structure with data members only (no member functions), all of which have public access so that the format of the data members is what the application program views.

Object-oriented purists would contend that by following that rule, there is no valid application for the C++ *struct*. If you fall into that category, C++ supports your beliefs. Use classes exclusively. If you lean toward the pragmatic approach, C++ permits you to write code using either idiom. C++ has something for everyone.

Virtually none of the exercises that follow in this book use *structs*. In Chapter 9 we shift to the C++ class, not because we are object-oriented purists but because you have now learned all you need to know about *structs*.

Unions

Unions share some of the structure attributes that you learned in this chapter. A union can have function members, but it cannot be a part of a class hierarchy. You will learn about class hierarchies in Chapter 11. A union can have constructor and destructor functions (Chapter 9), but it cannot have virtual functions (Chapter 11).

Unions can have private and public members. You will learn more about the private and public access specifiers in Chapter 9.

Summary

This chapter taught you about data abstraction and the C++ structure, its members, and its access specifiers. Chapter 9 is about the C++ class, a variation on the structure. Beginning with Chapter 9, this book will use the class mechanism exclusively for declaring user-defined data types and building object-oriented class hierarchies.

CHAPTER 9

C++ Classes

C++ classes support data abstraction and object-oriented programming, both of which involve the design and implementation of data types. When you begin programming with classes, you should use them to extend the C++ language by designing and implementing custom data types: small types that the language lacks but that a typical application might need, such as dates, times, and currency. This approach allows you to learn the syntax and behavior of the class mechanism without worrying about new and exotic programming paradigms. Rather than trying to learn a complex and highly abstract concept such as object-oriented programming, you will learn about the language features that support it. Later you can apply this new-found knowledge of C++ classes to learning about object-oriented programming. In this chapter you will learn about:

- Designing a class
- Data members
- Member functions
- Constructors and destructors

- Class conversion functions
- Friends
- References
- Assignment functions
- The *this* pointer
- Arrays of class objects
- Static class members
- The heap
- Copy constructors
- mutable data members
- *const* objects and member functions

DESIGNING A CLASS

Consider again the intrinsic numerical data types that C++ supports. These integer and floating-point types suffice for most of a programmer's numerical needs, but there are times when you need to extend the language to support more-complex data types. In C, you would organize the intrinsic types into a structure and write functions to manipulate that structure. With C++, you do the same thing, but you bind the data representations and their algorithms into a new data type by defining a class. A C++ *class* becomes a data type that you, the programmer, define. It is C++'s data abstraction mechanism. The class consists of data members, member functions, and custom operators.

Class Declaration

Let's begin by considering a simple class design. Let's look at an example of a class that describes the geometrical box form.

NOTE

Before proceeding, ask yourself why you might want to build a class that describes a box. Perhaps you are writing a program that deals with three-dimensional containers of some kind, and the box is a basic unit that the program must deal with. Any data entity that your program might process is a candidate to be a class in C++. This begins to answer the question, "What are the objects?" This is the first question asked by most functionally oriented programmers when they first encounter object-oriented programming.

Exercise 9.1 introduces classes by declaring the *Box* class.

Exercise 9.1 *The* Box *class.*

```
#include <iostream>
using namespace std;


// ----------- a Box class
class Box    {
private:
    int height, width, depth;    // private data members
public:
    Box(int, int, int); // constructor function
    ~Box();              // destructor function
    int volume();        // member function (compute volume)
};
// ---------- the constructor function
Box::Box(int ht, int wd, int dp)
{
    height = ht;
    width = wd;
    depth = dp;
}
// ---------- the destructor function
Box::~Box()
{
    // does nothing
}
// ------- member function to compute the Box's volume
int Box::volume()
{
    return height * width * depth;
}
```

Exercise 9.1 *The* Box *class. (continued)*

```
// -------- an application to use the box
main()
{
    Box thisbox(7, 8, 9);       // declare a Box
    cout << thisbox.volume();   // compute & display volume
}
```

Many new C++ features are packed into Exercise 9.1. The program begins by declaring the *Box* class. The class has three private data members—the integers *height, width,* and *depth*—and three public functions: a constructor named *Box*, a destructor named *~Box*, and a member function named *volume.* You learn about each of these kinds of functions as the chapter progresses.

Class Members

A class, as you learned in Chapter 8, is a souped-up C structure. As such, a class has members, just as a structure does. A class's members are defined by the class declaration and consist of data members, the constructor and destructor functions, overloaded operator functions, and other member functions.

Class Member Visibility

The *private* and *public* access specifiers specify the visibility of the members that follow the access specifiers. The access mode set by an access specifier continues until another access specifier occurs or the class declaration ends. Private members can be accessed only by member functions of the same class. Public members can be accessed by member functions and by other functions that declare an instance of the class. There are exceptions to these general rules. The discussion later in this chapter of *friend* classes and functions addresses some of those exceptions.

The *Box* class, therefore, specifies that its three integer data members are visible only to the constructor and destructor functions and to the *volume* member function, all three of which are visible to outside functions. You can use the *private* and *public* access specifiers as often as you want in a class declaration, but many programmers group private and public members separately.

All class declarations begin with *private* as the default access mode, so you could omit it in Exercise 9.1. The exercise includes it for readability and to demonstrate its purpose. Chapter 8 discussed C++ structures briefly, deferring the complicated aspects to this chapter. There are only a few small differences between the structure and the class. First, the structure begins with public access as the default, and the class begins with private access as the default. Second, if the structure is derived from a base class, the base class is public by default. If the class is derived from a base class, the base class is private by default. You have already learned about access specifiers. Chapter 11 discusses public and private base classes and class derivation—inheritance—in detail. Many programmers adopt a style in which they define a structure when its form complies with the C definition of a structure. Otherwise, they define a class.

A third access specifier, the *protected* keyword, works the same as the *private* keyword except when you use class inheritance. For now, you will not use the *protected* access specifier.

Data Members

The data members of the class are the ones that are instances of data types. A data member can be of any valid C++ data type, including an instance of another another class or a pointer or reference. The *Box* class has three data members: the integers *height, width,* and *depth.*

Initialization

The declaration of a class object can contain a list of initializers in parentheses. The declaration of *thisbox* in Exercise 9.1 contains three integer values. These values are passed as arguments to the class's constructor function, described soon. However, if the class has no private or protected members, has no *virtual* functions (discussed in Chapter 11), and is not derived from another class (also discussed in Chapter 11), you can initialize an object of the class with a brace-delimited, comma-separated list of initializers, just as you initialize a C structure:

```
class Date {
public:
    int mo, da, yr;
};
main()
{
    Date dt = {1,29,92};
    // ...
}
```

The same restrictions apply to structures, by the way. You cannot use a brace-delimited initializer list if a structure has any of the attributes just mentioned.

Member Functions

Member functions are the functions that you declare within the class definition. You must provide the code for these functions just as you did for the functions in structures in Chapter 8.

There are several categories of member functions. The constructor and destructor, discussed soon, are two of them. The others are regular member functions, overloaded operator functions, *friend* functions, and *virtual* functions. You learn about overloaded operator functions in chapter 10. You learn about *friend* functions later in this chapter and *virtual* functions in Chapter 11. For now, observe that the *Box* class has one regular member function, named *volume*, which is neither *friend* nor *virtual*.

Member functions, when defined outside the class declaration, are named with the class name followed by the :: operator followed by the function name. The name of the *Box* class's *volume* member function is, therefore, *Box::volume*.

The *Box::volume* function returns the product of the *Box* object's three dimensions. The program in Exercise 9.1 calls the *volume* function by using the same convention for calling a structure's function. Use structure member notation with the period operator, as illustrated in the following example:

```
int vol = thisbox.volume();
```

You can call the *volume* member function anywhere an object (or pointer or reference to an object) of type *Box* is in scope. Member functions of a class can call one another by using the function name without the object name prefix. The compiler assumes that the call is being made for the same object that the calling member function was called for.

When a member function is private, only other member functions within the same class can call it.

Object-Oriented Class Design

Exercise 9.1 follows a convention that many C++ programmers consider to be sound C++ object-oriented design: When you're designing a class, make all the data members private. Make public only those member functions necessary to implement the public interface of the class.

Let's review some of what you learned in Chapter 8: A class design encapsulates the data members and algorithms into a user-defined abstract data type. The class hides the details of the type's implementation within the class's private members. The class's public interface, which is provided by public member functions, defines the user's perception of the type. A class's hidden implementation can use private member functions, too, but these functions are not included in the public interface.

If you need to allow the class user to view or modify a private data value, do it with a public member function. This convention is not a hard and fast rule, and there will be times when you find it necessary to do otherwise. But if you use the convention as a guideline, your programs will be more object-oriented and, consequently, of stronger design.

Is *Box* in Exercise 9.1 an object? No, *Box* is a *type*. The class declaration merely defines the class's format. It does not set aside any memory to hold an instance of the class. No instance of the class exists until a program declares one within the scope of the class declaration. A declared instance of a data type is an *object*. A class is a user-defined data type. Therefore, an instance of a class is an object. The *thisbox* variable in Exercise 9.1 is an object of type *Box*. These distinctions are important in object-oriented programming.

The Scope of a Class Object

A class object is like any other instantiated data type with respect to scope. An *automatic* object comes into scope when the program defines it and goes out of scope when the program exits the block in which the class object is defined.

An *extern* class object comes into scope when the program begins running and goes out of scope when the program exits to the operating system.

The scope of a *static* local class object appears to be the same as that of an automatic object, but its actual existence is the same as that of an *extern* object. Understanding this behavior is important, because classes include special functions called constructor and destructor functions.

inline Functions

A class can have inline member functions. You learned about regular inline functions in Chapter 3. The compiler compiles an inline copy of the function every time the program calls the function. The same guidelines apply when you decide whether a class member function should be inline. As a general rule, inline functions should be small.

There are two notations for defining inline functions for a class. In the first one, you code the body of the function directly into the class declaration rather than coding a prototype. Both the *Box* constructor function and the *Box's volume* member function are small enough to be inline functions. Coding them as inline and removing the unnecessary destructor function significantly reduces the size of the program's source code.

Exercise 9.2 illustrates inline class member functions.

Exercise 9.2 *The* Box *class with* inline *functions.*

```
#include <iostream>
using namespace std;


// ----------- a Box class
class Box    {
    int height, width, depth;    // private data members
public:
    // ------ inline constructor function
    Box(int ht, int wd, int dp)
        { height = ht; width = wd; depth = dp; }
    // ----- inline member function
    int volume()
        { return height * width * depth; }
};

main()
{
    Box thisbox(7, 8, 9);       // declare a Box
    cout << thisbox.volume();   // compute & display volume
}
```

You often see inline class functions coded on a single line., a convention that reinforces the idea that inline functions should be small. If you cannot get the function's body on a single line, perhaps the function should not be inline.

The second notation for inline member functions uses the *inline* keyword in the function's definition outside the class. The *volume* function could be defined this way:

```
inline int Box::volume()
{
    return height * width * depth;
}
```

When you code an inline member function this way, put it in the same source code file with the class declaration—usually a header file—so that the function is visible to all source-code modules that use the class.

CONSTRUCTORS

When an instance of a class comes into scope, a special function called the *constructor* function executes. You can declare one or more constructor functions when you declare the class. If you do not declare at least one constructor function, the compiler provides a hidden default constructor function for the class, which may or may not do anything. See the section, "Default Constructors" later in this chapter.

The *Box* class has a constructor function named *Box*. Constructor functions always have the same name as the class, and they specify no return value, not even *void*.

The runtime system allocates enough memory to contain the data members of a class when an object of the class comes into scope. The system does not necessarily initialize the data members. Like objects of intrinsic data types, the data members of external objects are initialized to all zeros. The runtime system does not initialize local objects. Their data members may be assumed to contain garbage values. The class's constructor function must do any initialization that the class requires. The data memory returns to the system when the automatic class object goes out of scope. Dynamically allocated class objects work the same way except that you must use the *new* and *delete* operators to allocate and free the memory for the object. This subject is addressed in more detail later in this chapter.

The constructor function initializes the class object. The *Box* constructor function in Exercise 9.2 accepts three integer parameters and uses them to assign to the data members the values that describe the *Box* object.

Observe the declaration of *thisbox* in Exercise 9.2. It follows the C syntax for declaring a variable. First comes the data type—*Box*, in this case—and then comes the name of the object, *thisbox*. That's the same way you would declare, for example, an *int*, . The declaration of a class object can contain an argument list in parentheses. This list represents class object initializers and contains the arguments that are passed to the constructor function. The class declaration must contain a constructor function with a parameter list of data types that match those of the argument list in the class object declaration.

If the constructor function has an empty parameter list, the declaration of the object does not require the parentheses.

A constructor function returns nothing. You do not declare it as *void*, but it is *void* by default.

You may define multiple, overloaded constructor functions for a class. Each of them would have a distinct parameter list. More discussion of this feature follows later.

Constructors with Default Arguments

You may want to initialize a *Box* with dimensions, as you did in Exercise 9.1, but at other times you want a *Box* with default dimensions.

Exercise 9.3 shows a *Box* class that defaults to specified dimensions if you do not supply initializers.

Exercise 9.3 *Constructor with default parameters.*

```
#include <iostream>
using namespace std;


// ----------- a Box class
class Box    {
    int height, width, depth;     // private data members
public:
    // ----- constructor function with default initializers
    Box(int ht = 1, int wd = 2, int dp = 3)
        { height = ht; width = wd; depth = dp; }
    // ----- member function
    int volume() { return height * width * depth; }
};
```

Exercise 9.3 Constructor with default parameters. (continued)

```
main()
{
    Box thisbox(7, 8, 9);       // declare a Box
    Box defaultbox;             // no initializers
    cout << thisbox.volume();   // volume of the Box
    cout << endl;
    cout << defaultbox.volume(); // volume of the default
}
```

Default Constructors

A constructor with no parameters or a constructor with default arguments for all its parameters is called a *default constructor*. If you do not provide any constructors, the compiler provides a public default constructor, which usually does nothing. If you provide at least one constructor of any kind, the compiler does not provide a default constructor. Default constructors are important, as you will learn later. You cannot, for example, instantiate arrays of objects of a class that has no default constructor.

Overloaded Constructors

A class can have more than one constructor function. The several constructor functions for a class must have different parameter lists with respect to the number and types of parameters so that the compiler can tell them apart. You would code multiple constructors in cases in which the declarations of a class can occur with different initialization parameters. You may want to initialize a *Box* object with dimensions, as you did in Exercise 9.1, but at other times you simply want an empty *Box* with no initial dimensions—for example, to be on the receiving end of an assignment.

Exercise 9.4 shows the *Box* with two constructor functions.

Exercise 9.4 *A class with two constructors.*

```
#include <iostream>
using namespace std;


// ------------ a Box class
class Box    {
    int height, width, depth;      // private data members
public:
    // ------ constructor functions
    Box() { /* does nothing */ }
    Box(int ht, int wd, int dp)
        { height = ht; width = wd; depth = dp; }
    // ----- member function
    int volume() { return height * width * depth; }
};


int main()
{
    Box thisbox(7, 8, 9);     // declare a Box
    Box otherbox;             // a Box with no initializers
    otherbox = thisbox;
    cout << otherbox.volume();
    return 0;
}
```

This exercise uses the simplest of differences between constructors: One constructor has initializers and the other one does not. The differences between constructors can be much greater, depending on the types of the class's data members and the algorithms that associate with the constructor function. You will see more-complex constructor functions in later chapters.

Exercise 9.4 is an example of a weak class design. It permits you to instantiate and then use an uninitialized *Box* object. There is no way to determine in advance what the *volume* member function would return if the program failed to assign the *thisbox* object to the *otherbox* object before calling *volume*. In a better design, the constructor with the empty paramter list would assign default values to the object:

```
class Box    {
    int height, width, depth;
public:
    Box()
        { height = 0; width = 0; depth = 0; }
    Box(int ht, int wd, int dp)
        { height = ht; width = wd; depth = dp; }
    int volume() { return height * width * depth; }
};
```

An even better design uses default arguments to eliminate altogether the constructor with the empty parameter list:

```
class Box    {
    int height, width, depth;
public:
    Box(int ht = 0, int wd = 0, int dp = 0)
        { height = ht; width = wd; depth = dp; }
    int volume() { return height * width * depth; }
};
```

DESTRUCTORS

When a class object goes out of scope, a special function called the *destructor* is called. You define the destructor when you define the class. The destructor function name is always that of the class with a tilde character (~) as a prefix. Exercise 9.1 demonstrated the syntax of the Box class's destructor function.

There is only one destructor function for a class. A destructor function takes no parameters and returns nothing. The destructor's purpose is to undo whatever the class object has done that needs to be undone, such as releasing allocated dynamic heap memory.

The destructor function for the *Box* class in Exercise 9.1 does nothing. The exercise included the destructor to show its format. You could omit it and get the same result. However, on other occasions destructors are necessary. For example, some classes allocate memory from the heap in their constructor functions or elsewhere during the life of the class object and return the memory to the heap in the destructor function. Later exercises in this chapter demonstrate this principle.

CLASS CONVERSIONS

C++ intrinsic data types obey implicit type conversion rules. Suppose, for example, that an expression uses a *short int* variable in a context in which the compiler expects to see a *long int* variable. The compiler automatically invokes a type conversion rule to convert the short integer value to the long integer format. The compiler knows such implicit conversions for all pairs of data types that are compatible with respect to conversions. These implicit conversions occur in assignments, function arguments, return values, initializers, and expressions.

You can provide equivalent conversion rules for your classes.

Conversion Functions

You build an implicit conversion rule into a class by building a *conversion function,* a member function that converts between objects of any data type and objects of the class. The conversion function's declaration tells the compiler to call the conversion function when the syntax of a statement implies that the conversion should take effect—that is, when the compiler expects an object of one type and sees instead an object of the other data type.

There are two ways to write conversion functions. The first is to write a conversion constructor function; the second is to write a member conversion function. Which kind of conversion function you write depends on whether you are converting to or from an object of the class.

Conversion Constructors

A constructor function with only one entry in its parameter list is a *conversion constructor* if the parameter is a different type than the class of the constructor. A conversion constructor converts from an object of the type of the constructor's argument to an object of the class. The conversion constructor works like any other constructor when you declare an object of the class type with a matching initializer argument. It is an implicit conversion constructor when you use the argument type in a context in which the class type is expected.

Exercise 9.5 demonstrates a constructor conversion function that converts the *time_t* value returned by the Standard C *time* function to an object of the *Date* class.

Exercise 9.5 *Constructor conversion function.*

```
#include <iostream>
#include <ctime>
using namespace std;


class Date {
    int mo, da, yr;
public:
    Date(time_t);    // constructor conversion function
    void display();
};
// ----- member function to display the date
void Date::display()
{
    cout << mo << '/' << da << '/' << yr;
}
// ------ constructor conversion function
Date::Date(time_t now)
{
    tm* tim = localtime(&now);
    da = tim->tm_mday;
    mo = tim->tm_mon + 1;
    yr = tim->tm_year;
}
```

Exercise 9.5 Constructor conversion function. (continued)

```
int main()
{
    time_t now = time(0); // today's date and time
    Date dt(now);    // invoke the conversion constructor
    dt.display();    // display today's date
    return 0;
}
```

Chapter 6 explained the **<ctime>** header file and the Standard C time functions and data structures. Exercise 9.5 calls the *time* function to retrieve the current time expressed as a *time_t* object. Then the program constructs a *Date* object by invoking the *Date* class's conversion constructor function, which accepts a *time_t* object. In this exercise, the conversion constructor is the class's only constructor. That constructor function passes the *time_t* object to the Standard C *localtime* function, which returns a pointer to an object of type *struct tm* (declared in the Standard C **<ctime>** header file). The constructor then copies the structure members for day, month, and year to the *Date* object's data members, thus constructing a Date object from a *time_t* object.

Member Conversion Functions

A *member conversion function* converts an object of a class in which you define the function to an object of a different data type. A member conversion function uses the C++ *operator* keyword in its declaration. You declare a member conversion function in the class declaration:

```
operator long();
```

The *long* in this example is the type specifier of the converted data type. The type specifier can be any valid C++ type, including another class. You would define the member conversion function with the following notation:

```
Classname::operator long()
```

The *Classname* identifier is the type specifier of the class in which the function is declared. The function converts objects of this class into, in this example, *long* objects. The function returns an object of the data type to which it is converting, in this case a *long*.

The *Date* class that you have been using does not contain enough information to convert an object of that class back to the *time_t* variable, but you can convert one to, for example, a long integer containing the number of days since the beginning of the 20th century.

Exercise 9.6 shows how you would use a member function to make such a conversion.

Exercise 9.6 Member conversion function.

```
#include <iostream>
using namespace std;


class Date {
    int mo, da, yr;
public:
    Date(int m, int d, int y) { mo = m; da = d; yr = y; }
    operator long();    // member conversion function
};


// ---- the member conversion function
Date::operator long()
{
    static int dys[]={31,28,31,30,31,30,31,31,30,31,30,31};
    long days = yr - 1900;
    days *= 365;
    days += yr / 4;
    for (int i = 0; i < mo-1; i++)
        days += dys[i];
    days += da;
    return days;
}
```

Exercise 9.6 Member conversion function. (continued)

```
int main()
{
    Date xmas(12, 25, 1997);
    long since = xmas;
    cout << since << endl;
    return 0;
}
```

When the compiler sees the assignment of the *xmas* object to a *long* object, the compiler searches for valid ways to make that conversion. The compiler finds the *Date::operator long()* function, which satisfies its requirements for specification of a conversion rule. Then the compiler generates a call to that function, which assigns at runtime the return value from that function to the *long* integer object.

Converting Classes

The conversion examples so far have converted class objects to and from intrinsic C++ data type objects. You can also define conversion functions that convert from one class object to another.

Exercise 9.7 shows you how to convert class objects.

Exercise 9.7 Converting classes.

```
#include <iostream>
using namespace std;


// -------- Julian date class
class Julian {
public:
    int da, yr;
    Julian(int d = 0, int y = 0) { da = d; yr = y;}
    void display(){ cout << endl << yr << '-' << da; }
};
```

Exercise 9.7 Converting classes. (continued)

```
// ------- date class
class Date {
    int mo, da, yr;
public:
    Date(int m = 0, int d = 0, int y = 0)
        { mo = m; da = d; yr = y; }
    Date(const Julian&);  // constructor conversion function
    operator Julian();    // member conversion function
    void display(){cout << endl << mo << '/' << da
                        << '/' << yr;}
};


static int dys[] = {31,28,31,30,31,30,31,31,30,31,30,31};
// ---- constructor conversion function (Date <- Julian)
Date::Date(const Julian& jd)
{
    yr = jd.yr;
    da = jd.da;
    for (mo = 0; mo < 11; mo++)
        if (da > dys[mo])
            da -= dys[mo];
        else
            break;
    mo++;
}
// ---- member conversion function (Julian <- Date)
Date::operator Julian()
{
    Julian jd(0, yr);
    for (int i = 0; i < mo-1; i++)
        jd.da += dys[i];
    jd.da += da;
    return jd;
}
```

Exercise 9.7 *Converting classes. (continued)*

```
int main()
{
    Date dt(11,17,97);
    Julian jd;
    // ------- convert Date to Julian
    jd = dt;
    jd.display();
    // ------- convert Julian to Date
    dt = jd;
    dt.display();
    return 0;
}
```

This exercise has two classes: *Julian* and *Date*. A *Julian* date contains the year and the day of the year expressed as an integer value from 1 to 365 (366 in leap years). The conversion functions in Exercise 9.7 convert between the two date formats.

NOTE The date conversion algorithms in these exercises do not consider things such as the millennium or the leap year. These intentional omissions keep the exercises simple. Always cover all such possibilities when you design a class, particularly one that others might use. There is no telling how it might be used by other programmers.

Both kinds of conversion functions are built into the *Date* class in Exercise 9.7. This approach works because you convert from the *Date* type to the *Julian* type with the member conversion function, and from the *Julian* type to the *Date* type with the conversion constructor.

You cannot have both a *Date*-to-*Julian* member conversion function in the *Date* class and a *Date*-to-*Julian* conversion constructor function in the *Julian* class. The compiler could not know which function to call to perform the conversion and would, consequently, generate an error message.

The conversion constructor that constructs a Date object from a Julian object has as its parameter a *const* reference to a Julian object. This usage passes a reference rather than a copy to the constructor, a technique that eliminates argument-passing overhead for large objects. The parameter is *const* to specify that the constructor function does not modify any of the data members of the Julian object.

NOTE

Do not be concerned about the public data members in the *Julian* class. We will deal with that issue in due time.

Invoking Conversion Functions

There are three C++ forms that invoke a conversion function. The first is implicit conversion. For example, when the compiler expects to see a *Date* and the program supplies a *Julian*, the compiler calls the appropriate conversion function. The other two forms involve explicit conversions that you write into the code. The first of these conversions is implied by the C++ cast. The second is an explicit call to the conversion constructor or member conversion function.

Exercise 9.8 illustrates the three class conversion forms.

Exercise 9.8 *Invoking conversions.*

```
#include <iostream>
using namespace std;



// -------- Julian date class
class Julian {
public:
    int da, yr;
    Julian(int d = 0, int y = 0) { da = d; yr = y;}
    void display(){cout << endl << yr << '-' << da;}
};
```

Exercise 9.8 *Invoking conversions. (continued)*

```
// ------- date class
class Date {
    int mo, da, yr;
public:
    Date(int m, int d, int y) { mo = m; da = d; yr = y; }
    operator Julian(); // conversion function.
};


// ---- member conversion function (Julian <- Date)
Date::operator Julian()
{
    static int dys[] = {31,28,31,30,31,30,31,31,30,31,30,31};
    Julian jd(0, yr);
    for (int i = 0; i < mo-1; i++)
        jd.da += dys[i];
    jd.da += da;
    return jd;
}

int main()
{
    Date dt(11,17,89);
    Julian jd;
    // ------- convert Date to Julian via implicit conversion
    jd = dt;
    jd.display();
    // ------- convert Date to Julian via cast
    jd = (Julian) dt;
    jd.display();
    // ------- convert Date to Julian via constructor
    jd = Julian(dt);
    jd.display();
    return 0;
}
```

The cast in Exercise 9.8 uses traditional C language casting notation, which works in C++. C++, however, includes improved notations for casting. Chapter 14 discusses these new casting conventions.

The Contexts in Which Conversions Occur

So far the exercises have invoked conversion functions through assignment. The assignment of one object to another object of a different type invokes the appropriate conversion function. The following list identifies other contexts that invoke conversion functions:

- Function arguments
- Initializers
- Return values
- Statement expressions

Exercise 9.9 illustrates some of the ways you can cause a conversion function to be called.

Exercise 9.9 Contexts for conversions.

```
#include <iostream>
using namespace std;


// -------- Julian date class
class Julian {
public:
    int da, yr;
    Julian() {}
    Julian(int d, int y) { da = d; yr = y;}
    void display() {cout << endl << yr << '-' << da;}
};
```

Exercise 9.9 *Contexts for conversions. (continued)*

```
// ------- date class
class Date {
    int mo, da, yr;
public:
    Date(int m, int d, int y) { mo = m; da = d; yr = y; }
    operator Julian(); // conversion function
};



// ---- member conversion function (Julian <- Date)
Date::operator Julian()
{
    static int dys[] = {31,28,31,30,31,30,31,31,30,31,30,31};
    Julian jd(0, yr);
    for (int i = 0; i < mo-1; i++)
        jd.da += dys[i];
    jd.da += da;
    return jd;
}
// ----- a class that expects a Julian date as an initializer
class Tester {
    Julian jd;
public:
    explicit Tester(Julian j) { jd = j; }
    void display() { jd.display(); }
};
// -------- a function that expects a Julian date
void dispdate(Julian jd)
{
    jd.display();
}
```

Exercise 9.9 Contexts for conversions. (continued)

```
// --------- a function that returns a Julian Date
Julian rtndate()
{
    Date dt(10,11,88);
    return dt;             // this will be converted to Julian
}


int main()
{
    Date dt(11,17,89);
    Julian jd;
    // ------- convert Date to Julian via assignment
    jd = dt;
    jd.display();
    // ------- convert Date to Julian via function argument
    dispdate(dt);
    // ------- convert Date to Julian via initializer
    Tester ts(dt);
    ts.display();
    // ------- convert Date to Julian via return value
    jd = rtndate();
    jd.display();
    return 0;
}
```

Explicit Constructors

Observe the *explicit* qualifier in the *Tester* class's constructor in Exercise 9.9. Without that keyword, the compiler would treat the constructor as a conversion constructor to be invoked whenever the program uses an object of type *Julian* and the compiler expects to see an object of type *Tester*. Recall that conversion constructors have only one parameter (or only one without default argument values declared) with a type that is other than the type of the constructor. There will be times when you do not want a constructor with only one parameter to be used in conversions—when instead you want the constructor to be used only for explicit construction of instantiated objects. In these cases, use the *explicit* qualifier in the constructor's declaration. The following line of code, when placed after the declaration of the *Tester* object in Exercise 9.9, produces a compiler error:

```
ts = jd; // error
```

This error tells you that even though the *Tester* class has a constructor that accepts a *Date* argument, the compiler does not treat it as a *Date*-to-*Tester* conversion constructor because the constructor is declared to be *explicit*.

Conversion within an Expression

Conversion within an expression occurs in expressions in which one type is expected and another type is found. This process is easily illustrated when the conversion is to a numeric type instead of to another class.

Exercise 9.10 uses the conversion of a *Date* object to a long integer to illustrate how the integral representation of a class can, through conversion, contribute directly to an expression.

Exercise 9.10 Conversion in an expression.

```
#include <iostream>
using namespace std;


class Date {
    int mo, da, yr;
public:
    Date(int m, int d, int y) { mo = m; da = d; yr = y; }
    operator long();    // member conversion function
};
```

Exercise 9.10 *Conversion in an expression. (continued)*

```
// ---- the member conversion function
Date::operator long()
{
    static int dys[]={31,28,31,30,31,30,31,31,30,31,30,31};
    long days = yr;
    days *= 365;
    days += yr / 4;
    for (int i = 0; i < mo-1; i++)
        days += dys[i];
    days += da;
    return days;
}


int main()
{
    Date today(2, 12, 90);
    const long ott = 123;
    long sum = ott + today;      // today is converted to long
    cout << ott << " + " << (long) today << " = " << sum;
    return 0;
}
```

The implicit conversion from within an expression occurs if the converted object can be converted to a numerical type or if the expression invokes an overloaded operator that works with the class. Chapter 10 discusses overloading operators.

MANIPULATING PRIVATE DATA MEMBERS

All the data members in the *Julian* class in Exercises 9.7, 9.8, and 9.9 are public. This approach allows the conversion functions in the *Date* class to read and write the data members of the *Julian* object. Making the members public is one way to allow this access, but, when you do, you also make the members public to all other functions. You might not want to do that. Remember our object-oriented convention for keeping data members private and interface member functions public. To get their point across, these exercises violated that convention. Now you should consider alternative ways to get the same results without violating convention.

Getter and Setter Member Functions

To repeat our object-oriented convention: As a general rule, make all data members private. How, then, does a user of the class access an object's data values? The class design includes a public interface that contains public member functions to read and write data values. Some programmers call these functions *getter* and *setter* functions.

The values returned from getter functions and passed to setter functions are not necessarily one-for-one matches to the types of all the data members. You should instead provide getter and setter functions that represent the public interface, permitting the class user to extract data values from the class object and provide data values that modify the content and behavior of the class object.

You will not usually have a getter and setter function for every data member. If you did that, you might as well make the data members public. Furthermore, if the public interface consists only of getter and setter functions for every data member, you might just as well use a C *struct* instead of a class.

Exercise 9.11 shows how the *Date* class can have member functions that provide controlled access to the data members.

Exercise 9.11 Manipulating data members through member functions.

```
#include <iostream>
using namespace std;



class Date {
    int mo, da, yr;
public:
    Date(int m, int d, int y) { mo = m; da = d; yr = y; }
    // ---- a member function to return the year
    int getyear() const { return yr; }
    // ---- a member function to allow the year to be changed
    void setyear(int y) { yr = y; }
};
```

Exercise 9.11 Manipulating data members through member functions. (continued)

```
int main()
{
    // -------- set up a Date
    Date dt(4, 1, 89);
    // ------- use a member function to read the year value
    cout << "The year is: " << dt.getyear() << endl;
    // ------ use a member function to change the year
    dt.setyear(97);
    cout << "The new year is: " << dt.getyear();
    return 0;
}
```

By consistently using this approach, you ensure that accesses and changes to the data of a class are managed by member functions that are bound to the class. This binding strengthens a software design and makes it easier to maintain. Suppose, for example, that you changed the internal data representation of the *Date* class. You would also then modify the *getyear* and *setyear* functions to deal with that other data representation. However, users of the class would not have to change their code. They could recompile their programs, and, if both you and they did everything right, their programs would continue to work the same way they did before you modified the class.

const Member Functions

Observe that the *getyear* function in Exercise 9.11 is declared as *const*. You can guarantee that a member function never modifies the object for which it is called by declaring it with the *const* qualifier. No change to the *Date::getyear* function is permitted that modifies the data members in the object. This approach ensures that the member function accesses data values from the object, only to retrieve the data for the user, display the data, or perform some other nonmutating operation.

Furthermore, if the program declares a *Date* object as *const*, the program cannot call any non-*const* member functions for the object whether or not those functions actually change the object's data values. By declaring all functions that do not change values as *const*, you permit users of *const* objects to call those functions.

An Improved Member Conversion Function

Exercise 9.12 eliminates public data members and uses getter and setter member functions to improve the member conversion function that converts a *Date* object to a *Julian* object.

__Exercise 9.12__ Conversions with proper data hiding.

```
#include <iostream>
using namespace std;


// -------- Julian date class
class Julian {
    int da, yr;
public:
    Julian() {}
    Julian(int d, int y) { da = d; yr = y;}
    void display() const
        {cout << endl << yr << '-' << da;}
    // ------ member functions to read and write a day
    int getday() const { return da; }
    void setday(int d) { da = d; }
};


// ------- date class
class Date {
    int mo, da, yr;
public:
    Date(int m, int d, int y) { mo = m; da = d; yr = y; }
    operator Julian() const; // conversion function
};
```

Exercise 9.12 Conversions with proper data hiding. (continued)

```
// ---- member conversion function (Julian <- Date)
Date::operator Julian() const
{
    static int dys[] = {31,28,31,30,31,30,31,31,30,31,30,31};
    Julian jd(0, yr);
    int day = da;
    for (int i = 0; i < mo-1; i++)
        day += dys[i];
    jd.setday(day);
    return jd;
}


int main()
{
    Date dt(11,17,89);
    Julian jd;
    // ------- convert Date to Julian via assignment
    jd = dt;
    jd.display();
    return 0;
}
```

Observe that the *Date::operator Julian()* function in Exercise 9.12 is declared as *const*. This is valid usage, because the function does not modify the data values of the *Date* object for which it is running. Instead it modifies the data values of the temporary *Julian* object that it constructs to return to its caller.

FRIENDS

Having learned that hidden access to data members is best, you must now consider exceptions to that rule. There are times when a class declaration must allow specific outside functions to directly read and write the class's private data members.

The *friend* keyword in a class specifies that a particular function or all the member functions of another class can read and write the original class's private data members. This technique allows a class to maintain a private implementation while granting to specific classes and functions controlled access to that implementation.

Friend Classes

The first kind of friend is the class *friend*. A class can specify that all the member functions of another class can read and write the first class's private data members by identifying the other class as a friend.

Exercise 9.13 illustrates the use of the *friend* class.

Exercise 9.13 friend *classes.*

```
#include <iostream>
using namespace std;


class Date;        // tells compiler a Date class is coming
// -------- Julian date class
class Julian {
    int da, yr;
public:
    Julian(int d = 0, int y = 0)
        { da = d; yr = y;}
    void display() const
        {cout << endl << yr << '-' << da;}
    friend Date;    // allows Date member functions to see
                    // Julian private members
};
// ------- date class
class Date {
    int mo, da, yr;
public:
    Date(int m, int d, int y) { mo = m; da = d; yr = y; }
    operator Julian();
};
```

Exercise 9.13 friend *classes. (continued)*

```
// ---- member conversion function (Julian <- Date)
Date::operator Julian()
{
    static int dys[] = {31,28,31,30,31,30,31,31,30,31,30,31};
    Julian jd(0, yr);
    for (int i = 0; i < mo-1; i++)
        jd.da += dys[i];
    jd.da += da;
    return jd;
}


int main()
{
    Date dt(11,17,89);
    Julian jd(dt);
    jd.display();
    return 0;
}
```

Observe this new construct in the *Julian* class of Exercise 9.13 in the following example:

```
friend Date;
```

This statement tells the compiler that all member functions of the *Date* class have access to the private members of the *Julian* class. The conversion functions of the *Date* class need to see the individual data components of the *Julian* class, so the entire *Date* class is named as a friend of the *Julian* class.

Implied Construction

Observe the call to the *Julian* constructor in Exercise 9.13. It would seem that the *Julian* class would need a conversion constructor such as this one:

```
Julian(Date& dt);
```

Yet the only constructor is this one:

```
Julian(int d = 0, int y = 0);
```

Here's what happens. The compiler sees a need to construct a *Julian* object from a *Date* object. There is no such conversion constructor defined for the *Julian* class. There is, however, a member conversion function defined for the Date class that converts *Date* objects to *Julian* objects. The compiler looks to see whether the *Julian* class includes a constructor that constructs a *Julian* object from an existing *Julian* object. Such a constructor, called a *copy constructor* is discussed later in this chapter. A copy constructor takes as its only argument an object of the same type. There is no *Julian* copy constuctor, so the compiler provides a default one that simply copies each of the members from the existing *Julian* object to the new *Julian* object. Now, given that the compiler can convert a *Date* object to a *Julian* object and can construct a *Julian* object from a *Julian* object, the compiler compiles a call to the conversion function to construct a hidden, temporary, anonymous *Julian* object from the *Date* object. The compiler uses this temporary object as the argument to a call to its default copy constructor, and the new *Julian* object is thus constructed.

Forward References

Exercise 9.13 contains another C++ construct that you haven't seen yet. The beginning of the program has the following statement:

```
class Date;
```

This statement is a *forward reference.* It tells the compiler that a class named *Date* is defined later. The compiler needs to know that information because the *Julian* class refers to the *Date* class, and the *Date* class refers to the *Julian* class. One of them must be declared first, so the statement serves to resolve the forward reference to *Date* that occurs in the *Julian* class.

By using forward references, you can declare friends for and pointers and references to as-yet undefined classes. You cannot include any statements that require the compiler to know the details of the definition of the forward referenced class. For example, you cannot declare an instance of the class or refer to any members of the class.

Explicit *friend* Forward Reference

You can eliminate the need for the forward reference by including the *class* keyword in the *friend* declaration.

Exercise 9.14 modifies the Exercise 9.13 program by using the *class* keyword.

Exercise 9.14 friend *classes, forward reference.*

```
#include <iostream>
using namespace std;

// -------- Julian date class
class Julian {
    int da, yr;
public:
    Julian(int d = 0, int y = 0)
        { da = d; yr = y;}
    void display() const
        {cout << endl << yr << '-' << da;}
    friend class Date;    // allows Date member functions to see
                          // Julian private members
};
// ------- date class
class Date {
    int mo, da, yr;
public:
    Date(int m, int d, int y) { mo = m; da = d; yr = y; }
    operator Julian() const;
};
```

Exercise 9.14 friend *classes, forward reference. (continued)*

```
// ---- member conversion function (Julian <- Date)
Date::operator Julian() const
{
    static int dys[] = {31,28,31,30,31,30,31,31,30,31,30,31};
    Julian jd(0, yr);
    for (int i = 0; i < mo-1; i++)
        jd.da += dys[i];
    jd.da += da;
    return jd;
}


int main()
{
    Date dt(11,17,89);
    Julian jd(dt);
    jd.display();
    return 0;
}
```

Friend Functions

Sometimes you do not want an entire class to be a friend of another class. Unless it is necessary to access data in such a broad way, you should not do so. What you need is a way to specify that only selected member functions of another class may read and write the data members of the current class. In these cases, you may specify that a particular function rather than an entire class is a friend of a class.

Exercise 9.15 restricts the access to the data members of the *Julian* class to only the member function of the *Date* class that needs it.

Exercise 9.15 friend *functions in a class.*

```cpp
#include <iostream>
using namespace std;

class Julian;
// ------- date class
class Date {
    int mo, da, yr;
public:
    Date(const Julian&);  // conversion constructor
    void display() const
        {cout << endl << mo << '/' << da << '/' << yr;}
};
// -------- Julian date class
class Julian {
    int da, yr;
public:
    Julian(int d = 0, int y = 0)
        { da = d; yr = y; }
    friend Date::Date(const Julian&); // friend conversion function
};
// ---- conversion constructor (Date <- Julian)
Date::Date(const Julian& jd)
{
    static int dys[] = {31,28,31,30,31,30,31,31,30,31,30,31};
    yr = jd.yr;
    da = jd.da;
    for (mo = 0; mo < 11; mo++)
        if (da > dys[mo])
            da -= dys[mo];
        else
            break;
    mo++;
}
```

Exercise 9.15 friend *functions in a class. (continued)*

```
int main()
{
    Date dt(Julian(123, 89));
    dt.display();
    return 0;
}
```

Anonymous Objects

Observe the instantiation of the *Date* object in the main function of Exercise 9.15. It uses notation that calls the *Julian* constructor to construct an anonymous (unnamed) *Julian* object to be used to construct the instantiated *Date* object. This is a common C++ idiom. The *Julian* object is not needed except as an initializer to construct the *Date* object, Therefore, the program does not need to instantiate a named object of type *Date*.

Nonmember Friend Functions

Sometimes the function that is to be a friend is not a member of another class at all. Such a function has the special privilege of reading and writing a class object's private data members, yet the function is not a member of any class. This feature is particularly useful when you're overloading operators, the subject of Chapter 10.

A common use of nonmember *friend* functions is to bridge classes. A function that is friend to two classes can have access to the private members of both. Suppose you have a *Time* class and a *Date* class and you want a function that displays both.

Exercise 9.16 shows how a *friend* function that has access to the private data members of both classes can bridge the two.

Exercise 9.16 Bridging classes with a friend *function.*

```
#include <iostream>
using namespace std;

class Time;
// ------- date class
class Date {
    int mo, da, yr;
public:
    Date(int m, int d, int y) { mo = m; da = d; yr = y;}
    friend void display(const Date&, const Time&); // bridge function
};
// ------- time class
class Time {
    int hr, min, sec;
public:
    Time(int h, int m, int s) { hr = h; min = m; sec = s;}
    friend void display(const Date&, const Time&); // bridge function
};
// -------- a bridge friend function
void display(const Date& dt, const Time& tm)
{
    cout << dt.mo << '/' << dt.da << '/' << dt.yr;
    cout << ' ';
    cout << tm.hr << ':' << tm.min << ':' << tm.sec;
}

int main()
{
    Date dt(2,16,97);
    Time tm(10,55,0);
    display(dt, tm);
    return 0;
}
```

USING DESTRUCTORS

Until now, the exercises in this chapter have not included destructor functions, because the classes in them have not required anything in the way of custom destruction.

To illustrate how destructors work, a new *Date* class includes a pointer to a string that contains the month spelled out. Exercise 9.17 shows the destructor function for the new *Date* class.

Exercise 9.17 Destructors.

```cpp
#include <iostream>
#include <cstring>
using namespace std;


// ------- date class
class Date {
    int mo, da, yr;
    char *month;
public:
    Date(int m = 0, int d = 0, int y = 0);
    ~Date();
    void display() const;
};
Date::Date(int m, int d, int y)
{
    static char *mos[] = {
        "January", "February", "March", "April", "May",
        "June", "July", "August", "September", "October",
        "November", "December"
    };
```

Exercise 9.17 Destructors. (continued)

```
    mo = m; da = d; yr = y;
    if (m != 0)   {
        month = new char[strlen(mos[m-1])+1];
        strcpy(month, mos[m-1]);
    }
    else
        month = 0;
}
// ---- destructor
Date::~Date()
{
    delete [] month;
}
// ----------- display member function
void Date::display() const
{
    if (month != 0)
        cout << month << ' ' << da << ", " << yr;
}


int main()
{
    Date birthday(6,24,1940);
    birthday.display();
    return 0;
}
```

The constructor function for the *Date* object uses the *new* operator to allocate dynamic memory for the string name of the month. Then the constructor copies the name from its internal array into the *Date* object's *month* character pointer.

The constructor could have simply copied the pointer from the constructor's array into the class, but the point of the exercise is to discuss destructors. If you had copied the pointer, the object would have had nothing that needed destroying.

The destructor function deletes the *month* pointer, and this is where you can get into trouble. As programmed, the exercise has no problems, but as designed, the *Date* class can cause trouble when used in an assignment. Suppose you added the following code to the *main* function in Exercise 9.17:

```
Date newday;
newday = birthday;
```

You would construct an empty *Date* variable named *newday* and then assign the contents of *birthday* to it. That looks reasonable, but when you consider what the destructor function does, you see the problem.

If you do not tell the compiler otherwise, it assumes that class assignment is implemented as a member-by-member copy. In this example, the *birthday* variable has *month*, a character pointer that was initialized by the constructor's use of the *new* operator. The destructor uses the *delete* operator to release the memory when *birthday* goes out of scope. But when that happens, *newday* goes out of scope, too, and the destructor also executes for it. The *month* pointer in *newday* is a copy of the *month* pointer in *birthday*. The constructor deletes the same pointer twice, giving unpredictable results, and that is a problem that you must deal with in class design.

Furthermore, suppose that *newday* is an external object and *birthday* is automatic. When *birthday* goes out of scope, it deletes the *month* pointer in the *newday* object.

Now suppose that you had two initialized *Date* variables and you assigned one to the other, as in the following example:

```
Date birthday(6,24,40);
Date newday(7,29,41);
newday = birthday;
```

The problem compounds itself. When the two variables go out of scope, the *month* value originally assigned in *birthday* is in *newday* as a result of the assignment. The *month* value that the constructor's *new* operation put into *newday* has been overwritten by the assignment. Not only does the *month* value in *birthday* get deleted twice, but also the one that was originally in *newday* never gets deleted.

OVERLOADED ASSIGNMENT OPERATORS

The solution to the problems just posed lies in recognizing when they occur and writing a special assignment operator function to deal with them. You can overload the assignment operator for assigning an object of a class to another object of the same class. It is with this technique that you solve the problem of assignment and destruction of free-store pointers in a class. (Chapter 10 discusses overloaded operators in further detail.)

In the technique you are about to learn, your class assignment function uses the *new* operator to get a different pointer from the heap. Then it takes the value pointed to in the assigning object and copies it into the area pointed to in the assigned object.

You declare an overloaded assignment function by using the following notation within the class definition:

```
void operator=(const Date&); // overloaded assignment operator
```

Later we'll modify this usage to permit compound assignments. For now, the overloaded assignment function returns *void*. The overloaded assignment operator function is a member function of the class, in this case the Date class. The function's name is always *operator=* , and its parameter is always a reference to an object of the same class. The parameter represents the object being assigned from. The overloaded operator function runs as a member function of the object being assigned to.

Exercise 9.18 is an example of how the overloaded assignment operator works.

Exercise 9.18 Class assignment.

```
#include <iostream>
#include <cstring>
using namespace std;


// ------- date class
class Date {
    int mo, da, yr;
    char *month;
public:
    Date(int m = 0, int d = 0, int y = 0);
    ~Date();
    void operator=(const Date&); // overloaded assignment operator
    void display() const;
};
Date::Date(int m, int d, int y)
{
    static char *mos[] = {
        "January", "February", "March", "April", "May",
        "June", "July", "August", "September", "October",
        "November", "December"
    };
    mo = m; da = d; yr = y;
    if (m != 0)  {
        month = new char[strlen(mos[m-1])+1];
        strcpy(month, mos[m-1]);
    }
    else
        month = 0;
}
Date::~Date()
{
    delete [] month;
}
```

Exercise 9.18 Class assignment. (continued)

```
// ---------- display member function
void Date::display() const
{
    if (month != 0)
        cout << month << ' ' << da << ", " << yr << endl;
}
// ---------- overloaded Date assignment
void Date::operator=(const Date& dt)
{
    if (this != &dt)  {
        mo = dt.mo;
        da = dt.da;
        yr = dt.yr;
        delete [] month;
        if (dt.month != 0)    {
            month = new char [strlen(dt.month)+1];
            strcpy(month, dt.month);
        }
        else
            month = 0;
    }
}

int main()
{
    // ------ first date
    Date birthday(6,24,1940);
    birthday.display();
    // ------ second date
    Date newday(7,29,1941);
    newday.display();
    // ------ assign first to second
    newday = birthday;
    newday.display();
    return 0;
}
```

This exercise is just like Exercise 9.17 except that the overloaded assignment operator function is added to the *Date* class definition. The assignment function makes all necessary data member assignments and then uses the *delete* operator to return to the heap the string memory pointed to by the *month* pointer of the receiver—the object being assigned to. Then, if the sending object's *month* pointer has been initialized, the function uses *new* to allocate memory for the receiving object and copies the sending object's *month* string to the receiver. (If the sending object's *month* pointer has not been initialized, it means that the sender was never initialized.).

The first statement in the overloaded *Date* assignment operator compares the address of the sending object to the *this* pointer (discussed next). This operation protects against the occasion when a program assigns an object to itself.

N O T E

THE *this* POINTER

The *this* pointer is a special pointer that exists for a class while a nonstatic member function is executing. The *this* pointer is a pointer to an object of the type of the class, and it points to the object for which the member function is currently executing.

The *this* pointer is always named *this*. It is a hidden argument that is passed to every member function as if the member function were declared as shown in this example:

```
void Date::myFunction(Date* this);
```

The function declaration does not really contain the parameter when you write the code. I am showing it here to help you understand the underlying mechanism that supports the *this* pointer.

When your program calls a member function for an object, the compiler inserts the address of the object into the argument list for the function as if the function were declared as just shown and as if the function call looked like this example:

```
dt.myFunction(&dt);
```

Once again, you do not include the object's address as an argument when you write code that calls a member function. This example shows what the compiler generates as the hidden argument for the member function's hidden *this* pointer parameter.

N O T E

The *this* pointer does not exist in static member functions (see the discussion on static members later in this chapter).

When you call a member function for an object, the compiler assigns the address of the object to the *this* pointer and then calls the function. Therefore, every reference to any member from within a member function implicitly uses the *this* pointer. Both output statements in the following example are the same.

In this example, the second statement explicitly uses the pointer notation that the first statement uses implicitly:

```
void Date::month_display()
{
    cout << mo;        // these two statements
    cout << this->mo; // do the same thing
}
```

You can include the *this* pointer, as does the second statement in the function just shown. To do so, however, is redundant, beacuse the compiler provides the *this* pointer reference by default.

Returning *this

One use of the *this* pointer allows member functions to return the invoking object (or its address or a reference to it) to the caller. The overloaded assignment operator function in Exercise 9.18 returns nothing. With that function you would not be able to string assignments together in the C++ format as follows:

```
a = b = c;
```

Let's review some of what you learned in Chapter 2, in particular the discussion associated with Exercise 2.11. A compound assignment expression such as the one just shown works in C++ because every expression returns something—unless, of course, the expression is a call to a function returning *void*. The assignment can be expressed the following way:

```
b = c;
a = b;
```

Because the first statement is an expression that returns the value assigned, the two expressions can be combined as follows:

```
a = (b = c);
```

Because the rightmost assignment operator has higher precedence than the leftmost one, the parentheses are not required, and the preceding example is thus expressed in the following way:

```
a = b = c;
```

That concludes our review of Chapter 2.

To make your overloaded class assignments work in the same way that conventional, non-overloaded assignments do, you must make the assignment function return the result of the assignment, which happens to be the object being assigned to. This also happens to be what the *this* pointer points to while the overloaded assignment function is executing.

Exercise 9.19 modifies Exercise 9.18 by having the overloaded assignment function return a reference to a *Date*. The value returned is the object pointed to by the *this* pointer.

Exercise 9.19 The this *pointer.*

```
#include <iostream>
#include <cstring>
using namespace std;


// ------- date class
class Date {
    int mo, da, yr;
    char *month;
public:
    Date(int m = 0, int d = 0, int y = 0);
    ~Date();
    Date& operator=(const Date&); //overloaded assignment operator
    void display() const;
};
Date::Date(int m, int d, int y)
{
    static char *mos[] = {
        "January", "February", "March", "April", "May",
        "June", "July", "August", "September", "October",
        "November", "December"
    };
    mo = m; da = d; yr = y;
    if (m != 0)  {
        month = new char[strlen(mos[m-1])+1];
        strcpy(month, mos[m-1]);
    }
    else
        month = 0;
}
Date::~Date()
{
    delete [] month;
}
```

Exercise 9.19 The this *pointer. (continued)*

```
// ----------- display member function
void Date::display() const
{
    if (month != 0)
        cout << month << ' ' << da << ", " << yr << endl;
}
// ---------- overloaded Date assignment
Date& Date::operator=(const Date& dt)
{
    if (this != &dt)    {
        mo = dt.mo;
        da = dt.da;
        yr = dt.yr;
        delete [] month;
        if (dt.month != 0)    {
            month = new char [strlen(dt.month)+1];
            strcpy(month, dt.month);
        }
        else
            month = 0;
    }
    return *this;
}

int main()
{
    // ------ original date
    Date birthday(6,24,40);
    Date oldday, newday;
    // ------ assign first to second to third
    oldday = newday = birthday;
    birthday.display();
    oldday.display();
    newday.display();
    return 0;
}
```

This use of the *this* pointer is sometimes difficult to grasp, because it applies several C++ constructs that are unfamiliar to programmers of other languages, including C. Picture what is happening when you make the following assignment:

```
newday = birthday;
```

The assignment executes the overloaded assignment operator function for the *Date* class. That function has two parameters. The first parameter is implied. It is the address of the object for which the function is being called. In this case, the function is being called for the object on the left side of the assignment: the *newday* object. The second parameter is supplied as an argument and is the object on the right side of the assignment, in this case the *birthday* object. In the function, the *birthday* argument becomes the *dt* parameter. The first assignment statement in the function is as follows:

```
mo = dt.mo;
```

The preceding statement can also be read the following way:

```
this->mo = dt.mo;
```

The statement assigns the value in the *mo* data member of the *birthday* object to the *mo* data member of the *newday* object. The other assignments work the same way. When the function is finished, it returns a reference to what *this* points to: the *newday* object. Consequently, the overloaded assignment operator function, in addition to performing the assignment, returns a reference to the object that received the assignment, making possible the following statement:

```
oldday = newday = birthday;
```

By understanding this mechanism and the subject of operator overloading (as discussed in Chapter 10), you can see how the chained *cout* statements used in previous exercises work. In many of the exercises, you have been using statements similar to the following example:

```
cout << a << b << c;
```

Using *this* to Link Lists

The *this* pointer is convenient in applications in which a data structure uses self-referential members. An example is the simple linked list.

Exercise 9.20 builds a linked list from a class named *ListEntry*. The class supports a list entry that contains a name string.

Exercise 9.20 this *and the linked list.*

```cpp
#include <iostream>
#include <cstring>
using namespace std;


class ListEntry {
    char* listvalue;
    ListEntry* preventry;
public:
    ListEntry(char*);
    ~ListEntry()
        { delete [] listvalue; }
    ListEntry* PrevEntry() const
        { return preventry; };
    void display() const
        { cout << endl << listvalue; }
    // ---------- use the 'this' pointer to chain the list
    void AddEntry(ListEntry& le)
        { le.preventry = this; }
};


ListEntry::ListEntry(char* s)
{
    listvalue = new char[strlen(s)+1];
    strcpy(listvalue, s);
    preventry = 0;
}
```

Exercise 9.20 this *and the linked list. (continued)*

```
int main()
{
    ListEntry* prev = 0;
    // ---------- read in some names
    while (1)    {
        cout << endl << "Enter a name ('end' when done): ";
        char name[25];
        cin >> name;
        if (strncmp(name, "end", 3) == 0)
            break;
        // -------- make a list entry of the name
        ListEntry* list = new ListEntry(name);
        if (prev != 0)
            // -------- add the entry to the linked list
            prev->AddEntry(*list);
        prev = list;
    }
    // ------- display the names in reverse order
    while (prev != 0)    {
        prev->display();
        ListEntry* hold = prev;
        prev = prev->PrevEntry();
        // -------- delete the ListEntry
        delete hold;
    }
    return 0;
}
```

Exercise 9.20 displays prompting messages. You enter names until you are finished and then enter the word **end**. The program displays the names in the reverse order in which you entered them.

The class in Exercise 9.20 has a string value and a pointer to the previous entry in the list. The constructor function gets memory for the string from the heap, copies the string value to the memory, and sets the *preventry* pointer to null. The destructor deletes the string memory.

If you wanted to use this class in a broader scope to include assignments of objects of the class to one another, you would need to build an overloaded assignment operator like the one in Exercise 9.18.

A member function named *PrevEntry* returns the pointer to the previous entry in the list. Another member function displays the current entry.

The member function of concern here is *AddEntry*. It builds the list by putting the address of the current entry into the pointer of the next entry. It does this by copying the *this* pointer into the *preventry* pointer of the argument entry.

The *AddEntry* function makes no changes to the *ListEntry* object for which it is running; instead, it assigns the object's address to the *preventry* pointer of the *ListEntry* object referenced by the function's parameter. Furthermore, even though the function does not modify its own object, the function is not *const*. This is because it copies its object's address—the contents of the *this* pointer—to a non-const object. The compiler assumes that the non-const object might subsequently be permitted to modify the current object through the address that is being copied. Consequently, the *AddEntry* function should not be declared as *const*.

The *main* function of the program prompts you to enter some names at the console. After the last name, you enter the word **end**. Then the function navigates the list and displays the entries. Because the list pointers point from the current to the previous entry, the names display in the opposite order in which you entered them.

Observe the use of the *new* operator to allocate memory for the *ListEntry* object to which the list pointer points. Chapter 5 addressed *new* and *delete* but did not discuss those operators with respect to classes, because you had not learned about classes. A later section in this chapter discusses the heap as it pertains to objects of classes.

ARRAYS OF CLASS OBJECTS

Class objects are just like any other C++ data type in that you can declare pointers to them and arrays of them. The array notation is the same as that of an array of structures.

Exercise 9.21 shows an array of *Date* structures.

Exercise 9.21 *Arrays of classes.*

```
#include <iostream>
using namespace std;


// ------- date class
class Date {
    int mo, da, yr;
public:
    Date(int m = 0, int d = 0, int y = 0)
        { mo = m; da = d; yr = y;}
    void display() const
        { cout << mo << '/' << da << '/' <<yr << endl; }
};



int main()
{
    Date dates[2];
    Date temp(6,24,40);

    dates[0] = temp;
    dates[0].display();
    dates[1].display();
    return 0;
}
```

The constructor function in Exercise 9.21 uses default arguments to initialize the three data members to zero. This constructor serves as a default constructor as well as one that constructs a Date object from three integer arguments (or two, or one, depending on how many arguments you provide).

Class Object Arrays and the Default Constructor

Recall from earlier in this chapter that a constructor with no parameters or a constructor with default arguments for all its parameters is a default constructor. If you provide no constructors for a class, the compiler provides one public default constructor that does nothing. If you provide at least one constructor of any kind, the compiler provides no default constructor.

You cannot instantiate an array of objects of a class that has no default constructor. The notation for instantiating an array of class objects does not permit an initializer list that conforms to the format of constructor function arguments.

The *main* function in Exercise 9.21 declares an array of two *Dates* and a single date with initialized values. It assigns the initialized *Date* to the first of the two *Dates* in the array and then displays both dates. The first date in the array has a valid date value, and the second has all zeros.

When you declare an array of objects of a class, the compiler calls the default constructor function once for each element in the array. It is important that you understand this relationship when you design constructor functions.

Exercise 9.22 repeats Exercise 9.21, but it removes the default argument values and adds a default constructor with a display message to demonstrate that the default constructor gets called twice, once for each element in the array.

Exercise 9.22 *Constructors for arrays of classes.*

```
#include <iostream>
using namespace std;


// ------- date class
class Date {
    int mo, da, yr;
public:
    Date();
    Date(int m, int d, int y)
        { mo = m; da = d; yr = y;}
    void display() const
        { cout << mo << '/' << da << '/' << yr << endl; }
};
```

Exercise 9.22 Constructors for arrays of classes. (continued)

```
// constructor that is called for each element in a Date array
Date::Date()
{
    cout << "Date constructor running" << endl;
    mo = 0; da = 0; yr = 0;
}


int main()
{
    Date dates[2];
    Date temp(6,24,40);

    dates[0] = temp;
    dates[0].display();
    dates[1].display();
    return 0;
}
```

Exercise 9.22 displays the following messages:

```
Date constructor running
Date constructor running
6/24/40
0/0/0
```

As you can see, the default constructor function executes twice—once for each of the elements in the array. No message is displayed for the constructor of the *temp* object, because it uses the constructor function that accepts initializers, and that function has no message.

Class Object Arrays and Destructors

When an array of objects of a class goes out of scope, the compiler calls the destructor function once for each element of the array.

Exercise 9.23 illustrates how to call destructors for class array elements.

Exercise 9.23 Destructors for arrays of classes.

```
#include <iostream>
using namespace std;


// ------- date class
class Date {
    int mo, da, yr;
public:
    Date(int m = 0, int d = 0, int y = 0)
        { mo = m; da = d; yr = y;}
    ~Date()
        { cout << "Date destructor running" << endl; }
    void display() const
        { cout << mo << '/' << da << '/' << yr << endl; }
};


int main()
{
    Date dates[2];
    Date temp(6,24,40);


    dates[0] = temp;
    dates[0].display();
    dates[1].display();
    return 0;
}
```

Exercise 9.23 has a Date destructor function that does nothing except display
its execution on the console to prove that it runs more than once for an array

of objects. The following display shows that the destructor runs three times—twice for the two elements in the *dates* array and once for the *temp* object:

```
6/24/40
0/0/0
Date destructor running
Date destructor running
Date destructor running
```

STATIC MEMBERS

You can declare that a member of a class is *static*, in which case only one instance of it exists. It is accessible to all the member functions. No instance of the class needs to be declared for the static members to exist, although a static member that is not public cannot be accessed by the rest of the program.

The declaration of a static member in a class does not, however, automatically define the variable. You must define it outside the class definition for it to exist.

Static Data Members

You would use a static data member to maintain a global value that applies to all instances of the class. Member functions can access and modify this value. If the static member is public, all code in the scope of the class declaration, inside and outside of the class, can access the member. As an example, consider the simple linked list used in Exercise 9.20. The class merely defined the list entries. It was up to the using program to keep track of the end of the list.

Exercise 9.24 improves the linked-list example in Exercise 9.20 with static data members that hold the address of the list's first and last entries—the list head.

Exercise 9.24 *Static members and the linked list.*

```cpp
#include <iostream>
#include <cstring>
using namespace std;


class ListEntry {
public:
    static ListEntry* firstentry; // static list head pointer
private:
    static ListEntry* lastentry;  // static list head pointer
    char* listvalue;
    ListEntry* nextentry;
public:
    ListEntry(char*);
    ~ListEntry()
        { delete [] listvalue;}
    ListEntry* NextEntry() const
        { return nextentry; };
    void display() const
        { cout << listvalue << endl; }
};


ListEntry* ListEntry::firstentry; // static list head pointer
ListEntry* ListEntry::lastentry;  // static list head pointer


ListEntry::ListEntry(char* s)
{
    if (firstentry == 0)
        firstentry = this;
    if (lastentry != 0)
        lastentry->nextentry = this;
    lastentry = this;
    listvalue = new char[strlen(s)+1];
    strcpy(listvalue, s);
    nextentry = 0;
}
```

Exercise 9.24 *Static members and the linked list. (continued)*

```
int main()
{
    // ---------- read in some names
    while (1)    {
        cout << "\nEnter a name ('end' when done): ";
        char name[25];
        cin >> name;
        if (strncmp(name, "end", 3) == 0)
            break;
        // -------- make a list entry of the name
        new ListEntry(name);
    }
    ListEntry* next = ListEntry::firstentry;
    // ------- display the names
    while (next != 0)    {
        next->display();
        ListEntry* hold = next;
        next = next->NextEntry();
        // -------- delete the ListEntry
        delete hold;
    }
    return 0;
}
```

Exercise 9.24 displays prompting messages. You enter names until you are finished and then enter **end**. The program displays the names in the order in which you entered them.

This exercise represents an improved linked-list class. By using static data members to keep a record of the beginning and end of the list, the class assumes all the responsibility for list integrity.

The constructor function for a list entry adds the entry to the list, so there is no need for the *AddEntry* function of Exercise 9.20. Exercise 9.24 uses the *new* operator to declare a new entry, but it does not assign to a pointer the address returned by the *new* operator. The constructor function records the address of the entry in the *nextentry* pointer of the previous entry, and the program does not need to otherwise remember the address.

Finally, the linked-list class defined in Exercise 9.24 allows the program to retrieve the entries in the same order in which they were added. After you enter all the names and type **end**, the program displays those names in their original order rather than in reverse order as did earlier versions of this program.

Exercises 9.20 and 9.24 do not represent the best way in C++ to implement a linked-list data structure. For one thing, the *ListEntry* class supports only character strings. If you wanted a linked list of integers, for example, you would have to implement a separate class. Chapter 13 discusses the C++ template, which provides a more generic mechanism for creating container classes. Chapter 16 discusses the Standard Template Library, which provides several generic container classes, including a linked list, ready for you to use.

For the *main* function in Exercise 9.24 to retrieve the *ListEntry::firstentry* value to begin iterating the list, we had to make *ListEntry::firstentry* a public data member, a practice that violates our object-oriented guidelines for keeping data members private. We'll deal with that situation next.

Static Member Functions

Member functions can be static. You can use static member functions to perform tasks in the name of the class or an object when the function does not need access to the members of any particular instance of the class. Usually you use a static member function when you need to access only the static data members of a class.

Static member functions have no *this* pointer. Inasmuch as they have no access to the nonstatic members, they cannot use the *this* pointer to point to anything.

Exercise 9.25 adds a *FirstEntry* static member function to the *ListEntry* class to retrieve the address of the first entry added to the list from the *lastentry* data member, which is now declared private, as it should be.

Exercise 9.25 *Static member functions.*

```
#include <iostream>
#include <cstring>
using namespace std;


class ListEntry {
    static ListEntry* firstentry; // static list head pointer
    static ListEntry* lastentry;  // static list head pointer
    char* listvalue;
    ListEntry* nextentry;
public:
    ListEntry(char*);
    ~ListEntry()
        { delete [] listvalue;}
    static ListEntry* FirstEntry() // static member function
        { return firstentry; }
    ListEntry* NextEntry() const
        { return nextentry; };
    void display() const
        { cout << listvalue << endl; }
};


ListEntry* ListEntry::firstentry; // static list head pointer
ListEntry* ListEntry::lastentry;  // static list head pointer


ListEntry::ListEntry(char* s)
{
    if (firstentry == 0)
        firstentry = this;
    if (lastentry != 0)
        lastentry->nextentry = this;
    lastentry = this;
    listvalue = new char[strlen(s)+1];
    strcpy(listvalue, s);
    nextentry = 0;
}
```

Exercise 9.25 *Static member functions. (continued)*

```
int main()
{

    // ---------- read in some names
    while (1)     {
        cout << "\nEnter a name ('end' when done): ";
        char name[25];
        cin >> name;
        if (strncmp(name, "end", 3) == 0)
            break;
        // -------- make a list entry of the name
        new ListEntry(name);
    }
    ListEntry* next = ListEntry::FirstEntry();
    // ------- display the names
    while (next != 0)     {
        next->display();
        ListEntry* hold = next;
        next = next->NextEntry();
        // -------- delete the ListEntry
        delete hold;
    }
    return 0;
}
```

Exercise 9.25 displays prompting messages. You enter names until you are finished and then enter **end**. The program displays the names in the order in which you entered them.

The *ListEntry::FirstEntry* function is static. It returns the value stored in the static *firstentry* data member.

Public Static Members

If a static member is public, as the one in Exercise 9.25 is, it is accessible to the entire program. You can call a public static member function from anywhere without associating it with a particular instance of the class. A public static member function is not quite global. It exists only within the scope of the class in which it is defined. You can, however, call it from anywhere within that scope by prefixing it with the class name and using the :: scope resolution operator.

CLASSES AND THE HEAP

In Chapter 5, you learned about the C++ heap and the *new* and *delete* memory management operators. This section discusses those operators and their special relationship to classes.

Constructors and *new;* Destructors and *delete*

You used *new* and *delete* in earlier exercises to get and release memory for class objects. When you use *new* to get memory for a class object, the compiler executes the *new* operator function first to allocate the memory and then calls the class's constructor function. When you use *delete* to return the memory, the compiler calls the class's destructor function and then calls the *delete* operator function.

The *new* and *delete* operator functions are usually provided by the compiler. They are the same functions that allocate and return memory for intrinsic type objects.

Exercise 9.26 demonstrates the relationships between *new* and the constructor functions and *delete* and the destructor function.

Exercise 9.26 new = *constructor,* delete = *destructor.*

```
#include <iostream>
using namespace std;


class Date    {
    int mo, da, yr;
public:
    Date()
        { cout << "Date constructor" << endl; }
    ~Date()
        { cout << "Date destructor" << endl; }
};


main()
{
    Date* dt = new Date;
    cout << "Process the date" << endl;
    delete dt;
}S
```

The exercise defines a *Date* class with a constructor and a destructor. These functions display messages that say they are running. When the *new* operator initializes the *dt* pointer, the constructor function executes. When the *delete* operator deletes the memory pointed to by the pointer, the operation calls the destructor function.

Exercise 9.26 displays messages to demonstrate the order in which the constructor and destructor functions are executed.

The Heap and Class Arrays

You learned earlier that constructor and destructor functions are called once for every element in an array of class objects.

Exercise 9.27 illustrates an incorrect way to delete arrays of new classes.

Exercise 9.27 Deleting arrays of new *classes.*

```
#include <iostream>
using namespace std;


class Date    {
    int mo, da, yr;
public:
    Date()
        { cout << "Date constructor" << endl; }
    ~Date()
        { cout << "Date destructor" << endl; }
};



main()
{

    Date* dt = new Date[5];
    cout << "Process the dates" << endl;
    delete dt;                    // Not enough deletes!

}
```

The *dt* pointer points to an array of five dates. The *Date* constructor function executes five times from the *new* operator, because that is what the array notation tells the compiler to do. But the compiler has no indication from the call to *delete* that the pointer points to more than one *Date* object, so it builds only one call to the destructor function.

Exercise 9.27 displays the following messages to demonstrate that the destructor executes only once:

```
Date constructor
Date constructor
Date constructor
Date constructor
Date constructor
Process the dates
Date destructor
```

To solve this problem, C++ allows you to tell the *delete* operator that the pointer being deleted points to an array. You do so by adding the [] subscript operator to the *delete* operator like this:

```
delete [] pointername;
```

Exercise 9.28 illustrates the correct use of the *delete* operator where an array is involved.

***Exercise 9.28** Correctly deleting arrays of new classes.*

```
#include <iostream>
using namespace std;


class Date    {
    int mo, da, yr;
public:
    Date()
        { cout << "Date constructor" << endl; }
    ~Date()
        { cout << "Date destructor" << endl; }
};

main()
{
    Date* dt = new Date[5];
    cout << "Process the dates" << endl;
    delete [] dt;;                    // deleting 5 items
}
```

Exercise 9.28 displays the following messages to demonstrate that the destructor is called once for each element in the array:

```
Date constructor
Date constructor
Date constructor
Date constructor
Date constructor
Process the dates
Date destructor
Date destructor
Date destructor
Date destructor
Date destructor
```

If you use the [] notation in the *delete* of an object that has no destructors, the compiler ignores the notation. However, by convention you should include the [] notation whenever you're deleting memory that was allocated for an array even when the objects being deleted are not class objects or do not have destructors. The programs in this chapter have been doing just that.

Overloaded Class *new* and *delete* Operators

Chapter 5 taught you how to manage dynamic memory by using the *new* and *delete* operator functions. Those examples used the global *new* and *delete* operators. You can overload global *new* and *delete*, but, unless you are involved in low-level systems or embedded programming, it is not usually a good idea. As always, there are exceptions to any guideline. This book neither teaches nor encourages overloading global *new* and *delete*.

You can, however, quite justifiably overload the *new* and *delete* operators from within the scope of a class declaration. This feature allows a class to have its own custom *new* and *delete* operators. You typically use this feature to gain a performance benefit from class-specific knowledge about the memory requirements of a class that can avoid the general-purpose overhead of the global *new* and *delete* operators. Global heap operations often rely on operating system functions to allocate and free memory. These operations can be inefficient, particularly in a program that frequently allocates and frees many small blocks of memory in tight iterations.

Suppose you know that there are never more than a certain small number of instances of a class at any one time. You can allocate the necessary memory for all instances of that class and use class-specific *new* and *delete* operators to manage the memory.

Exercise 9.29 illustrates a class with overloaded *new* and *delete* operators that are specific to the class.

Exercise 9.29 *Class-specific* new *and* delete *operators.*

```
#include <iostream>
#include <cstring>
#include <cstddef>
#include <stdexcept>
using namespace std;


const int maxnames = 5;
class Names   {
    char name[25];
    static char Names::pool[];
    static bool Names::inuse[maxnames];
public:
    Names(char* s)
        { strncpy(name, s, sizeof(name)); }
    void* operator new(size_t) throw(bad_alloc);
    void operator delete(void*) throw();
    void display() const
        { cout << name << endl; }
};
// -------- simple memory pool to handle fixed number of Names
char Names::pool[maxnames * sizeof(Names)];
bool Names::inuse[maxnames];
```

Exercise 9.29 Class-specific new *and* delete *operators. (continued)*

```cpp
// -------- overloaded new operator for the Names class
void* Names::operator new(size_t) throw(bad_alloc)
{
    for (int p = 0; p < maxnames; p++)  {
        if (!inuse[p])    {
            inuse[p] = true;
            return pool+p*sizeof(Names);
        }
    }
    throw bad_alloc();
}
// --------- overloaded delete operator for the Names class
void Names::operator delete(void* p) throw()
{
    if (p != 0)
        inuse[((char*)p - pool) / sizeof(Names)] = false;
}

int main()
{
    Names* nm[maxnames];
    int i;
    for (i = 0; i < maxnames; i++)     {
        cout << endl << "Enter name # " << i+1 << ": ";
        char name[25];
        cin >> name;
        nm[i] = new Names(name);
    }
    for (i = 0; i < maxnames; i++)     {
        nm[i]->display();
        delete nm[i];
    }
    return 0;
}
```

Exercise 9.29 prompts you for five names and then displays them. A class of *Names* is defined in Exercise 9.29. The constructor initializes the name value of an object of the class. The class defines its own *new* and *delete* operators. Because the program is guaranteed never to exceed *maxnames* names at one time, the programmer has decided to improve execution speed by overriding the default *new* and *delete* operators.

The simple memory pool that supports names is a *pool* character array with enough space to hold all the concurrent *Names* the program expects. The associated *inuse bool* array contains a true/false value for each *Name* to indicate whether an entry in the pool is in use.

The overloaded *new* operator finds an unused entry in the pool and returns its address. The overloaded *delete* operator marks the specified entry as unused.

Overloaded *new* and *delete* functions within a class definition are always static and have no *this* pointer associated with the object being created or deleted. This is because the compiler calls the *new* function before it calls the class's constructor function, and it calls the *delete* function after it calls the destructor.

The *new* function executes before the class's constructor function. The *new* function cannot access any of the class's members, because no memory exists for them until *new* allocates it and because the constructor function has not yet performed any other class-specific initializations. The *delete* operator executes after the destructor function. Consequently, the *delete* operator cannot have access to the class members.

Testing for Exceptions

The design in Exercise 9.29 lacks the bulletproofing that you would want to include in a real program. For example, the overloaded *delete* operator function does not test its parameter argument to ensure that it falls within the boundaries of the memory pool. If you are absolutely positive that your program never passes a bad pointer value to the *delete* operator, you can omit such validations in the interest of efficiency, particularly when efficiency is the motive for overloading the operators in the first place. You should consider, however, installing such tests for a debug version of your software, using the preprocessor's compile-time conditional statements (described in Chapter 7) to remove the tests from the production version of the program.

Overloaded *new* and *delete* Exceptions

Both overloaded operator functions in Exercise 9.29 use *exception handling*, a C++ feature that you have not yet learned. The *throw* expressions in the function declarations and headers and the throw statement at the bottom of the overloaded *new* operator function implement the standard exception handling mechanism for memory allocation. Do not worry about how it works just now. You will learn about exception handling in Chapter 14. For now, accept the fact that these operations are required. If you were to change Exercise 9.29 so that the program tried to allocate more *Names* buffers than the memory pool contains, the overloaded *new* operator function would throw that exception, and the program would terminate. Chapter 14 explains how you can catch and process such exceptions.

Overloaded Class *new[]* and *delete[]*

When a class design includes overloaded *new* and *delete* operators such as those in Exercise 29, the overloaded operator functions are not called for allocations of arrays of objects of the class. Suppose that the program in Exercise 9.29 included these statements:

```
Names *nms = new Names[10];
// ...
delete [] nms;
```

These statements would call the global *new* and *delete* operators rather than the overloaded ones. To overload the *new* and *delete* operators for array allocations, you must overload the *new[]* and *delete[]* operator functions, as Exercise 9.30 demonstrates.

Exercise 9.30 *Class-specific* new[] *and* delete[] *operators.*

```
#include <iostream>
#include <cstring>
#include <cstddef>
#include <stdexcept>
using namespace std;


const int maxnames = 5;
class Names    {
    char name[25];
    static char Names::pool[];
    static short int Names::inuse[maxnames];
public:
    Names(char* s = 0)
        { if (s) strncpy(name, s, sizeof(name)); }
    void* operator new[](size_t) throw(bad_alloc);
    void operator delete[](void*) throw();
    void display() const
        { cout << name << endl; }
};
// -------- simple memory pool to handle fixed number of Names
char Names::pool[maxnames * sizeof(Names)];
short int Names::inuse[maxnames];
// -------- overloaded new[] operator for the Names class
void* Names::operator new[](size_t size) throw(bad_alloc)
{
```

Exercise 9.30 Class-specific new[] *and* delete[] *operators. (continued)*

```
    int elements = size / sizeof(Names);
    for (int p = 0; p < maxnames; p++) {
        if (!inuse[p])    {
            int i;
            for (i = 0; i < elements && p+i < maxnames; i++)
                if (inuse[p+i])
                    break;
            if (i == elements && p+i < maxnames)  {
                for (i = 0; i < elements; i++)
                    inuse[p+i] = elements;
                return pool+p*sizeof(Names);
            }
        }
    }
    throw bad_alloc();
}
// --------- overloaded delete[] operator for the Names class
void Names::operator delete[](void* b) throw()
{
    if (b != 0)  {
        int p = ((char*)b - pool) / sizeof(Names);
        int elements = inuse[p];
        for (int i = 0; i < elements; i++)
            inuse[p + i] = 0;
    }
}
```

Exercise 9.30 Class-specific new[] *and* delete[] *operators. (continued)*

```
int main()
{
    Names* np = new Names[maxnames+1];
    int i;
    for (i = 0; i < maxnames; i++)    {
        cout << endl << "Enter name # " << i+1 << ": ";
        char name[25];
        cin >> name;
        *(np + i) = name;
    }
    for (i = 0; i < maxnames; i++)
        (np + i)->display();
    delete [] np;
    return 0;
}
```

When you overload *new[]* and *delete[]*, you have more things to worry about than you do for overloaded *new* and *delete*. Inasmuch as the *new* operator is allocating memory for an array, it needs a way to remember the size of the array so that the overloaded *delete* operator can return the proper number of buffers to the pool. In this simple example, we replace the *bool* array that flagged buffers in use, substituting an array of integers. Into each element of the array, the *new* operator puts the number of buffers allocated instead of a simple true value. Then, when the *delete* operator function is asked to return buffers to the pool, the function uses the value in the array to determine how many buffers to return. This technique is extremely simple and serves to support the small example program in Exercise 9.30. A more complex buffer requirement might demand a more complex solution.

COPY CONSTRUCTORS

A *copy constructor* is a constructor that executes in these cases: when you initialize a new object of the class with an existing object of the same class, when you pass a copy of an object of the class by value as an argument to a function, and when you return an object of the class by value. The copy constructor is similar to the conversion constructor function that you learned about earlier in this chapter. Conversion constructors convert the values in one class object to the format of an object of a different class. Copy constructors initialize the values from an existing object of a class to a new, instantiated object of that same class.

Earlier in this chapter you learned how to overload the assignment operator (=) to manage the assignment of an object of a class to another object of the same class when the default assignment provided by the compiler would cause problems. Similar problems occur when you initialize an object with the contents of another object, so you must have copy constructor functions.

How does initialization of an object with another object differ from assignment of one object to another? Assignment assigns the value of an existing object to another existing object; initialization creates a new object and initializes it with the contents of the existing object. The compiler can distinguish between the two by using your overloaded assignment operator for assignments and your copy constructor for initializations.

Initializing an object with the contents of another object of the same class requires the use of a copy constructor function, which is a constructor that can be called with a single argument of an object of the same class as the object being constructed.

A copy constructor is always declared as taking a reference to the object being copied from. By convention, that parameter is *const*.

If you do not provide a copy constructor, the compiler always provides one by default. The default copy constructor performs a simple member-by-member copy of the class's data members.

Exercise 9.31 demonstrates the copy constructor.

Exercise 9.31 copy constructor.

```
#include <iostream>
#include <cstring>
using namespace std;


// ------- date class
class Date {
    int mo, da, yr;
    char* month;
```

Exercise 9.31 copy constructor. (continued)

```
public:
    Date(int m = 0, int d = 0, int y = 0);
    Date(const Date&);  // copy constructor
    ~Date();
    void display() const;
};


Date::Date(int m, int d, int y)
{
    static char* mos[] = {
        "January", "February", "March", "April", "May",
        "June", "July", "August", "September", "October",
        "November", "December"
    };
    mo = m; da = d; yr = y;
    if (m != 0)  {
        month = new char[strlen(mos[m-1])+1];
        strcpy(month, mos[m-1]);
    }
    else
        month = 0;
}
// ---------- Date copy constructor
Date::Date(const Date& dt)
{
    mo = dt.mo;
    da = dt.da;
    yr = dt.yr;
    if (dt.month != 0)  {
        month = new char [strlen(dt.month)+1];
        strcpy(month, dt.month);
    }
    else
        month = 0;
}
```

Exercise 9.31 copy constructor. (continued)

```
// Destructor for a Date
Date::~Date()
{
    delete [] month;
}
// ---------- display member function
void Date::display() const
{
    if (month != 0)
        cout << month << ' ' << da << ", " << yr << endl;
}
int main()
{
    // ------ first date
    Date birthday(6,24,1940);
    birthday.display();
    // ------ second date
    Date newday = birthday;
    newday.display();
    // ------ third date
    Date lastday(birthday);
    lastday.display();
    return 0;
}
```

The copy constructor in this exercise resembles the overloaded assignment operator in Exercise 9.18. The difference is that the copy constructor function executes when you declare a new *Date* object that is to be initialized with the contents of an existing *Date* object. The exercise shows that there are two ways to do this. One way uses the usual C++ variable initializer syntax:

```
Date newday = birthday;
```

The second way uses the constructor calling convention, in which the initializing object is an argument to the function's parameter:

```
Date lastday(birthday);
```

REFERENCES IN CLASSES

Chapter 5 taught you about references. Everything that you learned about using references with the standard C++ data types and structures applies equally to objects of classes. Using references to class objects as function parameters and return values adds a measure of efficiency that would not exist if you had to pass every object by value.

You can also declare references as class data members, but there are some things to consider. First, remember that a reference must be initialized. You do not usually initialize a class object with a brace-surrounded initialization list as you do a structure; instead, you initialize it with a constructor. Therefore, class member references must be initialized by the class constructor. Remember, too, that references are aliases. References in classes behave just as if they were data members of the class with the same notational syntax, but operations on member references actually operate on the objects that are used to initialize them. Exercise 9.32 shows the use of a class that has reference data members.

Exercise 9.32 *A class with a reference.*

```
#include <iostream>
using namespace std;


class Date  {
    int da, mo, yr;
public:
    Date(int d,int m,int y)
        { da = d; mo = m; yr = y; }
    void Display() const
        { cout << da << '/' << mo << '/' << yr; }
};
```

Exercise 9.32 A class with a reference. (continued)

```
class Time  {
    int hr, min, sec;
public:
    Time(int h, int m, int s)
        { hr = h; min = m; sec = s; }
    void Display() const
        { cout << hr << ':' << min << ':' << sec; }
};


class DateTime {
    const Date& dt;        // reference to Date
    const Time& tm;        // reference to Time
public:
    // --- constructor with reference initializers
    DateTime(const Date& d, const Time& t) : dt(d), tm(t)
        { /* empty */ }
    void Display() const
        { dt.Display(); cout << ' '; tm.Display(); }
};


int main()
{
    Date today(25,3,93);
    Time now(4,15,0);
    DateTime dtm(today, now);
    dtm.Display();
    return 0;
}
```

Observe the *DateTime* constructor specification. The colon operator specifies that a list of initializers—the *parameter initialization list*—follows. You must initialize reference data members in this manner. You cannot wait and do it in the body of the constructor. If the constructor is not *inline*, as this one is, you put the colon and initializer list in the constructor's definition rather than in its prototype in the class declaration like this:

```
class DateTime {
    const Date& dt;        // reference to Date
    const Time& tm;        // reference to Time
public:
    DateTime(const Date& d, const Time& t);
};
DateTime::DateTime(const Date& d, const Time& t) : dt(d), tm(t)
{
    // ... empty
}
```

You can use the constructor's parameter initialization list to initialize any data member. You should use it to initialize any *const* data members; as with references, you cannot assign values to *const* data members from within the constructor's statement body. (It is possible to cast away *constness*—a word coined by the C++ community for just this occasion—a subject that Chapter 15 addresses.)

NOTE You cannot write a complete overloaded assignment operator function for a class that has reference data members, because you cannot modify the value of a reference once it has been instantiated and initialized.

CONSTRUCTOR PARAMETER INITIALIZATION LISTS

You must use the constructor's parameter initialization list to initialize any class object data member that does not have a default constructor. Otherwise, the compiler would not know how to initialize the empty object awaiting assignment from within the constructor.

Some programmers use the parameter initialization list to initialize all class object data members. Consider this code:

```
class Date {
    int mo, da, yr;
public:
    Date(int m = 0, int d = 0, int y = 0);
};
class Employee {
    int empno;
    Date datehired;
public:
    Employee(int en, Date& dh);
};
```

The *Employee* constructor could be coded either of the following ways:

```
// --- Employee constructor, version 1
Employee ::Employee(int en, Date& dh)
{
    empno = en;
    datehired = dh;
}

// --- Employee constructor, version 2
Employee ::Employee(int en, Date& dh) : empno(en),datehired(dh)
{
}
```

The first version of the *Employee* constructor uses two logical steps to construct and initialize the *datehired* data member. The second version uses only a construction step specified in the member initialization list. Depending on the complexity of the *Date* object's default constructor, the difference between the two versions could be significant.

A Brief Essay on *const*

If you declare an object as *const*, you cannot call any of the class's member functions (except the constructor and destructor, which are called implicitly by the compiler) that are not also *const*. Consider this code fragment:

```
class Date {
    int month, day, year;
public:
    Date(int m, d, y) : month(m), day(d), year(y)
        { }
    void display()
        { cout << month << '/' << day << '/' << year; }
};


int main()
{
    const Date dt(6, 24, 1940);
    dt.display();       // --- error!
}
```

The call to the *display* member function generates a compiler error message, because you are calling a non-*const* function for a *const* object. Even though the function does not actually change the data members of the object, the compiler has no way of knowing that, and it generates the error.

Why, you might ask, does the compiler not look at the code in the body of the *display* function and figure out for itself that the function makes no changes? The answer is that the compiler is looking only at the function's declaration and not at its implementation. The implementation could, in fact, be elsewhere in the program, in another source-code file perhaps, and out of view of the compiler. The following example shows three separate source-code files:

```
// ----- date.h
class Date {
    int month, day, year;
public:
    Date(int m, d, y);
    void display();
};

// ----- date.cpp
#include <iostream>
using namespace std;
#include "date.h"

Date::Date(int m, d, y) : month(m), day(d), year(y)
{
}
void Date::display()
{
    cout << month << '/' << day << '/' << year;
}

// ----- program.cpp
#include <iostream>
using namespace std;
#include "date.h"

int main()
{
    const Date dt(6, 24, 1940);
    dt.display();        // --- error!
}
```

The solution, as you learned earlier, is to make the *display* function *const*:

```
// ---- in date.h
    void display() const;


// ---- in date.cpp
void Date::display() const
{
    cout << month << '/' << day << '/' << year;
}
```

Another solution is to omit the *const* qualifier from the declaration of the *Date* object:

```
Date dt(6, 24, 1940);
```

This solution, however, has a cost. There are times when you want to declare a *const* object to ensure that your program does not change its value after it has been constructed and initialized. Sure, you can promise yourself that you'll never intentionally mess with the object, but these features are built into the C++ language to provide a measure of protection against mistakes. You might as well take advantage of them.

Here's another scenario:

```
void foobar(const Date& dt)
{
    // ...
    dt.display(); // error if Date::display is not const
}
```

The *foobar* function declares a *const* reference to a *Date* object, meaning that the function has no intentions of ever modifying the caller's copy of the argument. If the *Date::display* function is not *const*, the *foobar* function cannot call it, because the compiler senses the potential for *Date::display* to modify an object that *foobar* has promised not to modify.

Some compilers issue warning messages in these cases and compile the program nonetheless. Others issue error messages and refuse to compile the program until you correct the error.

NOTE

Now let's consider the situation in which a class object must modify a data member in all cases, whether or not the objects are *const*. With earlier versions of C++ you had to cast away the constness of an object, which Chapter 15 explains. The ANSI committee considered this situation and invented the *mutable* keyword.

MUTABLE DATA MEMBERS

Suppose that you want to keep a count of every time an object is reported, irrespective of its constness. The class includes an integer data member to record that count. A *const* member function may modify a data member only if the data member is declared with the *mutable* qualifer. Exercise 9.33 is an example of that idiom.

Exercise 9.33 mutable *data members.*

```
#include <iostream>
using namespace std;


class AValue {
    int val;
    mutable int rptct;  // number of times the object is reported
public:
    AValue(int v) : val(v), rptct(0) { }
    ~AValue()
        { cout << "Avalue: " << val
               << " was reported " << rptct << " times."; }
    void report() const;
};


void AValue::report() const
{
    rptct++;        // modify data member even though const
    cout << val << endl;
}
```

Exercise 9.33 mutable *data members. (continued)*

```
int main()
{
    const AValue aval(123);
    aval.report();
    aval.report();
    aval.report();
    return 0;
}
```

THE MANAGEMENT OF CLASS SOURCE AND OBJECT FILES

In most of the exercises to this point, each program has been a single, stand-alone source-code module. The entire program was contained in one source-code file that represented the exercise. In practice, you do not usually organize a C++ source program that way. You use the traditional C convention of having common definitions in header files, common executable code in separately compiled object libraries, and separately compiled source-code files for the code that supports your application.

Class Definitions in a Header

The convention for C++ header files resembles that of C. Put things in header files that do not reserve memory but that declare structures, classes, and externally declared items to the source modules that include header files. When a class uses the definitions of other classes, its include file includes those of the other classes. This arrangement opens the possibility for multiple or circular inclusions. You should use a code convention that prevents the errors that can occur if a source file is included twice or if source file A includes source file B, which includes source file C, which includes source file A.

If you have a class named *Date*, for example, you might put its definition in a header file named **date.h**. If you use the *#ifndef* preprocessor directive shown in the following listing, you can prevent those cases in which a header file might be included more than once or header file inclusion wraps around:

```
#ifndef DATE_H
#define DATE_H
// --- the contents of date.h
#endif
```

Class Member Functions in a Library

As a rule, you should separately compile the member functions of your classes and maintain them as separate object files, perhaps in object library files. The source files for the member functions include the header files that define the classes to which the functions belong, as well as those for any classes that they may use and that might not be included from within the class header.

SUMMARY

This chapter taught you about C++ classes. Chapter 10 is about overloaded operators, a feature touched on in this chapter. In this chapter you learned how to overload the *new* and *delete* operators within a class definition. You also learned how to overload the assignment operator to build conversion functions and to manage class copying when member-by-member copy would not work.

The potential for overloaded operators extends beyond the uses you've learned so far. With them you can perform arithmetic, comparisons, and many other operations on your classes as if they were standard C++ data types. Chapter 10 describes these features.

CHAPTER 10

Overloaded Operators

This chapter is about extending the C++ language by adding operators to user-defined data types—classes. You learned in Chapters 8 and 9 how to add dates and other such types by binding data structures and functions. Now you will add to those classes the behavior of C++ operators.

C++ lets you build operators that implement unary and binary operations on objects of classes. This feature is called *operator overloading*, and with it you add member functions to the class to implement the overloaded operators.

In this chapter, you will learn how to overload:

- Arithmetic operators
- Relational operators
- Assignment operators
- Auto-increment and decrement operators
- Unary operators
- The subscript operator
- The pointer-to-member operator

TO OVERLOAD OR NOT TO OVERLOAD

A wise man named P.J. Plauger once observed that C++ programmers first learn to overload operators and then they learn not to. I'll reinterpret that wisdom and tell you that after you learn how to overload operators, you must then learn when to do it and how to do it appropriately.

Here are some guidelines to follow:

- Overload the assignment operator to assign objects of your types to one another.

- Overload the arithmetic operators for numerical types to give them arithmetic properties.

- Overload relational operators when objects of your class can be logically compared.

- When you overload arithmetic operators, bear in mind the commutative properties of arithmetic and logical operations. If, in your operator overloading scheme, A + B = C, then include overloaded operators so that B + A = C, C − B = A, and so on. Likewise, if B < A, then A > B, A != B, and so on. You'll more about this as we continue in this chapter.

- Overload the subscript bracket operators to retrieve elements from container classes.

- Overload the << insertion and >> extraction operators to allow you to read and write objects of your class from and to *iostreams*, the subject of Chapter 16.

- Overload the pointer-to-member -> operator to implement so-called smart pointers.

- On rare occasions, overload the *new* and *delete* operators as Chapter 9 discussed.

- Don't overload any other operators.

Any operator overloading outside those guidelines might seem natural and intuitive to you when you devise it, but it will probably seem abstruse to others when they first see it and will likely seem alien and, perhaps, contrived to you when you take another look at later. I strongly counsel you to view operator overloading with much skepticism and distrust. Anything that you can do with an overloaded operator, you can do just as well with a member function. C++ is an extensible language, but don't extend it beyond recognition.

You implement overloaded operators by writing special functions that the compiler calls when it sees matching operators associated with objects of types for which the operators are overloaded. You will learn about these functions in this chapter. But be warned. Nothing says that an overloaded binary addition operator function, for example, must perform addition. In one notable exception, the Standard C++ *string* class (Chapter 16) overloads the addition (+) operator to concatenate strings the way that Basic does, and that has nothing to do with addition. Everyone accepts that usage, because tradition has accustomed us to the idiom. But an overloaded operator function, being nothing more than a function, does whatever you code it to do. The compiler generates a call to the overloaded operator function when the program applies the operator in a context that fits the function's parameter types. You may have guessed by now that you could overload the addition operator to perform subtraction. Yes, you could, but it is not a wise thing to do.

A Case for Overloaded Operators

Consider a class that implements a numerical type. Let's articulate some requirements for the class:

- The program computes the sum of a column of objects of the type.
- The program increments, decrements, and adds and subtracts other numerical types to and from objects of the class.
- The program compares two of the objects to see whether they are equal or which is greater.

You could build class member functions to perform these operations and call them the way you call, for example, the standard C function *strcmp*. Or you can overload the arithmetic and relational operators to achieve the same effect.

In Chapter 9 you overloaded the *new* and *delete* operators to build custom memory management; you also overloaded the assignment operator for your classes. You have already used overloaded operators extensively in most of the exercises. Every time you display a value on the *cout* object, you use the << bitwise shift left operator, which is overloaded by the *ostream* class.

Overloading an operator means that you write a function to execute when your program uses the operator in prescribed ways with an object of your class. For example, you can do these operations with a *Date* class:

```
Date dt1(1,2,83);
Date dt2(2,4,93);
dt1 += 100;              // add 100 days
int dif = dt2-dt1;       // compute the delta
if (dt2 < dt1)           // compare two dates
    dt1 = dt2;           // assign dates
cout << dt1 << ' ' << dt2; // display the dates
```

Look at the last of the examples just shown. You will learn how to overload the << and >> operators in Chapters 11 and 16.

THE RULES OF OPERATOR OVERLOADING

Overloaded operators must obey some rules.

1. The overloaded operator must comply with the syntax of the language. For example, as you cannot do the following in C++:

    ```
    int a;
    / a;    // error: / is not a unary operator
    ```

    You therefore cannot overload the / operator to do the following:

    ```
    Date dt(1,2,83);
    / dt;    // error: / is not a unary operator
    ```

2. If you can put an operator between two identifiers, you can overload it for custom use with your classes even if the operator would not otherwise be acceptable to the compiler. Consider the following statement:

    ```
    cout << "Hello";
    ```

Without an overloaded << operator, that expression seems to shift *cout* a number of bits equal to the value of the pointer to the string, none of which would have passed the compiler's syntax check. But the statement is correct grammar—it is legitimate in some cases to have two identifiers separated by the << operator—so you can write an overloaded operator function that executes when this construct appears. The compiler sees the overloaded operator in the context of the two data types and associates the statement with the overloaded operator function.

3. You cannot overload the way an operator works with the intrinsic C++ data types. For example, you cannot overload the binary integer addition operator.

4. You cannot invent new operators that do not exist in the C++ language. For example, the dollar sign ($) is not a C++ operator, so it cannot be an overloaded operator.

5. You cannot overload these operators:

Operator	Definition
.	Class member operator
.*	Pointer-to-member operator
::	Scope resolution operator
?:	Conditional expression operator

6. You cannot change the precedence of operator evaluation.

BINARY ARITHMETIC OPERATORS

Consider a *Date* class such as the ones we used in Chapter 9. Suppose that you wanted to compute a new *Date* object by adding an integer number of days to an existing one. You could write a member function and call it as shown here:

```
newdate.AddToDate(100);
```

Rather than call a function to make the addition, you might prefer to use this more intuitive syntax:

```
newdate = newdate + 100;
```

Assuming that *newdate* is an object of type *Date* with a valid data value already assigned to it and assuming that you have correctly overloaded the binary addition operator (+) in this context, the result would be the *newdate* object of type *Date* with the effective month, day, and year incremented by 100 days.

CLASS MEMBER OPERATOR FUNCTIONS

To perform addition on objects of a class, you would write a class member function that overloads the binary addition (+) operator when it appears between a *Date* object and an integer. Here is how that function is declared in the class definition:

```
Date operator+(int) const;      // overloaded + operator
```

The function declaration says that the function returns an object of type *Date*, that the function's name is *operator+*, that it has one parameter of type *int*, and that the function is *const*. Whenever the compiler sees a function named *operator* suffixed by a real operator, the compiler treats that function as an overloaded operator function to be called when, in the case of binary operators such as the + operator, an expression has an object of the class type on the left side of the operator and an object of the parameter on the right. Consequently, the function just declared would be called in the following case:

```
Date dt(2,3,99);   // declare a date object
dt = dt + 100;     // invoke the overloaded operator
```

Incidentally, rather than have the compiler infer the overloaded operator function call from the context of an expression, you can explicitly call the overloaded operator function:

```
dt.operator+(100);
```

Exercise 10.1 overloads the binary addition operator to compute the sum of an integer and an object of the *Date* class, returning an object of the *Date* class.

Exercise 10.1 *Overloading the + operator.*

```
#include <iostream>
using namespace std;


class Date {
    int mo, da, yr;
    static int dys[];
public:
    Date(int m=0, int d=0, int y=0)
        { mo = m; da = d; yr = y; }
    void display() const
        { cout << mo << '/' << da << '/' << yr; }
    Date operator+(int) const;        // overloaded + operator
};


int Date::dys[]={31,28,31,30,31,30,31,31,30,31,30,31};
// -------- overloaded + operator
Date Date::operator+(int n) const
{
    Date dt = *this;
    n += dt.da;
    while (n > dys[dt.mo-1])    {
        n -= dys[dt.mo-1];
        if (++dt.mo == 13)    {
            dt.mo = 1;
            dt.yr++;
        }
    }
    dt.da = n;
    return dt;
}
```

Exercise 10.1 Overloading the + operator. (continued)

```
int main()
{
    Date olddate(2,20,1997);
    Date newdate;
    newdate = olddate + 21;     // three weeks hence
    newdate.display();
    return 0;
}
```

Here is how the overloaded operator function works. When the compiler sees the expression *olddate + 21*, it recognizes that *olddate* is an object of type *Date* and that the *Date* class includes an overloaded binary addition operator function. The compiler substitutes a call to the overloaded operator function with the integer value as the argument. You could code the substituted call yourself this way:

```
newdate = olddate.operator+(21);
```

The *operator+* part of the statement is the name of the member function. The 21 is the integer argument. Although you can call an overloaded operator function this way, these functions are meant to be used in the context of an expression that uses the operator, as in this statement:

```
newdate = olddate + 21;
```

Remember the discussion on the overloaded assignment operator in Chapter 9. If the *Date* class had an overloaded assignment operator function, the statement just shown would call it after calling the overloaded binary addition operator function to assign the result to *newdate*. Exercise 10.1 has no overloaded assignment operator, so the compiler creates a default one to make a copy of the original.

Observe that the overloaded binary addition operator function in Exercise 10.1 does not modify the *Date* object in the expression, and, therefore, the function can be declared *const*. The *olddate* object declared in the *main* function retains its value. This behavior mimics that of similar expressions with intrinsic numerical types. This is a valuable lesson. Strive to overload operators in intuitive ways.

NONMEMBER OPERATOR FUNCTIONS

Recall the guideline to overload operators to preserve the commutative properties of arithmetic operations. Exercise 10.1 provides for an expression permitting a *Date* object on the left side of the operator and an integer on the right. But suppose you also wanted to support the following expression:

```
Date newdate = 100 + olddate;
```

There is no way to design a class member overloaded operator function to support such an expression. Class member overloaded operator functions for binary operators always assume that the object for which the function is executing is on the left of the operator. You can, however, write a nonmember function to overload the operator with a different type on the left and a *Date* object on the right. Here is how you would declare such a function outside any class definition:

```
Date operator+(int n, Date& dt)
```

This declaration tells the compiler to call this function when it sees an expression involving an integer object to the left of the + operator and a *Date* object to the right.

Exercise 10.2 adds such a nonmember function to the program in Exercise 10.1 to overload the binary addition (+) operator.

Exercise 10.2 *Overloading + with a nonmember function.*

```
#include <iostream>
using namespace std;


class Date {
    int mo, da, yr;
    static int dys[];
public:
    Date(int m=0, int d=0, int y=0)
        { mo = m; da = d; yr = y; }
    void display() const
        { cout << mo << '/' << da << '/' << yr; }
    // ----- overloaded + operators
    Date operator+(int) const;
};

int Date::dys[]={31,28,31,30,31,30,31,31,30,31,30,31};
// -------- overloaded + operator: Date + int
Date Date::operator+(int n) const
{
    Date dt = *this;
    n += dt.da;
    while (n > dys[dt.mo-1])     {
        n -= dys[dt.mo-1];
        if (++dt.mo == 13)     {
            dt.mo = 1;
            dt.yr++;
        }
    }
    dt.da = n;
    return dt;
}
// ----- overloaded operator: int + Date
Date operator+(int n, Date& dt)
{
    return dt + n;
}
```

Exercise 10.2 Overloading + with a nonmember function. (continued)

```
int main()
{

    Date olddate(2,20,1997);
    Date newdate;
    newdate = 11 + olddate + 10;  // three weeks hence
    newdate.display();
    return 0;

}
```

The overloaded nonmember function in Exercise 10.2 uses the class's over-loaded *operator+* function to perform the addition. If the class did not have such a function, the overloaded nonmember operator function would have needed to access the class's private data members to compute the addition. The class would have had to declare the overloaded nonmember *operator+* function to be a friend, as shown here:

```
class Date {
    friend Date operator+(int n, Date& );
    // ...
};
```

Overloaded operator functions such as the one in Exercise 10.2 have both parameters declared. The function is not a member of a class. Because it does not execute as a class member function, there is no implied object.

N O T E

You could also have written the first overloaded binary addition function as a *friend* function. Some programmers overload all their class operators as *friend* functions by convention.

Observe that the expression in the program now uses two integer constants to compute the result. The effective expression is *(11+olddate)+10.* The first part uses the overloaded nonmember function, and the second part uses the over-loaded member function. Using these two overloaded functions you can write an expression that consists of a *Date* object and any number of integer expres-sions and compute the effective new *Date* object. You could not add two dates, because there is no overloaded operator function that permits that usage. The result would not be meaningful anyway. You could, however, use overloaded subtraction to compute the number of days between two dates, remembering the commutative properties of addition and subtraction.

The examples just given deal with addition. You can use the same approaches to develop overloaded subtraction, multiplication, division, relational, modulus, Boolean, and shifting operator functions. Once again, nothing requires you to make those functions perform intuitively, and many C++ programs have wildly overloaded operators that only their creators can understand. If you must overload arithmetic and relational operators, always try to overload them so that they perform operations that resemble their use with intrinsic data types in the C++ language.

RELATIONAL OPERATORS

Suppose you want to compare dates. Perhaps you need to use an expression such as the following one:

```
if (newdate < olddate)
// ....
```

You can overload relational operators in the same way that you overloaded the addition operator.

Exercise 10.3 shows the *Date* class with overloaded operators that compare dates.

Exercise 10.3 Overloading relational operators.

```
#include <iostream>
using namespace std;

class Date {
    int mo, da, yr;
public:
    Date(int m=0, int d=0, int y=0)
        { mo = m; da = d; yr = y; }
    void display() const
        { cout << mo << '/' << da << '/' << yr; }
```

Exercise 10.3 *Overloading relational operators. (continued)*

```
    // ----- overloaded operators
    int operator==(Date& dt) const;
    int operator<(Date&) const;
};
// ----- overloaded equality operator
int Date::operator==(Date& dt) const
{
    return (this->mo == dt.mo &&
            this->da == dt.da &&
            this->yr == dt.yr);
}
// ----- overloaded less than operator
int Date::operator<(Date& dt) const
{
    if (this->yr == dt.yr)    {
        if (this->mo == dt.mo)
            return this->da < dt.da;
        return this->mo < dt.mo;
    }
    return this->yr < dt.yr;
}
int main()
{
    Date date1(12,7,1941),
         date2(2,22,1990),
         date3(12,7,1941);


    if (date1 < date2)    {
        date1.display();
        cout << " is less than ";
        date2.display();
    }
```

Exercise 10.3 Overloading relational operators. (continued)

```
    cout << '\n';
    if (date1 == date3)    {
        date1.display();
        cout << " is equal to ";
        date3.display();
    }
    return 0;
}
```

The *Date* class in Exercise 10.3 has two overloaded relational operators: the equal to (==) and the less than (<) operators. The *main* function declares three dates, compares them, and displays the following messages:

```
12/7/41 is less than 2/22/90
12/7/41 is equal to 12/7/41
```

You could easily build the other relational operators as variations on the two in the exercise. For example, the != (not equal) operator could be coded the following way:

```
int operator!=(Date& dt) { return !(*this == dt); }
```

MORE ASSIGNMENT OPERATORS

You learned how to overload the assignment operator (=) in the discussion on class assignment in Chapter 9. C++ has other assignment operators (+=, -=, <<=, >>=, |=, &=, ^=) in which the assignment includes an arithmetic, Boolean, or shift operation applied to the receiving field. You can overload these operators to work with your classes.

Exercise 10.4 adds the overloaded += operator to the *Date* class by using the overloaded + operator that the class already has.

Exercise 10.4 *Overloading the += operator.*

```
#include <iostream>
using namespace std;


class Date {
    int mo, da, yr;
    static int dys[];
public:
    Date(int m=0, int d=0, int y=0)
        { mo = m; da = d; yr = y; }
    void display() const
        { cout << mo << '/' << da << '/' << yr; }
    // --------- overloaded + operator
    Date operator+(int) const;
    // --------- overloaded += operator
    Date operator+=(int n)
        { *this = *this + n; return *this; }
};


int Date::dys[]={31,28,31,30,31,30,31,31,30,31,30,31};
// -------- overloaded + operator
Date Date::operator+(int n) const
{
    Date dt = *this;
    n += dt.da;
    while (n > dys[dt.mo-1])    {
        n -= dys[dt.mo-1];
        if (++dt.mo == 13)    {
            dt.mo = 1;
            dt.yr++;
        }
    }
    dt.da = n;
    return dt;
}
```

Exercise 10.4 Overloading the += operator. (continued)

```
int main()
{

    Date olddate(2,20,1997);
    olddate += 21;              // three weeks hence
    olddate.display();
    return 0;

}
```

Observe that the overloaded *operator+=* function in Exercise 10.4 is not *const*. It cannot be, because it modifies its own object.

AUTO-INCREMENT AND AUTO-DECREMENT

You can overload the auto-increment (++) and the auto-decrement (—) operators and specify whether these operators are prefix or postfix.

```
Date dt;
++dt;   // calls the overloaded prefix ++ operator
dt++;   // calls the overloaded postfix ++ operator
```

Exercise 10.5 adds the overloaded auto-increment (++) prefix and postfix operators to the *Date* class by using the overloaded binary addition operator that the class already has.

Exercise 10.5 Overloading the ++ operator.

```
#include <iostream>
using namespace std;


class Date {
    int mo, da, yr;
    static int dys[];
```

Exercise 10.5 *Overloading the ++ operator. (continued)*

```
public:
    Date(int m=0, int d=0, int y=0)
        { mo = m; da = d; yr = y; }
    void display() const
        { cout << '\n' << mo << '/' << da << '/' << yr;}
    Date operator+(int) const;        // overloaded +
    // --------- overloaded prefix ++ operator
    Date operator++()
        { *this = *this + 1; return *this; }
    // --------- overloaded postfix ++ operator
    Date operator++(int)
        { Date dt=*this; *this=*this+1; return dt; }
};


int Date::dys[]={31,28,31,30,31,30,31,31,30,31,30,31};
// -------- overloaded + operator
Date Date::operator+(int n) const
{
    Date dt = *this;
    n += dt.da;
    while (n > dys[dt.mo-1])     {
        n -= dys[dt.mo-1];
        if (++dt.mo == 13)     {
            dt.mo = 1;
            dt.yr++;
        }
    }
    dt.da = n;
    return dt;
}
```

Exercise 10.5 *Overloading the ++ operator. (continued)*

```
int main()
{
    Date olddate(2,20,1997);
    olddate++;
    olddate.display();
    ++olddate;
    olddate.display();
    return 0;
}
```

As the exercise shows, you can specify that the auto-increment and auto-decrement operators are prefix or postfix, as shown here:

```
Date operator++();      // prefix ++ operator
Date operator++(int);   // postfix ++ operator
```

The compiler will call the overloaded prefix operator function when it sees the prefix notation. The unnamed *int* parameter in the overloaded postfix operator function declaration tells the compiler to call this function for the postfix operator. Note that the compiler makes no further distinction except to call the correct function. The code in the functions is responsible for supporting prefix or postfix operations. In Exercise 10.5, the overloaded *operator++()* function increments the object and returns it. The overloaded *operator++(int)* function saves the value of the object before incrementing it and then returns the saved object.

UNARY PLUS AND MINUS OPERATORS

You can overload the unary plus and minus operators to work with a class. You declare the overloaded function with no parameters, telling the compiler to use the function when the plus or minus operator is used as a unary operator. The function declaration looks like this:

```
int operator-() const;
```

Suppose you have a class that describes an inventory quantity and you need to express that quantity with the plus and minus unary operators. Exercise 10.6 is an example of how overloading the unary minus operator might work.

Exercise 10.6 *Overloaded unary minus*

```cpp
#include <iostream>
#include <cstring>
using namespace std;


class ItemQty {
    int onhand;
    char desc[25];
public:
    ItemQty(int oh, char *d)
        { onhand = oh; strcpy(desc, d); }
    void display() const
        { cout << '\n' << desc << ": " << onhand; }
    // ---- overloaded unary - operator
    int operator-() const
        { return -onhand; }
};


int main()
{
    ItemQty item1(100, "crankshaft");
    ItemQty item2(-50, "driveshaft");
    item1.display();
    cout << '\n' << -item1;    // invoke the overloaded -
    item2.display();
    cout << '\n' << -item2;    // invoke the overloaded -
    return 0;
}
```

The exercise declares two *ItemQty* objects: one with a positive *onhand* value and one with a negative. It calls the *display* function to display the record contents and then uses the overloaded unary minus operator to display the quantity with the unary minus operator applied, as shown in the following display:

```
crankshaft: 100
-100
driveshaft: -50
50
```

SUBSCRIPT OPERATOR

Overloading the subscript ([]) operator is sometimes useful. You can use it to provide access to elements of list data structures. For example, a *String* class that stores a string value can overload the subscript operator to provide subscripted access to the character positions of the string value.

Exercise 10.7 overloads the [] operator in a small string class.

Exercise 10.7 Overloaded [] subscript operator.

```cpp
#include <iostream>
#include <cstring>
using namespace std;


class String    {
    char* sptr;
public:
    String(char* s = 0);
    ~String() { delete sptr; }
    void display()
        { cout << sptr << endl; }
    // --- overloaded [] operator
    char& operator[](int n)
        { return *(sptr + n); }
    const char& operator[](int n) const
```

Exercise 10.7 *Overloaded [] subscript operator. (continued)*

```
String::String(char* s)
{
    if (s)  {
        sptr = new char[strlen(s)+1];
        strcpy(sptr, s);
    }
    else
        sptr = 0;
}


int main()
{
    String string1("The Ides of March");
    string1.display();


    // --- change some string chars
    string1[4] = '1';
    string1[5] = '5';
    string1[6] = 't';
    string1[7] = 'h';
    string1.display();


    // --- change a substring
    strncpy(&string1[4], "21st", 4);
    string1.display();


    // -- const string, cannot be modified
    const String string2("Et tu, Brute?");
    for (int i = 0; i < 13; i++)
        cout << string2[i];
    return 0;
}
```

The exercise declares and displays a *String* object with a value. Then the program uses the *String* class's first overloaded [] operator function to change individual character values in the *String* object. Because the [] operator function returns a non-*const* reference to the character being subscripted, the program can use the expression on the left side of an assignment. With that notation, the program inserts the value *'15th'* one character at a time into the string. Then, by using the address of the returned character reference, the program uses *strncpy* to insert the value *'21st'* into the string.

You could use the same overloaded [] operator function to retrieve characters only if all *String* objects were not *const*. To support *const String* objects, the class adds a second overloaded [] operator function. The function returns a *const* reference to the subscripted character, and the function itself is declared *const*, so the program can use that function to retrieve characters from a *const String* object.

Overloaded [] subscript operator functions must be nonstatic member functions. Furthermore, you cannot implement them as *friend* functions as you can other operators.

POINTER-TO-MEMBER OPERATOR

The -> operator, when overloaded, is always a postfix unary operator with the class object (or reference to same) on its left. The overloaded operator function returns the address of an object of some class.

Although the overloaded -> operator is postfix unary, its use requires the name of a class member on the right side of the expression. That member must be a member of the class for which the overloaded operator returns an address.

You can overload the -> operator to ensure that a pointer to a class object always has a value—in other words, to create a smart pointer to an object. The pointer always guarantees that it points to something meaningful, and you avoid problems associated with dereferencing null and garbage pointers.

To illustrate the need for a smart pointer, consider the following program, which assumes the existence of the *Date* class from earlier exercises and, at the beginning of the program, a pointer to an object of the *Date* class.

```
main()
{
    Date *dp;              // date pointer with garbage in it
    Date dt(3,17,90);      // Date
    dp = &dt;              // put address of date in pointer
    dp->display();         // display date through the pointer
}
```

The program declares a *Date* object, puts its address in the pointer, and calls the *display* member function through the pointer. Nothing is wrong with that. However, if the programmer neglects to assign a valid address of a *Date* object to the pointer, the program crashes because the pointer points nowhere meaningful. Whatever gets executed by that function call is not likely to be a valid function.

Exercise 10.8 overloads the -> operator to add a so-called smart pointer to the program.

Exercise 10.8 Overloaded -> operator.

```
#include <iostream>
using namespace std;


class Date {
    int mo, da, yr;
public:
    Date(int m=0, int d=0, int y=0)
              { mo = m; da = d; yr = y; }
    void display()
        { cout << '\n' << mo << '/' << da << '/' << yr; }
};
```

Exercise 10.8 Overloaded -> operator. (continued)

```
// ----------- "smart" Date pointer
class DatePtr {
    Date* dp;
public:
    DatePtr(Date* d = 0) { dp = d; }
    Date* operator->()
    {
        static Date nulldate(0,0,0);
        if (dp == 0)                // if the pointer is null
            return &nulldate;       // return the dummy address
        return dp;                  // otherwise return the pointer
    }
};
int main()
{
    DatePtr dp;         // date pointer with nothing in it
    dp->display();      // use it to call display function
    Date dt(3,17,90);   // Date
    dp = &dt;           // put address of date in pointer
    dp->display();      // display date through the pointer
    return 0;
}
```

An object of the *DatePtr* class is a pointer that knows whether a value has ever been assigned to it. If the program tries to use the pointer without first assigning the address of a *Date* object to it, the pointer contains the address of a null *Date* instead of garbage. The *DatePtr* object always returns the address of a *Date* object or the address of the null *Date* , because the *DatePtr* conversion constructor function accepts no value that is not the address of a *Date* and substitutes zero if a *DatePtr* is constructed without a parameter. When the overloaded -> operator function sees that the *dp* pointer is 0, it returns the address of the null *Date* object rather than the value in the pointer.

Note that the overloaded -> pointer operator must be a nonstatic member function. You cannot implement it as a *friend* function in the manner of other operators.

The smart pointer in Exercise 10.8 is by no means complete. It should include overloaded +, -, ++, —, +=, and -= operators so that objects of the class can react to addition and subtraction just as real pointers do. It should include overloaded relational operators, too.

Summary

This chapter showed you how to overload C++ operators to work with your classes.

You can overload other operators that this chapter did not address. The function call () operator and the address-of & operator are two examples. The notation for overloading these operators is the same as for others. I did not include examples of them for two reasons. First, I do not think it is a good idea to overload these operators except in the most extreme circumstances. Second, I could not contrive believable examples of circumstances under which a programmer would want to overload these operators. There is one notable exception: The Standard Template Library (Chapter 16) overloads the function call operator to implement container call back function objects called *predicates*.

CHAPTER 11

Class Inheritance

Class inheritance is what you use to construct specialized classes from existing ones and to design and implement object-oriented class hierarchies. This chapter describes these processes by using classes and class hierarchies to demonstrate how inheritance works and how you will use it.

Many introductory C++ books explain C++'s behavior with respect to inheritance by using small problems and classes that few programmers are likely ever to see. This chapter leads you through the complex subject of inheritance by building classes that use inheritance to form specialized data abstractions. Then we use those classes in an object-oriented class hierarchy. Finally, we use inheritance to build an application within an application framework class library. You will learn about:

- Specialization of data abstractions
- Base and derived classes
- Object-oriented problem domain class hierarchies
- Abstract base classes

- Virtual functions
- Polymorphism
- Inheritance and application frameworks

INHERITANCE

Inheritance is one of the four identifying characteristics of an object-oriented design. The other three are abstraction, encapsulation, and polymorphism. Chapter 17 provides an overview of object-oriented design and programming. You learned about abstraction in Chapter 8. This chapter is about how the C++ language supports inheritance and polymorphism.

With inheritance, you derive a new class from an existing class. The class from which you derive is called the *base class*, and the class that you derive is called the *derived class*. The act of designing a derived class is sometimes called *subclassing*. Figure 11.1 shows the relationship between a base class and a derived class.

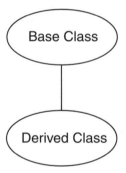

Figure 11.1 *Base and derived classes.*

Figure 11.1 shows the architecture of a simple, two-class design. In more complex designs, a base class has multiple derived classes, each of which can itself be the base of other derived classes, all of which forms a *class hierarchy*. With *multiple inheritance*, discussed in Chapter 12, a derived class can have more than one base class, each of which can have one or more base classes of its own. For now we'll keep it simple.

Figure 11.2 shows the C++ syntax for coding base and derived classes.

```
class Base {                      // the base class
    // ...
};
class Derived : public Base {    // the derived class
    // ...
};
```

Figure 11.2 *Base and derived class code syntax.*

As Figure 11.2 shows, a derived class names its base class in the class declaration header. The colon tells the compiler that a base class specification is next. The *public* keyword specifies which of the base class's members the derived class may access. More about that later.

A derived class inherits the characteristics of its base class, and that accounts for the term *inheritance*. The derived class automatically includes the data members and member functions of the base class. This means that a program can instantiate an object of the derived class and access the public members of the base class. The derived class can add its own data members and member functions, and it can override the member functions of the base. Adding and overriding members is the way you specialize the behavior of a base class to form a derived class. Figure 11.3 illustrates this concept.

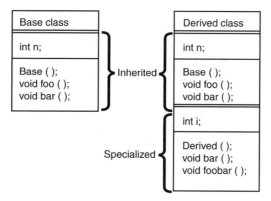

Figure 11.3 *Base and derived classes.*

The base class in Figure 11.3, which is named *Base* for this discussion, has one data member and three member functions. Those are the characteristics of the class, and a program can instantiate an object of type *Base* and call the *foo* and *bar* member functions. The derived class in Figure 11.3 is named *Derived*. It inherits all the members of the Base class, adds its own data member, adds a member function named *foobar*, and provides a specialization of the base class's *bar* function. As you soon learn, both *bar* functions are available to the program that uses this class. Figure 11.4 is an example of how these two classes might be declared.

```
class Base {                    // the base class
    int n:
public:
    Base();
    void foo();
    void bar();
};
class Derived : public Base {   // the derived class
    int i:
public:
    Derived();
    void bar();
    void foobar();
};
```

Figure 11.4 Base and derived class Declarations.

You have been dealing with potential base classes since Chapter 8. Any C++ structure or class that has public (or protected) constructors and destructors can have derived classes. The base class does not define its participation in an inheritance; the derived class does. The base class has nothing in it that tells it which classes, if any, inherit from it.

Do not be confused by my use of the names *Derived* and *Base* in these examples. They are not keywords or anything else tied to the C++ language. They are merely identifiers that I arbitrarily chose as the names of the two classes for the examples.

A derived class specifies the base class from which it inherits data members and behavior. The *public Base* notation following the semicolon in the *Derived* class declaration specifies that *Derived* is deriving itself from *Base*. (This association somewhat violates the inheritance metaphor. Outside object-oriented programming, heirs do not usually associate themselves with the estates of their benefactors.) But even though the derived class has the responsibility for declaring derivation, a class can include constructs that make it work better as a base class. Furthermore, some classes are designed to serve as base classes only.

Why Inheritance?

Why use inheritance to create a custom class based on an existing class? Why not just change the existing class, making it do what you want it to do? There are several reasons.

First, the base class might be used by other parts of your program and by other programs, and you want its original behavior to remain intact for those objects that already use it. By deriving a class from the base, you define a new data type that inherits all the characteristics of the base class without changing the base class's operation in the rest of the program and in other programs.

Second, the source code for the base class might not be available to you. To use a class, all you need are its class declaration in a header file and the object code for its member functions in a relocatable object file. If you are using class libraries from other sources, you might not have the source code for the member functions and thus could not change it.

Third—and this is a common reason—the base class might define a component in a class library that supports a wide community of users. Consequently, you must not modify the base class even if you could. One prominent example is the application framework class library, which this chapter addresses.

Fourth, the base class might be an *abstract base class*: one that is designed to be a base class only. A class hierarchy can contain general-purpose classes that do nothing on their own. Their purpose is to define the behavior of a generic data structure to which derived classes add implementation details.

Fifth, you might be building a class hierarchy to derive the benefits of the object-oriented approach. One of these benefits is the availability of general-purpose class methods that modify their own behavior based on the characteristics of the subclasses that use them. The class hierarchy approach supports this ability through the virtual function mechanism. You will learn about this technique later in the chapter.

There are two reasons to derive a class. One reason is that you want to specialize the behavior of an existing class. Specialization is the act of creating a new data type by leveraging the effort that went into the development of an earlier data type. The classes in Figure 11.4 show the mechanics of specialization.

The other reason for derivation is that you are building a well-organized, object-oriented class hierarchy in which custom data types that model the application's problem domain descend from a common base class. These two reasons are design approaches, but the class inheritance behavior of C++ that supports them is the same, with the same rules and boundaries. We'll look at both reasons in this chapter.

SPECIALIZED DATA ABSTRACTION CLASS DESIGN

Let's consider a realistic example of class specialization. Suppose your project uses a *Date* class similar to the ones that we used in the exercises of Chapters 9 and 10. This *Date* class has it all: the ability to display itself, a copy constructor, and overloaded operators to support assignment, arithmetic, and comparisons. But suppose that you need a *Date* class that displays itself in a different way. The boring old *Date* class that everyone else on the project uses displays itself in the boring old mm/dd/yyyy format. Your requirements are for a date class that has all the features of the project's *Date* class but that displays itself in the snazzy "Month dd, yyyy" format. You also want to be able to determine whether a date object has a null value as opposed to a valid date value, a feature that the current *Date* class does not support.

You could design a completely new class to support your new requirements, or you could use inheritance to take advantage of the fact that the existing *Date* class already does much of what you need. You could design a derived class that inherits the characteristics of the *Date* class and adds some specialized behavior of its own. Figure 11.5 illustrates the relationships between the *Date* base class and the *SpecialDate* specialized derived class.

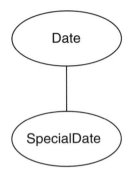

Figure 11.5 *Base and derived classes.*

In these figures, I use the vertical proximity of the two balloon symbols to represent the base and derived classes. The higher symbol is the base class. You cannot always do this in a complex class hierarchy design, particularly when you need to depict other relationships between classes that do not involve inheritance. Class designers often use arrowhead notations to show the direction of inheritance and use other symbols to represent other relationships.

The Base Class

Let's start by defining the *Date* class that, in our make-believe scenario, the entire programming staff uses. This design combines many of the components of the *Date* classes used in previous exercises.

Figure 11.6 is the source-code header file, **date.h**, that declares the *Date* class. This file is included along with the exercise source-code files for Chapter 11 on the accompanying CD-ROM and, if you installed the software, in the subdirectory for Chapter 11's source-code files.

Figure 11.6 Date.h.

```
#ifndef DATE_H
#define DATE_H

class Date  {
protected:
    static const int dys[];
    long int ndays; // days inclusive since Jan 1,1 (1/1/1 == 1)
public:
    // --- default and initializing constructor
    Date(int mo = 0, int da = 0, int yr = 0)
        { SetDate(mo, da, yr); }
    // --- copy constructor
    Date(const Date& dt)
        { *this = dt; }
    // --- destructor
    virtual ~Date() {}
    // --- overloaded assignment operator
    Date& operator=(const Date& dt)
        { ndays = dt.ndays; return *this; }
    // --- overloaded arithmetic operators
    Date  operator+(int n) const
        { Date dt(*this); dt += n; return dt; }
    Date  operator-(int n) const
        { Date dt(*this); dt -= n; return dt; }
    Date& operator+=(int n)
        { ndays += n; return *this; }
    Date& operator-=(int n)
        { ndays -= n; return *this; }
    Date& operator++()         // prefix
        { ++ndays; return *this; }
    Date  operator++(int)  // postfix
        { Date dt(*this); dt.ndays++; return dt; }
    Date& operator--()         // prefix
        { --ndays; return *this; }
```

Figure 11.6 Date.h. (continued)

```
Date  operator--(int)   // postfix
    { Date dt(*this); dt.ndays--; return dt; }
long int operator-(const Date& dt) const
    { return ndays-dt.ndays; }
// --- overloaded relational operators
bool operator==(const Date& dt) const
    { return ndays == dt.ndays; }
bool operator!=(const Date& dt) const
    { return ndays != dt.ndays; }
bool operator< (const Date& dt) const
    { return ndays <  dt.ndays; }
bool operator> (const Date& dt) const
    { return ndays >  dt.ndays; }
bool operator<=(const Date& dt) const
    { return ndays <= dt.ndays; }
bool operator>=(const Date& dt) const
    { return ndays >= dt.ndays; }
// --- getter and setter functions
void SetDate(int mo, int da, int yr);
void SetMonth(int mo)
    { *this = Date(mo, GetDay(), GetYear()); }
void SetDay(int da)
    { *this = Date(GetMonth(), da, GetYear()); }
void SetYear(int yr)
    { *this = Date(GetMonth(), GetDay(), yr); }
void GetDate(int& mo, int& da, int& yr) const;
int  GetMonth() const;
int  GetDay()   const;
int  GetYear() const;
// --- display method
virtual void Display() const;
// --- test for leap year
bool IsLeapYear(int yr) const
    { return ((yr % 4)==0 && (yr % 1000)!=0); }
bool IsLeapYear() const
    { return IsLeapYear(GetYear()); }
};
```

Figure 11.6 Date.h. *(continued)*

```
// ----- overloaded (int + Date)
inline Date operator+(int n, const Date& dt)
{
    return dt + n;
}

#endif
```

The implementation of the *Date* class defined in **date.h** includes constructs that support using the class as a base. The *protected* access specifier for both data members and the *virtual* qualifier on the destructor and *Display* member functions are all measures that class designers use to support subsequent derivation from a class. The designer of the *Date* class was not compelled to include these things merely to make *Date* objects work. The designer was, instead, looking ahead to the possibility that this class could someday become a base. You will learn about protected members and virtual functions later in this chapter.

Observe the two *IsLeapYear* member functions in Figure 11.6, **date.h**. One is a member function that determines whether the date object falls within a leap year. The other *IsLeapYear* function takes an integer year argument. There are occasions when member functions of the class (and, later, of derived classes) need to test to see whether a year's value is a leap year before the *Date* object is fully formed, such as during construction of the object.

Designing for Efficiency

The *Date* class's data representation uses a long integer value to store the number of days inclusive since January 1, AD 1, for the *Date* object. This implementation is designed for efficiency in a system in which programs perform a lot of date arithmetic and comparison. Observe that the overloaded operator functions are all inline and that they are relatively small. It is a trivial matter to add and subtract dates and integers when the date representation is itself a single integer datum.

This approach represents a conscious design decision. If the *Date* class were to be used instead in an application that mostly initialized and displayed the month, day, and year data values, you would probably design the class with separate integer data members for the three date components. That *Date* class would look more like those we used in earlier chapters.

The potential of this decision teaches an important lesson. If you decide to use the earlier *Date* class data representation—even if you decide to change it after many programs use the current design—the public interface to the class is the same. The calling conventions for such a *Date* class's member functions are no different from those of Figure 11.6's **date.h**. The differences, of course, are seen in private and protected data members and in member function code—the so-called hidden details of implementation.

Incidentally, the overloaded assignment operator function and the copy constructor function are unnecessary in the class as it is currently designed. The compiler-supplied default functions would do exactly the same thing. I include them here to remind myself that such functions might be necessary if someday I modify the data representation to include pointers to allocated memory resources. Inasmuch as I implemented them as inline functions, there is no performance penalty for defining them myself.

Figure 11.7 is **date.cpp**, the source-code file that implements the *Date* class's member functions that are not inline.

Figure 11.7 Date.cpp.

```
#include <iostream>
using namespace std;

#include "Date.h"

const int Date::dys[]={31,28,31,30,31,30,31,31,30,31,30,31};

void Date::SetDate(int mo, int da, int yr)
{
    if (mo < 1 || mo > 12 || yr < 1) {
        ndays = 0;  // invalid month or year or null date
        return;
    }
```

Figure 11.7 Date.cpp. (continued)

```
    // compute days thru last year
    ndays = (yr-1) * 365 + (yr-1) / 4 - (yr-1) / 1000;
    for (int i = 0; i < mo; i++) {
        int dy = dys[i];
        if (i == 1 && IsLeapYear(yr))
            dy++;              // make Feb's days 29 if leap year
        if (i < mo-1)         // add in all but this month's days
            ndays += dy;
        else if (da > dy) {
            ndays = 0;        // invalid day
            return;
        }
    }
    ndays += da;  // add in this month's days
}

void Date::GetDate(int& mo, int& da, int& yr) const
{
    da = ndays;
    if (ndays == 0) {
        yr = mo = 0;
        return;
    }
    for (yr = 1;; yr++) {
        int daysthisyear = IsLeapYear(yr) ? 366 : 365;
        if (da <= daysthisyear)
            break;
        da -= daysthisyear;
    }
```

Figure 11.7 Date.cpp. (continued)

```
    for (mo = 1; mo < 13; mo++)       {
        int dy = dys[mo-1];
        if (mo == 2 && IsLeapYear(yr))
            dy++;    // make Feb's days 29 if leap year
        if (da <= dy)
            break;
        da -= dy;
    }
}
int Date::GetMonth() const
{
    int mo, da, yr;
    GetDate(mo, da, yr);
    return mo;
}
int Date::GetDay()   const
{
    int mo, da, yr;
    GetDate(mo, da, yr);
    return da;
}
int Date::GetYear()    const
{
    int mo, da, yr;
    GetDate(mo, da, yr);
    return yr;
}
void Date::Display() const
{
    int mo, da, yr;
    GetDate(mo, da, yr);
    cout << mo << '/' << da << '/' << yr;
}
```

As you can see from Figure 11.7, the majority of the class's processing occurs when you construct a *Date* object from month, day, and year integers and when you extract those data values from the integer data representation of the *Date* class. Compare the details of the constructor and *Display* member functions to those of the *Date* classes in Chapters 9 and 10. This comparison reinforces the concept that you must consider all alternatives to class design by paying close attention to the requirements of the programs that use objects of the class.

Single Inheritance

The class hierarchy that we are using in this discussion represents a design that employs *single inheritance*, which means that all derived classes have no more than one base class. We'll address multiple inheritance in Chapter 12. For now, let's consider our derived class, the one that specializes the behavior of the base *Date* class.

The Derived Class

Figure 11.8 is **SpecialDate.h**, the header source-code file that declares the specialized *SpecialDate* class, which is derived from the *Date* class. There are several lessons to be learned from this derivation.

Figure 11.8 SpecialDate.h.

```
#ifndef SPECIALDATE_H
#define SPECIALDATE_H

#include "Date.h"

class SpecialDate : public Date  {
    static char* mos[];
public:
    SpecialDate(int da, int mo, int yr) : Date(mo, da, yr)
        { }
    virtual void Display() const;
    bool IsNullDate() const
        { return ndays == 0; }
};

#endif
```

Protected Members

Observe the *protected* access specifier that appears ahead of the *ndays* data member in **date.h,** Figure 11.6. You learned about public and private members in Chapter 9. Protected members are private to users of the class. If the program instantiated an object of type *Date*, the program could not access the protected *ndays* data member. In this respect, protected members are the same as private members.

If a base class has private members, those members are not accessible to the derived class. Protected members, however, are public to derived classes but, as I just explained, private to the rest of the program. Use of the *protected* keyword is one acknowledgment by the *Date* class in **date.h** that it might be used as a base class.

When you're designing a class, consider whether the class might someday be derived from—even if you have no such intentions at the start. Specify the *protected* keyword for members that could be accessible to derived classes.

Derived and Specialized Members

The *SpecialDate* class has one static data member of its own: the *mos* array of pointers. The class inherits two other data members from the *Date* class: the protected static *dys* array of integers and a long integer named *ndays*. If the *dys* array member were private to the *Date* class, the member functions of the *SpecialDate* class would not be able to read or write the array except through public member functions of the *Date* class. Inasmuch as no such accessing public member functions exist in this particular design, the *dys* array would be a hidden detail of implementation of the *Date* class, hidden even from derived classes. The *dys* array is protected, however, so that later exercises in derivation can use it. It is also *const* so that the values in the array cannot be changed after the array has been initialized.

The *Date* class's *ndays* data member, on the other hand, is protected, so member functions of the derived *SpecialDate* class can indeed read and write that data member.

Public and Private Base Classes

The *SpecialDate* class declares that it is publicly derived from the *Date* class. A derived class can specify that a base class is public or private by using the *public* or *private* access specifier in the definition of the derived class:

```
class SpecialDate : public Date  { /* ... */ };
class OtherDate : private Date { /* ... */ };
```

The *public* access specifier in this context means that the protected members of the base class are protected members of the derived class and that the public members of the base class are public members of the derived class. The *private* access specifier in this context means that the protected and public members of the base class are private members of the derived class. This distinction is important if the class hierarchy is ever extended with classes derived from the current derived class.

If you do not provide an access specifier, the compiler assumes that the access is private unless the base class is a *struct*, in which case the compiler assumes that the access is public.

Constructors in the Base and Derived Classes

When you declare an object of a derived class, the compiler executes the constructor function of the base class followed by the constructor function of the derived class.

The parameter list for the derived class's constructor function could be different from that of the base class's constructor function. Therefore, the constructor function for the derived class must tell the compiler which values to use as arguments to the constructor function for the base class.

The derived class's constructor function specifies the arguments to the base class's constructor function in **SpecialDate.h** by using a parameter initialization list for the base class:

```
SpecialDate(int da, int mo, int yr) : Date(mo, da, yr)
    { }
```

The colon (:) operator after the derived constructor's parameter list specifies that a parameter initialization list follows. You learned to use parameter initialization lists to initialize *const* and reference data members in Chapter 9. You use the same syntax to specify the arguments for a base class's constructor. The argument list is in parentheses and follows the name of the base class.

Unless the base class has a default constructor (one that expects no arguments), you must provide a base class parameter initialization list. It follows then that if the base class does not have a default constructor, the derived class must have a constructor if only to provide arguments for a base class constructor.

The arguments to the base class constructor function are expressions that may use constants, global variables, and the arguments from the parameter list of the derived class's constructor function. The base class arguments can be any valid C++ expressions that match the types of the base constructor's parameters. In the *SpecialDate* example, the constructor passes its own arguments to the *Date* constructor, changing their order according to the following requirements: The designer of the *SpecialDate* class has decided that date class users prefer to express date values in the day, month, year order rather than the month, day, year order that the *Date* class mandates. Consequently, the *SpecialDate* constructor function declares those parameters in a different order from those of the *Date* class and reorders them in the parameter initialization list for the *Date* class constructor.

When a base class has more than one constructor function, the compiler decides which one to call based on the types of the arguments in the derived class constructor's parameter initialization list for the base constructor.

Specializing with New Member Functions

Class specialization through inheritance often includes the addition of member functions to the derived class that the base class does not have. The *SpecialDate* class in this example includes a member function named *IsNullDate*. The *Date* class has no such member function. If you instantiate an object of type *Date*, you cannot call the *IsNullDate* function for that object, because the class has no such member function. However, if you instantiate an object of type *SpecialDate*, you can indeed call the *IsNullDate* function for that object.

The *IsNullDate* function takes advantage of the fact that the base *Date* class specifies the *ndays* data member as protected and tests that data member for a zero value. If the *SpecialDate* class could not access *ndays*, the *IsNullDate* function would have to call one of the *Date* class's member functions—*GetDay*, *GetMonth*, or *GetYear*—and test the return value for zero. The overhead required to extract a date component from the long integer data representation makes it more efficient to use the actual long integer data value.

Specializing by Overriding Base Class Member Functions

When a base and a derived class have member functions with the same name, parameter list types, and *const* specification, the function in the derived class overrides that in the base class when the function is called as a member of the derived class object. This technique allows the derived class to provide specialized behavior for a particular method.

Both the base *Date* class and the derived *SpecialDate* class in our example have functions named *Display*. A program that declares an object of type *Date* can call the *Display* function for that object, and the *Date* class's version of that member function executes. A program that declares an object of type *SpecialDate* can call the *Display* function for that object, and the *SpecialDate*'s version of that member function executes. We'll see an example of that behavior soon.

Figure 11.9 is **SpecialDate.cpp**, the source-code file that implements the static data member and non-inline member function of the *SpecialDate* class.

Figure 11.9 SpecialDate.cpp.

```cpp
#include <iostream>
using namespace std;
#include "SpecialDate.h"

char* SpecialDate::mos[] = {
    "January", "February", "March", "April",
    "May", "June", "July", "August",
    "September", "October", "November", "December"
};

void SpecialDate::Display() const
{
    if (!IsNullDate())
        cout << mos[GetMonth()-1] << ' ' << GetDay()
             << ", " << GetYear();
}
```

Building the Program

The exercises in this book have, until now, been independent, stand-alone programs. That approach works well for simple example programs, but you will seldom find yourself working in such a small environment. To learn about inheritance, you will define classes in header files, put member functions in separate, class-specific source files, and link the object code compiled from those multiple source files to make running programs—in other words, you will view these examples from an environment that is more like those in which you do real programming.

A program that uses the *SpecialDate* class must include the **SpecialDate.h** header file and link the program's compiled object file with the object files that the compiler generates when you compile **Date.cpp** and **SpecialDate.cpp**. You don't need to include **date.h**, because **SpecialDate.h** does that for you.

Most C++ development systems permit you to compile and link with multiple object files. Most systems also support libraries of object files. We don't need to use libraries for these exercises (except, of course, the standard ones that come with the compiler). If you are using Quincy to run the exercises, the tutorial includes special project files for the programs that are built from more than one object file. You used such a setup in Chapters 3 and 5 when you worked with Exercises 3.10 and 5.8.

Exercise 11.1 instantiates an object of a derived class and uses that class's specialized behavior.

Exercise 11.1 Class specialization.

```
#include <iostream>
using namespace std;
#include "SpecialDate.h"

int main()
{
```

Exercise 11.1 Class specialization. (continued)

```
    for (;;) {
        cout << "Enter dd mm yyyy (0 0 0 to quit): ";
        int da, mo, yr;
        cin >> da >> mo >> yr;
        if (da == 0)
            break;
        SpecialDate dt(da, mo, yr);
        if (dt.IsNullDate())
            cout << "Try again";
        else
            dt.Display();
        cout << endl;
    }
    return 0;
}
```

The real lesson of Exercise 11.1 is found not in the application program but in the source-code files **SpecialDate.h**, Figure 11.8, and **SpecialDate.cpp**, Figure 11.9, which demonstrate how an abstract data type can be specialized through inheritance.

Scope Resolution Operator with Base and Derived Classes

A program can use the scope resolution operator (::) to bypass the override of a base class member that a derived class has overridden. You express the call to the base class function by coding the base class name and the double colons ahead of the member name to bypass the overridden member:

```
    SpecialDate dt(29, 6, 1990);
    dt.Date::Display();
```

Exercise 11.2 demonstrates this usage with the *Date* class's *Display* function.

Exercise 11.2 Class scope resolution.

```
#include <iostream>
using namespace std;
#include "SpecialDate.h"

int main()
{
    SpecialDate dt(29, 6, 1990);
    dt.Display();
    cout << endl;
    dt.Date::Display();
    cout << endl;
    return 0;
}
```

The program in Exercise 11.2 instantiates an object of the derived type *SpecialDate* and uses the *SpecialDate* class's *Display* member function to display the date. Then the program uses the scope resolution operator to display the same date object by using the base *Date* class's *Display* member function.

N O T E

Using the scope resolution operator without specifying a type on its left from within a member function compiles a call to a global, nonmember function with the same name and parameter list.

More Than One Derived Class

A program can derive more than one class from a single base class. Recall the *JulianDate* class from the exercises in Chapter 9. A Julian date is one that is expressed as the year and a day value representing the 1-based number of days since January 1. Inasmuch as the *Date* class in this chapter records the date information in an integer data member, we can implement the *JulianDate* class by deriving from *Date*, forming a simple object-oriented class hierarchy. Figure 11.10 shows that relationship.

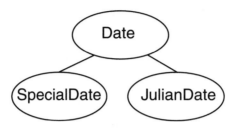

Figure 11.10 Multiple derived classes.

A Second Derived Class

Figures 11.11 and 11.12 are **JulianDate.h** and **JulianDate.cpp**, which implement a second class derived from the base *Date* class.

Figure 11.11 JulianDate.h.

```
#ifndef JULIANDATE_H
#define JULIANDATE_H

#include "Date.h"

class JulianDate : public Date  {
public:
    JulianDate(int yr, int da);
    int GetDay() const;
    virtual void Display() const;
};

#endif
```

Figure 11.12 JulianDate.cpp.

```cpp
#include <iostream>
using namespace std;
#include "JulianDate.h"

JulianDate::JulianDate(int yr, int da)
{
    if (yr < 1 || da < 1 || da > (IsLeapYear(yr) ? 366 : 365))
        return;
    int mo;
    for (mo = 1; mo < 13; mo++)      {
        int dy = dys[mo-1];
        if (mo == 2 && IsLeapYear(yr))
            dy++;
        if (da <= dy)
            break;
        da -= dy;
    }
    SetDate(mo, da, yr);
}
int JulianDate::GetDay() const
{
    int mo, da, yr;
    GetDate(mo, da, yr);
    int day = 0;
    for (int m = 1; m < mo; m++)      {
        day += dys[m-1];
        if (m == 2 && IsLeapYear(yr))
            day++;
    }
    return day + da;
}
void JulianDate::Display() const
{
    cout << GetDay() << '-' << GetYear();
}
```

Observe that the *JulianDate* constructor in Figure 11.12 has no parameter initialization list for the base *Date* class. It cannot provide all three arguments, because it has no month argument and because its day argument is a different data representation from the day argument of the *Date* constructor. You can omit a base class parameter initialization list when the base class has a default constructor, one that accepts no arguments. Look back at **date.h** in Figure 11.6. The *Date* class constructor has default argument values for all its parameters. This means that the constructor function serves two purposes: It is an initializing constructor, and it is the default constructor. The *JulianDate* constructor builds the three date values that initialize a *Date* object and then calls the base *Date* class's *SetDate* member function, passing those three date values as arguments.

The *JulianDate* class's *GetDay* member function overrides the base *Date* class's *GetDay* member function to compute and return the Julian version of the day rather than the traditional day of the month value. The *Date* class's *GetYear* member function works without being overridden, because the year value is computed the same way for both kinds of dates. A program could also call the *GetMonth* member function for a *JulianDate* object, and the *Date* class's *GetMonth* member function would execute and return the proper month. You could prevent this usage by overriding *GetMonth* in the *JulianDate* class to return a zero.

Using the Base Class and Both Derived Classes

Exercise 11.3 uses all three date variations to display the birthdates of my children.

Exercise 11.3 Multiple derived classes.

```
#include <iostream>
using namespace std;
#include "SpecialDate.h"
#include "JulianDate.h"

int main()
{
    // ---- process a Date
    Date dt(4,6,1961);
    cout << endl << "Alan:    ";
    dt.Display();
```

Exercise 11.3 Multiple derived classes. (continued)

```
// ---- process a JulianDate
JulianDate jdt(1962, 285);
cout << endl << "Sharon: ";
jdt.Display();
cout << " (";
jdt.Date::Display();
cout << ')';
// ---- process a SpecialDate
SpecialDate sdt(28, 4, 1965);
cout << endl << "Wendy:  ";
sdt.Display();
return 0;
}
```

Exercise 11.3 instantiates and displays three dates by using three date classes. Two of those classes are derived from the third. Inasmuch as most of us are unfamiliar with the Julian date format, I added a parenthetical display of Sharon's birthdate in the *Date* class format by calling the *Date* class's *Display* member function. (Sharon would want everyone to know that she is 35 this year.)

The Lack of a Relationship between Derived Classes

The only thing in common between the *SpecialDate* and *JulianDate* classes is that they have the same base class. The two classes have no knowledge of or relationship with each other. You cannot call the specialized member functions of one class for an object of the other class. You cannot cast an object of one type to the other type. You cannot initialize or copy between objects of these two classes. You cannot do these things because the classes do not have the necessary conversion and copy constructor member functions. You must explicitly provide these things, as you learned to do in Chapter 9. It is important to understand that no implied relationships exist between classes derived from a common base class.

Classes Derived from Derived Base Classes

You can derive a class from a base class that was itself derived from another base class. Suppose that the *JulianDate* class is not exactly what you want every time. Perhaps you need a specialized Julian date class, called *SpecialJulianDate*, that displays its objects in the same way that the *SpecialDate* class does. Assuming that you do not want to modify an existing class for the reasons mentioned earlier in this chapter, you have these three design choices:

- Derive a class from *SpecialDate* and add the *JulianDate* construction behavior.
- Derive a class from *JulianDate* and add the *SpecialDate* display behavior.
- Use multiple inheritance and derive a class from both *SpecialDate* and *JulianDate*.

Figure 11.13 illustrates all three design choices.

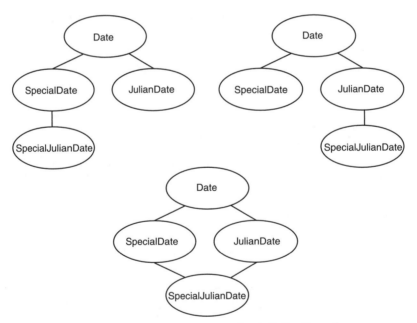

Figure 11.13 *Design choices for the SpecialJulianDate class.*

The third choice (at the bottom of Figure 11.13), which uses multiple inheritance, is not a viable one at this time. First, it has some inherent design problems that are typically encountered with multiple inheritance. Also, you won't learn about multiple inheritance until you get to Chapter 12.

Either of the first two choices (at the top of Figure 11.13 from left to right) involves some amount of duplication. The second choice involves duplicating the array of pointers that the *SpecialDate* class uses for the names of the months. That class provides no apparent easy way for a nonderived class to get to that array. Remember that you cannot modify the *SpecialDate* class, so you cannot declare this new class to be a friend. A possible solution to that problem is to declare a class derived from *SpecialDate* with the sole purpose of returning a pointer to the static array. Let's explore that possibility. Consider this class:

```
class MonthArray : public SpecialDate {
public:
    static const char* GetMonth() const
        { return mos; }    // Error. Why?
};
```

Remember that *SpecialJulianDate*, in this discussion, is derived from *JulianDate*. The *SpecialJulianDate* class's *Display* function would get the address of *SpecialDate*'s static array of month names this way:

```
const char* months = MonthArray::GetMonth();
```

Can you see why this does not work? The designer of the *SpecialDate* class did not have the foresight to make the static array a protected data member. We'll give the developer the benefit of the doubt and assume that he or she had good reason to completely hide that detail of the implementation. Whatever the reason, the *MonthArray* class cannot access that member, and the compiler issues an error when the *MonthArray::GetMonth* function is declared. That eliminates this solution from our consideration. If you still want to derive *SpecialJulianDate* from *JulianDate*, you must provide a second, identical array for the new class. There is something unappealing about solutions that duplicate design features and that duplicate what is stored in memory, and most programmers look for other ways. Fortunately, one is close at hand. The first choice in Figure 11.13 derives *SpecialJulianDate* from *SpecialDate*, and that solution works if we add some creative design components. Figure 11.14 shows the effective class hierarchy for the *SpecialJulianDate* class.

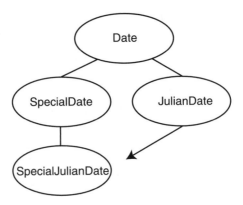

Figure 11.14 SpecialJulianDate class hierarchy.

Figure 11.14 illustrates the relationship that now exists between the classes. *SpecialJulianDate* is directly derived from *SpecialDate* and indirectly derived from *Date* through *SpecialDate*'s derivation. *SpecialJulianDate*, therefore, inherits the properties of both classes. *SpecialJulianDate* also uses the services of *JulianDate*, as Figure 11.14 shows. Figure 11.14 uses a bold arrow symbol to differentiate this interclass relationship from that of inheritance.

> Even though *SpecialJulianDate* inherits from both classes, this relationship is not what is called multiple inheritance. *SpecialJulianDate* is indirectly derived from *Date* only because SpecialJulianDate's direct base class, *SpecialDate*, is itself directly derived from *Date*. You will learn about multiple inheritance in Chapter 12.

Figure 11.15 is **SpecialJulianDate.h**, the header file that implements the *SpecialJulianDate* class.

Figure 11.15 SpecialJulianDate.h.

```
#ifndef SPECIALJULIANDATE_H
#define SPECIALJULIANDATE_H

#include "SpecialDate.h"
#include "JulianDate.h"

class SpecialJulianDate : public SpecialDate  {
public:
    SpecialJulianDate(int yr, int da) : SpecialDate(0,0,0)
    {
        JulianDate jd(yr, da);
        SetDate(jd.GetMonth(),jd.Date::GetDay(),jd.GetYear());
    }
};

#endif
```

The *SpecialJulianDate* class needs only a constructor. The constructor is inline, so no **.cpp** file is needed. The *SpecialJulianDate* class is derived from *SpecialDate*, so the base class *SpecialDate::Display* function serves to display the date in the required format. The constructor must build the object from the constructor arguments usually provided for a *JulianDate* object. We could have copied the *JulianDate* class constructor code here, but there is a better way. The *SpecialJulianDate* constructor function instantiates a *JulianDate* object from the year and month constructor arguments. (This instantiation represents the relationship mentioned earlier wherein the *SpecialJulianDate* class uses the services of the *JulianDate* class.) Then the constructor calls the indirect base *Date* class's *SetDate* function, passing the values returned from the *JulianDate* object's *GetMonth*, *GetDay*, and *GetYear* functions, except that the call to the *GetDay* function uses the scope resolution operator to call the *Date* class's *GetDay* function rather than the *JulianDate* class's *GetDay* function.

The *SpecialJulianDate* constructor must provide a parameter initialization list for the *SpecialDate* constructor—in this case, all zero arguments—because the designer of the *SpecialDate* class lacked the foresight to provide a default constructor. Someone should to talk to that designer.

Exercise 11.4 instantiates an object of the *SpecialJulianDate* class.

Exercise 11.4 A class derived from a derived class.

```
#include <iostream>
using namespace std;
#include "SpecialJulianDate.h"

int main()
{
    // ---- process a SpecialJulianDate
    SpecialJulianDate sjdt(1941, 321);
    cout << endl << "Judy:    ";
    sjdt.Display();
}
```

When the object in Exercise 11.4 calls its *Display* member function, the compiler generates a call to the *Display* member function of the *SpecialDate* class because the *SpecialJulianDate* class does not have an overriding *Display* member function. The object could call the *Date::Display* member function, too, by using the *Date* class name and the scope resolution operator.

PROBLEM DOMAIN CLASS HIERARCHY DESIGN

Now we are ready for some object-oriented design. Any program supports what programmers call the *problem domain*. The idea is to model the data components of a problem domain in an object-oriented class hierarchy. Figure 11.16 is a small example of such a class hierarchy.

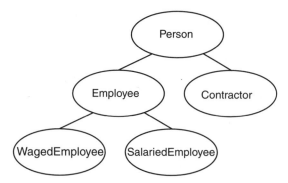

Figure 11.16 An object-oriented class hierarchy.

Each balloon in Figure 11.16 represents a class. Derived classes are below their base classes on the chart and are connected to their base classes by a single line. These base and derived classes represent the major components of the problem domain, in this case a personnel accounting system such as one you might see in payroll and labor distribution applications. We will build these classes in this chapter and use them as examples for learning the behavior of C++ and object-oriented class hierarchies.

The *Person* class is the root base class. Everything in this hierarchy is related to people, so the *Person* class encapsulates the data and behavior related to personnel accounting that all people have in common.

Two classes are derived from *Person*. The *Employee* class specializes the *Person* class with data and behavior specific to employees, and the *Contractor* class does the same thing for workers that the organization hires on a temporary basis from temp agencies and job shops as well as workers hired as private consultants. Employees are further specialized by the *WagedEmployee* and *SalariedEmployee* classes.

So far, we haven't considered what the common and specialized behaviors are or how they affect our application. For now we are looking at the overall design.

N O T E The hierarchy in Figure 11.16—and any class hierarchy—is not the same as a hierarchical database. When you instantiate an object of type *Contractor*, for example, only one object exists, and it contains all the members of both classes. A database hierarchy, on the other hand, represents the relationships between different objects, such as department objects, project objects, and employee objects. The significant difference is that a *WagedEmployee* is an *Employee*, which is a *Person*, whereas a department contains employees who work on projects, which are in the province of departments.

C++ versus Pure Object-Oriented Design

Pure object-oriented design, a subject of much debate, employs one class hierarchy; everything descends from a common root class. The data types, the data structures, and even the program itself are all classes in the hierarchy, and they all descend from the common root. Figure 11.17 is an example of that concept.

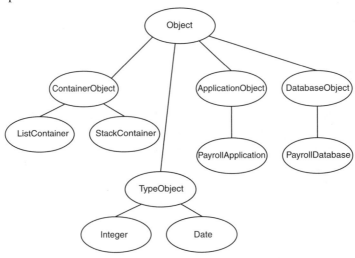

Figure 11.17 *A pure object-oriented hierarchy.*

A pure object-oriented application begins running when its application object is created, usually as the result of the object's declaration somewhere in the program. This arrangement is analogous to the declaration of the single *main* function somewhere in a C++ program. The pure object-oriented program's application object communicates with the other objects by instantiating them and sending them messages—an approach that is analogous to a C++ program declaring class objects and calling the member functions of those classes through the objects.

C++ programs do not usually reflect pure object-oriented programming. Depending on the application's requirements, they typically have several unrelated class hierarchies: one or more for the problem domain, another for the application framework, perhaps a few data abstractions, and some data structure and container classes.

C++ programs tend to reflect a combination of object-oriented and functional (also called *procedural*) programming models. (Object-oriented purists might argue, then, that C++ programs are not object-oriented at all.) A C++ program launches from its *main* function rather than from the instantiation of an application object. Some application framework class libraries start with an application object, but even when using such an application framework, a C++ program instantiates the application object in or below its *main* function.

Do not worry, therefore, when you see C++ class hierarchies that do not descend from a common, all-encompassing root object. That multiple-hierarchy idiom is the norm in C++ programs rather than the exception.

More Data Abstractions

As you might expect, it takes more classes than Figure 11.16 shows to implement the personnel application. You do not depict every class in a design diagram. It is not necessary to show the relationship between problem domain classes and classes from the Standard C++ library. Other data abstraction classes may or may not be on the diagram. A personnel application certainly needs to represent dates for different reasons. We developed a *Date* class earlier in this chapter, and we will modify it to make it more appropriate for general-purpose use. We will build two other data abstractions to encapsulate the data and behavior of money and Social Security numbers. Figure 11.18 expands the personnel application's problem domain class hierarchy to include three data abstraction classes.

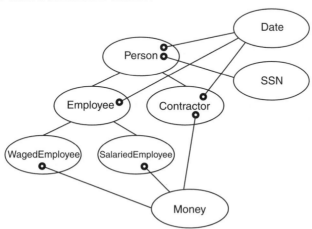

Figure 11.18 *Class hierarchy with data abstraction classes.*

Observe the bold lines that have small circles at the end. This notation represents a relationship in which the class at the circle end of the line has, as a data member, one or more instances of the class at the other end of the line.

As you can see, such a diagram can become complex. That is why you often stop diagramming at the level of detail that Figure 11.16 shows and allow the source code of your class hierarchy design to document relationships such as those added by Figure 11.18.

Overloading << and >>

For the exercises in the rest of this and subsequent chapters, we will do away with the functions named *Display* that we used to display objects on the console. That mechanism was convenient for learning about member functions, but it has a problem: The display functions bind the classes to the *cout* object. What if you wanted to display the object on the *cerr* device? What if you wanted to print it? What if you wanted to record the object in a stream file (explained in Chapter 16)? The display functions do not do any of that. A more practical approach, and one that is commonly used, is to make such display functions work with an object of type *ostream*, which is a Standard C++ library class declared when you include **<iostream>** in your program. The *cout, cerr,* and printer devices are objects of type *ostream*. You might modify the *Date::Display* function to work like this:

```
void Date::Display(ostream& os) const
{
    int mo, da, yr;
    GetDate(mo, da, yr);
    os << mo << '/' << da << '/' << yr;
}
```

The *Display* function just shown accepts a reference to type *ostream* and sends its data members and slash separators to the object referred to by the function parameter's argument. You call the *Display* function to display an object on the console like this:

```
Date dt(1/28/97);
dt.Display(cout);
```

Having learned all this, you won't be surprised to discover that the standard *ostream* class overloads the << operator to send to its object whatever arguments the overloaded operator functions receive. Figure 11.19 shows the overloaded << operator functions as they are declared in the *ostream* class declaration.

Figure 11.19 Overloaded ostream::operator<< functions.

```
ostream& operator<<(char c);
ostream& operator<<(unsigned char c);
ostream& operator<<(signed char c);
ostream& operator<<(const char *s);
ostream& operator<<(const unsigned char *s);
ostream& operator<<(const signed char *s);
ostream& operator<<(const void *p);
ostream& operator<<(int n);
ostream& operator<<(unsigned int n);
ostream& operator<<(long n);
ostream& operator<<(unsigned long n);
ostream& operator<<(short n);
ostream& operator<<(unsigned short n);
ostream& operator<<(bool b);
ostream& operator<<(double n);
ostream& operator<<(float n);
ostream& operator<<(long double n);
```

As Figure 11.19 shows, the *ostream* class overloads the << operator for all the intrinsic types. The corresponding *istream* class, of which *cin* is an object, similarly overloads the >> operator. These two sets of overloaded operators allow the input and output operations, such as the following, that many of our exercises have used:

```
int n;
cin >> n;    // read a value into n from the console
cout << n;   // display the value from n on the console
```

We will overload << and >> for any classes that need to display themselves from this point on. To begin, we will specialize the *Date* class to add this behavior. Figure 11.20 is **PDate.h**, which overloads << and >> to work with objects of type *Date*.

Figure 11.20 PDate.h.

```
#ifndef PDATE_H
#define PDATE_H

#include <iostream>
using namespace std;
#include "Date.h"

inline ostream& operator<<(ostream& os, const Date& dt)
{
    os << dt.GetMonth() << '/'
       << dt.GetDay()   << '/'
       << dt.GetYear();
    return os;
}
inline istream& operator>>(istream& is, Date& dt)
{
    int mo, da, yr;
    is >> mo >> da >> yr;
    dt.SetDate(mo, da, yr);
    return is;
}
#endif
```

We do not use inheritance to overload the << and >> operators for the *Date* class. These overloaded operator functions must be nonmember functions, because they are executed with objects of type *ostream* and *istream* on the left side of the expression; therefore, they cannot be members of the *Date* class. The *Date* class conveniently provides member functions to get and set the day, month, and year values, so overloaded << and >> operator functions do not need access to the protected data members of the class they are working for; therefore, the overloaded operator functions do not need to be friends of the *Date* class. You specialize the *Date* class to overload << and >> simply by including the **PDate.h** header file.

At this point I would visit the person in charge of the project-wide *Date* class and strongly suggest that he or she include the contents of **PDate.h** at the bottom of **date.h**. That way, everyone can use the overloaded operators without being concerned about finding and using the specializing **PDate.h** header file.

Exercise 11.5 shows the use of the overloaded << and >> operators with the *Date* class. This is the technique that classes and exercises use from this point on.

Exercise 11.5 *Using overloaded << and >> operators.*

```
#include "PDate.h"

int main()
{
    Date dt;
    cout << "Enter date: (mm dd yy) ";
    cin >> dt;
    cout << "The date is " << dt << endl;
    return 0;
}
```

SSN and Money: Two More Data Abstractions

To complete our preparations for the personnel class library, we will develop the *SSN* and *Money* classes to implement data abstractions of Social Security numbers and money. Figures 11.21 and 11.22 are **Ssn.h** and **Ssn.cpp**, the files that implement the *SSN* class.

Figure 11.21 Ssn.h.

```
#ifndef SSN_H
#define SSN_H

#include <iostream>

class SSN  {
    long unsigned int ssn;
public:
    explicit SSN(long unsigned int sn = 0);
    friend ostream& operator<<(ostream& os, const SSN& ssn);
};

#endif
```

Figure 11.22 Ssn.cpp.

```
#include <ssn.h>

SSN::SSN(long unsigned int sn) : ssn(sn)
{
    if (ssn > 999999999L)
        ssn = 0;
}

ostream& operator<<(ostream& os, const SSN& sn)
{
    int lssn = sn.ssn / 1000000L;
    int mssn = (sn.ssn - (lssn * 1000000L)) / 10000;
    int rssn = sn.ssn - (lssn * 1000000L) - (mssn * 10000);
    os << lssn << '-' << mssn << '-' << rssn;
    return os;
}
```

The *SSN* constructor ensures that no Social Security number has more than nine decimal digits. A more comprehensive class would use the Social Security Administration's rules for forming Social Security numbers to more properly validate the constructor's argument.

The nonmember overloaded operator<< function is a friend of the *SSN* class so that it can read the long unsigned integer data member. The purpose of the function is to display the Social Security number in the familiar nnn-nn-nnnn format.

Figures 11.23 and 11.24 are **Money.h** and **Money.cpp**, the source-code files that implement the *Money* class.

Figure 11.23 Money.h.

```
#ifndef MONEY_H
#define MONEY_H

#include <iostream>
using namespace std;

class Money {
    double value;
public:
    Money(double val = 0);
    operator double() const
        { return value; }
    friend ostream& operator<<(ostream&, const Money&);
};

#endif
```

Figure 11.24 Money.cpp.

```
#include <iomanip>
#include <Money.h>

Money::Money(double val)
{
    // ensure that the value is only 2 decimal places
    // and rounded up to the nearest penny
    long int nval = ((val + .005) * 100);
    float cents = nval % 100;
    cents /= 100;
    value = (nval / 100) + cents;
}


ostream& operator<<(ostream& os, const Money& curr)
{
    os << '$'
        << setw(10)
        << setprecision(2)
        << setiosflags(ios::fixed)
        << curr.value;
}
```

The *Money* class has enough intelligence built-in to ensure that its data representation is always two decimal places and that it displays itself properly. A more comprehensive money class would overload all the arithmetic and relational operators. To keep everything simple, we will neglect that part of the design for these exercises.

Including Headers

The **Ssn.cpp** and **Money.cpp** files include **Ssn.h** and **Money.h**, the headers that declare the data abstraction classes. Observe that the #*include* preprocessing directives use the angle bracket notation, whereas previous includes of header files associated with exercises used the double-quote character around the file name. The angle bracket notation means that the compiler should not look for the header file in the same subdirectory where it finds the **.cpp** file. You will learn the implications of that usage later in this chapter.

The Standard C++ *string* Class

Ever since C++ became a public resource, programmers have used classes to add custom data types that are missing from the C language. Programmers who came to C from BASIC, for example, often complained that C has no *string* data type. When those programmers made the move to C++, the first thing that many of them did was to use the C++ class mechanism to build a string class. Many C++ books use string classes to demonstrate data abstraction and the principles of class design. The ANSI committee eventually defined a standard string class named, of course, *string*, with many of the best properties from all those prior designs. You can concatentate, compare, assign, display, and make substrings of C++ *string* objects. I'll discuss the standard *string* class in more detail in Chapter 16. Until then, we will use the string class to make the classes in this chapter easier to design and understand.

PERSON: THE BASE CLASS

The top of the class hierarchy in Figure 11.16 is the *Person* class, the class from which all the other classes in the hierarchy descend. The *Person* class encapsulates those data and behavioral traits that are common to all people and of interest to this problem domain. Figures 11.25 and 11.26 are **Person.h** and **Person.cpp**, the source-code files that implement the *Person* class.

Figure 11.25 Person.h.

```
#ifndef PERSON_H
#define PERSON_H

#include <iostream>
#include <string>
using namespace std;
#include <Date.h>
#include <Ssn.h>

class Person {
public:
    enum Sex {unknown, male, female};
    enum MaritalStatus {single, married, divorced, widowed};
```

Figure 11.25 Person.h. *(contiued)*

```
protected:
    string name;
    string address;
    string phone;
    SSN ssn;
    Date dob;
    Sex sex;
    MaritalStatus mstatus;

public:
    Person(const string& nm = "")
            : name(nm), sex(unknown), mstatus(single)
        { }
    virtual ~Person() { }
    // --- setter functions
    void SetName(const string& nm)
        { name = nm; }
    void SetAddress(const string& addr)
        { address = addr; }
    void SetPhone(const string& phon)
        { phone = phon; }
    void SetSSN(SSN sn)
        { ssn = sn; }
    void SetDob(const Date& dtb)
        { dob = dtb; }
    void SetSex(Sex sx)
        { sex = sx; }
    void SetMaritalStatus(MaritalStatus st)
        { mstatus = st; }
```

Figure 11.25 Person.h. *(contiued)*

```
    // --- getter functions
    const string& GetName() const
        { return name; }
    const string& GetAddress() const
        { return address; }
    const string& GetPhone() const
        { return phone; }
    SSN GetSSN() const
        { return ssn; }
    const Date& GetDob() const
        { return dob; }
    Sex GetSex() const
        { return sex; }
    MaritalStatus GetMaritalStatus() const
        { return mstatus; }
    virtual void FormattedDisplay(ostream& os) = 0;
};

ostream& operator<<(ostream& os, const Person& person);

#endif
```

Figure 11.26 Person.cpp.

```
#include <Person.h>

void Person::FormattedDisplay(ostream& os)
{
    os << "Name:          " << name    << endl;
    os << "Address:       " << address << endl;
    os << "Phone:         " << phone   << endl;
    os << "SSN:           " << ssn     << endl;
    os << "Date of birth: " << dob     << endl;
    os << "Sex:           ";
    switch (sex)  {
```

Figure 11.26 Person.cpp. *(continued)*

```cpp
        case Person::male:
            os << "male" << endl;
            break;
        case Person::female:
            os << "female" << endl;
            break;
        default:
            os << "unknown" << endl;
            break;
    }
    os << "Marital status: ";
    switch (GetMaritalStatus()) {
        case Person::single:
            os << "single" << endl;
            break;
        case Person::married:
            os << "married" << endl;
            break;
        case Person::divorced:
            os << "divorced" << endl;
            break;
        case Person::widowed:
            os << "widowed" << endl;
            break;
        default:
            os << "unknown" << endl;
            break;
    }
}
```

Figure 11.26 Person.cpp. (continued)

```
stream& operator<<(ostream& os, const Person& person)
{
    os << person.GetName() << endl
       << person.GetAddress() << endl
       << person.GetPhone() << endl
       << person.GetSSN() << endl
       << person.GetDob() << endl
       << person.GetSex() << endl
       << person.GetMaritalStatus() << endl;
    return os;
}
```

Enums in a Class

The *Person* class declares two enumerated data types—*Sex* and *MaritalStatus*—as public. They are public so that programs that use the *Person* class can refer to the enumerated constant values. They are declared within the class declaration so that their identifiers are not in the global scope. This practice avoids any potential for name collisions with other parts of the program. Member functions of the class can refer to the enumerated values without qualification, but a program that uses them from outside the class must use the scope resolution operator to specify the values:

```
empl.SetSex(Person::male);
```

Virtual Functions

Two of the functions in the *Person* class are declared with the *virtual* qualifier. A virtual function indicates that the class designer expects the function to be overridden in a derived class by a function with the same function name and parameter types. We will revisit this subject and examine the effects of virtual and nonvirtual function overrides when we discuss this class hierarchy's derived classes. The *Person* class's destructor function is one of the two virtual functions, a significant characteristic that you will soon learn about.

Abstract Base Class: The Pure Virtual Function

The *Person* class's *FormattedDisplay* member function declaration includes an equal sign followed by a zero (= 0). This notation specifies that the member function is a *pure virtual* function. This means that the base class is an abstract base class, and the class designer intends the class to be used only as a base class. The base class may or may not provide a function body for the pure virtual function. In either case, a program that uses this class may not directly declare any objects of an abstract base class. If the program declares an object of a class directly or indirectly derived from the abstract base class, the pure virtual function must be overridden, either in the class of the object being declared or in a class above the object's class and below the abstract base class in the hierarchy.

Two Ways to Display

The *Person* class includes two display techniques. The *FormattedDisplay* member function displays the *Person* data in a format conducive to query responses and report fields. I use it here to demonstrate the behavior of virtual functions. The overloaded << operator nonmember function displays raw data. We will use that function for writing to disk files in Chapter 16.

DERIVED CLASSES

The class hierarchy in Figure 11.16 includes several derived classes, which we will discuss now.

The *Employee* Class

Figures 11.27 and 11.28 are **Employee.h** and **Employee.cpp**, the source-code files that implement the *Employee* class, which is derived directly from the *Person* class.

Figure 11.27 Employee.h.

```cpp
#ifndef EMPLOYEE_H
#define EMPLOYEE_H

#include <person.h>

class Employee : public Person   {
protected:
    Date datehired;
public:
    Employee(const string& nm = "") : Person(nm)
        {  }
    virtual ~Employee() {  }
    Date GetDateHired() const
        { return datehired; }
    void SetDateHired(Date date)
        { datehired = date; }
    virtual void FormattedDisplay(ostream& os) = 0;
};

ostream& operator<<(ostream& os, Employee& empl);

#endif
```

Figure 11.28 Employee.cpp.

```cpp
#include <Employee.h>

void Employee::FormattedDisplay(ostream& os)
{
    Person::FormattedDisplay(os);
    os << "Date hired:     " << datehired << endl;
}
```

Figure 11.28 Employee.cpp. *(continued)*

```
ostream& operator<<(ostream& os, Employee& empl)
{
    os << ((Person&)empl) << endl;
    os << empl.GetDateHired() << endl;
    return os;
}
```

The *Employee* class, like its base *Person* class, is an abstract base class through its pure virtual *FormattedDisplay* member function; to use the *Employee* class, you must derive a class from it. The *Employee* class, specializes the *Person* class by adding a *datehired* data member. All employees have been hired, but not all persons have been hired. Contrast this specialization with that of the *Contractor* class discussed later.

Overriding a Function Override

The *Employee::FormattedDisplay* member function begins by calling the *Person::FormattedDisplay* member function by using the *Person* class name and the scope resolution operator. This technique allows the derived class to use the base class's overridden behavior. Recall that the *SpecialDate* class (early in this chapter) totally overrode its base *Date* class's *Display* function to provide custom specialization for the derived class. *SpecialDate* objects display differently from *Date* objects. The *Employee* class, on the other hand, needs only to add to the base class's behavior by displaying the specialized *datehired* data member.

The overloaded << operator function similarly calls the overloaded << function for the *Person* class by casting the *Employee* reference argument to a reference to type *Person*. In this case, you cannot use the scope resolution operator to call an overridden member function because the overloaded << operator functions are not members of any class. Instead, they are functions to be called when the compiler sees an *ostream* object on the left of the << operator and a *Person* or *Employee* object on the right. The cast coerces the compiler into treating the *Employee* reference as if it referred to its base *Person* class. The cast also calls the overloaded << operator function that deals with *Person* objects. That function works correctly because the *Employee* object, being derived from the *Person* class, includes all the data members and member functions of the *Person* class.

The *WagedEmployee* Class

Figures 11.29 and 11.30 are **WagedEmployee.h** and **WagedEmployee.cpp**, the source-code files that implement the *WagedEmployee* class.

Figure 11.29 WagedEmployee.h.

```
#ifndef WAGEDEMPLOYEE_H
#define WAGEDEMPLOYEE_H

#include <Employee.h>
#include <Money.h>

class WagedEmployee : public Employee  {
    Money hourlywage;
public:
    WagedEmployee(const string& nm = "") : Employee(nm)
        { }
    virtual ~WagedEmployee() { }
    Money GetHourlyWage() const
        { return hourlywage; }
    void SetHourlyWage(Money wage)
        { hourlywage = wage; }
    virtual void FormattedDisplay(ostream& os);
};

ostream& operator<<(ostream& os, WagedEmployee& cntr);

#endif
```

Figure 11.30 WagedEmployee.cpp.

```
#include <WagedEmployee.h>

void WagedEmployee::FormattedDisplay(ostream& os)
{
    os << "----Waged Employee----" << endl;
    Employee::FormattedDisplay(os);
    os << "Hourly wage:    " << hourlywage << endl;
}

ostream& operator<<(ostream& os, WagedEmployee& cntr)
{
    os << ((Employee&)cntr) << endl
       << cntr.GetHourlyWage() << endl;
    return os;
}
```

The *WagedEmployee* class is the first of what is called a *concrete data type*, which is a data type defined by a class for which you can instantiate an object. The *WagedEmployee* class specializes the *Employee* class by adding the *hourlywage* data member. Not all employees work for an hourly wage, so this behavior must be represented by a specialized derived class. Contrast this behavior with that of the *SalariedEmployee* class, discussed in the next section.

By deriving from the *Employee* class, the *WagedEmployee* class directly inherits all the data and behavior of the *Employee* class and, because *Employee* is derived from *Person*, indirectly inherits all the data and behavior of the *Person* class. A *WagedEmployee*, therefore, is a specialized *Employee*, which is a specialized *Person*.

The *SalariedEmployee* Class

Figures 11.31 and 11.32 are **SalariedEmployee.h** and **SalariedEmployee.cpp**, the source-code files that implement the *SalariedEmployee* class.

Figure 11.31 SalariedEmployee.h.

```
#ifndef SALARIEDEMPLOYEE_H
#define SALARIEDEMPLOYEE_H

#include <Employee.h>
#include <Money.h>

class SalariedEmployee : public Employee  {
    Money salary;
public:
    SalariedEmployee(const string& nm = "") : Employee(nm)
        { }
    virtual ~SalariedEmployee() { }
    Money GetSalary() const
        { return salary; }
    void SetSalary(Money sal)
        { salary = sal; }
    virtual void FormattedDisplay(ostream& os);
};

ostream& operator<<(ostream& os, SalariedEmployee& empl);

#endif
```

Figure 11.32 SalariedEmployee.cpp.

```
#include <SalariedEmployee.h>

void SalariedEmployee::FormattedDisplay(ostream& os)
{
    os << "----Salaried Employee----" << endl;
    Employee::FormattedDisplay(os);
    os << "Salary:         " << salary << endl;
}
```

Figure 11.32 SalariedEmployee.cpp. (continued)

```
ostream& operator<<(ostream& os, SalariedEmployee& empl)
{
    os << ((Employee&)empl) << endl
        << empl.GetSalary() << endl;
    return os;
}
```

The *SalariedEmployee* class is also a concrete data type. It specializes the *Employee* class by adding the *salary* data member. Not all employees work for an annual salary, so this behavior must be represented by a specialized derived class. Contrast this behavior with that of the *WagedEmployee* class, discussed in the previous section.

By deriving from the *Employee* class, the *SalariedEmployee* class directly inherits all the data and behavior of the *Employee* class and, because *Employee* is derived from *Person*, indirectly inherits all the data and behavior of the *Person* class. A *SalariedEmployee*, therefore, is a specialized *Employee*, which is a specialized *Person*.

We now have two specialized *Employee* derivations having individual behavior and behavior in common that they inherit from their common base class.

The *Contractor* Class

Figures 11.33 and 11.34 are **Contractor.h** and **Contractor.cpp**, the source-code files that implement the *Contractor* class.

Figure 11.33 Contractor.h.

```
#ifndef CONTRACTOR_H
#define CONTRACTOR_H

#include <Person.h>
#include <Money.h>

class Contractor : public Person  {
    Date startdate;
    Date enddate;
    Money hourlyrate;
```

Figure 11.33 Contractor.h. (continued)

```cpp
public:
    Contractor(const string& nm = "") : Person(nm)
        { }
    virtual ~Contractor() { }
    Date GetStartDate() const
        { return startdate; }
    Date GetEndDate() const
        { return enddate; }
    Money GetHourlyRate() const
        { return hourlyrate; }
    void SetStartDate(Date date)
        { startdate = date; }
    void SetEndDate(Date date)
        { enddate = date; }
    void SetHourlyRate(Money rate)
        { hourlyrate = rate; }
    virtual void FormattedDisplay(ostream& os);
};

ostream& operator<<(ostream& os, Contractor& cntr);

#endif
```

Figure 11.34 Contractor.cpp.

```cpp
#include <Contractor.h>

void Contractor::FormattedDisplay(ostream& os)
{
    os << "----Contractor----" << endl;
    Person::FormattedDisplay(os);
    os << "Start date:    " << startdate << endl;
    os << "End date:      " << enddate   << endl;
    os << "Hourly rate:   " << hourlyrate << endl;
}
```

Figure 11.34 Contractor.cpp. *(continued)*

```
ostream& operator<<(ostream& os, Contractor& cntr)
{
    os << ((Person&)cntr) << endl
        << cntr.GetStartDate() << endl
        << cntr.GetEndDate() << endl
        << cntr.GetHourlyRate() << endl;
    return os;
}
```

The *Contractor* class is a concrete data type derived from the *Person* class. A contractor is not an employee and, therefore, does not have a date hired, an hourly wage, or a salary. A contractor has start and end dates for the contracted period and, in this example, an hourly rate. The difference between a contractor's hourly rate and a waged employee's hourly wage might seem inconsequential in this small example, but a personnel accounting system more comprehensive than this example would surely include other differences that would more dramatically distinguish the two classes.

Building Object Libraries

A typical software development project compiles its problem domain classes separately and stores them in object libraries. An object library is a file that contains compiled object files that are usually related. A program can link with an object library, and the linker includes in the executable program only those object files from the library that define functions and variables that the program refers to.

Applications programs include the header files that declare the classes and that link with the compiled object libraries to use the non-inline member functions in the class declaration. This is the same way that you link programs to the Standard C++ library classes and functions. The difference is that your project-specific libraries and header files are maintained in private subdirectories rather than in the public ones that contain the Standard C++ files.

If you look at the subdirectory structure for the tutorial exercises, you will see that it has several subdirectories. The Include subdirectory contains all the header files for the libraries, which are to be included in the applications program exercises in this and later chapters. The other subdirectories contain source code, object libraries, and Quincy 97 project files that you use to build the object libraries from the source code. The DataTypes subdirectory contains **Date.cpp**, **Money.cpp**, **DataTypes.prj**, and **DataTypes.a**. These files represent generic user-defined data types that any application might use. The Personnel subdirectory contains **Personnel.prj**, **Personnel.a**, and the **.cpp** files for the *Person* class and its derived classes.

The project files (**.prj**) in these subdirectories are configured to search the Include subdirectory for header files and to build their associated object libraries (**.a**).

The project files for the applications programs are configured to search the Include subdirectory for header files to include and to search the other subdirectories for object library files to link. They are also configured to link with the particular object file libraries that contain class methods for the classes that the programs use.

Using the Problem Domain Class Hierarchy

We now have a problem domain class hierarchy to support a personnel system. That hierarchy uses other general-purpose data abstraction classes, which we have built. Now we need an application to use the classes. We begin with a straightforward application program, as shown in Exercise 11.6.

Exercise 11.6 A personnel application program.

```
#include <WagedEmployee.h>
#include <SalariedEmployee.h>
#include <Contractor.h>

string ReadString(const string& prompt)
{
    string str;
    cout << prompt << ": ";
    getline(cin, str);
    return str;
}
```

Exercise 11.6 A personnel application program. (continued)

```
Date ReadDate(const string& prompt)
{
    Date dt;
    cout << prompt << " (mm dd yy): ";
    cin >> dt;
    return dt;
}

Money ReadMoney(const string& prompt)
{
    double mn;
    cout << prompt << ": ";
    cin >> mn;
    return mn;
}

void PersonInput(Person* pPerson)
{
    static string str;
    getline(cin, str); // flush the input buffer

    pPerson->SetName(ReadString("Name"));
    pPerson->SetAddress(ReadString("Address"));
    pPerson->SetPhone(ReadString("Phone"));
    pPerson->SetDob(ReadDate("Date of birth"));

    long int ssn;
    cout << "SSN: ";
    cin >> ssn;
    pPerson->SetSSN(SSN(ssn));

    char sx;
    do {
        cout << "Sex (m/f) ";
        cin >> sx;
    } while (sx != 'm' && sx != 'f');
    pPerson->SetSex(sx == 'm' ? Person::male : Person::female);
}
```

Exercise 11.6 A personnel application program. (continued)

```
void EmployeeInput(Employee* pEmployee)
{
    pEmployee->SetDateHired(ReadDate("Date hired"));
}

void WagedEmployeeInput(WagedEmployee* pWagedEmployee)
{
    pWagedEmployee->SetHourlyWage(ReadMoney("Hourly wage"));
}

void SalariedEmployeeInput(SalariedEmployee* pSalariedEmployee)
{
    pSalariedEmployee->SetSalary(ReadMoney("Salary"));
}

void ContractorInput(Contractor* pContractor)
{
    pContractor->SetStartDate(ReadDate("Start date"));
    pContractor->SetEndDate(ReadDate("End date"));
    pContractor->SetHourlyRate(ReadMoney("Hourly rate"));
}

int main()
{
    Person* pPerson = 0;
    cout << "1 = Salaried employee" << endl
         << "2 = Waged employee"    << endl
         << "3 = Contractor"        << endl
         << "Enter selection: ";
    int sel;
    cin >> sel;
    switch (sel)  {
```

Exercise 11.6 A personnel application program. (continued)

```
        case 1:
            pPerson = new SalariedEmployee;
            PersonInput(pPerson);
            EmployeeInput((Employee*)pPerson);
            SalariedEmployeeInput((SalariedEmployee*)pPerson);
            break;
        case 2:
            pPerson = new WagedEmployee;
            PersonInput(pPerson);
            EmployeeInput((Employee*)pPerson);
            WagedEmployeeInput((WagedEmployee*)pPerson);
            break;
        case 3:
            pPerson = new Contractor;
            PersonInput(pPerson);
            ContractorInput((Contractor*)pPerson);
            break;
        default:
            cout << "\aIncorrect entry";
            break;
    }
    if (pPerson != 0)  {
        pPerson->FormattedDisplay(cout);
        delete pPerson;
    }
    return 0;
}
```

The program in Exercise 11.6 is a strong mix of object-oriented and functional programming. The object-oriented part uses the personnel system's class hierarchy to instantiate and display objects of type *SalariedEmployee,* *WagedEmployee,* and *Contractor.* The functional part uses nonmember functions for the user interface.

The first three functions in the program are generic user-input functions to prompt for and read data values into objects of the *string, Date,* and *Money* classes. The next five functions, which call the first three, prompt for and read data values into objects of the *Person, Contractor, Employee, WagedEmployee,* and *SalariedEmployee* classes. Because *Person* and *Employee* are abstract base classes, these functions are not called for objects of those classes but instead are called for objects of classes derived from those abstract base classes.

The *main* function displays a menu, reads the user input, and uses *case* statements to process the user's selection. Each case instantiates an object of the type selected by the user. The instantiation allocates memory from the heap by using the *new* operator and assigns that memory to a pointer of type *Person,* which is the root base class of the hierarchy. Then each case calls a set of the class input functions, passing the pointer. The function calls to those functions that expect pointers to type *Contractor, Employee,* and *WagedEmployee* use casts to cast the *Person* pointer to a pointer of the correct type. C++ does not automatically convert a pointer to a base class into a pointer to one of its derived classes, although the opposite conversion is acceptable; you could pass the address of an object of a derived class to a function that expects the address of an object of one of the class's base classes.

Calling Virtual Functions by Reference

When a pointer or reference to a base class refers to a derived class object, a call to a virtual function through the pointer or reference calls the function that is a member of the class of the object—if the object has overridden the virtual function. Exercise 11.6 demonstrates this behavior, and the following code fragment highlights what Exercise 11.6 does:

```
Person* pPerson = new SalariedEmployee;  // instantiate object
pPerson->FormattedDisplay(cout);         // call object's func
```

The call through the *pPerson* pointer—which is declared to be of type *Person*—to the *FormattedDisplay* member function calls the one associated with the class of the object itself rather than with the base class. When the program calls *FormattedDisplay* through *pPerson,* the function that is called depends on the type of the object that *pPerson* points to. When the object is of type *Contractor,* the program calls *Contractor::FormattedDisplay().* When the object is of type *SalariedEmployee,* the program calls *SalariedEmployee::FormattedDisplay().* When the object is of type *WagedEmployee,* the program calls *WagedEmployee::FormattedDisplay().*

Calling Nonvirtual Functions by Reference

If *Person::FormattedDisplay()* were a nonvirtual member function, Exercise 11.6 would always call the *FormattedDisplay()* member function in the *Person* class irrespective of the type of the object that *pPerson* pointed to.

Overriding the Virtual Function Override

If you want a base class's virtual function to execute even when the calling object is of a derived class that has an overriding function, use the base class name and scope resolution operator to specify that the base class function is to execute:

```
pPerson->Person::FormattedDisplay(cout);
```

The overriding function call does not have to specify the topmost base class with the scope resolution operator; it can name any class up the hierarchy. If the named class does not override the virtual function, the compiler searches up the hierarchy until it finds a class that does, and that is the function that is executed. If, for example, the *Employee* class did not have a *FormattedDisplay* member function—it does, but pretend for this discussion that it does not— the following code would execute the *Person::FormattedDisplay* function:

```
Person* pPerson = new WagedEmployee;
//...
pPerson->Employee::FormattedDisplay(cout);
```

Virtual Functions without Derived Overrides

If the derived class has no function to override the base class's virtual function, the base class's function executes regardless of the pointer or reference type.

Virtual Destructors

Usually, when an object of a derived class is destroyed, the destructor for the derived class executes and then the destructor for the base class executes. But suppose that an object is declared with the *new* operator and that the pointer type is that of a base class with a nonvirtual destructor. When the program destroys the object by using the *delete* operator with the pointer as an argument, the base destructor executes instead of the derived destructor. Exercise 11.7, which departs from the personnel class hierarchy to make its point, demonstrates this behavior.

Exercise 11.7 *Nonvirtual base class destructor.*

```
#include <iostream>
using namespace std;

class Shape {
public:
    Shape() {}
    ~Shape()
        { cout << "Executing Shape dtor" << endl; }
};

class Circle : public Shape {
public:
    Circle() {}
    ~Circle()
        { cout << "Executing Circle dtor" << endl; }
};

int main()
{
    Shape* pShape = new Circle;
    // ...
    delete pShape;
    return 0;
}
```

When you run Exercise 11.7, observe that only the *Shape* destructor message is displayed on the console. Even though the object is a *Circle*, the *delete* operator does not know at runtime the type of the object pointed to by *pShape*. This is not usually what you want. You must assume that derived classes can require custom destruction and that their destructors must be called when their objects are destroyed.

When a base class destructor is virtual, the compiler calls the correct destructor function irrespective of the type of the pointer. The version of Exercise 11.8 on the companion CD-ROM duplicates Exercise 11.7 except that the *Shape* destructor is virtual. Exercise 11.8, as displayed here, shows only the *Shape* class definition.

Exercise 11.8 *Virtual base class destructor.*

```
class Shape {
public:
    Shape() {}
    virtual ~Shape()
        { cout << "Executing Shape dtor" << endl; }
};
```

Making the *Shape* destructor virtual solves the problem. The *delete* operator now knows to execute the *Circle* destructor. When you run Exercise 11.8, observe that it displays first the message from the *Circle* destructor and then the message from the *Shape* destructor. A derived class destructor calls its base class destructor after the derived class destructor has done everything else.

If the base class needs no custom destruction, you must still provide a virtual destructor (with an empty statement block) to permit the proper destructor calls for dynamically allocated objects. All the classes in the personnel class hierarchy have virtual destructors.

Even though destructor functions can be virtual, constructor functions cannot be virtual.

NOTE

Which Member Functions Should Be Virtual?

Using virtual functions in your class design is not without some cost. When a class has at least one virtual function, the compiler builds a table of virtual function pointers for that class. This table, commonly called the *vtbl*, contains an entry for each virtual function in the class. Programmers do not usually have to worry about the *vtbl* except to know that its presence is a consequence of having virtual functions. Each object of the class in memory includes a variable called the *vptr*, which points to the class's common *vtbl*. Therefore, don't simply make every function in your class a virtual function just to cover the possibility that someone will someday derive another class from your class.

When you design a class hierarchy, consider each member function with respect to whether it should be virtual. Ask first whether the class is ever likely to be a base class. If it is, make sure that you provide a virtual destructor even if it does nothing. Then ask whether any derived class might have overriding functions (the same name and parameter list as your potential base class's functions). Next, ask whether calls to those functions will always be in the name of the actual object or whether they might be through a pointer or reference to your base class. Answering all that, you can determine whether such calls need the services of the function that is a member of the base class or whether they need a virtual function that finds its way to the member function of the actual class of which the object is a type. These are the kinds of decisions that face the designer of an object-oriented class hierarchy.

POLYMORPHISM

Polymorphism is the ability of different objects in a class hierarchy to exhibit unique behavior in response to the same message. It is the name given to the behavior of the *FormattedDisplay* member functions in the personnel class library just discussed. Polymorphism is from the Greek *poly*, meaning "many," and *morph*, meaning "shape." An object referred to from the perspective of its base class can assume one of *many shapes* depending on the nature of the base class's derived classes and depending on which of these classes the object is an object of.

As you just learned, *Employee* and *Contractor* classes derived from the base *Person* class have different behavior when a member function is called for one of their objects through a pointer or reference to the base *Person* class. It's one thing to understand the behavior of a polymorphic class. It's quite another matter to imagine a realistic scenario wherein the concept might apply. The *Contractor* class in our example class hierarchy assumes the existence of only one kind of contractor. In reality a company can employ several kinds of contractor personnel: subcontractors, independent contractors, contractors from temporary agencies, contractors from job shops, and so on. The company's accounting requirements could vary for each of these kinds of contractors.

You might need to derive more classes from the concrete *Contractor* class, as Figure 11.35 shows, to support these various requirements.

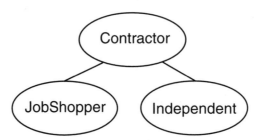

Figure 11.35 *Deriving from a concrete data type class.*

We will not implement these classes in exercises. Instead, we will discuss them briefly. It would be good experience for you to use what you have learned and try now to implement one or more classes derived from *Contractor*.

You might need to add virtual functions to the *Contractor* class. Consider the application function in Figure 11.36, which iterates through a list of *Contractor* objects and calls a function to report contractor compensation. This function does not exist in the *Contractor* class that we implemented earlier in this chapter. You would have to add the function and then provide overriding functions in your derived classes.

Figure 11.36 *Iterating base class pointers.*

```
void ReportCompensationForAll(const Contractor *ctrs[])
{
    while (*ctrs)
        *(ctrs++)->ReportCompensation();
}
```

The *ReportCompensationForAll* function assumes that all the pointers in the argument array point to *Contractor* objects when in fact some of them might point to *Contractor* objects, others to *JobShopper* objects, and the rest to *Independent* objects. Depending on the type of the object, the effects of the member function call can vary. The object itself provides the polymorphic behavior through its overriding *ReportCompensation* member function. The calling *ReportCompensationForAll* function does not care about the details of the report, only that it gets done. In some cases, the effect could be that no action is taken. To override the behavior of a base class virtual function to do nothing at all, you can provide an overriding function with an empty statement list. For example, there might be no requirement to report compensation to a *JobShopper* object. Some other part of your accounting system—accounts payable, perhaps—receives an invoice and pays the bill to the job shop company.

INHERITANCE AND FRAMEWORKS

An application framework class library encapsulates an *application programming interface* (API), which is the set of function-calling conventions that implement applications on a particular operating system platform. The most familiar such platform is Microsoft Windows, and the most commonly used framework is found in the library of the Microsoft Foundation Classes (MFC), which encapsulate the Win32 API. When a Windows C++ MFC programmer needs to display a command button on the screen, the programmer derives a specialized class from the generic MFC *CButton* class, providing specialized text for the button's label and specialized behavior in the form of member functions to execute when the user clicks the button.

Many programmers use inheritance primarily to specialize framework classes to implement a user interface that suits the application. Some of the elements of Exercise 11.6 are user-interface components that are built into the application program. An application framework generalizes such operations into reusable classes to relieve the application programmer of the burden of writing user-interface code for every application program.

To illustrate this principle, I prepared a simple framework that implements a generic, text-based user interface on the console. The *Application* class encapsulates the application and data entry functions, and the *Menu* class encapsulates the menu functions.

Figure 11.37 is **menu.h**, the header file that defines the generic Menu class. This class supports menus with a maximum of 10 commands and assumes that each menu command can be executed by a function that returns *void* and takes no arguments. The program instantiates a menu object, passing the constructor a menu title and a variable number of command arguments that consist of a text label and a function address for each command.

Figure 11.37 Menu.h.

```
#ifndef MENU_H
#define MENU_H

#include <string>

const int maxcommands = 10;

class Menu {
    typedef void (*Mfunc)();
    int cmdcount;
    string title;
    string cmdlabels[maxcommands];
    Mfunc cmdfuncs[maxcommands];
public:
    Menu(char* ttl, ...);
    void Execute();
};

#endif
```

Figure 11.38 is **menu.cpp**, the source-code file that implements the member functions of the generic *Menu* class.

Figure 11.38 Menu.cpp.

```
#include <cstdarg>
#include <iostream>
using namespace std;
#include <Menu.h>

Menu::Menu(char* ttl, ...) : title(ttl)
{
    cmdcount = 0;
    va_list ap;
    va_start(ap, ttl);
    while (cmdcount < maxcommands)  {
```

Figure 11.38 Menu.cpp. (continued)

```
        char* cmdstr = va_arg(ap, char*);
        if (cmdstr == 0)
            break;
        cmdlabels[cmdcount] = cmdstr;
        cmdfuncs[cmdcount++] = va_arg(ap, Mfunc);
    }
    va_end(ap);
}
void Menu::Execute()
{
    unsigned int selection;
    do   {
        // --- display the menu
        int sel;
        cout << endl << title << endl;
        for (sel = 1; sel <= cmdcount; sel++)
            cout << sel
                << " = "
                << cmdlabels[sel-1] << endl;
        cout << sel << " = quit" << endl;
        cout << "Enter selection: ";
        cin >> selection;
        --selection;
        if (selection < cmdcount)
            (*cmdfuncs[selection])();
    } while (selection != cmdcount);
}
```

The *Menu* class constructor uses the Standard C++ **<cstdarg>** variable argument feature (Chapter 6, Exercise 6.4) to initialize the *Menu* object's data members. The anchor argument is the menu title. The following arguments are pairs of *char* pointers and function pointers, one pair for each menu command. The terminal argument is a null pointer.

The *Menu::Execute* function executes a *Menu* object. First, it displays the menu selection text labels, prefixing each one with a numeric selection number. The user will enter this number to select an item from the menu. The last selection is always labeled **quit**, and its selection number is 1 greater than the last command selection number. The *Execute* function iterates the menu until the user enters the **quit** selection number.

Figure 11.39 is **application.h**, the header file that defines the *Application* class.

Figure 11.39 Application.h.

```
#ifndef APPLICATION_H
#define APPLICATION_H

#include <string>
#include <Date.h>
#include <Money.h>
#include <SSN.h>
#include <Menu.h>

class Application {
    Menu& menu;
public:
    Application(Menu& mn) : menu(mn)
        { }
    virtual ~Application() { }
    void ReadData(string& str, const string& prompt);
    void ReadData(Date& date, const string& prompt);
    void ReadData(Money& money, const string& prompt);
    void ReadData(SSN& ssn, const string& prompt);
    void ExecuteMenu()
        { menu.Execute(); }
};
#endif
```

Figure 11.40 is **application.cpp**, the source-code file that implements the member functions of the *Application* class.

Figure 11.40 Application.cpp.

```
#include <iostream>
using namespace std;
#include <Application.h>

void Application::ReadData(string& str, const string& prompt)
{

    cout << prompt << ": ";
    getline(cin, str);


}
void Application::ReadData(Date& date, const string& prompt)
{

    cout << prompt << " (mm dd yy): ";
    cin >> date;
}
void Application::ReadData(Money& money, const string& prompt)
{

    double mn;
    cout << prompt << ": ";
    cin >> mn;
    money = mn;
}
void Application::ReadData(SSN& ssn, const string& prompt)
{

    long sn;
    cout << "SSN: ";
    cin >> sn;
    ssn = SSN(sn);
}
```

An application program instantiates and initializes a *Menu* object. Then it instantiates an *Application* object (usually an object of a class derived from *Application*) with the *Menu* object as an initializer. The *Application::Execute* function executes the *Menu* object, which runs the application from the menu. The *Application* class's *ReadData* member functions prompt for and read data values into objects of the *string, Date, Money,* and *SSN* data abstraction types discussed earlier in this chapter.

We begin by deriving a class from the generic *Application* class. Figure 11.41 is the *PersonnelAppl* class, which encapsulates those components unique to a personnel data entry application.

Figure 11.41 PersonnelAppl.h.

```
#ifndef PERSONNELAPPL_H
#define PERSONNELAPPL_H

#include <Application.h>
#include <WagedEmployee.h>
#include <SalariedEmployee.h>
#include <Contractor.h>

class PersonnelAppl : public Application  {
    Person* pPerson;
    void PersonInput();
    void EmployeeInput();
    void WagedEmployeeInput();
    void SalariedEmployeeInput();
    void ContractorInput();
public:
    PersonnelAppl(Menu& mn) : Application(mn)
        { }
    void GetSalariedInput();
    void GetWagedInput();
    void GetContractorInput();
};
#endif
```

The *PersonnelAppl* class's public interface includes a constructor and three public member functions for collecting data into *SalariedEmployee*, *WagedEmployee*, and *Contractor* objects. The class has private member functions for getting the unique data values for the *Person, Employee, WagedEmployee, SalariedEmployee,* and *Contractor* components of the three basic object types. Figure 11.42 is **PersonnelAppl.cpp**, the source-code file that implements the *PersonnelAppl* class member functions.

Figure 11.42 PersonnelAppl.cpp.

```cpp
#include "PersonnelAppl.h"

void PersonnelAppl::PersonInput()
{
    static string str;
    getline(cin, str); // flush the input buffer

    ReadData(str, "Name");
    pPerson->SetName(str);
    ReadData(str, "Address");
    pPerson->SetAddress(str);
    ReadData(str, "Phone");
    pPerson->SetPhone(str);

    Date dob;
    ReadData(dob, "Date of birth");
    pPerson->SetDob(dob);

    SSN ssn;
    ReadData(ssn, "SSN");
    pPerson->SetSSN(ssn);

    char sx;
    do {
        cout << "Sex (m/f) ";
        cin >> sx;
    } while (sx != 'm' && sx != 'f');
    pPerson->SetSex(sx == 'm' ? Person::male : Person::female);
}
```

Figure 11.42 PersonnelAppl.cpp. *(continued)*

```cpp
void PersonnelAppl::EmployeeInput()
{
    Date date;
    ReadData(date, "Date hired");
    ((Employee*)pPerson)->SetDateHired(date);
}
void PersonnelAppl::WagedEmployeeInput()
{
    Money money;
    ReadData(money, "Hourly wage");
    ((WagedEmployee*)pPerson)->SetHourlyWage(money);
}
void PersonnelAppl::SalariedEmployeeInput()
{
    Money money;
    ReadData(money, "Salary");
    ((SalariedEmployee*)pPerson)->SetSalary(money);
}
void PersonnelAppl::ContractorInput()
{
    Date date;
    ReadData(date, "Start date");
    ((Contractor*)pPerson)->SetStartDate(date);
    ReadData(date, "End date");
    ((Contractor*)pPerson)->SetEndDate(date);
    Money money;
    ReadData(money, "Hourly rate");
    ((Contractor*)pPerson)->SetHourlyRate(money);
}
```

Figure 11.42 PersonnelAppl.cpp. (continued)

```
void PersonnelAppl::GetSalariedInput()
{
    pPerson = new SalariedEmployee;
    PersonInput();
    EmployeeInput();
    SalariedEmployeeInput();
    pPerson->FormattedDisplay(cout);
    delete pPerson;
}
void PersonnelAppl::GetWagedInput()
{
    pPerson = new WagedEmployee;
    PersonInput();
    EmployeeInput();
    WagedEmployeeInput();
    pPerson->FormattedDisplay(cout);
    delete pPerson;
}
void PersonnelAppl::GetContractorInput()
{
    pPerson = new Contractor;
    PersonInput();
    ContractorInput();
    pPerson->FormattedDisplay(cout);
    delete pPerson;
}
```

Having designed and implemented an *Application*-derived class that encapsulates the data entry behavior for the personnel data types, we next write a program that uses that class. Exercise 11.9 is such a program.

Exercise 11.9 The PersonnelAppl class in use.

```
#include "PersonnelAppl.h"

int main()
{
    Menu menu(
        "Personnel Data Entry",
        "Salaried employee", PersonnelAppl::GetSalariedInput,
        "Waged employee",    PersonnelAppl::GetWagedInput,
        "Contractor",        PersonnelAppl::GetContractorInput,
        0
    );
    PersonnelAppl* appl = new PersonnelAppl(menu);
    appl->ExecuteMenu();
    delete appl;
    return 0;
}
```

SUMMARY

This chapter taught you how to use inheritance for data abstraction, for designing an object-oriented class hierarchy, and for integrating your application into an application framework class library. Chapter 12 carries these concepts a step further by addressing multiple inheritance, a language feature that permits a class to be derived directly from more than one base class.

CHAPTER 12

Multiple Inheritance

This chapter is about multiple inheritance (MI), an object-oriented design technique that is the subject of much debate and disagreement. Many object-oriented programmers believe that you should avoid using MI at all times because of inherent problems associated with the design model. This belief finds its way into new language design; Java, for example, does not support MI for class design. Other programmers view MI as a tool to be used when appropriate. C++ supports MI, so this chapter explains it. I leave it to you to choose which side of the debate you prefer to join. You will learn about:

- Deriving from multiple base classes
- MI design ambiguities
- Base class constructor and destructor execution
- Virtual base classes

MULTIPLE BASE CLASSES

In multiple inheritance, a derived class has more than one base class. This technique allows you to define a new class that inherits the characteristics of several unrelated base classes. Figure 12.1 illustrates this principle with a simple property accounting system.

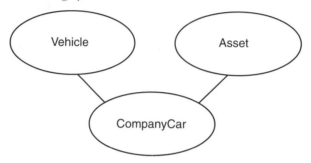

Figure 12.1 *Multiple inheritance.*

Figure 12.1 illustrates the design model under which you would apply MI. This example suggests a class design that supports an organization's vehicles and assets. The *Vehicle* class encapsulates the data and behavior that describe vehicles. Date acquired, useful life, and maintenance schedules might be included in the *Vehicle* class. Classes that support specific kinds of vehicles—trucks, airplanes, cars—would be derived from the *Vehicle* class. The *Asset* class encapsulates the data and behavior of the organization's assets, including date acquired and depreciation schedule data for accounting purposes. A company car, being both a vehicle and an asset, is represented by a class that derives from both base classes.

You might wonder why the design does not simply put the vehicle and asset data and behavior into the *CompanyCar* class. The reason is two-fold. First, not all vehicles are assets. The company might use lease cars, for example, which are expensed rather than depreciated for tax purposes. Those vehicles are not assets in the accounting sense of the word. Second, not all assets are vehicles. The company has other depreciable assets—office furniture, copiers, computers, and so on.

For this discussion, assume that the *Vehicle* and *Asset* classes are defined as shown here:

```
class Vehicle {
public:
    Vehicle(int vehno);
    // ...
};

class Asset {
public:
    Asset(int assetno);
    // ...
};
```

You specify more than one base class when you define a derived class with multiple inheritance. The following code shows how you define the *CompanyCar* class given that the *Vehicle* and *Asset* class definitions are in scope:

```
class CompanyCar : public Vehicle, public Asset {
    // ...
};
```

As with single inheritance (Chapter 11), the colon operator after the class identifier specifies that base class specifications follow. The comma operator separates the base classes.

The constructor function declaration in a class derived from multiple bases specifies the arguments for the constructors of all the base classes, as shown here:

```
CompanyCar::CompanyCar(int vehicleno, int assetno)
              : Vehicle(vehicleno), Asset(assetno)
{
    // ...
}
```

CONSTRUCTOR EXECUTION WITH MULTIPLE INHERITANCE

When the program declares an object of a class that is derived from multiple bases, the constructors for the base classes are called first. The order of execution is the order in which the base classes are declared as bases to the derived class.

In the case of the *CompanyCar* class, the constructor for the *Vehicle* class executes first, followed by the constructor for the *Asset* class. The constructor for the *CompanyCar* class executes last.

If the class definition includes an object of another class as a data member, that class's constructor executes after the constructors for the base classes and before the constructor for the class being defined. Consider the following example:

```
class CompanyCar : public Vehicle, public Asset {
    Date NextOilChange;
    // ...
};
```

The order of constructor execution is *Vehicle, Asset, NextOilChange,* and *CompanyCar.*

DESTRUCTOR EXECUTION WITH MULTIPLE INHERITANCE

When an object of a class goes out of scope, the destructors execute in the reverse order of the constructors.

REFINING THE PROPERTY SYSTEM DESIGN

We won't implement these classes in an exercise until we understand more about the requirements from a practical point of view. The relationships we just discussed are an oversimplification of the real problem domain.

To follow these examples it helps to know that an organization's physical property is divided into two categories for accounting purposes: depreciable assets and expensed items. To deduct from taxes the cost of a depreciable asset, which the organization owns, you distribute the asset's cost over several years. This distribution is called *depreciating* the asset. The number of years and the amount to be written off each year are written into tax law and are a function of the kind of asset you are depreciating. Computers, vehicles, and office buildings, for example, are depreciated according to distinct formulas. Expenses, on the other hand, are not depreciated; you write off the total cost of each expense in the year that you incur the expense. Expensed items include office supplies, leased items, and other tangible property that is not depreciated; these items are accounted for along with nontangible expenses such as labor, professional fees, insurance, and rent. The IRS provides guidelines as to which kinds of property to expense and which kinds to depreciate. The accounting procedures for depreciable assets and expenses differ, so an automated accounting system must provide different behavior for objects of the two categories.

With that in mind, we take a different view of the problem. Depreciable assets and expensed items, being property, have some things in common. Each category of property has a control number, name, date acquired, and cost. These shared attributes can be represented by a *Property* base class. Figure 12.2 shows these relationships in a single-inheritance class hierarchy.

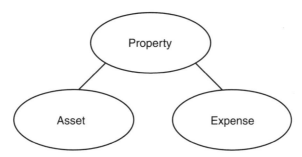

Figure 12.2 *Asset and Expense derived from Property.*

Vehicles have common characteristics unrelated to whether they are assets or expenses, so the *Vehicle* class is not derived from anything but serves instead as a base class for the various kinds of vehicle classes, which must then be further specialized according to their property category.

Given that we must account for vehicle and nonvehicle assets and expenses, the class hierarchy for our property system might look like Figure 12.3.

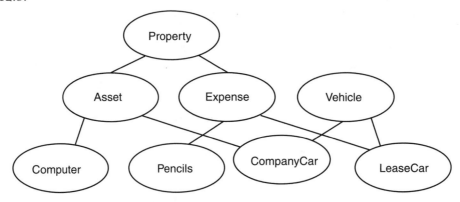

Figure 12.3 *An MI class hierarchy.*

The design shown in Figure 12.3 uses MI in two places. The *CompanyCar* class is derived from *Vehicle* and *Asset*, and the *LeaseCar* class is derived from *Vehicle* and *Expense*. These models reflect the design objective that derived classes are specializations of their base classes.

OVERRIDING MEMBERS WITH MULTIPLE INHERITANCE

Suppose that the *Property*, *Vehicle*, and *LeaseCar* classes all have functions with the same name and argument list and that some of the base classes have data members with the same name, as shown here:

```
class Property {
public:
    int ctlno;
    virtual void Display();
    // ...
};

class Expense : public Property {
    // ...
};
```

```
class Vehicle  {
public:
    int ctlno;
    virtual void Display();
    // ...
};

class LeaseCar : public Expense, public Vehicle  {
public:
    virtual void Display();
    // ...
};
```

The *LeaseCar::Display* function overrides both base class *Display* functions just as it would in a single-inheritance hierarchy. The *LeaseCar::Display* function can call the two base class *Display* functions by using the scope resolution operator, as shown here:

```
void LeaseCar::Display()
{
    Expense::Display();
    Vehicle::Display();
    // ...
}
```

Notice that the *LeaseCar::Display* function calls *Expense::Display* even though the *Expense* class has no *Display* member function. The compiler searches up the hierarchy until it finds a matching member function. In this case, the compiler finds the *Display* member function in the *Property* class.

AMBIGUITIES WITH MULTIPLE INHERITANCE

The class hierarchy that Figure 12.3 represents appears to be solid with no ambiguities. One potential data member ambiguity exists in the code, however, and we will contrive another ambiguity: a member function to demonstrate how to deal with and resolve ambiguities.

The problems represented by the ambiguous behavior we are about to discuss are among the reasons that many programmers disapprove of using MI in class design.

Ambiguous Member Functions

Suppose that the *LeaseCar* class had no *Display* function to override the virtual *Display* functions of the two base classes:

```
class LeaseCar : public Expense, public Vehicle  {
public:
    // ...
};
```

This omission introduces a potential ambiguity into the design: A call to *LeaseCar::Display* does not work, because the compiler does not know which of the base class *Display* functions to call. The ambiguity is not a problem if you do not attempt to call the *Display* function directly through an object of type *LeaseCar* or a pointer or reference to one. But suppose that you want to call one of the *Display* functions. You can resolve the ambiguity by using the scope resolution operator to specify which class's *Display* function to call:

```
LeaseCar myChevy;
myChevy.Vehicle::Display();
myChevy.Expense::Display();
```

Ambiguous Data Members

The class design has another potential ambiguity not related to ambiguous member functions. Both base classes have a public integer data member with the name *ctlno,* and the derived class has no such data member. In this case, the member functions of the derived class must use the scope resolution operator to resolve which base class's data member to use:

```
void LeaseCar::Display()
{
    cout << Vehicle::ctlno;
    // ...
}
```

In this example the ambiguous members are public. The program that instantiates an object of the class cannot access such an ambiguous member directly through the object. The program must use the scope resolution operator and the base class name:

```
LeaseCar myChevy;
myChevy.Vehicle::ctlno = 123;
myChevy.Vehicle::Display();
```

Resolving Ambiguities in the Design

Generally, you try to resolve ambiguities in the class design. In this case, you would put member functions into the *LeaseCar* class that provide the necessary access to the base classes. The first version of *LeaseCar* in this discussion did just that for the *Display* member function. Because data members are typically private and are accessed through member functions, the class design would probably look like this:

```
class Property  {
protected:
    int ctlno;
public:
    virtual void Display();
    // ...
};

class Expense : public Property {
    // ...
};

class Vehicle  {
protected:
    int ctlno;
public:
    virtual void Display();
    // ...
};
```

```
class LeaseCar : public Expense, public Vehicle  {
public:
    virtual void Display();
    void SetVehicleCtlNo(int cno)
        { Vehicle::ctlno = cno; }
    void SetExpenseCtlNo(int cno)
        { Expense::ctlno = cno; }
    int GetVehicleCtlno() const
        { return Vehicle::ctlno; }
    int GetExpenseCtlno() const
        { return Expense::ctlno; }
    // ...
};
```

The ambiguous *ctlno* data members are protected, and that means that only member functions of the classes can access them. The *LeaseCar* public interface includes getter and setter member functions that resolve the ambiguity by providing specific access to the base class data members.

Unavoidable Ambiguities

Would you intentionally introduce such ambiguities into a class design? Would you design *Property* and *Vehicle* classes with member names that collide? Probably not, but suppose that you are deriving the *LeaseCar* class from two existing classes that other programs and other applications use extensively. Maybe you are extending the application's design to support leased cars because the organization recently decided to lease cars. Maybe the *Vehicle* class comes from a completely different application, such as a maintenance management system. All these factors can contribute to circumstances under which class designs involve ambiguities beyond your control. You must be prepared to understand and deal with them.

VIRTUAL BASE CLASSES

With multiple inheritance, the potential exists for a derived class to have too many instances of one of the bases. Suppose that the property system class hierarchy is designed in a pure object-oriented environment and all classes are derived directly or indirectly from a common base class. For this example we will use a class called *DisplayObject*. Its purpose—contrived for this example—is to store and report on demand the date and time the object was created, perhaps as a debugging aid. Figure 12.4 updates the class hierarchy diagram accordingly.

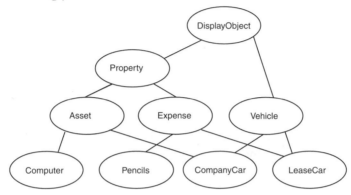

Figure 12.4 *An object-oriented MI class hierarchy.*

The *DisplayObject* class is an abstract base class from which the *Property* and *Vehicle* classes are derived. Because all the other classes in the hierarchy descend from one of these two, all the classes inherit the characteristics of the *DisplayObject* class.

   This MI design has a built-in problem. *LeaseCar* and *CompanyCar* are multiply derived from classes that are themselves derived from *DisplayObject*. Consequently, *LeaseCar* and *CompanyCar* inherit *DisplayObject*'s data members twice. You do not want that to happen. Objects of those derived classes do not need two copies of *DisplayObject*'s data members. Furthermore, any attempt to address a *DisplayObject* data member for a *LeaseCar* or *CompanyCar* object would result in a compile-time ambiguity that the program could resolve only by applying the scope resolution operator to associate the member with one of the intermediate base classes. The two copies of *DisplayObject*'s data members would, no doubt, represent compromised integrity of the design when they are modified and accessed from different places in the hierarchy.

   The problem just revealed is another of the reasons that many programmers disapprove of using MI in a design. C++ addresses the problem with the *virtual base class*. C++ allows you to specify in the definition of a derived class that a base class is virtual. All virtual occurrences of the base class throughout the class hierarchy share one actual occurrence of it when an object of a derived class is instantiated. To specify a virtual base class in the derived class definition, use the following notation:

```
class Vehicle : public virtual DisplayObject   {
    // ...
};
```

There are rules, however, about how a virtual base class can itself be specified. A class whose constructor has parameters cannot be a virtual base class. If this restriction did not exist, the compiler would not know which constructor argument list from which derived class to use. Another restriction: A pointer to a virtual base class cannot be cast to a class that is derived from it either directly or further down the class hierarchy.

IMPLEMENTING THE DESIGN

To demonstrate that all these theories work, we implement and use the class hierarchy that we just designed. The classes are small, and we use header files and inline member functions to keep the example as simple as possible.

The *DisplayObject* Class

We begin with the class definition of the root base class, *DisplayObject*, shown in Figure 12.5 as the source-code file **DisplayObject.h**.

Figure 12.5 DisplayObject.h.

```
#ifndef DISPLAYOBJECT_H
#define DISPLAYOBJECT_H

#include <iostream>
using namespace std;
#include <ctime>

class DisplayObject {
    time_t tm;
protected:
    DisplayObject()
        { tm = time(0); }
public:
    ReportTime()
        { cout << "Obj constructed: "<< ctime(&tm); }
};
#endif
```

The *DisplayObject* class constructor uses the Standard C *ctime* function (Chapter 6) to record in a *time*_t data member the time the object was constructed. The constructor is protected, and that makes the class an abstract base class.

The *Vehicle* Class

Figure 12.6, **Vehicle.h**, implements the *Vehicle* class.

Figure 12.6 Vehicle.h.

```
#ifndef VEHICLE_H
#define VEHICLE_H

#include <string>
#include "DisplayObject.h"

class Vehicle : public virtual DisplayObject   {
    int year;
    string model;
public:
    Vehicle(int yr, const string& md) : year(yr), model (md)
        { }
    virtual ~Vehicle() { }
    void MaintenanceSchedule()
    {
        cout << "Maintenance Schedule" << endl;
        cout << year << " " << model << endl;
    }
};
#endif
```

The *Vehicle* class is derived from the virtual base *DisplayObject* class. *Vehicle* includes data members to store the vehicle model year and name. This class is typical of one that represents cars. In a real system you would probably have a *Vehicle* base class with derived classes named *Car, Truck, Forklift, Airplane, Tugboat,* and so on.

The *Property* Class

Figure 12.7, Property.h, implements the Property class.

Figure 12.7 Property.h.

```
#ifndef PROPERTY_H
#define PROPERTY_H

#include <string>
#include <Date.h>
#include <Money.h>
#include "DisplayObject.h"

class Property : public virtual DisplayObject  {
    int idnbr;          // id number
    string name;        // property name
    Date dateacquired;  // date acquired
    Money cost;         // cost

protected:
    Property(int id) : idnbr(id)
        { }
    virtual ~Property() { }
public:
    int GetNbr() const
        { return idnbr; }
    void SetName(const string& nm)
        { name = nm; }
    const string& GetName()
        { return name; }
```

Figure 12.7 Property.h. (continued)

```
    void SetDate(Date dt)
        { dateacquired = dt; }
    const Date& GetDate() const
        { return dateacquired; }
    void SetCost(Money cst)
        { cost = cst; }
    Money GetCost() const
        { return cost; }
};
#endif
```

The *Property* class is derived from the virtual base *DisplayObject* class. It includes data members that store the property's identification number, the name of the property item, the date it was acquired, and its cost. Its public interface includes getter and setter functions that provide access to the data members. The constructor and destructor are protected, so *Property* is an abstract base class.

The *Asset* and *Expense* Classes

Figure 12.8, **Asset.h**, implements the *Asset* class, and Figure 12.9, **Expense.h**, implements the *Expense* class.

Figure 12.8 Asset.h.

```
#ifndef ASSET_H
#define ASSET_H

#include "Property.h"

class Asset : public Property  {
public:
    enum type { straight, sliding };
private:
    int type;
```

Figure 12.8 Asset.h. (continued)

```
public:
    Asset(int id, type ty) : Property(id), type(ty)
        { }
    virtual ~Asset() { }
    virtual void Schedule()
        { cout << "Schedule for " << GetName() << endl; }
};
#endif
```

Figure 12.9 Expense.h.

```
#ifndef EXPENSE_H
#define EXPENSE_H

#include "Property.h"

class Expense : public Property  {
public:
    Expense(int id) : Property(id)
        { }
    virtual ~Expense() { }
};
#endif
```

The *Asset* and *Expense* classes are derived from the *Property* class. The principal differences are that the *Asset* class includes an asset type initializer and data member that presumably would be used in computing its depreciation schedule, a process that is simulated in this example by the *Schedule* member function. The *Expense* class has no type or *Schedule* members.

The *Computer* and *Pencils* Classes

We won't implement the *Computer* and *Pencils* classes as a part of this exercise even though they are included in the class hierarchy diagram in Figure 12.4.

Their behavior is trivial in this context, and they do not employ MI, so they have nothing to add to this lesson that you did not already learn in Chapter 11.

The *CompanyCar* and *LeaseCar* Classes

Now we get to the part of the example that involves MI. Figure 12.10, **Cars.h**, implements the *CompanyCar* and *LeaseCar* classes.

Figure 12.10 Cars.h.

```
#ifndef CARS_H
#define CARS_H

#include "Vehicle.h"
#include "Asset.h"
#include "Expense.h"

class CompanyCar : public Vehicle, public Asset {
public:
    CompanyCar(int id, int year, const string& model) :
            Vehicle(year, model), Asset(id, Asset::straight)
        {  }
};

class LeaseCar : public Vehicle, public Expense {
public:
    LeaseCar(int id, int year, const string& model) :
                Vehicle(year, model), Expense(id)
        {  }
};
#endif
```

The *CompanyCar* class is multiply derived from *Vehicle* and *Asset*. The *LeaseCar* class is multiply derived from *Vehicle* and *Expense*. Remember that *Asset* and *Expense* are each derived from *Property* and that *Property* and *Vehicle* are each derived from *DisplayObject*. That is why *DisplayObject* must be a virtual base class in this hierarchy.

The Application

Exercise 12.1 represents the application that uses the class hierarchy we just formed.

Exercise 12.1 *Using multiple inheritance.*

```
#include "cars.h"

int main()
{
    CompanyCar car1(1, 1996, "Chevy");
    LeaseCar   car2(2, 1997, "Ford");
    car1.MaintenanceSchedule();
    car1.ReportTime();
    car2.MaintenanceSchedule();
    car2.ReportTime();
    return 0;
}
```

Exercise 12.1 does not use all the features of the class hierarchy. It does not add costs, names, or dates acquired, and it does not report all the data values. It calls the *Vehicle::MaintenanceSchedule* function for both objects to identify the object. Then it calls the *ReportTime* member function of the root base class *DisplayObject* to demonstrate the behavior of the virtual base class.

SOME PRACTICE

Return now to Chapter 11 and review Figure 11.13, where we discussed design choices for the *SpecialJulianDate* class. We chose a design approach that did not involve MI, because you had not yet learned about MI. Given what you have learned in this chapter, redesign the *SpecialJulianDate* class with MI, as diagrammed in Figure 12.11.

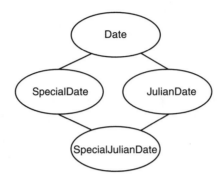

Figure 12.11 *Revising the* SpecialJulianDate *class.*

SUMMARY

Now that you understand the behavior of MI in a class hierarchy, you can decide for yourself whether the model suits your programming style. When base classes are not virtual, the potential ambiguities and duplicate data members can make for designs that are complex and difficult to comprehend. The two preeminent application frameworks for Windows are the Microsoft Foundation Classes (MFC) and Borland's Object Windows Library (OWL). OWL makes extensive use of MI, whereas MFC contains no MI. These two class hierarchy designs represent opposite design philosophies for solving the same problem. Both of them work well.

CHAPTER 13

Templates

This chapter is about C++ *templates*, a mechanism that supports a programming idiom called *parameterized data types*. The ANSI Standard C++ library (Chapter 16) depends heavily on templates, although not all contemporary C++ compilers have implemented the library through that mechanism. They have not implemented the changes to the template mechanism to support the library standard. The GNU compiler that accompanies this book on the companion CD-ROM is among those compilers that are not yet fully compliant with the proposed ANSI standard specification. Consequently, this chapter discusses traditional templates as they were implemented before the template innovations of the ANSI committee. Eventually, most compilers will comply, and a future edition of this book will describe templates as they are defined in the standard specification.

This chapter shows you how and when to use templates. You will learn about:

- Class templates
- Template specialization
- Function templates

CLASS TEMPLATES

Class templates allow you to describe a generic data type to manage other data types. Class templates are typically used to build general-purpose container classes, such as stacks, lists, and queues, in which the maintenance of the container is generic but the item in the container is specific. The Standard C++ library (Chapter 16) includes many such template container classes.

Consider the *ListEntry* linked list class that you used in Chapter 9 in Exercises 9.20 and 9.24. These particular linked list classes manage lists of character pointers. A program might need several linked lists, each one managing a different data type.

By using a class template, you can define a generic linked list class with an unspecified data type to be in the list. You can then associate specific classes with the template.

The format of a class template specification is shown in this example:

```
template<class T>
class LinkedList {
    T& p;
    // ...
public:
    // ...
    void AddEntry(T &entry);
};
```

The template specifies objects of type *LinkedList* with an unspecified data type as a parameter. Users of the template specify the data type to be managed by the list.

The first part of a class template definition and its member function definitions is the template specifier:

```
template<class T>
```

The *T* identifier represents the parameterized data type throughout the definition. The identifier can be any C++ data type, including intrinsic types and classes. The use of *T* for the primary template parameter is a convention. You can use any valid C++ identifier instead.

As with normal classes, you must provide the member functions for a class template. The *LinkedList* example has an *AddEntry* member function. You define the function as shown here:

```
template<class T>
void LinkedList<T>::AddEntry(T &entry)
{
    // ...
}
```

These function definitions are in the header file that contains the class definition. They must be visible to the program that declares objects of the class template. They do not generate any code until they are used.

You declare an object of a class template by specifying the name of the class and its parameterized data type:

```
LinkedList<int> IntList;
```

This statement declares an object from the *LinkedList* template with the *int* data type as the parameter.

Think of C++ templates as macros. The compiler uses the object declaration to build the class definition and functions. The compiler substitutes the template argument, which is *int* in the example just shown, for the template parameter, which is *T* in the *LinkedList* template example.

You can declare more than one object of a class template in the same program. For example, given the *LinkedList* template just shown, a program can declare two different linked lists:

```
LinkedList<char*> StrList;
LinkedList<Date> DateList;
```

These statements declare two *LinkedList* objects. The first one is a list of character pointers. The second one is a list of *Date* objects. These two statements cause the compiler to generate two copies of the member functions in the template. Each copy is customized to work with the type specified in the declaration. In this example, there is a copy of the code for character pointers and a second one for the *Date* class. Wherever the template definition uses *T*, the compiler substitutes *char** for the first object and *Date* for the second. This means that the code in the template's member functions must work in the context of those types.

If you use the same data types for two different objects of the same template, as shown next, the compiler generates only one set of code for the two objects.

```
LinkedList<int> monthList;
LinkedList<int> yearList;
```

The using program calls a class template's member functions just as it calls member functions of other classes. For example, you can add entries to the *LinkedList* objects with these calls:

```
Date dt(6,24,93);        // a date
DateList.AddEntry(dt);   // add the date to DateList

char* name = "Dolly";    // a string
StrList.AddEntry(name);  // add the string to StrList

int n = 123;             // an int
IntList.AddEntry(n);     // add the int to IntList
```

A template can contain more than one data type parameter, making it possible to build parameterized data types of considerable complexity. The parameters can be classes, which are identified by the *class* keyword. Other parameters can be specific data types, as shown here:

```
template <class T, class S, int b>
```

At least one parameter should be a class. When you declare an object of the class template, you must use actual types where they are called for. In the example just shown, you can use any type for the first two parameters, but the third type must be an *int*.

Exercise 13.1 illustrates how a class template works.

Exercise 13.1 A simple class template.

```
#include <iostream>
using namespace std;

template<class T1, class T2>
class MyTemp {
    T1 t1;
    T2 t2;
public:
    MyTemp(T1 tt1, T2 tt2)
        { t1 = tt1; t2 = tt2; }
    void display()
        { cout << t1 << ' ' << t2 << endl; }
};

int main()
{
    int a = 123;
    double b = 456.789;
    MyTemp<int, double> mt(a, b);
    mt.display();
    return 0;
}
```

The template in Exercise 13.1 builds a parameterized type from two parameters. The class template stores and displays values. The main function declares an object of the type with an *int* and a *double* as the parameters. Then it tells the object to display itself. Exercise 13.1 displays this output:

```
123 456.789
```

Exercise 13.1 calls attention to something to consider when you use a template. The template sends its parameterized types to the *cout* object by using the << insertion operator. Therefore, any type that you use with the template must be compatible with that operation, and this means that there must be an overloaded << operator function that accepts *ostream* objects on the left and objects of the parameterized type on the right. Exercise 13.1 works because the *ostream* class can accept *ints* and *doubles* with the << operator. If a class template uses relational operators to compare objects of the parameterized type, the type must be able to use those operators, too. C++ intrinsic types would work with such a template, but user-defined types would not work if you have not overloaded the relational operators.

A Bounded Array Class Template

C and C++ programmers often build bugs into their programs because the language does not test whether an array subscript is within the bounds of the array. The following code passes the compiler's error tests and executes with no run time bounds-checking.

```
int main()
{
    int array[10];
    for (int i = 0; i <= 10; i++)
        array[i] = 123;
    return 0;
}
```

The problem with the code is that the subscript is allowed to go beyond the end of the array. The array has 10 elements. The subscript is allowed to go as high as 10, which references the 11th element, which does not exist. However, the program writes an integer into the next integer position in memory beyond the array. The result depends on the program and the compiler. If you are lucky, the program aborts early in testing and you find the problem. If you are not so lucky, the 11th array element is in a harmless position, and you do not encounter the bug until much later when it is more difficult to isolate.

Other languages have bounded arrays. The runtime systems of those languages do not allow you to address an array with a subscript that is beyond the array's boundaries. The cost is in runtime efficiency.

You can use a template to add bounded arrays to your programs without adding much overhead. The technique depends on your understanding not only of templates but also of the Standard C *assert* macro (Chapter 6). Figure 13.1 is **barray.h**, the class template for the bounded array.

Figure 13.1 Barray.h.

```
// ------ barray.h
#ifndef BARRAY_H
#define BARRAY_H

#include <cassert>
using namespace std;

// --- a bounded array template
template <class T, int b>
class Array    {
    T elem [b];
public:
    Array() { /* ... */ }
    T& operator[] (int sub)
    {
        assert(sub >= 0 && sub < b);
        return elem[sub];
    }
};
#endif
```

This simple template has one purpose: to check all subscripted references to array elements and abort the program if a subscript is out of bounds. Observe that the template specifier has two parameter types:

```
template <class T, int b>
```

NOTE

If the template included non-inline member functions, the statement just shown would immediately precede the function definitions as well.

The overloaded subscript operator ([ ]) function in the *Array* class template grants read-write subscripted access to elements of the array. The *assert* macro validates the subscript's value. If the value is less than zero or greater than the array's dimension minus 1, the *assert* macro displays an error message on the *stderr* device and aborts the program.

Exercise 13.2 uses the bounded array template.

Exercise 13.2 *Using a bounded array template.*

```
#include <iostream>
#include <iomanip>
using namespace std;
#include <Date.h>
#include "Barray.h"

int main()
{
    // ---- a bounded array of dates
    Array<Date, 5> dateArray;

    // ----- some dates
    Date dt1(12,17,37);
    Date dt2(11,30,38);
    Date dt3(6,24,40);
    Date dt4(10,31,42);
    Date dt5(8,5,44);

    // ----- put the dates in the array
    dateArray[0] = dt1;
    dateArray[1] = dt2;
    dateArray[2] = dt3;
    dateArray[3] = dt4;
    dateArray[4] = dt5;
```

Exercise 13.2 Using a bounded array template. (continued)

```
    // ------ display the dates
    for (int i = 0; i < 5; i++)
        cout << dateArray[i] << endl;
    cout << flush;
    // ---- try to put a date in the array
    //      outside the range of the subscript
    Date dt6(1,29,92);
    dateArray[5] = dt6;  // template's assertion aborts
    return 0;
}
```

The program declares an *Array* object of *Date* objects with a subscript limit of 5. Then it declares five *Date* objects, which it puts into the array. After displaying all five objects, the program flushes *cout* and then tries to put another *Date* object into the array's sixth position, which does not exist. The *assert* macro's test is false, and the program aborts. Exercise 13.2 displays this output:

```
12/17/37
11/30/38
6/24/40
10/31/42
8/5/44
Assertion "sub >= 0 && sub < b" failed: file "Barray.h", line 16
```

The format of the error message depends on the compiler's implementation of the Standard C *assert* macro, but the information displayed is the same.

After your program is fully tested, you can remove the assertion code by inserting this line before the include of <cassert>:

```
#define NDEBUG
```

When to Use Class Templates

Templates surround other types with generic management. The types that you provide as parameters have their own behavior. The class templates provide a way to contain objects of those classes in general-purpose containers. The details of their containment are unrelated to their purposes. A *Date* class has its own behavior. So does a *string* class. So does a class that encapsulates a person's name, address, and phone number. Their participation in a queue, list, bag, linked list, balanced tree, or any other kind of container is unrelated to their purpose. It is natural and proper to use the features of a programming language to separate these two unrelated behaviors.

Before C++ supported templates, programmers used inheritance to associate data types with container classes. In other cases, they built cumbersome classes that used *void* pointers and casts to manage the containment of unrelated types in various containers. These approaches worked well enough, but they are not always the best ones. As a rule you should use inheritance when the derived class modifies the functional behavior of the base. When the relationship manages objects of the class without changing the class's behavior, you should use templates.

There are, however, other considerations. If the management algorithm entails a lot of code in the class definition and its member functions and if you plan to instantiate many different parameterized versions of the template, think twice before you build the entire algorithm as a template. Remember that each distinct use of the template generates a new copy of the code. If the template manages a significant number of different types, the executable program can be big. Programmers often separate the common code that is not influenced by the parameterized type into a base class from which they derive the class template. The base class code is instantiated only once irrespective of the number of discrete type instantiations of the derived class template.

A Linked List Template

We used the *LinkedList* class at the beginning of this chapter to see how templates work. Now we implement a complete *LinkedList* class template. Figure 13.2 is **Linklist.h**, the header file that defines the *LinkedList* template.

Figure 13.2 Linklist.h.

```
// ----------- linklist.h
#ifndef LINKLIST_H
#define LINKLIST_H

template <class T> class LinkedList;
template <class T>
// --- the linked list entry
class ListEntry    {
    T thisentry;
    ListEntry* nextentry;
    ListEntry* preventry;
    ListEntry(T& entry);
    friend class LinkedList<T>;
};
template <class T>
// ---- construct a linked list entry
ListEntry<T>::ListEntry(T &entry)
{
    thisentry = entry;
    nextentry = 0;
    preventry = 0;
}
template <class T>
// ---- the linked list
class LinkedList    {
    // --- the list head
    ListEntry<T>* firstentry;
    ListEntry<T>* lastentry;
    ListEntry<T>* iterator;
    void RemoveEntry(ListEntry<T> *lentry);
    void InsertEntry(T& entry, ListEntry<T> *lentry);
```

Figure 13.2 Linklist.h. (continued)

```
public:
    LinkedList();
    ~LinkedList();
    void AppendEntry(T& entry);
    void RemoveEntry(int pos = -1);
    void InsertEntry(T&entry, int pos = -1);
    T* FindEntry(int pos);
    T* CurrentEntry();
    T* FirstEntry();
    T* LastEntry();
    T* NextEntry();
    T* PrevEntry();
};
template <class T>
// ---- construct a linked list
LinkedList<T>::LinkedList()
{
    iterator = 0;
    firstentry = 0;
    lastentry = 0;
}
template <class T>
// ---- destroy a linked list
LinkedList<T>::~LinkedList()
{
    while (firstentry)
        RemoveEntry(firstentry);
}
template <class T>
// ---- append an entry to the linked list
void LinkedList<T>::AppendEntry(T& entry)
{
```

Figure 13.2 Linklist.h. (continued)

```
    ListEntry<T>* newentry = new ListEntry<T>(entry);
    newentry->preventry = lastentry;
    if (lastentry)
        lastentry->nextentry = newentry;
    if (firstentry == 0)
        firstentry = newentry;
    lastentry = newentry;
}
template <class T>
// ---- remove an entry from the linked list
void LinkedList<T>::RemoveEntry(ListEntry<T>* lentry)
{
    if (lentry == 0)
        return;
    if (lentry == iterator)
        iterator = lentry->preventry;
    // ---- repair any break made by this removal
    if (lentry->nextentry)
        lentry->nextentry->preventry = lentry->preventry;
    if (lentry->preventry)
        lentry->preventry->nextentry = lentry->nextentry;
    // --- maintain list head if this is last and/or first
    if (lentry == lastentry)
        lastentry = lentry->preventry;
    if (lentry == firstentry)
        firstentry = lentry->nextentry;
    delete lentry;
}
template <class T>
// ---- insert an entry into the linked list
void LinkedList<T>::InsertEntry(T& entry, ListEntry<T>* lentry)
{
```

Figure 13.2 Linklist.h. (continued)

```
    ListEntry<T>* newentry = new ListEntry<T>(entry);
    newentry->nextentry = lentry;
    if (lentry)     {
        newentry->preventry = lentry->preventry;
        lentry->preventry = newentry;
    }
    if (newentry->preventry)
        newentry->preventry->nextentry = newentry;
    if (lentry == firstentry)
        firstentry = newentry;
}
template <class T>
// ---- remove an entry from the linked list
void LinkedList<T>::RemoveEntry(int pos)
{
    FindEntry(pos);
    RemoveEntry(iterator);
}
template <class T>
// ---- insert an entry into the linked list
void LinkedList<T>::InsertEntry(T& entry, int pos)
{
    FindEntry(pos);
    InsertEntry(entry, iterator);
}
template <class T>
// ---- return the current linked list entry
T* LinkedList<T>::CurrentEntry()
{
    return iterator ? &(iterator->thisentry) : 0;
}
```

Figure 13.2 Linklist.h. (continued)

```
template <class T>
// ---- return a specific linked list entry
T* LinkedList<T>::FindEntry(int pos)
{
    if (pos != -1)    {
        iterator = firstentry;
        if (iterator)    {
            while (pos--)
                iterator = iterator->nextentry;
        }
    }
    return CurrentEntry();
}
template <class T>
// ---- return the first entry in the linked list
T* LinkedList<T>::FirstEntry()
{
    iterator = firstentry;
    return CurrentEntry();
}
template <class T>
// ---- return the last entry in the linked list
T* LinkedList<T>::LastEntry()
{
    iterator = lastentry;
    return CurrentEntry();
}
```

Figure 13.2 Linklist.h. (continued)

```
template <class T>
// ---- return the next entry in the linked list
T* LinkedList<T>::NextEntry()
{
    if (iterator == 0)
        iterator = firstentry;
    else
        iterator = iterator->nextentry;
    return CurrentEntry();
}
template <class T>
// ---- return the previous entry in the linked list
T* LinkedList<T>::PrevEntry()
{
    if (iterator == 0)
        iterator = lastentry;
    else
        iterator = iterator->preventry;
    return CurrentEntry();
}
#endif
```

This template definition builds a linked list of objects of any type. After the list is built, the user can navigate it by using the template's member functions, which return pointers to objects in the list.

There are two templates in the **Linklist.h** file. The first one is for the *ListEntry* class, which the *LinkedList* class uses. A using program cannot declare an object of this class. Observe that there is no public constructor. Only a friend of this class template can use it. The *LinkedList* class is its only friend. The *ListEntry* class contains a listed object and pointers to the next and previous objects in the list.

The *LinkedList* template contains the *list head*: a data structure that includes pointers to the first and last entries in the class and an *iterator* pointer that the class uses to navigate the list. These pointers point to *ListEntry* objects.

Two private member functions are used by the *LinkedList* class to insert and remove *ListEntry* objects from the list. The *LinkedList* class constructs and destroys these *ListEntry* objects.

The *LinkedList* class's public interface consists of a constructor and destructor, member functions to append, insert, and remove objects of the type, and member functions to navigate the list. The following exercises demonstrate this behavior.

A Linked List of Integers

Exercise 13.3 uses the *LinkedList* class to maintain a list of integers.

Exercise 13.3 Using a linked list template for integers.

```
#include <iostream>
using namespace std;
#include "linklist.h"

int main()
{
    LinkedList<int> IntList;
    // --- add 10 integers to the linked list
    for (int i = 0; i < 10; i++)
        IntList.AppendEntry(i);
    // --- iterate thru the 10 and remove #5
    int* ip = IntList.FirstEntry();
    while (ip)    {
        cout << *ip << ' ';
        if (*ip == 5)
            IntList.RemoveEntry();
        ip = IntList.NextEntry();
    }
    // --- iterate thru what's left
    cout << endl;
    while ((ip = IntList.NextEntry()) != 0)
        cout << *ip << ' ';
    return 0;
}
```

The program in Exercise 13.3 declares a *LinkedList* object with *int* as the type parameter. Then it adds 10 integers to the list. Next, the program uses a *FirstEntry* call and a series of *NextEntry* calls to iterate through the list, displaying each integer as it retrieves it. When it finds the list entry with the value 5, the program calls *RemoveEntry* to remove the entry from the list. When it is at the end, the program iterates through the list a second time, displaying the values to prove that number 5 was removed. Exercise 13.3 displays this output:

```
0 1 2 3 4 5 6 7 8 9
0 1 2 3 4 6 7 8 9
```

A Linked List of Dates

Exercise 13.4 uses the *LinkedList* template to build and maintain a list of *Date* objects. For this exercise you link the program with the *Date* class from Chapter 9.

Exercise 13.4 Using a linked list template for dates.

```
#include <iostream>
using namespace std;
#include <date.h>
#include "linklist.h"

int main()
{
    LinkedList<Date> DateList;
    Date dt1(12,17,37);
    Date dt2(11,30,38);
    Date dt3(6,24,40);
    Date dt4(10,31,42);
    Date dt5(8,5,44);
```

Exercise 13.4 Using a linked list template for dates. (continued)

```
// --- add 5 dates to the linked list
DateList.AppendEntry(dt1);
DateList.AppendEntry(dt2);
DateList.AppendEntry(dt3);
DateList.AppendEntry(dt4);
DateList.AppendEntry(dt5);
// --- iterate thru the dates
cout << "---Forward---" << endl;
Date* dp;
while ((dp = DateList.NextEntry()) != 0)
    cout << *dp << endl;
// --- insert a date
Date dt6(1,29,92);
DateList.InsertEntry(dt6, 3);
// --- iterate thru the dates
cout << "---Backward---" << endl;
dp = DateList.LastEntry();
while (dp != 0)    {
    cout << *dp << endl;
    dp = DateList.PrevEntry();
}
    return 0;
}
```

The program in Exercise 13.4 declares a *LinkedList* object with the *Date* type. Then it declares five *Date* objects, which it puts into the list by calling the *AppendEntry* function. The program iterates through the list and displays the *Date* objects. Then it inserts a date by calling the *InsertEntry* function with a *Date* object and the integer parameter 3. The integer parameter specifies that the insertion is to occur before the fourth entry in the list. A zero value would insert the object at the front of the list. Finally, the program iterates through the list in reverse order by calling *LastEntry* and then *PrevEntry* until no more entries are returned. The exercise displays the dates in reverse order to prove that the insertion worked. Exercise 13.4 displays this output:

```
---Forward---
12/17/37
11/30/38
6/24/40
10/31/42
8/5/44
---Backward---
8/5/44
10/31/42
1/29/92
6/24/40
11/30/38
12/17/37
```

Template Specialization

You can generate a specialized version of a complete class template or of selected member functions of a class template. Specialized templates and functions allow the programmer to define specific behavior related to a particular type. Using the specialized type, the specialized class or function overrides the class template or template member function when a template object is instantiated.

Class Template Specialization

Exercise 13.5 illustrates the specialization of a class template. This exercise defines a class template named *Set*, which has a constructor and a member function named *display*. The *display* function sends to the standard *cout* object the data value of the type being parameterized. Not all types, however, overload the << operator in that way. The *Date* class used in previous exercises is an example. The program in Exercise 13.5, therefore, provides a specialized class for instantiation of the *Set* template when the type being parameterized is a *Date*.

Exercise 13.5 *Class template specialization.*

```
#include <iostream>
using namespace std;
#include <date.h>

template <class T>
class Set    {
    T t;
public:
    Set(T st) : t(st) { }
    void display()
        { cout << t << endl; }
};
// ----- specialized class template
class Set<Date>    {
    Date t;
public:
    Set(Date st) : t(st) { }
    void display()
        { cout << "Date: " << t << endl; }
};

int main()
{
    Set<int> intset(123);
    Set<Date> dt = Date(1,2,3);
    intset.display();
    dt.display();
    return 0;
}
```

Exercise 13.5 displays these values:

```
123
1/2/3
```

Template Member Function Specialization

The program in Exercise 13.5 specializes the complete *Set* class template even though only the *display* member function changes in the specialization. An alternative approach is to specialize only the member functions that change. Exercise 13.6 modifies the program to eliminate the specialized class template and substitute a specialization of the *display* member function only.

Exercise 13.6 Template member function specialization.

```cpp
#include <iostream>
using namespace std;
#include <Date.h>

template <class T>
class Set     {
    T t;
public:
    Set(T st) : t(st) { }
    void display();
};
template <class T>
void Set<T>::display()
{
    cout << t << endl;
}
// ----- specialized class template member function
void Set<Date>::display()
{
    cout << "Date: " << t << endl;
}
```

Exercise 13.6 Template member function specialization. (continued)

```
int main()
{
    Set<int> intset(123);
    Set<Date> dt = Date(1,2,3);
    intset.display();
    dt.display();
    return 0;
}
```

Exercise 13.6 displays these values:

```
123
1/2/3
```

The member function being specialized cannot be inline in the original template definition.

NOTE

FUNCTION TEMPLATES

A template can define a parameterized nonmember function. A typical example substitutes templates for the *min* and *max* macros often defined in C. Before considering the function template, consider these C macros:

```
#define min(a,b) ((a)<(b)?(a):(b))
#define max(a,b) ((a)>(b)?(a):(b))
```

These macros have a problem related to side effects. Suppose you call one of the macros this way:

```
a = min(b++, --c);
```

The *min* macro would expand that expression into this:

```
a = (b++) < (--c) ? (b++) : (--c);
```

The side effects occur when either *b* gets incremented twice or *c* gets decremented twice depending on which one is greater. C++ programmers overcome that problem with an inline function as shown here:

```
inline int min(int a, int b)
{
    return (a < b ? a : b);
}
```

There are no side effects, but there is a problem. The *min* function now works with integers only. If your type cannot be converted to a meaningful integral value, it does not work with the inline *min* function. The apparent solution is to use a function template:

```
template<class T>
T& min(T& a, T& b)
{
    return (a < b ? a : b);
}
```

This solution isn't perfect either. It won't work unless both objects being compared are of the same type and are both non-*const*. To solve that problem, you must provide the same function with all combinations of *const* and non-*const* parameterized parameters:

```
template<class T>
T& min(const T& a, const T& b)
{
    return (a < b ? a : b);
}
template<class T>
T& min(T& a, const T& b)
{
    return (a < b ? a : b);
}
```

```
template<class T>
T& min(const T& a, T& b)
{
    return (a < b ? a : b);
}
```

Sorting with a Template

The next example sorts arrays of parameterized types. The Standard C *qsort* function does that by having you provide a call-back function that performs the comparisons of array elements. Using a template, however, is easier as long as the type supports comparisons by overloading relational operators. Figure 13.3 is **Quiksort.h**, the definition of the *quicksort* function template.

Figure 13.3 Quiksort.h.

```
// -------- quiksort.h
#ifndef QUIKSORT_H
#define QUIKSORT_H

// ---- function template for quicksort algorithm

template<class T>
inline void swap(T& t1, T& t2)
{
    T hold = t2;
    t2 = t1;
    t1 = hold;
}

template<class T>
void quicksort(T *array, int hi, int lo = 0)
{
```

Figure 13.3 Quiksort.h. (continued)

```
    while (hi > lo)    {
        int i = lo;
        int j = hi;
        //  sort everything higher than median above it
        //  and everything lower below it
        do    {
            while (array[i] < array[lo] && i < j)
                i++;
            while (array[--j] > array[lo])
                ;
            if (i < j)
                swap(array[j], array[i]);
        } while (i < j);
        swap(array[lo], array[j]);
        // --- sort the set with the fewer number of elements
        if (j - lo > hi - (j+1))    {
            // --- sort the bottom set
            quicksort(array, j-1, lo);
            lo = j+1;
        }
        else    {
            // --- sort the top set
            quicksort(array, hi, j+1);
            hi = j-1;
        }
    }
}
#endif
```

The template implements the *quicksort* algorithm, which sorts an array of types. Its parameters are the address of the array and the number of elements in the array.

The *quicksort* algorithm divides the array into two parts. First, it arbitrarily selects an element to represent the median value. (This implementation of the algorithm uses the first element in the array for the median value. As a guess, this approach is no better or worse than selecting any other element in the array.) Then the algorithm places all elements greater than that value in the upper part and all the lower elements in the lower part. Then it calls itself recursively, once for each of the two parts. When there is only one part left, the array is fully sorted.

Exercise 13.7 uses the *quicksort* function template to sort integers.

Exercise 13.7 Using the quicksort function template.

```
#include <iostream>
#include <iomanip>
#include <cstdlib>
using namespace std;
#include "quiksort.h"

int main()
{
    int dim;
    // --- get the number of integers to sort
    cout << "How many integers?" << endl;
    cin >> dim;
    // --- build an array of random integers
    int* arrs = new int[dim+1];
    int i;
    for (i = 0; i < dim; i++)
        arrs[i] = rand();
    // --- display the random integers
    cout << endl << "----- unsorted -----" << endl;
    for (i = 0; i < dim; i++)
        cout << setw(8) << arrs[i];
```

Exercise 13.7 Using the quicksort function template. (continued)

```
// --- sort the array
quicksort(arrs, dim);
// --- display the sorted integers
cout << endl << "----- sorted -----" << endl;
for (i = 0; i < dim; i++)
    cout << setw(8) << arrs[i];
delete arrs;
return 0;
}
```

The program in Exercise 13.7 builds an array of integers, reading the dimension for the array from the keyboard. It uses the Standard C *rand* function to fill the array with random numbers and displays the numbers in their random sequence. Then it calls the *quicksort* function template to sort the array. Finally, the program displays the array in its new sequence.

SUMMARY

Templates add *genericity* to C++, an object-oriented feature that was missing in traditional C++ and that many programmers judged to be a major deficiency in the language. Next, Chapter 14 describes exception handling.

CHAPTER 14

Exception Handling

Exception handling is a C++ feature that lets a program intercept and process exceptional conditions—errors, usually—in an orderly, organized, and consistent manner. In this chapter, you will learn about:

- Traditional C exception handling
- Why traditional methods do not work in C++
- The C++ try/throw/catch idiom
- Anomalies in C++ exception handling

Exception handling allows one section of a program to sense and dispatch error conditions, and another section to handle them. Usually one category of code, perhaps the classes and functions in a library, knows how to detect errors without knowing the appropriate handling strategy. It is just as usual for other categories of code to understand how to deal with errors without being able to detect them.

For example, a class library function may perform math, detecting overflow, underflow, divide-by-zero, and other exceptional conditions that are the result of user input. Selection of a strategy for handling the exception depends on the application. Some programs write error messages on the console; others display dialog boxes in a graphical user interface; still others request the user to enter better data; still others terminate the program. The error could result from a bug in the program or an invalid (and unvalidated) user input. A reusable library function should not presume to know the best exception handling strategy for all applications. On the other hand, an application cannot be expected to detect all possible exceptions.

An example of this relationship is the bounded array class template in Chapter 11. The class detects when an array subscript is out of range by using the *assert* macro, which terminates the program. A more appropriate behavior would be to detect and report the error to the class user and let the user determine how to handle it.

This relationship—that a distant function can report an error to the using program—has implications. Somehow, the detecting function must return control to the handling function through an orderly sequence of function returns. The detecting function can be many function calls deep. An orderly return to the higher level of the handler function requires, at the very least, a coordinated unwinding of the stack.

EXCEPTION HANDLING IN C

Traditional C programs take two approaches to exception handling: They follow each function call with a test for errors; and they use *setjmp* and *longjmp* (Chapter 6) to intercept error conditions. The first approach, which uses something like *errno* and *null* or *ERROR* function return values to report the nature of the error, is reliable but tedious. Programmers tend to avoid or overlook all the possibilities. The *setjmp* and *longjmp* approach is closer to what C++ exception handling strives for: an orderly and automatic way to unwind the stack to a state that was recorded at a specified place higher in the function-call hierarchy.

The *setjmp* and *longjmp* approach is intended to intercept and handle conditions that do not require immediate program termination.

The syntax checker of a programming language translator, for example, can be in the depths of a recursive descent parser when it detects a syntax error. The program does not need to terminate. It should simply report the error and find its way back to where it can read the next statement and continue. The program uses *setjmp* to identify that place and *longjmp* to get back to it. Figure 14.1 is a code fragment that represents that process.

Figure 14.1 *Using* setjmp *and* longjmp.

```
#include <setjmp.h>
jmp_buf jb;
void Validate()
{
    int err;
    err = setjmp(jb);
    if (err)
        /* An exception has occurred */
        ReportError(err);
    while (getInput())
        parse();
}
// --- parse a line of input
void parse()
{
    /* parse the input */
    /* ... */
    if (error)
        longjmp(jb, ErrorCode);
}
```

The *longjmp* call unwinds the stack to its state as recorded in the *jmp_buf* by the *setjmp* call. The initial *setjmp* call returns zero. The *longjmp* call jumps to a return from the *setjmp* call and causes *setjmp* to seem to return the specified error code, which should be nonzero.

This scheme, however, contains anomalies. And, as you will soon learn, C++ exception handling does not solve all of them. Suppose that the parse function looked like this:

```
void parse()
{
    FILE *fp = fopen(fname, "rt");
    char *cp = malloc(1000);
    /* parse the input */
    /* ... */
    if (error)
        longjmp(jb, ErrorCode);
    free(cp);
    fclose(fp);
}
```

Ignore for the moment that in a real program the function would test for exceptions to the *fopen* and *malloc* calls. The two calls represent resources that the program acquires before and releases after the *longjmp* call. The calls could be in interim functions that are called after the *setjmp* operation and that themselves called the *parse* function. The point is that the *longjmp* call occurs before those resources are released. Therefore, every exception in this program represents two system resources that are lost: a heap segment and a file handle. In the case of the *FILE** resource, subsequent attempts to open the same file would fail. If each pass through the system opened a different file—for example, a temporary file with a system-generated file name—the program would fail when the operating system ran out of file handles. Programmers traditionally solve this problem by structuring their programs to avoid it. Either they manage and clean up resources before calling *longjmp* or they do not use *longjmp* where interim resources are at risk. In the function just shown, the problem is solved by moving the *longjmp* call below the *free* and *fclose* calls. However, it is not always that simple.

Unwinding the stack in a C program involves resetting the stack pointer to where it pointed when *setjmp* is called. The *jmp_buf* stores everything that the program needs to know to do that. This procedure works because the stack contains automatic variables and function return addresses. Resetting the stack pointer essentially discards the automatic variables and forgets about the function return addresses. All this is correct behavior, because the automatic variables are no longer needed and the interim functions are not to be resumed.

EXCEPTION HANDLING IN C++

Using *longjmp* to unwind the stack in a C++ program does not work, because automatic variables on the stack include objects of classes, and those objects need to execute their destructor functions. Consider this modification to the *parse* function, which is now in a C++ program:

```
void parse()
{
    string str("Parsing now");
    // parse the input
    // ...
    if (error)
        longjmp(jb, ErrorCode);
}
```

Assume that the constructor for the *string* class allocates memory for the string value from the heap. Its destructor returns that memory to the heap. In this program, however, the *string* destructor does not execute, because *longjmp* unwinds the stack and jumps to the *setjmp* call before the *str* object goes out of scope. The memory used by the *str* object itself is returned to the stack, but the heap memory pointed to by a pointer in the string is not returned to the heap.

The problem just shown is one that C++ exception handling solves. The unwinding of the stack in the exception handling *throw* operation—the analog to *longjmp*—includes calls to the destructors of automatic objects. Furthermore, if the *throw* occurs from within the constructor of an automatic object, its destructor is not called, although the destructors of objects embedded in the throwing object are called.

The *try* Block

C++ functions that can sense and recover from errors execute from within a *try* block that looks like this:

```
try {
    // C++ statements
}
```

Code executing outside any *try* block cannot detect or handle exceptions. *Try* blocks may be nested. The *try* block typically calls other functions that are able to detect exceptions.

The *catch* Exception Handler

A *try* block is followed by a *catch* exception handler with a parameter list:

```
try  {
    // C++ statements
}
catch(int err)   {
    // error-handling code
}
```

There can be multiple *catch* handlers with different parameter lists:

```
try  {
    // C++ statements
}
catch(int err)   {
    // error-handling code
}
catch(char *msg)   {
    // error-handling code with char *
}
```

The *catch* handler is identified by the type in its parameter list. The parameter in the *catch* parameter list does not have to be named. If the parameter is named, it declares an object with that name, and the exception-detection code can pass a value in the parameter. If the parameter is unnamed, the exception-detection code can jump to the *catch* exception handler merely by naming the type.

The *throw* Statement

To detect an exception and jump to a *catch* handler, a C++ function issues the *throw* statement with a data type that matches the parameter list of the proper *catch* handler:

```
throw "An error has occurred";
```

This *throw* statement would jump to the *catch* exception handler function that has the *char** parameter list.

The *throw* statement unwinds the stack, cleaning up all objects declared within the *try* block by calling their destructors. Next, *throw* calls the matching *catch* handler, passing the parameter object.

The *try/throw/catch* Sequence

Exercise 14.1 begins to bring it all together.

Exercise 14.1 Throwing *and* catching *an exception.*

```
using namespace std;

void foo();
class Bummer {}; // an exception to be thrown

int main()
{
    // --- the try block
    try  {
        cout << "calling foo" << endl;
        foo();
        cout << "return from foo << endl";
    }
```

Exercise 14.1 Throwing *and* catching *an exception. (continued)*

```
    // --- catch exception handler
    catch(Bummer)   {
        // error-handling code
        cout << "catching Bummer" << endl;
    }
    cout << "done" << endl;
    return 0;
}
// --- program function
void foo()
{
    int error = 1;
    // C++ statements to do stuff
    if (error)   {
        cout << "throwing Bummer" << endl;
        throw Bummer();
    }

}
```

Exercise 14.1 displays this output:

```
calling foo
throwing Bummer
catching Bummer
done
```

In Exercise 14.1, the program enters a *try* block, and this means that functions called directly or indirectly from within the *try* block can throw exceptions. In other words, the *foo* function can throw exceptions and so can any function called by *foo* and so on.

The *catch* exception handler function immediately following the *try* block is the only handler in this example. It catches exceptions that are thrown with a *Bummer* parameter. *Bummer* is a class set up specifically to identify the exception.

Catch handlers and their matching *throw* statements can have a parameter of any type. For example:

```
catch(ErrorCode ec) { ... }
// ...
throw ErrorCode(123);
```

This example assumes that there is a class named *ErrorCode* that can be constructed with an integer parameter list. The *throw* statement builds a temporary object of type *ErrorCode* and initializes the object with the value given in the *throw* statement. The parameter may be an automatic variable within the block that uses *throw* even if the *catch* uses a reference, as shown here:

```
void bar()
{
    try  {
        foo();
    }
    catch(ErrorCode& ec)   {
        // ...
    }
}
// ...
void foo()
{
    // ...
    if (error) {
        ErrorCode dt(234);
        throw dt;
    }
}
```

The *throw* statement builds a temporary *ErrorCode* object to pass to the *catch* handler. The automatic *ErrorCode* object in the *foo* function is allowed to go out of scope. The temporary *ErrorCode* object is not destroyed until the *catch* handler completes processing.

When a *try* block has more than one *catch* handler, a *throw* executes the one that matches the parameter list. That handler is the only one to execute unless it throws an exception to execute a different *catch* handler. When the executing *catch* handler exits, the program proceeds with the code following the last *catch* handler. Exercise 14.2 demonstrates this behavior.

Exercise 14.2 *Multiple* catch *handlers.*

```
#include <iostream>
using namespace std;

void foo();
class Bummer {}; // an exception to be thrown
class Dumber {}; // an exception to be thrown

int main()
{
    // --- the try block
    try {
        cout << "calling foo" << endl;
        foo();
        cout << "return from foo" << endl;
    }
    // --- catch exception handler
    catch(Bummer) {
        // error-handling code
        cout << "catching Bummer" << endl;
    }
    catch(Dumber) {
        // error-handling code
        cout << "catching Dumber" << endl;
    }
    cout << "done" << endl;
    return 0;
// --- program function
void foo()
{
    int error = 1;
    // C++ statements to do stuff
    if (error) {
        cout << "throwing Dumber" << endl;
        throw Dumber();
    }
}

}
```

Exercise 14.2 displays this output:

```
calling foo
throwing Dumber
catching Dumber
done
```

Exception Specification

You can specify the exceptions that a function may throw when you declare the function, as shown here:

```
void f() throw(Dumber, Killer)
{
    // C++ statements
    if (err1)
        throw Dumber();
    if (err2)
        throw(Killer());
}
```

The exception specification is part of the function's signature. You must include it in the prototype and in the function's definition header block. Otherwise, the compiler reports a type mismatch when it encounters the second declaration of the function.

Unexpected Exceptions

If a function includes an exception specification as shown previously and if the function throws an exception not given in the specification, the exception is passed to a system function named *unexpected*. The *unexpected* function calls the latest function named as an argument in a call to the *set_unexpected* function, which returns its current setting. A function with no exception specification can throw any exception.

Catch-all Exception Handlers

A *catch* handler with ellipses for a parameter list, shown next, catches all uncaught exceptions:

```
catch(...)   {
    // error-handling code
}
```

In a group of catches associated with a *try* block, the catch-all handler must appear last. Exercise 14.3 demonstrates the catch-all handler.

Exercise 14.3 A catch-all handler.

```
#include <iostream>
using namespace std;

void foo();

class Bummer {}; // an exception to be thrown
class Dumber {}; // an exception to be thrown
class Killer {}; // an exception to be thrown

int main()
{
    // --- the try block
    try {
        cout << "calling foo" << endl;
        foo();
        cout << "return from foo" << endl;
    }
    // --- catch exception handler
    catch(Bummer)   {
        // error-handling code
        cout << "catching Bummer" << endl;
    }
    catch(Dumber)   {
        // error-handling code
        cout << "catching Dumber" << endl;
    }
    catch(...)     {
```

Exercise 14.3 A catch-all handler. (continued)

```
        // catching leftovers
        cout << "catching Killer" << endl;
    }
    cout << "done" << endl;
    return 0;
}
// --- program function
void foo()
{
    int error = 1;
    // C++ statements to do stuff
    if (error)    {
        cout << "throwing Killer" << endl;
        throw Killer();
    }
}
```

The catch-all handler in Exercise 14.3 catches the *Killer* exception, because none of the other *catch* handlers has a matching *Killer* parameter list. Exercise 14.3 displays this output:

```
calling foo
throwing Killer
catching Killer
done
```

Throwing an Exception from a Handler

You can code a *throw* with no operand in a *catch* handler or in a function called by one. The *throw* with no operand rethrows the original exception. Exercise 14.4 demonstrates this behavior.

Exercise 14.4 Rethrowing exceptions.

```cpp
#include <iostream>
using namespace std;

void foo();
class Bummer {}; // an exception to be thrown

int main()
{
    // --- the try block
    try {
        // --- an inner try block
        try    {
            cout << "calling foo" << endl;
            foo();
        }
        catch(...)    {
            cout << "rethrowing Bummer" << endl;
            throw;    // rethrow the exception
        }
    }
    // --- catch exception handler
    catch(Bummer)    {
        // error-handling code
        cout << "catching Bummer" << endl;
    }
    cout << "done" << endl;
    return 0;
}
```

Exercise 14.4 Rethrowing exceptions. *(continued)*

```
// --- program function
void foo()
{
    int error = 1;
    // C++ statements to do stuff
    if (error)    {
        cout << "throwing Bummer" << endl;
        throw Bummer();
    }
}
```

Exercise 14.4 displays this output:

```
calling foo
throwing Bummer
rethrowing Bummer
catching Bummer
done
```

Uncaught Exceptions

An uncaught exception is one for which there is no *catch* handler specified or one thrown by a destructor that is executing as the result of another throw. Such an exception causes the *terminate* function to be called, which calls *abort* to terminate the program. Exercise 14.5 illustrates this behavior.

Exercise 14.5 Uncaught exceptions.

```
#include <iostream>
using namespace std;

void foo();
class Bummer {}; // an exception to be thrown
class Killer {}; // an exception to be thrown

int main()
{
    // --- the try block
    try  {
        cout << "calling foo" << endl;
        foo();
    }
    // --- catch exception handler
    catch(Bummer)   {
        // error-handling code
        cout << "catching Bummer" << endl;
    }
    cout << "done" << endl;
    return 0;
}
// --- program function
void foo()
{
    int error = 1;
    // C++ statements to do stuff
    if (error)    {
        cout << "throwing Killer" << endl;
        throw Killer();
    }
}
```

Exercise 14.5 displays this output:

```
calling foo
throwing Killer
Abnormal program termination
```

N O T E   The last part of the output depends on what the compiler's *abort* function displays before it terminates the program. The GNU compiler that accompanies this book on the companion CD-ROM aborts the program without displaying the "Abnormal program termination" message.

You can specify a function for *terminate* to call by calling the *set_terminate* function, which returns its current value. Exercise 14.6 demonstrates that usage.

Exercise 14.6 Catching uncaught exceptions.

```cpp
#include <iostream>
#include <cstdlib>
#include <exception>
using namespace std;

class Bummer {}; // an exception to be thrown
class Killer {}; // an exception to be thrown

// --- to catch uncaught exceptions
void terminator_2()
{
    cout << "catching the uncaught" << endl;
    exit(-1);
}
```

Exercise 14.6 *Catching uncaught exceptions. (continued)*

```
int main()
{
    set_terminate(&terminator_2);
    // --- the try block
    try  {
        cout << "throwing Killer" << endl;
        throw Killer();
    }
    // --- catch exception handler
    catch(Bummer)   {
        // error-handling code
        cout << "catching Bummer" << endl;
    }
    cout << "done" << endl;
    return 0;
}
```

Exercise 14.6 displays this output:

```
throwing Killer
catching the uncaught
```

SELECTING AMONG THROWN EXCEPTIONS

To review: A *try* block is followed by one or more *catch* handlers, which are distinguished by their parameter lists. You must decide in your design how to differentiate the exceptions. You might code only one *catch* handler with an *int* parameter and let the value of the parameter determine the error type. This approach, illustrated next, makes the unlikely assumption that you have control of all the *throw*s in all the functions in all the libraries that you use.

```
catch(int exception_code)
{
    switch (exception_code)   {
        case 0:
            // process code 0
            break;
        case 1:
            // process code 1
            break;
        // ....
    }
}
```

Throwing intrinsic types is not the best approach. If all libraries threw *int*s, for example, the *catch* handlers would become a hodgepodge of collisions and conflicts. No doubt conventions will emerge. One possibility uses class definitions to distinguish exceptions and categories of exceptions. A *throw* with a publicly derived class as its parameter is caught by a *catch* handler with the base class as its parameter. Consider this example:

```
class FileError {
public:
    virtual void HandleException() = 0;
};
class Locked : public FileError {
public:
    void HandleException();
};
class NotFound : public FileError {
public:
    void HandleException();
};
```

```
void bar()
{
    try {
        foo();
    }
    catch(FileError& fe) {
        fe.HandleException();
    }
}
void foo()
{
    // ...
    if (file_locked)
        throw NotFound();
}
```

FileError is a public virtual base class. Its derived classes are *NotFound* and *Locked*. The only *catch* handler for this category of exception is the one with the *FileError* reference parameter. It does not know which of the exceptions was thrown, but it calls the *HandleException* pure virtual function, which automatically calls the proper function in the derived class.

This approach is only one of many that you can use. Instead of classes, you can use enumerated types and have switches in the *catch* handlers. Publishers of libraries will document the conventions that they use to throw exceptions, and your *catch* handlers will use those conventions, perhaps several different conventions in one application. Eventually standards will emerge. Chapter 15 discusses the exception handling conventions being considered for the Standard C++ library.

EXCEPTIONS AND UNRELEASED RESOURCES

Recall the discussion at the beginning of this chapter about the *setjmp* and *longjmp* anomaly of unreleased resources. C++ exception handling does not solve that problem. Consider this condition:

```
void foo()
{
    string *str = new string("Hello, Dolly");
    // ...
    if (file_locked)
        throw NotFound();
    delete str;
}
```

The *string* object is allocated from the heap by the *new* operator. If the exception is thrown, the *delete* operation is not performed. In this case, there are two complications. The memory allocated on the heap for the *string* object is not released, and its destructor is not called. This means that the memory that its constructor allocated for the *string* data is also lost.

The same problem exists with dangling open file handles, unclosed screen windows, and other such unresolved system resources. If the program just shown seems easy to fix, remember that the *throw* could occur from within a library function far into a stack of nested function calls.

Programming idioms have been suggested that address this problem, and programmers must consider them. Dr. Stroustrup suggests that all such resources can be managed from within automatic instances of resource-management classes. Their destructors would release everything as the *throw* unwinds the stack. Another approach is to make all dynamic heap pointers and file and window handles global so that the *catch* handler could clean everything up. These methods sound cumbersome, however, and they work only if all the functions in all the libraries cooperate.

AN IMPROVED CALCULATOR PROGRAM

Exercise 5.48 in Chapter 5 demonstrated recursion by implementing a simple four-function calculator. Exercise 6.3 in Chapter 6 improved the calculator by using the Standard C *setjmp* and *longjmp* functions to handle errors. Now Exercise 14.7 further improves the calculator by applying much of what you have learned since Chapter 6, including the use of exception handling to manage the errors in the calculator.

Exercise 14.7 *A calculator with exceptions.*

```
#include <iostream>
#include <cstdlib>
#include <cctype>
#include <string>
using namespace std;

class Error {};

class Calculator {
    int pos;
    string expr;
    int addsubt();
    int multdiv();
    int number() throw(Error);
public:
    Calculator()
        { }
    int Compute(const string& str) throw(Error);
};

int Calculator::Compute(const string& str) throw(Error)
{
    int rtn = 0;
    try {
        pos = 0;
        expr = str;
        rtn = addsubt();
        if (pos < expr.length() && expr[pos] != '\0')
            throw Error();
    }
```

Exercise 14.7 *A calculator with exceptions. (continued)*

```
    catch(Error)  {
        cout << '\r';
        while (pos--)              // position error pointer
            cout << ' ';
        cout << "^ syntax error" << endl << '\a';
        throw;
    }
    return rtn;
}
// ---- top of recursive descent: add/subtract
int Calculator::addsubt()
{
    int rtn = multdiv();
    while (expr[pos] == '+' || expr[pos] == '-')      {
        int op = expr[pos++];
        int opr2 = multdiv();
        if (op == '+')
            rtn += opr2;
        else
            rtn -= opr2;
    }
    return rtn;
}
// ---- highest precedence: multiply/divide
int Calculator::multdiv()
{
    int rtn = number();
    while (expr[pos] == '*' || expr[pos] == '/')      {
        int op = expr[pos++];
        int opr2 = number();
        if (op == '*')
            rtn *= opr2;
        else
            rtn /= opr2;
    }
    return rtn;
}
```

Exercise 14.7 A calculator with exceptions. (continued)

```
// ---- extract a number
int Calculator::number() throw(Error)
{
    int rtn;
    if (expr[pos] == '(')  {
        // --- parenthetical expression
        pos++;
        rtn = addsubt();            // back to top
        if (expr[pos++] != ')')  // must have ')'
            throw Error();
    }
    else    {
        // --- extract the number
        if (!isdigit(expr[pos]))
            throw Error();
        char ans[80] = "0";
        int i = 0;
        while (isdigit(expr[pos]) && pos < expr.length())
            ans[i++] = expr[pos++];
        ans[i] = '\0';
        rtn = atoi(ans);
    }
    return rtn;
}
int main()
{
    int ans;
    do  {
        // ---- read an expression
        cout << "Enter expression (0 to quit):" << endl;
        string expr;
        cin >> expr;
        try   {
            Calculator calc;
            ans = calc.Compute(expr);
            if (ans != 0)
                cout << ans << endl;
        }
```

Exercise 14.7 A calculator with exceptions. *(continued)*

```
        catch(Error)  {
            cout << "Try again" << endl;
            ans = 1;
        }
    } while (ans != 0);
    return 0;
}
```

Exercise 14.7's first improvement over the earlier calculator programs is to implement the calculator in a class. The *main* function reads the arithmetic expression from the console, enters a *try* block and instantiates a *Calculator* object. The program calls the *Calculator*'s *Compute* function, passing the expression string as an argument. If everything goes properly, the *Compute* function returns an integer value that is the result of the expression. If the value is zero, the program terminates. Otherwise, the program displays the value and asks for another expression to compute.

If an error occurs during the computation, the *Calculator* throws an *Error* exception. The *main* function catches the exception, displays a "Try again" message, and asks for another expression.

All the recursive descent parsing algorithms are now member functions in the *Calculator* class. The *Compute* member function initializes a subscript data member into the expression string, enters a *try* block, and calls the *addsubt* member function at the top of the recursive descent. If any part of that process encounters an error in the expression, the function throws an *Error* exception, which the *Compute* member function catches. When it catches an exception, the *Compute* function uses the current subscript data member to display where in the expression string the error was found. Then the *Compute* function rethrows the exception so that the *main* function can catch it, too. If no exception is thrown, the *Compute* function returns the value returned by the *addsubt* member function. The rest of the program, which consists mainly of the recursive descent parsing algorithm, works just as it did in the two earlier calculator programs.

SUMMARY

Exception handling is a valuable addition to C++. Chapter 15 discusses namespaces, a new casting mechanism, and runtime type information—features that the ANSI committee added to Standard C++.

ANSI/ISO Language Innovations

The ANSI/ISO committee took advantage of its standardization charter to introduce modifications to the C++ language definition that enhance the language in ways proposed by committee members. This policy is different from that of the ANSI/ISO C standardization committee, which decided only to codify existing practice and resolve ambiguities and contradictions among existing translator implementations.

The C++ committee's changes are innovations. In most cases, the changes implement features that committee members admired in other languages, features that they view as deficiencies in traditional C++, or simply features that they've always wanted in a programming language. A great deal of thought and discussion have been invested in each change, and consequently the committee feels that the proposed Standard C++ is the best definition of C++ possible today.

Most C++ changes consist of language additions that should not affect existing code. Old programs should still compile with newer compilers as long as the old code does not coincidentally use any of the new keywords as identifiers. In this chapter, you will learn about:

- Namespaces
- New-style casts
- Runtime type information
- Digraphs and operator keywords

NAMESPACES

Namespaces have represented a problem in C and C++ since the language's inception in the early 1970s. In an interview in *Dr. Dobb's Journal* in 1989, Dennis Ritchie, the designer of C, addressed the namespace problem, saying that the ANSI/ISO X3J11 C standardization committee introduced "…a convention that helps, but it certainly didn't solve the real problem."

Here is the problem: External, global identifiers are in scope throughout a program. They are visible to all object modules in the application program, in third-party class and function libraries, and in the compiler's system libraries. When two variables in global scope have the same identifier, the linker generates an error. Programmers avoid such name collisions in their own code by assigning unique identifiers to each variable. Under Standard C (applying the convention mentioned by Dr. Ritchie), the compiler system prefixes its internal global identifiers with underscore characters, and programmers are told to avoid that usage to avoid conflicts. Third-party library publishers addressed their part of the problem with mnemonic prefixes to global identifiers. This strategy attempts to avoid conflicts with other libraries, but it is unsuccessful when two publishers use the same prefix. The problem is that the language had no built-in mechanism with which a library publisher could stake out a so-called namespace of its own—one that would insulate its global identifiers from those of other libraries being linked into the same program.

Programmers using multiple libraries with coincidental name collisions had three choices: Get the source code to the libraries and modify and recompile them; convince one of the publishers to rename identifiers and republish its library; or choose not to use one of the offending libraries. Often, none of the three choices was available.

The C++ committee approached this problem by introducing name-spaces, a feature wherein identifiers declared within a defined block are associated with the block's namespace identifier. All references from outside the block to the global identifiers declared in the block must, in one way or another, qualify the global identifier reference with the namespace identifier. Publishers of libraries specify the namespace identifiers for the libraries' global identifiers. This feature is no more effective than using prefixes; two library publishers could conceivably and unwittingly use the same namespace identifier. Identifiers, however, tend to be longer than the typical two- or three-character prefixes and stand a better chance of being unique.

The *namespace* Definition

You define a *namespace* by surrounding all the associated code with a name-space block:

```
namespace MyLibrary  {
    int counter;
    class Date { /* ... */ };
    // ...
}
```

References from within the *MyLibrary namespace*'s enclosing braces to the counter variable, *Date* class, and members of the *Date* class do not need to be qualified. References to those identifiers from outside the braces must be qualified with the *MyLibrary* identifier.

Library builders assign *namespaces* to their libraries and place the class definitions and function prototypes in *namespace* definitions in the header files. This usage is shown here:

```
// --- wincls.h
namespace WindowClasses  {
    class Window  { /* ... */ };
    class Desktop { /* ... */ };
    unsigned int OpenWindowCount;
}
```

The example shows how a library uses a *namespace* definition. You can similarly group your program's declarations within specific *namespaces* by using the same conventions.

Library users include the library header files and specify which names they intend to use from the *namespaces*. There are three ways for a program to qualify the reference to an identifier that is declared in a different *namespace* from that of the reference: explicit *namespace* qualification; the *using* declaration; and the *using* directive.

Explicit *namespace* Qualification

To explicitly qualify an identifier with its *namespace*, you use the :: scope resolution operator:

```
namespace MyLibrary  {
    int counter;
    // ...
}
main()
{
    MyLibrary::counter++;
}
```

Other identifiers named *counter* could be declared in other *namespaces* and would not collide with the usage in the example.

The *using* Declaration

A *using* declaration specifies that all the identifiers in the *namespace* are available to the program within the scope of the *using* declaration. The following example uses the **wincls.h** file shown earlier:

```
#include "wincls.h"
using namespace WindowClasses;
// ...
```

All the identifiers in the *namespace* are now available to the program without further qualification. Unlike the *using* directive, described next, the *using* declaration does not place the names in the local scope. Instead, it makes all the *namespace*'s identifiers available to the program in the context of their own outer scope. This is not usually what you want. The library in question will no doubt consist of many unknown identifiers that need to be hidden within the *namespace*. That is what *namespaces* are for. The principal use of *using* declarations is to support standard library interfaces that are well known. It is pointless to require programs to qualify, for example, the standard *strcpy* function or the *cout* object with their respective *namespaces*. The header files for those standard libraries should include appropriate *using* declarations. In that way, old programs still compile without needing *namespace* qualifiers, and new programs do not need *namespace* qualifications just to use the standard libraries.

The *using* Directive

The *using* directive tells the compiler that you intend to use specific identifiers within a *namespace*. The *using* directive places those specific identifiers in the directive's scope as if they had been declared where the directive appears. Here is an example:

```
#include "wincls.h"
using WindowClasses::Window;
using WindowClasses::Desktop;
// ...
```

The two *using* directives in the example just shown allow the program to use the *Window* and *Desktop* identifiers that are declared in the **wincls.h** header file. At the same time, other identifiers declared in the header file and in the library's object files remain under the protection of the *WindowClasses namespace* definition.

The *namespace* Alias

Most *namespace* identifiers used by third-party libraries are typically of sufficient length so that the *namespace* stands a better chance of being unique and so that it identifies the library to which it belongs. These long identifiers would be cumbersome as qualifiers in the program's code. To support more-readable coding styles, the *namespace* feature allows a program to assign an alias to a *namespace* identifier:

```
namespace SGL = SpiffyGraphicsLibrary;

main()
{
    using SGL::DoShape;
    DoShape(); // calls SpiffyGraphicsLibrary::DoShape()
    // ...
}
```

Namespace aliases combine the terse and readable syntax of the older prefix-qualifying style with the protection of a fully defining *namespace* identifier.

The Global *namespace*

Any identifier declared in global space outside any *namespace* definition is said to be in the *global namespace*. You can still reference global identifiers just as you could in the past. If the identifiers are the same as other identifiers in other *namespaces*, you can reference them by using the :: global scope resolution operator:

```
int amount;             // global amount
namespace Payroll  {
    int amount;         // Payroll::amount
    // ...
}
main()
{
    using Payroll::amount;
    amount++;   // increments Payroll::amount
    ::amount++; // increments global amount
}
```

Unnamed *namespace* Definitions

An unnamed *namespace* definition omits the *namespace* identifier. The compiler generates an internal identifier that is unique throughout the program. Identifiers declared within an unnamed *namespace* definition are available only within the translation unit within which they are declared. Here is an example:

```
namespace {
    int counter;
}
main()
{
    counter++;
}
```

The *main* function can reference the *counter* variable declared within the unnamed *namespace*. So can any other function in the same translation unit. Functions in other translation units in the same program cannot reference the *counter* variable. This usage can replace the *static* storage class specification for variables declared outside functions.

Namespaces Summarized

Namespaces are a complex but useful feature. You can nest *namespaces* and contrive all kinds of interesting, surprising resolutions by mixing and using them. I recommend a close reading of Dr. Stroustrup's *The Design and Evolution of C++*, Chapter 17, for a detailed discussion of the more arcane aspects of this feature and for an historical perspective of its development.

The committee has defined specific *namespaces* for all Standard library functions and classes (Chapters 6 and 16). Throughout this book, the exercises have included statements similar to these:

```
#include <iostream>
#include <cstdlib>
using namespace std;
```

The classes and functions in the Standard C++ library—including those that C++ inherits from C—are declared inside the *std* namespace. Without the *using* declaration, the program would have to qualify every reference to a standard class, object, or function with the *std* name like this:

```
#include <iostream>
#include <cstdlib>

void foo()
{
    std::cout << std::rand();
}
```

The *using* declaration permits the code just shown to be coded like this:

```
#include <iostream>
#include <cstdlib>
using namespace std;

void foo()
{
    cout << rand();
}
```

The *using* declaration effectively puts everything declared in the two header files into the global *namespace* from the point of the *using* declaration to the end of the source-code file. This usage is what C and C++ programmers are accustomed to. The disadvantage of this approach is that identifiers declared in the *std* namespace are no longer protected from *namespace* collisions with global identifiers that you declare or with global identifiers declared in other header files that you include.

There is an alternative. Every Standard C++ header file has an associated legacy header file that puts the header's declarations into the global *namespace*. Standard C++ compilers include these legacy header files so that old code compiles correctly. The program just shown could be coded like this:

```
#include <iostream.h>  // legacy C++ header file
#include <stdlib.h>    // legacy (and Standard C) header file

void foo()
{
    cout << rand();
}
```

 This book includes no namespace-specific exercises, because the GNU compiler on the accompanying CD-ROM supports only the *namespace* keywords and not the feature. A future edition will demonstrate this feature more conclusively.

NOTE

NEW-STYLE CASTS

New-style C++ casts replace traditional C typecast notation (Chapter 5), providing safer notation that reflects the design of polymorphic class hierarchies and that you can readily find in code by using text-searching tools such as the Unix grep command-line utility. C-style casts are still supported by the language, but their use is discouraged and they will gradually disappear as new programs replace old ones.

In a perfect universe, programs would need no casts at all, and the framers of the language would like to have eliminated them. Research shows, however, that many idioms require them, particularly in systems programming. The C-style cast is known to be unsafe, error-prone, difficult to spot when we read programs, and more difficult to ferret out in large bodies of source-code text. New-style casts are an attempt by the committee to improve the casting situation.

There are four new casting operators. Each one returns an object converted according to the rules of the operator. They use this syntax:

```
cast_operator <type> (object)
```

The *cast_operator* is one of the following: *dynamic_cast, static_cast, reinterpret_cast,* and *const_cast.* The *type* argument is the type being cast to. The *object* argument is the object being cast from.

dynamic_cast

The *dynamic_cast* operator casts a base class reference or pointer to a derived class reference or pointer and vice versa. You can use *dynamic_cast* only when the base class has at least one virtual function.

The *dynamic_cast* operator permits a program to determine at runtime whether a base class reference or pointer refers to an object of a specific derived class or to an object of a class derived from the specified class. This operation is called *downcasting.*

Downcasting Pointers

If a *dynamic_cast* operation on a pointer is not valid—if the type of the pointer being cast from is not a member of the class hierarchy being cast to—*dynamic_cast* returns a zero. Exercise 15.1 demonstrates downcasting pointers with the *dynamic_cast* operator.

Exercise 15.1 *Downcasting with* dynamic_cast *to pointer.*

```
#include <typeinfo>
#include <iostream>
using namespace std;

class Shape {
public:
    virtual void foo() {}  // to enable rtti
};
class Circle    : public Shape { };
class Rectangle : public Shape { };

void Process(Shape* sp)
{
```

Exercise 15.1 *Downcasting with* dynamic_cast *to pointer. (continued)*

```
    // --- downcast Shape* to Circle*
    Circle* cp = dynamic_cast<Circle*>(sp);
    if (cp != 0)  {
        cout << "Processing a Circle" << endl;
        return;
    }
    // --- downcast Shape* to Rectangle*
    Rectangle* rp = dynamic_cast<Rectangle*>(sp);
    if (rp != 0)  {
        cout << "Processing a Rectangle" << endl;
        return;
    }
    cout << "Unknown Shape, cannot process" << endl;
}

int main()
{
    // --- instantiate and process a Circle
    Circle circle;
    Process(&circle);
    // --- instantiate and process a Rectangle
    Rectangle rect;
    Process(&rect);
    // --- instantiate and process a generic Shape
    Shape shape;
    Process(&shape);
    return 0;
}
```

The *Process* nonmember function in Exercise 15.1 knows about objects derived from the *Shape* base class. *Process* is a nonmember function rather than a member of *Shape* so that the *Shape* class design does not need to be aware of all the present and future specializations of itself. This approach is an alternative to having a pure virtual or empty *Shape::Process* function that is overridden derived classes. *Process* represents some external generic process that does not implement any particular abstract data type's behavior but that needs to use the interfaces of the object's classes.

If the object whose address is passed to *Process* is not a *Circle*, the *dynamic_cast<Circle*>* operation returns a zero value, and *Process* knows not to call functions that are unique to *Circle*s. Similarly, if the object is not a *Rectangle*, the *dynamic_cast<Rectangle*>* operation returns a zero value, and *Process* knows not to call functions that are unique to *Rectangle*s.

A program that uses the *dynamic_cast* operator must include the **<typeinfo>** header and enable runtime type information as a compile option. The *dynamic_cast* operator uses internal runtime type information data structures to perform its checking and conversions. We'll discuss runtime type information later in this chapter.

Downcasting References

If you use references rather than pointers, *dynamic_cast* throws a *bad_cast* exception if the target is not of the specified class. Exercise 15.2 demonstrates this behavior.

Exercise 15.2 Downcasting with dynamic_cast *to reference.*

```
#include <typeinfo>
#include <iostream>
using namespace std;

class Control {
public:
    virtual void foo() {}
};
class TextBox : public Control { };
class EditBox : public TextBox { };
class Button  : public Control { };
```

Exercise 15.2 Downcasting with dynamic_cast to reference. (continued)

```
void Paint(Control& cr)
{
    try  {
        TextBox& ctl = dynamic_cast<TextBox&>(cr);
        cout << "Paint a TextBox" << endl;
    }
    catch(bad_cast)     {
        cout << "nonTextBox, can't paint" << endl;
    }
}

int main()
{
    // --- instantiate and paint Control
    Control ct;
    Paint(ct);
    // --- instantiate and paint Button
    Button bt;
    Paint(bt);
    // --- instantiate and paint TextBox
    TextBox tb;
    Paint(tb);
    // --- instantiate and paint EditBox
    EditBox eb;
    Paint(eb);
    return 0;
}
```

Exercise 15.2 also demonstrates that a *dynamic_cast* works when the object is derived from the type being cast from. *TextBox* is derived from *Control. EditBox* is derived from *TextBox.* A reference to *Control,* the topmost base class in the hierarchy, can refer to an object of type *EditBox,* the bottommost derived class. The *Control* reference, which refers to an *EditBox* object, can be downcast to a reference to type *TextBox,* the inner class in this particular hierarchy.

Upcasting

Upcasting casts a reference or pointer to a derived class to a reference or pointer to one of the base classes in the same hierarchy. Most upcasting is done by implicit conversion. When the main function in Exercise 15.1 passes the address of a *Circle* object as an argument to the *Process* function's pointer-to-*Shape* parameter, an implicit conversion occurs. The compiler performs a static type-check to ensure that the conversion is permitted and, if it is not permitted, issues a compile-time error message. You must fix the program's source code before you can compile it. The type-check in Exercise 15.1 passes, because *Circle* is derived from *Shape* and because derived class objects can be referenced through pointers and references to their base class (or classes).

Inasmuch as implicit conversion involves static, compile-time type-checking, it follows that the actual contents of a pointer involved in an implicit cast do not enter into the process. A pointer can contain a null value or might never have been initialized at all, and the compiler permits the conversion. You use *dynamic_cast* for upcasting when you need to determine at runtime whether a pointer to a derived class really contains the address of an object of that class and, at the same time, you want to coerce the address into a pointer of one of the object's base classes.

static_cast

Unlike *dynamic_cast*, the *static_cast* operator makes no runtime check and is not restricted to base and derived classes in the same polymorphic class hierarchy. You can use *static_cast* to invoke implicit conversions between types that are not in the same hierarchy. Type-checking is static, wherein the compiler checks to ensure that the conversion is valid as opposed to the dynamic runtime type-checking that *dynamic_cast* performs. Assuming that you did not subvert the type system with a C-style cast to coerce an invalid address into a pointer or to initialize a pointer with zero, *static_cast* is a reasonably safe type-casting mechanism. Exercise 15.3 compares *static_cast* with C-style casts.

Exercise 15.3 static_cast.

```
#include <iostream>
using namespace std;

class B {
    int i;
public:
    // --- conversion constructor
    B(int a) : i(a)      { }
    void display()  { cout << i; }
};

int main()
{
    // --- C-style cast int to B
    B bobj1 = (B)123;
    bobj1.display();
    cout << '/';
    // --- constructor notation
    B bobj2 = B(456);
    bobj2.display();
    cout << '/';
    // --- static_cast
    B bobj3 = static_cast<B>(789);
    bobj3.display();
    return 0;
}
```

If you are downcasting from a base to a derived type—a conversion that is not always safe—*static_cast* assumes that its argument is an object of (or pointer or reference to an object of) the base class *within an object of the derived class*. The cast can result in a different, possibly invalid address. Consider this code:

```
class C : public A, public B { };
B *bp;
// bp is somehow initialized ...
C *cp = static_cast<C*>(bp);
```

If the *bp* pointer points to an object of type *C*, the cast works correctly. If it points to an object of type *B*, the cast makes the conversion, but the address is incorrect; it resides in a pointer to *C* but really points to an object of type *B*.

Similarly, if the pointer points to an object of the base class, unpredictable behavior will result if you use the derived class pointer to dereference members of the nonexisting derived class object.

If you are unsure about the safety of the cast, use *dynamic_cast* to downcast a reference or pointer and check the result.

If you are casting from a derived to a base type—a practice that is safe—*static_cast* assumes that its argument is a valid object of the derived class or a pointer or reference to an object of the derived class.

reinterpret_cast

The *reinterpret_cast* operator replaces most other uses of the C-style cast except those in which you are casting away *const*ness (discussed next). The *reinterpret_cast* operator converts pointers into other pointer types, numbers into pointers, and pointers into numbers. You should know what you are doing when you use *reinterpret_cast*, just as you should when you use C-style casts. That is not to say that you should never use *reinterpret_cast*. There are times when nothing else (except C-style casts) will do. Exercise 15.4 demonstrates a simple memory allocator that returns the address of a 100-character buffer as a *void* pointer. The *main* function assigns the return to a *char* pointer. Under the conversion rules of C++ (and unlike those of C), you cannot implicitly convert *void** to *char**, so a cast is needed. Rather than use a C-style cast, the exercise uses *reinterpret_cast*.

Exercise 15.4 reinterpret_cast.

```
#include <iostream>
#include <cstring>
using namespace std;

void* getmem()
{
    static char buf[100];
    return buf;
}

int main()
{
    char* cp = reinterpret_cast<char*>(getmem());
    strcpy(cp, "Hello, Woody");
    cout << cp;
    return 0;
}
```

const_cast

The three cast operators just discussed respect *const*ness—that is, you cannot use them to cast away the *const*ness of an object. For that, use the *const_cast* operator. Its type argument must match the type of the object argument except for the *const* and *volatile* keywords.

When would you want to cast away *const*ness? Class designs should take into consideration users who declare a *const* object of the type. They do that by declaring as *const* any member functions that do not modify any of the object's data member values. Those functions are accessible through *const* objects. Other functions are not. Some classes, however, have data members that contribute to the management rather than the purpose of the objects. They manipulate hidden data that the user is unconcerned about, and they must do so for all objects regardless of *const*ness.

For example, suppose that there is a global counter that represents some number of actions taken against an object of the class, *const* or otherwise. Exercise 15.5 demonstrates such a program.

Exercise 15.5 const_cast.

```
#include <iostream>
using namespace std;

class A {
    int val;
    int rptct;  // number of times the object is reported
public:
    A(int v) : val(v), rptct(0) { }
    ~A()
        { cout << val << " was reported " << rptct << " times."; }
    void report() const;
};

void A::report() const
{
    const_cast<A*>(this)->rptct++;
    cout << val << endl;
}

int main()
{
    const A a(123);
    a.report();
    a.report();
    a.report();
    return 0;
}
```

If the declaration of the *A::report()* member function were not *const*, the using program could not use the function for *const* objects of the class. The function itself needs to increment the *rptct* data member, something it normally could not do from a *const* member function. *Const* functions cannot change data values. To cast away the constness of the object for that one operation, the function uses the *const_cast* operator to cast the *this* pointer to a pointer to a non-*const* object of the class.

C++ provides the *mutable* keyword to specify class members that are never *const* even when a *const* object of the class is instantiated. Chapter 9 discusses the *mutable* keyword.

N O T E

RUNTIME TYPE INFORMATION (RTTI)

The *typeid* operator supports the new C++ runtime type information feature. Given an expression or a type as an argument, the operator returns a reference to a system-maintained object of type *type_info,* which identifies the type of the argument. There are only a few things that you can do with the *type_info* object reference. You can compare it to another *type_info* object for equality or inequality. You can initialize a *type_info* pointer variable with its address. You cannot assign or copy a *type_info* object or pass it as a function argument. You can call the member function *type_info::name*( ) to get a pointer to the type's name. You can call the member function *type_info::before*( ) to get a zero or 1 integer that represents the order of the type in relation to another type. Exercise 15.6 demonstrates some of the *typeid* operator's behavior.

Exercise 15.6 typeid.

```
#include <typeinfo>
#include <iostream>
using namespace std;

class Control { };

int main()
{
```

Exercise 15.6 typeid. *(continued)*

```
// --- display name of type
Control ct;
cout << "ct is a " << typeid(ct).name() << endl;
// --- compare typeids and display type of expression
double counter = 1.23;
if (typeid(counter) != typeid(Control))
    cout << "counter is not a " << typeid(Control).name()
        << endl;
if (typeid(counter) == typeid(1.23))
    cout << "counter is a double" << endl;
if (typeid(counter) != typeid(int))
    cout << "counter is not an int" << endl;
return 0;
}
```

A program that uses the *typeid* operator must include the **<typeinfo>** header and must have the runtime type information compile option enabled.

How would you use *typeid?* What purpose is gained by determining the specific type of an object? The *dynamic_cast* operator is more flexible in one way and less so in others. It tells you that an object is of a specified class or, in some cases, of a class in the same class hierarchy as the specified class. But for you to be able to use dynamic_cast, there must be an object of the class already instantiated. Furthermore, *dynamic_cast* works only with pointers and references to polymorphic class objects; there must be at least one virtual function somewhere in the class hierarchy. The *typeid* operator works with instantiated objects, pointers and references to objects, intrinsic type names, function names, class members, class names, and expressions.

Consider a persistent object database manager. It scans the database files and constructs memory objects from data values that it finds. How does it determine which constructors to call? RTTI can provide that intelligence. If the first component of a persistent object record is the class name or an offset into an array of class names, the program can use RTTI to select the constructor. Consider the following example, in which the database scanner retrieves the class name of the next object and calls the *DisplayObject* function. In this example, only three classes are recorded in the database.

```
void DisplayObject(char *cname)
{
    if (strcmp(cname, typeid(Employee).name())==0) {
        Employee empl;
        empl.Display();
    }
    else if (strcmp(cname, typeid(Department).name())==0) {
        Department dept;
        dept.Display();
    }
    else if (strcmp(cname, typeid(Project).name())==0) {
        Project proj;
        proj.Display();
    }
}
```

The example assumes that the database manager knows how to construct each object when the file pointer is positioned just past the type identifier in the record. This technique assumes that the scanner program knows about all the classes in the database and is similar to one that I use in the Parody II object database manager in *C++ Database Development*, 2nd Edition.

OPERATOR KEYWORDS, DIGRAPHS, AND TRIGRAPHS

Not all international character sets include all the C++ operator characters. The eight-bit ASCII values assigned to those characters in the English language are used by special symbols in the alphabets of other languages. As a result, international keyboards might not include all the C++ operator characters. The C committee addressed this problem by providing *trigraphs*: three-character sequences consisting of common characters from the international character set and that substitute for the missing operators. Table 15.1 lists the C trigraphs.

Table 15.1 C Language Trigraphs.

TRIGRAPH	OPERATOR
??=	#
??(	[
??/	\
??)	]
??'	^
??<	{
??!	|
??>	}
??-	~

The C++ committee decided to adopt what it considered to be more readable *digraphs* as alternatives for some of the C trigraphs. Table 15.2 lists the C++ digraphs.

Table 15.2 C++ Language Digraphs

DIGRAPH	OPERATOR
%%	#
<:	[
:>	]
<%	{
%>	}

The C++ committee substituted keywords for the remaining trigraphs and assigned other keywords for operators formed from ASCII characters not addressed by the C trigraphs. Table 15.3 lists the C++ operator keywords.

Table 15.3 C++ Operator Keywords

KEYWORD	OPERATOR
and	&&
and_eq	&=
bitand	&
bitor	|
compl	~
not	!
or	||
or_eq	|=
xor	^
xor_eq	^=
not_eq	!=

The following three program fragments compare conventional C++ with the trigraphs of Standard C and the digraphs and keywords of Standard C++. I leave it to you to decide which alternative is more readable.

```
// --- conventional C++
#include <iostream>
void foo()
{
    int a, b, x[20];
    // ...
    if (a || b)
        x[3] |= 5^2;
}

// --- Standard C Trigraphs
??=include <iostream>
void foo()
??<
    int a, b, x??(20??);
    // ...
    if (a ??!??! b)
        x??(3??) ??!= 5 ??' 2;
??>
```

```
// --- Standard C++ Digraphs and Operator Keywords
%%include <iostream.h>
void foo()
<%
    int a, b, x<:20:>;
    // ...
    if (a or b)
        x<:3:> or_eq 5 xor 2;
%>
```

Summary

This chapter is a potpourri of new language features—innovations of the ANSI/ISO C++ committee. Many legacy C++ programs exist that use none of these features because of the relative newness of the features to the language. Many C++ programmers still code with traditional idioms that they trust, waiting to see whether all these new features pass muster in the industry. Some programmers have not figured how they might use some of the features. Such is the evolution of any significant programming language.

CHAPTER 16

The Standard C++ Library

This chapter is about the Standard C++ Library. You learned about the Standard C Library in Chapter 6; the C++ library consists of classes that implement common programming idioms.

The Standard C++ library is an enormous subject, and a comprehensive treatment is beyond the scope of this book. Until the final publication of the standard specification, the subject is a constantly moving target. At least one book was dedicated to this subject alone and was obsolete before its publication date.

This chapter addresses those elements of the library that seem to have settled in—elements that have, at least in the classes' public interfaces, survived the environment of constant innovation, change, and improvement that permeates the standardization activity. I try here to teach you a healthy subset of the library, one that will support you well in your C++ programming endeavors and one that is likely to remain relevant at least until the next edition of this book.

You will learn about:

- The *string* class
- *iostream*s
- *fstream*s
- *strstream*s
- The *complex* class
- The Standard Template Library
- Standard exceptions

THE *string* CLASS

When BASIC programmers switched *en masse* to C in the mid-1980s, virtually all of them had the same reaction: "What, no string data type?"

BASIC programmers loved the language's rich set of string operators for manipulating character strings. C's null-terminated character arrays, its so-called string literals, and its *strcpy* and *strcmp* family of functions seemed lame by comparison.

When those same C programmers switched to C++ in the early 1990s, they all seized upon the opportunity to use the C++ class mechanism to implement string classes and recover some of the convenience they gave up when they abandoned BASIC. Most early C++ books include string classes as examples. Most of the early C++ compilers included string classes among their other class libraries. No two of those early string classes were quite the same—or so it seemed—and there was no standard for anyone to follow.

Finally, C++ has a standard *string* class. The committee approved one, and most compilers now implement the Standard C++ *string* class. To use it, you include the **<string>** header. We have used the *string* class in exercises in several chapters, but all we've done is instantiate, intialize, display, and read data into *string* objects. The *string* class has much more functionality than that.

Rather than use specific exercises to demonstrate the *string* class, we will use *string* objects in the exercises that need them. Following is a description of the *string* class's primary characteristics for your reference.

Constructing Strings

You can construct an empty *string* object. You can construct a *string* object from another *string* object. You can construct a *string* object from a null-terminated character array. These constructors are shown here:

```
string s1;
string s2("this is a string");
string s3(s2);
```

Assigning Strings

You can assign the value of one string to another *string* object. You can assign a null-terminated character array to a *string* object. You can assign a single character to a *string* object:

```
s1 = s3;
s2 = "a different string";
s3 = 'X';
```

Concatenating Strings

You can build new strings by concatenating existing strings with other strings, null-terminated character arrays, and single characters. The concatenation operators, shown here, are + and +=:

```
string s4("hello ");  // "hello "
string s5("dolly");   // "dolly"
string s6 = s4 + s5;  // "hello dolly"
s4 += s2;             // "hello dolly"
s4 += '!';            // "hello dolly!"
```

Subscripting Strings

You can use the [ ] subscript operator or the *at(int)* member function to retrieve a single character from a string and to change a character in a string:

```
char ch1 = s4[1];      // ch1 = 'e'
char ch2 = s4.at(2);   // ch2 = 'l'
s4[5] = ',';           // "hello,dolly!"
s4.at(0) = 'J';        // "Jello,dolly!"
```

Comparing Strings

The *string* class supports all the relational operators. You can compare strings with one another and with null-terminated character arrays:

```
string s1("hello ");
if ("goodbye" < s1)
    // ...
if (s1 == "hello")
    // ...
```

Substrings

The *string::substr* function extracts a substring from a string and returns the extracted substring. The first argument is the zero-based position in the original string of the substring. The second argument is the number of characters in the substring:

```
string s1("my goodbye");
cout << s1.substr(3, 4);   // displays "good"
```

The *string* class has no *right* and *left* member functions to emulate the BASIC *right$* and *left$* operators, although most of the early ad hoc string classes included *right* and *left*. The left operation can be simulated by using the *substr* function with a zero value position argument:

```
string s2("hello dolly");
string s3(s2.substr(0, 5);   // emulates s2.left(5);
                             // initializes s3 with "hello"
```

You can use the *string* class's *length* function, which returns the length of the string to simulate the right operation:

```
string s4(s2.substr(s2.length()-5,5));  // emulates s2.right(5);
                                        // initializes s4 with "dolly"
```

Searching Strings

The *string* class includes several overloaded *find* and *rfind* functions. The *find* functions search forward starting at the beginning of the *string* object. The *rfind* functions search in reverse starting at the end of the *string* object. You can search for a matching substring, a single character, and a null-terminated character array. The functions return a zero-based index into the string or –1 if the search argument is not found. Following are some examples. The comments on each line specify the value returned by the function.

```
string s1("hello dolly");
int ndx;
ndx = s1.find("dolly");  // 6
ndx = s1.find("ll");     // 2
ndx = s1.rfind("ll");    // 8
ndx = s1.find('o');      // 4
ndx = s1.rfind('o');     // 7
ndx = s1.find("bye");    // -1
```

String Operations

The *string* class is implemented as a specialized Standard Template Library (STL) sequence container that contains character types. As such, *string* includes, in addition to the functions listed here, generic algorithms and iterators and the ability to work with STL allocators. These features are characteristic of the STL generic programming model. STL is discussed in more detail later in this chapter.

Following are a few of the *string* class's additional member functions:

clear()

The *clear()* function clears the *string* object to a zero-length value.

empty()

The *empty()* functions returns a *bool* that indicates whether the string is empty (*true*) or has string data (*false*).

length()

The *length()* function returns the number of characters in the string object.

c_str()

The *c_str()* function returns a *const* pointer to the string data buffer.

 The *wchar_t* version of *string* is named *wstring*.

N O T E

INPUT/OUTPUT STREAMS

The exercises in this book have used the C++ *iostream* class library to read input from the keyboard and display results on the screen. But the *iostream* class library has capabilities beyond those that read and write the console. The library is the C++ equivalent of the Standard C stream input/output functions, and you can use it to manage console and file input/output.

The *iostream* classes have many more features than this chapter describes. After mastering the usages in the exercises given here, you should refer to the *iostream* documentation that comes with your compiler to see how to use its more advanced features. This chapter provides sufficient knowledge to use the streams in ways that support most programming problems.

C++ has no input/output operators as intrinsic or integral parts of the language. Just as C relies on function libraries to extend the language with input/output functions, C++ depends on class libraries for its input and output.

C++ manages file and console input and output as streams of characters. C++ programs manage data values as data types such as integers, structures, classes, and so on. The *iostream* library provides the interface between the data types that a program views and the character streams of the input/output system.

When the first edition of this book was written, the *iostream* class library was relatively new. Compiler vendors implemented it according to their own interpretations of the AT&T specification. The implementations today tend to follow the emerging ANSI/ISO standard but with a few minor differences reflecting the compiler writers' interpretations of the standard. Not all compilers deliver the same output, so you might see different results from these exercises depending on which compiler you use. Do not worry about that. Learn the basics and then learn how your compiler behaves.

Stream Classes

Chapter 2 introduced the C++ *iostream* class library and showed some of the ways to use it. That introduction allowed you to proceed with the exercises in this book, most of which use console input/output. Without knowing about C++ classes, you were not prepared to understand how the classes and their objects are implemented. Now that you have classes, overloaded operators, and inheritance under your belt, you are ready to learn to use the features of the *iostream* libraries.

In Standard C++, the stream classes are implemented as template classes that can be specialized for different character types. Standard C++ specializes two sets of classes for the two standard character types—*char* and *wchar_t*, but the mechanism provides for the specialization of any character set of any character width. This chapter's exercises use the classes that are specialized for the *char* type.

The ios Class

C++ streams are implemented as classes. The *cout* and *cin* objects are global instances of those classes, which derive from a base class named *ios* and which are declared by the system. There is not much to know about *ios*, although later you will use constant values and functions that *ios* defines, including *ios::beg* and *ios::setprecision(int)*. A program deals mostly with objects of types derived from the *ios* class, such as *istream* and *ostream*. Many of the member functions that you use for objects of these classes are defined in the *ios* class.

The ostream Class

Stream output is managed by a class named *ostream*, which is derived from *ios*. You learned to display a message on the screen with a statement such as the following one:

```
cout << "Hello, Dolly";
```

The *cout* object is an external object of the *ostream* class. The *cout* object is declared in the library, and an *extern* declaration of it appears in **<iostream>** so that it is available to be used by any program that includes **<iostream>**.

In addition to *cout*, **<iostream>** declares other objects as instances of the *ostream* class. The *cerr* object writes to the standard error device and uses unbuffered output. The *clog* object also writes to the standard error device, but it uses buffered output. A later part of this chapter describes buffered output.

A program writes to an *ostream* object by using the overloaded << insertion operator. The exercises in this book have used this feature extensively. The *ostream* class provides sufficient overloaded << insertion operators to support writing most standard C++ data types to the output stream. Earlier you learned how to overload the << insertion operator to write your own classes to an *ostream* object.

The *wchar_t* version of *ostream* is named *wostream*.

N O T E

The istream Class

The *istream* class manages stream input in the same way that the *ostream* class manages output. The *istream* class is externally declared in **<iostream>**. The *cin* object reads data values from the standard input device.

The *istream* class uses the overloaded >> extraction operator to read input. There are sufficient overloaded extraction >> operators to support reading the standard C++ data types, and a user-defined class can overload the >> extraction operator to read data from an *istream* object.

The *wchar_t* version of *istream* is named *wistream*.

Buffered Output

The data characters written to an *ostream* object are usually buffered. For example, the *ostream* class collects output bytes into a buffer and does not write them to the actual device associated with the object until the one of the following events occurs: the buffer fills, the program tells the object to flush its buffer, the program terminates, or, if the output object is *cout*, the program reads data from the *cin* object. The *cout* and *clog* objects use buffered output. The *cerr* object does not.

Sometimes you need to tell the program to flush a stream's buffer. A program tells an *ostream* object to flush itself by sending it the *flush* manipulator as the following code fragment demonstrates.

```
cout << "Please wait..." << flush;
```

Formatted Output

Most of the exercises in this book display unformatted data. The C++ *iostream* class library includes techniques for managing the format of displayed data.

Chapter 2 included discussions on the *dec*, *oct*, and *hex* manipulators. These manipulators set the default format for input and output. If you insert the *hex* manipulator into the output stream, for example, the object translates the internal data representation of the object into the correct display. Exercise 2.18 in Chapter 2 demonstrated this behavior. Several other manipulators and functions are used to control the format of stream output. The following discussions demonstrate some of them. We return to our convention of showing you all the output displays; they are, after all, the point of these lessons.

We'll begin with Exercise 16.1, a simple program that displays an unformatted column of floating-point numbers.

Exercise 16.1 *Displaying columns of numbers.*

```
#include <iostream>
using namespace std;

int main()
{
    static double values[] =
        { 1.23, 35.36, 653.7, 4358.224 };
    for (int i = 0; i < 4; i++)
        cout << values[i] << endl;
    return 0;
}
```

Exercise 16.1 displays the following output:

```
1.23
35.36
653.7
4358.22
```

Now we will proceed to use the formatting features of the Standard C++ *iostream* system to modify the output in various ways.

Manipulators, Flags, and Member Functions

The exercises in this discussion use manipulators and member functions to change the various modes of display, which are controlled by flags. The *ios* class keeps the current settings of the flags and values in member data items. Many of the flags and values can be changed with either a manipulator or a member function. First we'll look at a few examples so that you can learn how manipulators and member functions change output formats. Later there are tables that explain all the variations.

The ios::width Function

By default, objects of type *ostream* write data without padding. The exercises in this book insert the space character between data values in the output stream to separate them. You might want some displays to be lined up in columns, and this means that displays need to be written with a fixed width.

A program can specify a default width for all following displays by calling the *ostream::width* member function. The *width* member function takes a width parameter. The width value remains in effect for the *ostream* object until you change it.

Exercise 16.2 demonstrates how the *width* member function manages output width. By calling the *width* function with an argument of 10, the program specifies that the displays are to appear in a column at least 10 characters wide.

Exercise 16.2 *The* width *member function.*

```
#include <iostream>
using namespace std;

int main()
{
    cout.setf(ios::fixed, ios::scientific);
    static double values[] = { 1.23, 35.36, 653.7, 4358.224 };
    for (int i = 0; i < 4; i++)    {
        cout.width(10);
        cout << values[i] << endl;
    }
    return 0;
}
```

Exercise 16.2 displays the following output:

```
      1.23
     35.36
     653.7
   4358.22
```

The setw Manipulator

Sometimes a report needs to use different widths for different data elements; it is more convenient to insert width commands into the stream than to interrupt the output to call formatting functions. The *setw* manipulator provides this capability.

Exercise 16.3 demonstrates the use of the *setw* manipulator to display columns that have data elements with different width requirements.

Exercise 16.3 The setw *manipulator.*

```cpp
#include <iostream>
#include <iomanip>
using namespace std;

int main()
{
    cout.setf(ios::fixed, ios::scientific);
    static double values[] =
        { 1.23, 35.36, 653.7, 4358.224 };
    static char *names[] =
        {"Zoot", "Jimmy", "Al", "Stan"};
    for (int i = 0; i < 4; i++)
        cout << setw(6)  << names[i]
             << setw(10) << values[i] << endl;
    return 0;
}
```

N O T E

You must include **<iomanip>** to use the *setw* manipulator.

Exercise 16.3 displays the following output:

```
  Zoot      1.23
 Jimmy     35.36
    Al     653.7
  Stan   4358.22
```

Note that using *setw* or *width* does not cause any truncation. If the data value being displayed is wider than the current width value, the entire data value displays and affects the format of the displays that follow on the same line. You should be aware of this behavior when you design well-formatted displays that use the *setw* manipulator or the *width* member function.

Note also that the default width you specify applies only to the object for which you specified it—in this case the *cout* object—and not for other objects of the class.

To return the object to the default width, use the *width* member function or the *setw* manipulator with a zero argument.

The ios::fill Function

You can use the *fill* member function to set the value of the padding character for output that has a width other than the default width.

Exercise 16.4 demonstrates this usage by padding a column of numbers with asterisks.

Exercise 16.4 The fill *member function.*

```
#include <iostream>
using namespace std;

int main()
{
    static double values[] =
        { 1.23, 35.36, 653.7, 4358.224 };
    for (int i = 0; i < 4; i++)    {
        cout.width(10);
        cout.fill('*');
        cout << values[i] << endl;
    }
    return 0;
}
```

Exercise 16.4 displays the following output:

```
******1.23
*****35.36
*****653.7
***4358.22
```

Output Justification

Suppose that you want the names in Exercise 16.3 to be left-justified and the number to remain right-justified. You can use the *setiosflags* manipulator to specify that the output is to be left- or right-justified.

Exercise 16.5 demonstrates *setiosflags* by modifying the display from Exercise 16.3 so that the names are left-justified.

Exercise 16.5 *The* setiosflags *and* resetiosflags *manipulators.*

```
#include <iostream>
#include <iomanip>
using namespace std;

int main()
{
    static double values[] =
        { 1.23, 35.36, 653.7, 4358.224 };
    static char* names[] =
        {"Zoot", "Jimmy", "Al", "Stan"};
    for (int i = 0; i < 4; i++)
        cout << setiosflags(ios::left)
             << setw(6)  << names[i]
             << resetiosflags(ios::left)
             << setiosflags(ios::right)
             << setw(10) << values[i] << endl;
    return 0;
}
```

Exercise 16.5 displays the following output:

```
Zoot          1.23
Jimmy        35.36
Al           653.7
Stan       4358.22
```

The exercise sets the left-justification flag by using the *setiosflags* manipulator with an argument of *ios::left*. This argument is a constant value defined in the *ios* class, so its reference must include the *ios::* prefix. The *resetiosflags* manipulator turns off the left-justification flag to return to the default right-justification mode.

The setprecision Manipulator

Suppose you wanted the floating-point numbers in Exercise 16.5 to display with only one decimal place. The *setprecision* manipulator tells the object to use a specified number of digits of precision.

Exercise 16.6 adds the *setprecision* manipulator to the program.

Exercise 16.6 The setprecision *manipulator.*

```
#include <iostream>
#include <iomanip>
using namespace std;

main()
{
    static double values[] = { 1.23, 35.36, 653.7, 4358.224 };
    static char* names[] = {"Zoot", "Jimmy", "Al", "Stan"};
    for (int i = 0; i < 4; i++)
        cout << setiosflags(ios::left)
             << setw(6)
             << names[i]
             << resetiosflags(ios::left)
             << setiosflags(ios::right)
             << setw(10)
             << setprecision(1)
             << values[i]
             << endl;
    return 0;
}
```

Exercise 16.6 displays the following output:

```
Zoot          1
Jimmy       4e+01
Al          7e+02
Stan        4e+03
```

Scientific and Fixed Notation

Floating-point numbers are displayed in either fixed-point or scientific (exponential) notation. Observe that Exercise 16.5 uses fixed point notation and Exercise 16.6 uses scientific notation. The default fixed-point notation mode is overridden when you use the *setprecision* manipulator.

N O T E

Not all *iostream* implementations let the *setprecision* manipulator change the *ios::fixed* notation default. But then again, not all *iostream* implementations have *ios::fixed* notation as the default display mode.

Scientific notation might not be what the program needs to display. The two flags *ios::fixed* and *ios::scientific* control the notation with which floating-point numbers display. A program can set and clear these flags with the *setiosflags* and *resetiosflags* manipulators.

Exercise 16.7 uses the *setiosflags* manipulator to set the *ios::fixed* flag so that the program does not display in scientific notation.

Exercise 16.7 *Setting the* ios::fixed *flag.*

```
#include <iostream>
#include <iomanip>
using namespace std;

int main()
{
    static double values[] = { 1.23, 35.36, 653.7, 4358.224 };
    static char* names[] = {"Zoot", "Jimmy", "Al", "Stan"};
    for (int i = 0; i < 4; i++)
```

Exercise 16.7 *Setting the* ios::fixed *flag. (continued)*

```
        cout << setiosflags(ios::left)
             << setw(6)
             << names[i]
             << resetiosflags(ios::left)
             << setiosflags(ios::fixed)
             << setiosflags(ios::right)
             << setw(10)
             << setprecision(1)
             << values[i]
             << endl;
    return 0;
}
```

Exercise 16.7 displays the following output:

```
Zoot       1.2
Jimmy     35.4
Al       653.7
Stan    4358.2
```

NOTE   The default notation in some C++ implementations is *ios::scientific*. In others, the default is *ios::fixed*. Until all compilers comply with the standard specification (and until the standard specification is clear on all such matters), it's wise to be specific if you expect your programs to be portable among compilers and operating platforms.

The ios::setf and ios::unsetf Functions

Exercise 16.7 inserts the *setiosflags* manipulator into the stream to control justification and notation. The *ios* class, from which *ostream* is derived also includes *unsetf* and *setf* member functions that clear and set flags that control output format. The following example uses *unsetf* to clear the *ios::scientific* flag and *setf* to set the *ios::fixed* flag.

```
cout.unsetf(ios::scientific);
cout.setf(ios::fixed);
```

The *setf* call shown next differs from the one just shown. This variation on the call has two parameters: the flag to set and a mask that defines the flags to clear.

```
cout.setf(ios::fixed, ios::scientific);
```

Formatting Flags

Table 16.1 lists the formatting flags that the *ios* class defines. These flags have mutually exclusive bit values that can be OR'd together to form a single bit mask. The *setiosflags* and *resetiosflags* manipulators and the *setf* and *unsetf* member functions accept OR'd masks of these flags as arguments.

Table 16.1 ios Formatting Flags

FLAG	ACTION IF ON	DEFAULT
ios::showbase	Display an integer's numeric base	off
ios::showpoint	Display decimal point and trailing zeros	off
ios::showpos	Display + for positive numeric values	off
ios::skipws	Bypass white space	off
ios::stdio	Stay in sync with **<cstdio>** functions	off
ios::unitbuf	Flush the stream after each insertion	off
ios::uppercase	Display A–F for hex values, E for scientific notation (instead of a–f and e)	off
ios::dec	Display integers in base 10	on
ios::hex	Display integers in base 16	off
ios::oct	Display integers in base 8	off
ios::fixed	Display floating-point numbers in fixed notation	on
ios::scientific	Display floating-point numbers in exponential notation	off
ios::left	Align fields on the left	on
ios::right	Align fields on the right	off
ios::boolalpha	Insert and extract *bool* type in alphabetic format	off
ios::internal	Fill between sign and value	off

Formatting Manipulators

Table 16.2 lists the manipulators that **<iomanip>** defines. Each of these manipulators compiles to an expression that returns an internal type (*smanip*) that the *ios* object (*cout*, for example) uses to manage the format of the data stream. You insert manipulators into output streams with the << insertion operator.

*Table 16.2 **<iomanip>** Manipulators*

MANIPULATOR	PURPOSE
setiosflags(int m)	Set (turn on) flags in OR'd mask m expression
resetiosflags(int m)	Reset (turn off) flags in OR'd mask m expression
setw(int w)	Set field width to w
setprecision(int p)	Set floating-point precision to p
setfill(int c)	Set padding fill character to c
setbase(int b)	Set numeric base to b (8, 10, or 16)

Table 16.3 lists the manipulators that **<iostream>** defines to control streams. You insert the first six manipulators in Table 16.3 into output streams using the << insertion operator. You insert the last manipulator (*ws*) into input streams with the >> extraction operator.

*Table 16.3 **<iostream>** Manipulators*

MANIPULATOR	PURPOSE
endl	Insert newline character ('\n'); flush the stream
ends	Insert null character ('\0')
flush	Flush the stream
dec	Display integers in base 10
hex	Display integers in base 16
oct	Display integers in base 8
ws	Skips white space in the input stream

Formatting Functions

The *ios* class includes several functions that control the format of a stream. You call these functions through an object of the class (*cout*, for example).

Table 16.4 ios Formatting Functions

FUNCTION	ACTION
int ios::fill()	Return current padding fill character
int ios::fill(int c)	Set padding fill character to c; return previous character
int ios::precision()	Return current floating point precision
int ios::precision(int p)	Set precision to p; return previous precision
int ios::setf(int m)	Turn on flags in OR'd mask m; return previous flags
int ios::setf(int m1, int m2)	Turn on flags in OR'd m1; Turn off flags in OR'd m2; return previous flags
void ios::unsetf(int m)	Turn off flags in OR'd m
int ios::width()	Return current width
int ios::width(int w)	Set width to w; return previous width

Output Member Functions

The *ostream* class includes two member functions that write characters and memory blocks to output stream objects as alternatives to the overloaded << insertion operator.

The put Member Function

The *put* member function writes a single character to the output stream. The following two statements are the same:

```
cout.put('A');
cout << 'A';
```

The write Member Function

The *write* member function writes any block of memory to the stream in binary format. Because *write* does not terminate when it sees a null, it is useful for writing the binary representations of data structures to stream files, which are discussed later. Exercise 16.8 illustrates the *write* function with the *cout* object.

Exercise 16.8 *The* ostream write *function.*

```
#include <iostream>
using namespace std;

int main()
{
    static struct    {
        char msg[23];
        int alarm;
        int eol;
    } data = { "It's Howdy Doody time!", '\a', '\n' };

    cout.write(static_cast<char*>(&data), sizeof data);
    return 0;
}
```

In Exercise 16.8, the message is displayed. The program writes the message, sounds the alarm, and advances to the next line.

Note the cast to *char** before the address of the structure object. The *write* function accepts *char* pointers and unsigned *char* pointers only. The address of the structure must be cast to one of these. See Chapter 15 for a discussion of casts.

Input Member Functions

The >> extraction operator has a limitation that programs sometimes need to overcome: It bypasses white space. If you type characters on a line that is being read by the extraction operator, only the nonspace characters come into the receiving character variable. The spaces are skipped. Similarly, if the program uses the extraction operator to read a string of words, the input stops when it finds a space character. The next word is read into the next use of the extraction operation on the *istream* object, and all spaces between the words are lost. You cannot override this behavior by resetting the *ios::skipws* flag. The >> extraction operator is not affected by that flag. You must use the *istream* class's *get* and *getline* member functions to read input characters that include white space.

The get Member Function

The *get* member function works just like the >> extraction operator except that white space characters are included in the input.

Exercise 16.9 demonstrates the difference between the two operations.

Exercise 16.9 *The* istream get *member function.*

```
#include <iostream>
using namespace std;

int main()
{
    char line[25], ch = 0, *cp;
    cout << " Type a line terminated by 'x'" << endl << '>';
    cp = line;
    while (ch != 'x')    {
        cin >> ch;
        *cp++ = ch;
    }
    *cp = '\0';
    cout << ' ' << line;

cout << "\n Type another one" << endl << '>';
    cp = line;
    ch = 0;
    while (ch != 'x')    {
        cin.get(ch);
        *cp++ = ch;
    }
    *cp = '\0';
    cout << ' ' << line;
    return 0;
}
```

In Exercise 16.9, two strings are read from the keyboard one character at a time. The first input uses the extraction operator, and the second one uses the *get* member function. If you typed **now is the timex** for both entries, the screen would look like the following display:

```
Type a line terminated by 'x'
now is the timex            (entered by you)
nowisthetimex               (echoed by the program)
Type another one
now is the timex            (entered by you)
now is the timex            (echoed by the program)
```

The extraction operator skips over the white space, and the *get* function does not. The program needs the **x** terminator because it needs to know when to stop reading. Because *cin* is a buffered object, the program does not begin to start seeing characters until you type the carriage return, and that character is not seen by the program.

A variation of the *get* function allows a program to specify a buffer address and the maximum number of characters to read.

Exercise 16.10 shows how the *get* function can specify a buffer address and length instead of a character variable to receive the input.

Exercise 16.10 *Using* get *with a buffer and length.*

```
#include <iostream>
using namespace std;

int main()
{
    char line[25];
    cout << " Type a line terminated by carriage return"
        << endl << '>';
    cin.get(line, 25);
    cout << ' ' << line;
    return 0;
}
```

Exercise 16.10 reads whatever you type into the structure and echoes it to the screen.

The length value minus 1 is the maximum number of characters that is read into the buffer. You can type more than that number, but the excess characters are discarded.

The getline Member Function

The *getline* function works the same as the variation of the *get* function demonstrated in Exercise 16.12. Both functions allow a third argument that specifies the terminating character for input. If you do not include that argument, its default value is the *newline* character.

Exercise 16.11 uses the *getline* function with a third argument to specify a terminating character for the input stream.

Exercise 16.11 *The* istream getline *member function.*

```
#include <iostream>
using namespace std;

int main()
{
    char line[25];
    cout << " Type a line terminated by 'q'"
        << endl << '>';
    cin.getline(line, 25, 'q');
    cout << ' ' << line;
    return 0;
}
```

If you type **after this I quit**, the console displays the following:

```
Type a line terminated by 'q'
after this I quit          (entered by you)
after this I               (echoed by the program)
```

Some compilers include the terminating character in the final string, as shown here:

```
after this I q             (echoed by the program)
```

The read Member Function

The *istream* class's *read* member function is the input equivalent of the *write* function. It reads the binary representation of the input data into the buffer without bypassing white space. It is usually used with file input/output, described next.

Exercise 16.12 is an example of using the *read* function to read a string of characters from the keyboard into a structure.

Exercise 16.12 *The* istream read *function.*

```
#include <iostream>
using namespace std;

int main()
{
    struct    {
        char msg[23];
    } data;

    cin.read(static_cast<char*>(&data), sizeof data);
    cout << data.msg;
    return 0;
}
```

Exercise 16.12 reads whatever you type into the structure and echoes it to the screen.

File Input/Output

A file stream is an extension of a console stream. File stream classes are derived from the console stream classes and inherit all the characteristics of the console. But files have some requirements of their own that character devices such as the console do not have. Files have distinct names. A program can append data to an existing file. A program can seek to a specified position in a file. The class inheritance facility of C++ is a natural way to build file classes from console classes, and that is how the file stream classes work.

A program that uses the file stream classes must include the **<fstream>** header file wherein the classes are defined. The program might also include

<iostream>, but it is not necessary because **<fstream>** itself includes **<iostream>**.

The ofstream Class

The *ofstream* class objects are files that a program can write to. In the most elementary use of *ofstream*, the program declares an object of type *ofstream*, passing a file name argument to the constructor. Then the program writes to the file through the object. When the object goes out of scope, the file closes.

Exercise 16.13 uses an *ofstream* object in its simplest form.

Exercise 16.13 File output.

```
#include <fstream>
using namespace std;

int main()
{
    ofstream tfile("test.dat");
    tfile << "These are test data";
    return 0;
}
```

The program creates a file and writes a string to it. To view the file and verify that the program works, drag the file's icon to the Windows 95 Notepad applet.

You can use the *ofstream* class to append to an existing file. Exercise 16.14 appends a string to the file that Exercise 16.13 created.

Exercise 16.14 Appending to an output file.

```
#include <fstream>
using namespace std;

int main()
{
    ofstream tfile("test.dat", ios::app);
    tfile << ", and these are more";
        return 0;
}
```

The *write* member function works well with *ofstream* classes. Exercise 16.15 shows how the *write* function can record the binary representation of a class object into a data file.

Exercise 16.15 *The* write *member function.*

```
#include <fstream>
using namespace std;
#include <Date.h>

int main()
{
    Date dat(6, 24, 1940);
    struct date {
        int mo, da, yr;
    } dt;
    dat.GetDate(dt.mo, dt.da, dt.yr);
    ofstream tfile("date.dat");
    tfile.write(static_cast<char*>(&dt), sizeof dt);
    return 0;
}
```

The program instantiates a *Date* object using the *Date* class that we created in Chapter 11. Then the program declares a *date* structure and uses *Date::GetDate* to load the *Date* object's month, day, and year values into the *date* structure's data member. The program creates the file and writes the binary value of the *struct date* object into it. The *write* function does not stop writing when it reaches a null character, so the complete class structure is written regardless of its content.

NOTE

The *wchar_t* version of *ofstream* is named *wofstream*.

Exercise 16.15 teaches another valuable lesson. You might wonder why the program uses an interim, contrived data structure instead of simply writing the *Date* object like this:

```
tfile.write(static_cast<char*>(&dat), sizeof dat);
```

There are several reasons you should not do that. Pay close attention to this lesson.

First, the *Date* class is an externally designed abstract data type. You might not know how the class implements its data representation. (Sure, you can always look at the **Date.h** header file, but read on.)

Second, if you depend on the details of that format and if the *Date* class designer changes the implementation, you must necessarily recompile all programs and convert all data files that depended on the previous data representation.

Third, and most important, the *Date* class might have one or more virtual functions. (It does.) A class that has virtual functions includes among its data members a hidden private pointer (*vptr*) to the class's virtual table (*vtbl*). If the class is derived from other classes, there are *vptr* data members for all the base classes. Those pointers' values are physical memory addresses based on where in memory the compiler put the class's *vtbl* for this particular program. The address-of operator (&) returns the memory address of the complete object, and the *sizeof* operator includes all *vptr* data members. There is no standard that specifies where in an object's memory the compiler must put *vtpr* data members, so you cannot get tricky and bypass it in any portable way. You cannot reference the *vptr* data member, not even from within a member function, so you cannot save and restore its value. Not only is the *vptr* data value meaningless to the storage of a date's value, but also if you were to read it from the file into a *Date* object in another program, you would probably trash the other program's pointer with a value that points to nowhere in particular. Later, when the program accessed the *vptr* to execute a virtual function or resolve a use of the *typeid* or *dynamic_cast* operator, the program would crash.

The ifstream Class

The *ifstream* class objects are input files. A program can declare an input file stream object and read it. A program can use the >> extraction operator, the *get* function, or the *getline* function just as if the stream were the console device rather than a file. A program can also use the *read* member function to read binary blocks into memory.

Exercise 16.16 reads the *Date* object from the file written by Exercise 16.15.

Exercise 16.16 The read *member function.*

```
#include <fstream>
using namespace std;
#include <Date.h>

int main()
{
    struct date {
        int mo, da, yr;
    } dt;
    ifstream tfile("date.dat");
    tfile.read(static_cast<char*>(&dt), sizeof dt);
    Date dat(dt.mo, dt.da, dt.yr);
    cout << dat;
    return 0;
}
```

Exercise 16.16 displays the date **6/24/1940** on the screen. Observe that the program uses the same protective convention that Exercise 16.15 used. It reads the file data into the structure object. Then it instantiates a *Date* object from the data members of the structure. An overloaded *ostream::operator<<(const Date&)* function is defined along with the *Date* class to permit displaying *Date* objects to *ostream* objects, and the program uses this mechanism to display the date on the console.

The *wchar_t* version of *ifstream* is named *wifstream*.

N O T E

Testing for End-of-File

The *istream::eof* member function returns a true value if the stream has reached the end of its character stream. A program typically uses this test to determine that a program has reached end of file and should try no more reads of the data.

Exercise 16.17 opens the text file that Exercise 16.13 created and Exercise 16.14 modified and reads the file data one character at a time. The program sends each character to *cout* as the character is read and stops at end-of-file.

Exercise 16.17 *Testing end-of-file.*

```
#include <fstream>
using namespace std;


int main()
{
    ifstream tfile("test.dat");
    while (!tfile.eof())     {
        char ch;
        tfile.get(ch);
         if (!tfile.eof())
            cout << ch;
    }
    return 0;
}
```

Assuming you ran Exercises 16.13 and 16.14, Exercise 16.17 displays this message:

```
These are test data, and these are more
```

Seeking

File streams support random access of binary files (more about that later). A program can modify the current position of a file stream by using one of the member functions *seekg* and *seekp*. The *seekg* function changes the position of the next input operation on a file opened for input. The *seekp* function changes the position of the next output operation on a file opened for output.

Exercise 16.18 opens a file, changes the input position, and then reads to end-of-file.

Exercise 16.18 *The* seekg *member function.*

```
#include <fstream>
using namespace std;

int main()
{
    ifstream tfile("test.dat", ios::binary);
    tfile.seekg(6);          // seek six characters in
    while (!tfile.eof())     {
        char ch;
        tfile.get(ch);
        if (!tfile.eof())
            cout << ch;
    }
    return 0;
}
```

Exercise 16.18 displays this message:

```
are test data, and these are more
```

Observe the *ios::binary openmode* argument in the *ifstream* object's initializer list. This argument specifies that the file is to open in *binary* rather than *text* mode. The functions that seek (*seekg* and *seekp*) and the functions that report a file's current position (*tellg* and *tellp*) work properly only when a file is opened for binary reads or writes. See "Binary and Text Files" later in this chapter for a discussion of the differences between binary and text files.

By adding an argument to the function call, a program can specify that a *seekg* or *seekp* operation occurs relative to the beginning of the file, the end of the file, or the current position. The argument is defined in the *ios* class. The following are examples of the function calls:

```
tfile.seekg(5, ios::beg);
tfile.seekg(10, ios::cur);
tfile.seekg(-15, ios::end);
```

If you do not provide the second argument, the seek occurs from the beginning of the file.

You can determine the current position for input with the *tellg* member function and the current position for output with the *tellp* member function.

Exercise 16.19 illustrates the *tellg* function.

Exercise 16.19 *The* tellg *function.*

```
#include <fstream.h>
main()
{
    ifstream tfile("test.dat", ios::binary);
    while (!tfile.eof())    {
        char ch;
        streampos here = tfile.tellg();
        tfile.get(ch);
        if (ch == ' ')
            cout << "\nPosition " << here << " is a space";
    }
}
```

Exercise 16.19 displays these messages:

```
Position 5 is a space
Position 9 is a space
Position 14 is a space
Position 20 is a space
Position 24 is a space
Position 30 is a space
Position 34 is a space
```

The program reads the file built by earlier exercises and displays messages showing the character positions where it finds spaces. The *tellg* function returns an integral value of type *streampos*, a *typedef* defined in one of the compiler's internal header files related to file streams.

Reading and Writing Stream Files

Sometimes a program needs to open a file for read/write access. Typical examples are database files in which a program reads records, updates them, and writes them back to the file.

To open a file for read/write access, you add an *openmode* argument to the *ifstream* constructor argument list. The *openmode* argument overrides the default read-only mode of *ifstream* objects. Following is an example of the syntax for opening a file with read/write access:

```
ifstream tfile(fname, ios::in | ios::out);
```

Next, you declare an object of type *ostream* (not *ofstream*) and initialize its constructor with the return value from the *ifstream* object's *rdbuf* member function. This function returns the file's buffer component. The *ostream* object can now be used for writing while the *ifstream* object is used for reading.

Exercise 16.20 reads the text file from the earlier exercises into a character array and writes an uppercase-only copy of the bytes at the end of the file.

Exercise 16.20 Reading and writing a stream file.

```
#include <fstream>
#include <cctype>
using namespace std;

int main()
{
    char* fname = "test.dat";
    // --- read the file into an array
    ifstream tfile(fname, ios::in | ios::out | ios::binary);
    ostream ofile(tfile.rdbuf());
    char tdata[100];
    int i = 0;
    while (!tfile.eof() && i < sizeof tdata)
        tfile.get(tdata[i++]);
    ofile.seekp(0, ios::end);
    ofile << "\r\n";
    for (int j = 0; j < i-1; j++)
        ofile.put(static_cast<char>(toupper(tdata[j])));
    return 0;
}
```

The program modifies the file so that it contains these contents:

```
These are test data, and these are more
THESE ARE TEST DATA, AND THESE ARE MORE
```

Observe that Exercise 16.20 uses the *seekp* function to change the output insertion location for the output component of the file.

Observe also that the program sends the string *"\r\n"* to the file as a line separator rather then the *endl* manipulator or the *newline* character. This procedure is because the file is opened with the *ios::binary openmode* and the exercises as distributed compile and run under Windows 95 or NT. See "Binary and Text Files" later in this chapter for a discussion of the differences between binary and text files.

NOTE   This program does not work as coded with the accompanying Quincy compiler. The gnu-win32 port of the GNU C++ compiler has a bug in its implementation of the *filebuf* class. This bug causes all files that do not specifically have an *openmode* argument of *ios::in* to be truncated to a zero length upon open unless the *openmode* argument includes the *ios::nocreate* value. To get around the bug, the program on the CD-ROM constructs the *ifstream* object as shown here:

```
ifstream tfile(fname, ios::in | ios::out | ios::nocreate);
```

The notation just shown does not hurt anything in a fully compliant *fstream* library, and it gets around the gnu-win32 bug, but you should not need to add the *ios::nocreate* flag to the *openmode* argument in a fully ANSI-compliant programming environment.

Opening and Closing a Stream File

A program can declare an *ifstream* or *ofstream* object without a name. When it does, the object exists but no file is associated with it. You must then use the *open* member function to associate a file with the *fstream* object. You can disassociate the file from the object by calling the *close* member function. This technique allows a single object to represent different files at different times.

Exercise 16.21 demonstrates the use of the *open* function to associate the stream object with a file and the *close* function to disassociate the object from a file.

Exercise 16.21 open *and* close *member functions.*

```
#include <fstream>
using namespace std;

int main()
{
    ofstream tfile;     // an ofstream object without a file
    tfile.open("test1.dat");
    tfile << "This is TEST1";
    tfile.close();
    tfile.open("test2.dat");
    tfile << "This is TEST2";
    tfile.close();
    return 0;
}
```

The *iostream* classes include conversion functions that return true or false values if you use the object name in a true/false conditional expression. Suppose you declare a file stream object without an initializing name and do not associate a name with that object. The following code shows how you might test for that condition:

```
fstream tfile;     // no file name given
if (tfile)         // this test returns false
    // ...
```

How to Open a File

The C and C++ stream facilities for opening files are less than instantly intuitive. Veteran programmers still have to stop and think when they are about to open a file. Does the file already exist? May the file already exist? If the file exists, should the program truncate it? Append to it? If the file does not exist, should the program create it? The variations on this theme go on and on.

The *open* member function and the implied open operation performed by the constructor take an *openmode* integer value as a parameter. The argument values for the *open_mode* parameter are defined in the *ios* class. You optionally provide one or more of these parameters in a logical OR expression depending on how you want the file to be opened.

Table 16.5 lists the *openmode* bits defined in the *ios* class.

Table 16.5 openmode Values

OPENMODE	DESCRIPTION
ios::app	Append to an output file. Every output operation is performed at the physical end-of-file, and the input and output file pointers are repositioned immediately past the last character written.
ios::ate	The open operation includes a seek to the end of the file. This mode can be used with input and output files.
ios::in	This is an input file and is an implied mode for *ifstream* objects. If you use *ios::in* as an *open_mode* for an *ofstream* file, it prevents the truncation of an existing file.
ios::out	This is an output file and is an implied mode for *ofstream* objects. When you use *ios::out* for an *ofstream* object without *ios::app* or *ios::ate*, *ios::trunc* is implied.
ios::nocreate	The file must exist; otherwise, the open fails.
ios::noreplace	The file must not exist; otherwise, the open fails.
ios::trunc	Delete the file if it already exists and re-create it.

There are seven of these bits and two types of objects: *ofstream* and *ifstream*. Therefore, there are many possible open statements for you to code. Not all of them would be logical, but you could code them all. For each of them, the file might exist or it might not. Consequently, there are even more possible circumstances. Covering them all is beyond the scope of this book. However, here are some of the most common circumstances:

- You want to create a file. If it exists, delete the old one.
  ```
  ofstream ofile("FILENAME");  // no open_mode
  ```
- You want to read an existing file. If it does not exist, an error has occurred.

```
ifstream ifile("FILENAME");  // no open_mode
if (ifile.fail())
// the file does not exist ...
```

- You want to read and write an existing file. This is an update mode. You might read records, seek to records, rewrite existing records, and add records to the end of the file.

```
ifstream ifile("FILENAME", ios::in | ios::out);
if (ifile.fail())
// the file does not exist ...
ostream ofile(ifile.rdbuf());
```

    (See the note that accompanies Exercise 16.20.)

- You want to write to an existing file without deleting it first.

```
ofstream ofile("FILENAME", ios::out | ios::nocreate);
```

- You want to append records to an existing file, creating it if it does not exist.

```
ofstream ofile("FILENAME", ios::out | ios::app);
```

Testing Errors

A program can and should test errors when it uses input/output file streams. Each stream object has its own set of condition flags that change according to the current state of the object. You used one of these flags when you tested for end-of-file with the *eof* member function. Other member functions that test for flag settings are *bad*, *fail*, and *good*. The *bad* function returns a true value if your program attempts to do something illegal, such as seek beyond the end of the file. The *fail* function returns a true value for all conditions that include the *bad* positive return plus any valid operations that fail, such as trying to open an unavailable file or trying to write to a disk device that is full. The *good* function returns true whenever *fail* would return false.

Exercise 16.22 attempts and fails to open a nonexisting file for input.

Exercise 16.22 File error checking.

```
#include <fstream>
using namespace std;

int main()
{
    ifstream ifile;
    ifile.open("noname.fil", ios::in | ios::nocreate);
    if (ifile.fail())
        cout << "Cannot open";
    else    {
        // ...
        ifile.close();
    }
    return 0;
}}
```

Exercise 16.26 displays the **Cannot open** message on the screen.

Observe the use of the *ios::nocreate* mode value as an argument to the *open* member function. This argument tells the *open* function to fail if the file does not exist. Therefore, the call to the *fail* member function returns true because the file does not exist. This function works the same way whether you open the file with the *open* member function or specify the file name as an initializer in the declaration of the stream object.

Binary and Text Files

The C++ **<fstream>** library recognizes two kinds of files: binary and text files. By default, all files are opened as text files. To open a binary file, you include the *ios::binary* value in the *openmode* argument for the *open* function or in the constructor's initializer list.

On some operating platforms—Unix, for example—there is no difference between binary files and text files, and the use of the *ios::binary* argument has no effect. Other platforms—MS-DOS, Windows 95, and Windows NT, for example—have a distinct difference.

Those platforms that differentiate between text files and binary files do so in these ways:

1. When the program writes a newline ('\n') character to a binary file, the file system writes the single newline character, which, on most platforms is the same as the linefeed (0x0a) character.

2. When the program writes a newline character to a text file, the file system writes two characters: a carriage return character (0x0d) followed by a linefeed character (0x0a).

3. When the program reads a newline character from a binary file, the file system reads the single newline character into memory.

4. When the program reads a carriage return/linefeed character pair from a text file, the file system translates the pair into a single newline character in memory.

5. When the program reads a single newline character—a linefeed that is not preceded by a carriage return character—from a text file, the file system inserts the newline character into memory.

This approach has significant implications, mainly involving file position operations—seeking and telling. A text file's data representation in memory has a different length than its data representation on disk because of the bidirectional translations between single newline memory characters and carriage return/linefeed character pairs on disk. Consequently, seeking and telling are unreliable operations when applied to text files.

strstream

The *strstream* classes—*istrstream*, *ostrstream*, and *strstream*—implement input/output streams by using the computer's memory (rather than the console or disk files as the input/output device). The classes provide a convenient way to use the *iostream* text-formatting system to convert objects to displayable character strings and vice versa. The draft standard specification relegates these classes to the deprecated category, which means that they discourage you from using them and encourage you to use the *stringstream* classes instead (described later in this chapter). However, many compilers (including the accompanying gnu-win32 port of the GNU compiler) do not yet implement the *stringstream* classes, so I am including a discussion of *strstream*s in this edition.

The *strstream* classes implement their internal buffers with a data member of the *strstreambuf* class. Many operations are made through that data member. The public *rdbuf()* member function in each of the *strstream* classes returns a pointer to the *strstreambuf* class. You will see that member function used in some of the exercises that follow.

The istrstream class

By using the *istrstream* class, you can extract from a character string into one or more objects. The objects must be of intrinsic C++ types or of classes in which an overloaded >> operator permits reading from an *istream* object into a type.

Let's begin with the simplest example. Recall from earlier chapters the Standard C *atoi* function that is declared in **<cstdlib>** and that converts a zero-terminated character string into an integer, as shown in the following code fragment:

```
#include <cstdlib>
using namespace std;

char *str = "1234";
int n = atoi(str);    // n == 1234
```

Exercise 16.23 demonstrates that you can extract from a text string into an object just as if you were extracting the string data from the console or an *ifstream* file object.

Exercise 16.23 The istrstream *class.*

```
#include <strstream>
#include <cstdlib>
using namespace std;

int main()
{
```

Exercise 16.23 *The* istrstream *class. (continued)*

```
    char instr[100];
    cout << "Enter an integer: " << flush;
    cin.getline(instr, 100);
    cout << "atoi returns " << atoi(instr) << endl;
    istrstream istr(instr);
    int n;
    istr >> n;
    cout << "extracted from istr: " << n;
    return 0;
}
```

Exercise 16.23 prompts for and reads an integer from the console. The integer is read into a character array. The program displays the integer result from calling the Standard C *atoi* function with the input string as an argument. Then the program constructs an *istrstream* object, initializing the object with the input string. Finally, the program uses the >> extraction operator to extract the integer value from the string into an integer variable, which the program displays. If you enter **123** in response to the prompt, this is what the console displays when the program has finished running:

```
Enter an integer: 123
atoi returns 123
Extracted from istr: 123
```

The *istrstream* class has even more functionality than that. Exercise 16.24 demonstrates its ability to extract several object values of different types from an *istrstream* object.

Exercise 16.24 Extracting from istrstream.

```
#include <strstream>
#include <cstdlib>
#include <string>
using namespace std;


int main()
{
    char instr[100];
    cout << "Enter an integer, a float, and a string: " << flush;
    cin.getline(instr, 100);
    istrstream istr(instr);
    int n;
    float f;
    string s;
    istr >> n >> f >> s;
    cout << "Extracted from istrstream: "
        << n << ' ' << f << ' ' << s << endl;
    return 0;
}
```

The *istrstream* object in Exercise 16.24 will contain three string values of different types separated by white space (assuming that you enter the values that way when you run the program). The program extracts those string values into three variables and displays the result. The console displays the following data if you enter **123 4.5 Hello** in response to the prompt.

```
Enter an integer, a float, and a string: 123 4.5 Hello
Extracted from istrstream: 123 4.5 Hello
```

Now let's consider an application for the *istrstream* class. Here's the problem: Read a sentence from the console. Allow the user to separate words with multiple spaces. Extract the words from the input and reconstruct the sentence with each space collapsed into a single period (.) character. Exercise 16.25 solves this problem.

Exercise 16.25 *Using* istrstream *to extract words.*

```
#include <strstream>
#include <string>
using namespace std;


int main()
{
    char sentence[100];
    cout << "Type a brief sentence: " << endl;
    cin.getline(sentence, 100);
    istrstream istr(sentence);
    int ct;
    // --- count the words
    string wd;
    for (ct = 0; !istr.eof(); ct++)
        istr >> wd;
    string* pwords = new string[ct];
    // --- seek to the beginning
    istr.clear();
    istr.seekg(0, ios::beg);
    // --- collect the words
    int i;
    for (i = 0; i < ct; i++)
        istr >> pwords[i];
```

Exercise 16.25 *Using* istrstream *to extract words. (continued)*

```
    // --- rebuild sentence; collapsed ws, period separators
    string strsent;
    for (int j = 0; j < i; j++)  {
        strsent += pwords[j];
        if (j < i-1)
            strsent += '.';
    }
    delete [] pwords;
    cout << "The reconstructed sentence is: " << strsent;
    return 0;
}
```

Exercise 16.25 assumes that the sentence will not exceed 100 characters. The user types the sentence, and the program counts the words by extracting them one at a time until the *istrstream* object reaches end-of-file. Then the program instantiates a dynamic array of *string* objects with enough array elements to contain all the words. Next, the program uses the *seekg* function to reset the *istrstream* object to the beginning of the stream and extracts each word one at a time into the elements of the array. The *clear* member function is necessary to reset the end-of-file indication. Otherwise, the *seekg* operation would fail. The extraction operator bypasses white space to find each word. Finally, the program reconstructs the sentence into a *string* object by concatenating to the object each word from the array and a period where white space would be. The concatenations use the *string* class's overloaded += operator.

If you type the sentence **now is the time for action** with extra white space between the words, the console displays these lines of data when the program is finished:

```
Type a brief sentence:
now  is  the  time  for  action
The reconstructed sentence is: now.is.the.time.for.action
```

The ostrstream class

The *ostrstream* class permits you to format objects into strings. The *ostrstream* class emulates a stream output device in memory. Programmers typically use this class to construct text messages from memory variables, perhaps to insert into reports or dialog boxes. We'll do the same thing here, but we'll display the results on the standard console output device.

Exercise 16.26 The ostrstream *class.*

```
#include <strstream>
using namespace std;
#include <Date.h>


int main()
{
    ostrstream ostr;
    Date dt(11,17,1997);
    ostr << "Judy's next birthday is ";
    ostr << dt;
    ostr << ". Let's have a party.";
    ostr << ends;
    // --- now display the ostrstream object
    cout << ostr.rdbuf();
    return 0;
}
```

Exercise 16.26 declares an empty *ostrstream* object. Then it declares a *Date* object using the *Date* class that we developed for earlier exercises. The program uses the << insertion operator to insert a zero-terminated character string value into the *ostrstream* object. Then the program inserts the *Date* object into the *ostrstream* object followed by another character string. These operations work just like sending objects to the *cout* object to display them on the console except that the formatted display string goes into the *ostrstream* object's internal buffer rather than to a device. The *ostrstream* class automatically resizes its buffer with each insertion to contain whatever you insert.

The *ends* manipulator inserts a zero value character ('\0') into the *ostrstream* object in case we want to use the buffer in an operation that requires a zero-terminated character array.

The *rdbuf()* function returns a pointer to the internal *strstreambuf* buffer object. You don't need to know the details of that implementation, but it helps to know that you can insert such a buffer object's address into an *ostream* object—in this case, *cout*—and the object displays the buffer.

The *ostrstream* object in Exercise 16.26 allocates memory from the heap to hold the string data. As you insert data into the object, it reallocates memory as required to hold the additional characters. Consequently, the physical memory address where the object stores the data can change with each insertion. When the object is destroyed, its destructor returns the most recent buffer memory to the heap.

You can retrieve the memory address by calling the *str()* member function. You would do that when you need to perform an operation that requires a character pointer rather than the buffer reference that *rdbuf()* returns.

When you call *str()*, the object assumes that because you asked for the address, you need the address to remain unchanged. Therefore, it "freezes" itself and does not allow you to do anything further that could change the address. You cannot, for example, insert any more characters into the object. Furthermore, the object abdicates its responsibility for freeing its allocated memory. It does not know how long you will keep the address that *str()* returned, so it does not free the memory when the object is destroyed. You must do that yourself.

The Standard definition of *ostrstream* is unspecific about what happens if you try to subvert its good intentions and add characters to a frozen object.

N O T E

Exercise 16.27 demonstrates the use of *str()* to get the buffer's address and freeze the object.

Exercise 6.27 *Freezing an* ostrstream *object.*

```
#include <strstream>
using namespace std;

int main()
{
    ostrstream ostr;
    ostr << "This is only a test" << ends;
    char* sp = ostr.str();  // freezes the object
    // --- now display the ostrstream object
    cout << sp;;
    delete [] sp;
    return 0;
}
```

You can unfreeze an *ostrstream* object explicitly by calling the *freeze* member function with a zero argument:

```
ostr.freeze(0);
```

Once you have unfrozen the object, you should not depend on the address that *str()* provided previously. You must not delete the pointer. Even if it was still valid, the object will delete its own buffer space when the object is destroyed. You cannot safely delete the same memory twice, and that is what would happen.

The *ostrstream* class allows you to instantiate an object and specify a memory buffer that you have allocated. In this case, the object takes no responsibility for returning the buffer to the heap. The buffer might not be allocated from the heap. It could be an automatic buffer on the stack or an extern or static buffer that remains in existence for the life of the program.

Exercise 6.28 demonstrates this behavior.

Exercise 6.28 Providing a buffer for ostrstream.

```
#include <strstream>
using namespace std;


int main()
{
    char buf[30];
    ostrstream ostr(buf, sizeof buf);
    ostr << "This is test # " << 12 << ends;
    // --- now display the ostrstream object
    cout << ostr.str();
    return 0;
}
```

The program instantiates the *ostrstream* object by passing a buffer address and a length. The object will accept only the number of characters that the length specifies.

Observe that Exercise 6.28 displays the text by calling the *str()* function rather than the *rdbuf()* function. The former returns a pointer to the character array buffer, which is null-terminated. The latter displays the entire contents of the buffer irrespective of null terminators, and the data string that the program inserts is shorter than the length of the buffer.

The strstream class

The *strstream* class supports reading and writing the same object. Exercise 6.29 demonstrates this class.

Exercise 6.29 *The* strstream *class.*

```
#include <strstream>
#include <string>
using namespace std;

int main()
{
    strstream sstr;
    sstr << "Number ";
    sstr << 666;
    sstr << ends;
    sstr.seekg(6);
    int n;
    sstr >> n;
    cout << "Extracted int: " << n << endl;
    sstr.seekg(0);
    string s;
    sstr >> s;
    cout << "Extracted string: " << s;
    return 0;
}
```

Exercise 6.29 instantiates a *strstream* object and uses the insertion (<<) opera-tor to write a string literal and an integer value to the object. The *seekg* func-tion call positions the input pointer to the seventh (relative to 1) character position of the object's character array, which is the space character just before the *666* characters. (Remember, even though you inserted an integer, this is a character-oriented stream object just like the console. Its internal data representation is an array of characters.) Then the program uses the extrac-tion (>>) operator to read the *666* value into an integer variable. The pro-gram displays the integer to prove that the extraction works. Finally, the program calls *seekg* again to position the input pointer to the beginning of the stream, extracts the string value from the stream into a *string* object, and dis-plays the *string* object on the console. Following are the lines that the program displays on the console:

```
Extracted int: 666
Extracted string: Number
```

Here's an interesting observation. If the string literal ("*Number*") that was first inserted into the *strstream* object did not have that final space character (and was "*Number*" instead), the internal string would be "*Number666*" after the program inserted the integer value *666*. The first extraction would still extract the integer 666, because that operation converts character digits into an integer value. The second extraction, which begins at the first position of the internal string and continues until it finds white space, a nondisplayable character, or end-of-file, would have extracted "*Number666*" into the *string* object.

stringstream

The *stringstream* classes are a new addition to the Standard C++ library, and few compilers implement them. Of the popular C++ compilers for PC platforms, only Microsoft's Visual C++ versions 4.2 and above implement the *stringstream* classes at the time of this writing. Consequently, the exercises that accompany this discussion do not compile with Quincy, the compiler environment included on the CD-ROM that accompanies this book. They do, however, compile with Visual C++ 4.2.

There are three classes: *istringstream*, *ostringstream*, and *stringstream*. They work essentially the same as the *istrstream*, *ostrstream*, and *strstream* classes with this exception: They read into and write from objects of the *string* class rather than a heap-allocated or user-supplied character array. Consequently, you do not have to concern yourself with memory allocation because *string* class objects take care of that for themselves. There is no such thing as a "frozen" object and no *freeze* member function. When you call the *str()* function, it returns a copy of the internal buffer object not the address of the character data.

Exercises 16.30, 16.31, and 16.32 are *stringstream* versions of Exercises 16.24, 16.27, and 16.29.

Exercise 16.30 The istringstream *class.*

```
#include <iostream>
#include <sstream>
#include <cstdlib>
#include <string>
//using namespace std; // out for VC++ 4.2, in for 5.0

int main()
{
    char instr[100];
    cout << "Enter an integer, a float, and a string: ";
    cin.getline(instr, 100);
    istringstream istr(instr);
    int n;
    float f;
    string s;
    istr >> n >> f >> s;
    cout << "Extracted from istringstream: "
         << n << ' ' << f << ' ' << s << endl;
    return 0;
}
```

Exercise 16.31 *The* ostringstream *class.*

```
#include <iostream>
#include <sstream>
// using namespace std;  // out for VC++ 4.2, in for 5.0

int main()
{
    ostringstream ostr;
    ostr << "This is only a test" << ends;
    const string& sp = ostr.str();
    // --- now display the ostringstream object
    cout << sp;;
    return 0;
}
```

Exercise 16.32 *The* stringstream *class.*

```
#include <iostream>
#include <sstream>
#include <string>
//using namespace std; // out for VC++ 4.2, in for 5.0

int main()
{
    stringstream sstr;
    sstr << "Number ";
    sstr << 666;
    sstr.clear();
    sstr.seekg(6);
    int n;
    sstr >> n;
    cout << "Extracted int: " << n << endl;
    sstr.clear();
    sstr.seekg(0);
    string s;
    sstr >> s;
    cout << "Extracted string: " << s;
    return 0;
}
```

The *wchar_t* versions of *istringstream*, *ostringstream*, and *stringstream* are named *wistringstream*, *wostringstream*, and *wstringstream*.

THE *complex* CLASS

The *complex* class is a template class that the library specializes for three intrinsic types: float, double, and long double. The class overloads the arithmetic and relational operators, the insertion and extraction operators, and the assignment operator. The overloaded arithmetic and relational operator functions can accept a single argument of any parameterized *complex* type or any combination of two arguments of the parameterized type and a parameterized *complex* type. The overloaded arithmetic operator functions can accept a *complex* argument and either another *complex* argument or a scalar variable of the type upon which the complex number is parameterized.

The *complex* class includes functions to extract values from a complex object, as shown in Table 16.6.

Table 16.6 complex Class Value Functions

FUNCTION	RETURNS
real()	Real part
imag()	Imaginary part
abs(x)	Magnitude of x
arg(x)	Phase angle of x
norm(x)	Squared magnitude of x
conj(x)	Complex conjugate of x
polar(rho,theta)	Complex value corresponding to a complex number whose magnitude is rho and whose phase angle is theta.

Exercise 16.33 is a small example of using the *complex* class

Exercise 16.33 The complex *class.*

```
#include <iostream>
#include <complex>
using namespace std;
int main()
{
    complex<float> cn(5, 3);
    cn += complex<float>(1, 2);
    cout << cn;
    return 0;
}
```

N O T E

Exercise 16.33 compiles and executes with Quincy, but the execution aborts Quincy when it completes. I had to modify one of the GNU header files (**complext.h**) to make the exercise compile properly. This indicates that the *complex* class had not been tested by the gnu-win32 library team as of the beta version that I integrated with Quincy. Exercise 16.33 compiles and executes properly with Visual C++ 4.2 when the *using* declaration is commented out.

THE STANDARD TEMPLATE LIBRARY

The Standard Template Library (STL) was developed at Hewlett-Packard Laboratories and accepted in 1994 as an addition to the Standard C++ library. The breadth of the scope of STL caused committee members to reconsider Standard library container classes that they had already accepted and published in the working paper. Most container-type data structures can be implemented with STL class templates. The bounded array and linked-list templates of Chapter 13 are examples. STL replaces both of them. This discussion provides an overview of STL's underlying concepts.

STL is a library of container class templates and algorithmic function templates. Remember from Chapter 13 that templates define generic container classes with which you manage sets of data objects. The containers are unconcerned about the details of the objects they contain, and the objects are unconcerned about the details of containment.

N O T E   STL is a rapidly moving target. The closest impementation that complies with the proposed standard is that of Visual C++ 5.0, but even that implementation is waiting for the compiler to implement changes to the template mechanism necessary to support STL as defined. Consequently, this discussion does not change much from the previous edition of the book except to add and explain some exercises that work with Quincy. Compiler vendors—and many book authors, too—are waiting for the standard specification to settle down before they invest a lot of effort in implementing and explaining STL.

This chapter does not go into much detail about STL. Complete books have been written on the subject, and you should read one or more of them. See the bibliography for a list. This chapter provides an overview of STL's concepts, describes in general terms the container data structures that STL supports, and provides a few small examples of their use.

STL Rationale

The rationale for STL is found in this observation: Given one set of data types, another set of container types, and a third set of common algorithms to support the containers, the amount of software to be developed with traditional C++ methods is a product of the number of elements in the three sets. If you have integer, *Date*, and *Personnel* objects to contain in lists, queues, and stacks, and if you need insert, extract, and sort algorithms for each object, then there are 27 (3×3×3) traditional C++ algorithms to develop. With templates, you can define the containers as generic classes and reduce the number to nine algorithms: three algorithms for each of the three containers.

If, however, you design the algorithms themselves as templates that perform generic operations on parameterized containers, there are only three algorithms. That is the underlying basis of STL.

That explanation is a simplification of the STL rationale, but it hints at larger advantages that cannot be ignored. If class template containers are sufficiently generic, they can support any user-defined data type that meets their requirements with respect to operator overloading and behavior. You can contain any data type within any kind of supported container without having to develop custom container code. Furthermore, if the algorithms are sufficiently generic, you can use them to process containers of objects of user-defined data types.

You can add containers of your own design by conforming to the rules of STL, and all the existing algorithms will automatically work with the new containers.

Finally, as you add conforming algorithms, you find that they work with all containers and all contained data types—those of the present and those that are not yet designed.

To summarize: If you stick to the rules, you can add to any of the three components that make up STL—the containers, the algorithms, and the contained data types—and all existing components automatically accept the new addition and work seamlessly with it.

The STL Programming Model

STL supports several container types categorized as *sequences* and *associative* containers. Access to containers is managed by a hierarchy of *iterator* objects that resemble C++ pointers. Iterators point to objects in the containers and permit the program to iterate through the containers in various ways.

All the containers have common management member functions defined in their template definitions: insert, erase, begin, end, size, capacity, and so on. Individual containers have member functions that support their unique requirements.

A standard suite of algorithms provides for searching for, copying, reordering, transforming, and performing numeric operations on the objects in the containers. The same algorithm is used to perform a particular operation for all containers of all object types.

As we discuss the container types, remember that they are implemented as templates; the types of objects they contain are determined by the template arguments given when the program instantiates the containers.

Sequences

A sequence is a container that stores a finite set of objects of the same type in a linear organization. An array of names is a sequence. You would use one of the three sequence types—*vector*, *list*, or *deque*—for a particular application depending on its retrieval requirements.

The vector Class

A *vector* is a sequence that you can access at random. You can append entries to and remove entries from the end of the *vector* without undue overhead. Insertion and deletion at the beginning or in the middle of the *vector* take more time, because they involve shifting the remaining entries to make room or to close the deleted object space. A *vector* is an array of contiguous objects with an instance counter or pointer to indicate the end of the container. Random access is a matter of using a subscript operation.

The list Class

A *list* is a sequence that you access bidirectionally; it allows you to perform inserts and deletes anywhere without undue performance penalties. Random access is simulated by forward or backward iteration to the target object. A *list* consists of noncontiguous objects linked with forward and backward pointers.

The deque Class

A *deque* is like a *vector* except that a *deque* allows fast inserts and deletes at the beginning as well as the end of the container. Random inserts and deletes take more time.

Container Adapters

A container adapter uses existing container classes and implements a unique interface. You select the existing container based on the requirements of the problem. You instantiate a container adapter class by naming the existing container in the declaration:

```
stack< list<int> > stackedlist;
```

The example just shown instantiates a *stack* container—one of the three adaptor containers supported by STL—by using the *list* container as the underlying data structure.

A container adaptor hides the public interface of the underlying container and implements its own. A stack data structure, for example, resembles a *list* but has its own requirements for its user interace.

Three adapter containers included in STL: the *stack*, the *queue*, and the *priority_queue*.

The stack Class

A stack is a data structure that exhibits push-down, pop-up behavior. The most recently inserted—pushed—element is the only one that can be extracted. Extraction of the logically topmost element pops that element from the stack—removes it so that the element that was inserted immediately before the popped element is now the next available element. The *stack* template class implements two accessor functions, *push()* and *pop()*, to insert and extract elements in the data structure.

The queue Class

A queue is a data structure wherein you insert elements at the end and extract elements from the beginning. The *queue* template class implements two accessor functions—*push()* and *pop()*—to insert and extract elements in the data structure.

The priority_queue Class

A priority queue is a data structure wherein you insert elements at the end and extract the element that has the highest priority. The *priority_queue* template class implements two accessor functions, *push()* and *pop()*, to insert and extract elements in the data structure.

Associative Containers

Associative containers provide for fast keyed access to the objects in the container. These containers are constructed from key objects and a compare function that the container uses to compare objects. Associative containers consist of *set, multiset, map,* and *multimap* containers. You would use associative containers for large dynamic tables that you can search sequentially or at random. Associative containers use tree structures—rather than contiguous arrays or linked lists—to organize the objects. These structures support fast random retrievals and updates.

The set and multiset Classes

The *set* and *multiset* containers contain objects that are key values. The *set* container does not permit multiple keys with the same value. The *multiset* container does permit equal keys.

The map and multimap Classes

The *map* and *multimap* containers contain objects that are key values and associate each key object with another parameterized type object. The *map* container does not permit multiple keys with the same value. The *multimap* container permits equal keys.

Iterators

Iterators provide a common method of access into containers. They resemble and have the semantics of C++ pointers. In fact, when the parameterized type is a built-in C++ type (*int, double*, and so on), the associated iterators are C++ pointers.

Each container type supports one category of iterator depending on the container's requirements. The categories are input, output, forward, bidirectional, and random access. STL defines a hierarchy of iterators as shown in Figure 16.1.

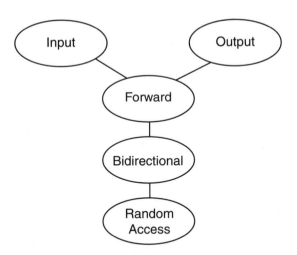

Figure 16.1 *STL iterator hierarchy.*

Each iterator category has all the properties of those above it in the hierarchy. Those properties specify the behavior that the iterator must exhibit in order to support the container. Iterators are so-called smart pointers. They are permitted to have values that represent one of a set of defined states. These states are listed and explained in Table 16.7.

Table 16.7 STL Iterator States

ITERATOR STATE	MEANING
singular	The iterator's value does not dereference any object in any container.*
dereferenceable	The iterator points to a valid object in the container.
past-the-end	The iterator points to the object position past the last object in the container.

* The iterator could be uninitialized or set to a logical null value.

Iterators can be initialized, incremented, and decremented, and their bounds can be limited by the current extent of the containers. If you can cause an iterator to be equal to another iterator by incrementing the first one, the second iterator is *reachable* from the first. The two iterators are also known to refer to the same container. The two iterators can therefore define a *range* of objects in the container.

Iterators can be set as the result of a search of the container or by subscripted reference into the container. Containers include member functions that return iterators that point to the first object and the past-the-end object position. Iterators are the objects with which STL algorithms work.

Algorithms

Algorithms, the backbone of STL, perform operations on containers by dereferencing iterators. Each algorithm is a function template parameterized on one or more iterator types. Table 16.8 lists the standard algorithms provided with STL.

Table 16.8 STL Algorithms

NONMUTATING SEQUENCE OPERATIONS	MUTATING SEQUENCE OPERATIONS	SORTING OPERATORS	GENERALIZED NUMERIC OPERATIONS
for_each	copy	sort	accumulate
find	copy_backward	stable_sort	inner_product
find_if	swap	partial_sort	partial_sum
adjacent_find	swap_ranges	partial_sort_copy	adjacent_difference
count	transform	nth_element	
count_if	replace	lower_bound	

Table 16.8 STL Algorithms (continued)

NONMUTATING SEQUENCE OPERATIONS	MUTATING SEQUENCE OPERATIONS	SORTING OPERATORS	GENERALIZED NUMERIC OPERATIONS
mismatch	replace_if	upper_bound	
equal	replace_copy	equal_range	
search	replace_copy_if	binary_search	
	fill	merge	
	fill_n	inplace_merge	
	generate	includes	
	generate_n	set_union	
	remove	set_intersection	
	remove_if	set_difference	
	remove_copy	set_symmetric_difference	
	remove_copy_if	push_heap	
	unique	pop_heap	
	unique_copy	make_heap	
	reverse	sort_heap	
	reverse_copy	min	
	rotate	max	
	rotate_copy	max_element	
	random_shuffle	min_element	
	partition	lexicographical_compare	
	stable_partition	next_permutation	
		prev_permutation	

Algorithms accept iterators as arguments. The iterators tell the algorithm which object or range of objects in a container to operate on. Every container has a fixed set of iterator values that the program can use by calling member functions that return the iterator values. For example, the *begin()* function returns the value that represents the first logical element in a sequence container, and the *end()* function returns a value that represents the container position one past the last element.

Exercise 16.34 builds and sorts a *vector* container of pseudorandom integers.

Exercise 16.34 *Using the* vector *STL class.*

```
#include <iostream>
#include <iomanip>
#include <vector>
#include <algorithm>
using namespace std;

int main()
{
    int dim;
    // --- get the number of integers to sort
    cout << "How many integers? ";
    cin >> dim;
    // --- a vector of integers
    vector<int> vct;
    // --- insert values into the vector
    for (int i = 0; i < dim; i++)
        vct.insert(vct.end(), rand());
    // --- display the random integers
    cout << endl << "----- unsorted -----" << endl;
    vector<int>::iterator iter;
    for (iter = vct.begin(); iter < vct.end(); iter++)
        cout << setw(8) << *iter;
    // --- sort the array with the STD sort algorithm
    sort(vct.begin(), vct.end());
    // --- display the sorted integers
    cout << endl << "----- sorted -----" << endl;
    for (iter = vct.begin(); iter < vct.end(); iter++)
        cout << setw(8) << *iter;
    return 0;
}
```

Exercise 16.34 instantiates a vector of integer objects named *vct*. Then it uses the vector template class member function named *insert* to insert random numbers into the vector. The program displays the vector's contents, retrieving each of the objects through an iterator object that iterates the vector. Next, the program uses the STL *sort* algorithm to sort the vector container. The *sort* function accepts a range of objects expressed as a pair of iterators. The second iterator must be reachable from the first one. The container *begin()* and *end()* member functions return iterators that refer to the first object in the container and the past-the-end position of the container. This pair constitutes a range that represents the entire container. Finally, the program displays the vector's sorted contents.

Exercise 16.34 iterates the vector using an iterator object. You can retrieve specific elements of the vector by using the overloaded [ ] subscript operator and an integer subscript that ranges from zero through 1 minus the number of elements in the vector:

```
for (int i = 0; i < vct.size(); i++)
    cout << setw(8) << vct[i];
```

Predicates

Algorithms also accept *predicates*, which are *function object* arguments. A function object is an object of a class that overloads *operator()* and that you pass to an algorithm as a call-back function argument. The algorithm calls the predicate for each object that it processes from the container. In some cases the predicate is a *bool* function that returns *true* or *false* to tell the algorithm whether to select the object. In other cases, the predicate processes the objects that the algorithm finds and returns an object of the type in the container. STL provides a set of standard arithmetic, comparison, and logical function objects that you can use as predicates.

The associative containers require predicates as an argument to the template instantiation. The predicate argument specifies how elements are stored and retrieved with respect to one another. Exercise 16.35 demonstrates the *set* container class and its predicate argument, the default *less<T>* predicate class.

Exercise 16.35 *The* set *class.*

```cpp
#include <iostream>
#include <iomanip>
#include <set>
#include <algorithm>
using namespace std;

typedef set<int, less<int> > IntSet;

int main()
{
    IntSet intset;

    intset.insert(1);
    intset.insert(2);
    intset.insert(3);
    intset.insert(5);
    intset.insert(8);
    intset.insert(13);
    intset.insert(21);

    IntSet::iterator iter;
    // --- retrieve from found position in forward sequential order
    for (iter = intset.find(5); iter != intset.end(); iter++)
        cout << *iter << endl;

    return 0;
}
```

Exercise 16.35 begins with a *typedef* that declares the name *IntSet* to be the same as referencing the *set* template class with an *int* parameterized type. The *typedef* makes the subsequent code easier to read and easier to modify if you determine later that you'd rather use a different container type for this problem.

The second template argument is the *less<int>* predicate, a standard class with an overloaded *operator()* that returns a *bool* based on the comparison between two elements in the *set*. STL uses this predicate to insert and locate specific elements in the set. Standard C++ specifies that you can omit this argument, and the class constructor will provide a default argument. Most compilers, however, do not support default template arguments, so most contemporary STL implementations require you to provide the predicate argument even when you are using the default.

Each *insert* call inserts an integer into the *set*. A *set* is an associative container, so its elements are retrieved by value—the element's *key*—rather than by position. The for loop calls the *set<int>::find* function to search for an element that has the key value 5. The *find* function returns an iterator object that points to the found element or to one past the last object in the *set* container if no object is found that matches the key. In this case, the object is found and the program uses the iterator to display that object and all the ones that logically follow the object in the container.

Exercise 16.36 demonstrates the *map* container and the application of a user-defined predicate. The *map* container stores elements that consist of a key and a value. The key is the half of the element with which elements are retrieved. The value is some data object that represents what the key element indexes. In this case, we store records of people's names and their birthdates. The key element is the name. The associated value is the birthdate.

Exercise 16.36 The map *class and predicates.*

```
#include <iostream>
#include <string>
#include <map>
#include <algorithm>
using namespace std;
#include <Date.h>

// ---- predicate to make a case-insensitive string compare
struct ltstr {
    bool operator()(const string& s1, const string& s2) const;
};
```

Exercise 16.36 *The* map *class and predicates. (continued)*

```
bool ltstr::operator()(const string& s1, const string& s2) const
{
    int i1 = 0, i2 = 0;
    short int df;
    char c1, c2;
    do {
        c1 = i1 == s1.length() ? 0 : s1[i1];
        c2 = i2 == s2.length() ? 0 : s2[i2];
        df = tolower(c1) - tolower(c2);
        i1++, i2++;
    } while (c1 && c2 && df == 0);
    return df < 0;
}

typedef map<string, Date, ltstr> Brothers;

void Show(Brothers& bromap, const string& s)
{
    if (bromap.find(s) != bromap.end())
        cout << (s + ": ") << bromap[s] << endl;
}

int main()
{
    Brothers bromap;


    bromap["Frederick"] = Date(12,17,1937);
    bromap["Joseph"]    = Date(10,30,1938);
    bromap["Alan"]      = Date( 6,24,1940);
    bromap["Walter"]    = Date(11,23,1942);
    bromap["Julian"]    = Date( 8, 5,1944);
```

Exercise 16.36 *The* map *class and predicates. (continued)*

```
    Show(bromap, "alan");
    Show(bromap, "frederick");
    Show(bromap, "julian");
    Show(bromap, "joseph");
    Show(bromap, "walter");
    Show(bromap, "herman");

    // --- retrieve from the map in reverse sequential order
    Brothers::reverse_iterator iter = bromap.rbegin();
    while (iter != bromap.rend())  {
        string nm = (*iter).first;
        Date dt = (*iter).second;
        cout << endl << nm << "'s dob = " << dt;
        iter++;
    }
    return 0;
}
```

The *ltstr* structure in Exercise 16.36 is a user-defined predicate. It does a case-insensitive compare of the contents of two *string* objects and returns a true value if the first string compares less than the second. If we had not needed case insensitivity, we could have used the standard *less<string>* predicate. This exercise demonstrates how a predicate works. A predicate needs an over-loaded *operator()* function that serves as a call-back function for the container to use to compare objects during insertion and searching.

The program uses the *Date* class that we built earlier in the book. The program inserts *Date* objects into the *map* container by subscripting with the quoted string values of the names. The container expects a *string* object as the key, so the compiler constructs one from the quoted string. The container expects a *Date* object as its data value, and each assignment constructs an unnamed *Date* object to include with the container element.

The program calls the *Show* function once for each name, except that the names are expressed with lowercase strings and there is one call to *Show* for a name that the program did not insert in the container. The *Show* function calls the container's *find* function to see whether the named object exists. If it does, the *Show* function retrieves and displays the object by using the string as a subscript.

Why does the *Show* function test first to see whether the object is in the container? If you try to dereference a *map* element with the overloaded subscript operator and the element does not exist in the container, the expression adds the element to the container by using the subscripted key value and an empty data value.

Each *map* container element consists of an object of type *pair<>*, which is instantiated with the two types used to instantiate the *map* container. In this case, the *pair* class is instantiated as *pair<string, Date>*. The *pair* object contains public data members named *first*, which contains the key, and *second*, which contains the data value. Iterators of *map* (and *multimap*) containers point to objects of type *pair<>*. The program dereferences the *first* and *second* data members to retrieve the key and data value from the *pair<>* object.

Exercise 16.36 iterates the *map* container by using a *reverse_iterator*, extracting and displaying the key and data values. Following is the display that Exercise 16.36 creates:

```
alan: 6/24/1940
frederick: 12/17/1937
julian: 8/5/1944
joseph: 10/30/1938
walter: 11/23/1942

Walter's dob = 11/23/1942
Julian's dob = 8/5/1944
Joseph's dob = 10/30/1938
Frederick's dob = 12/17/1937
Alan's dob = 6/24/1940
```

STL Summarized

STL consists of generic containers with iterators along with algorithms that operate on those containers through their iterators. STL is almost a different programming model—another paradigm, if you will. It flies in the face of pure object-oriented theory by apparently separating the data from the functions. Algorithms are not bound to classes. They are not methods. They are function templates. Their binding to the data occurs as a function of their parameterized argument types.

This treatment of STL is by no means an exhaustive study. It should serve, however, as an introduction to the underlying concepts of the library. After fully compliant implementations are in place, programmers will begin to use this powerful tool, and virtually all vendor-unique container class libraries can be forgotten.

STANDARD EXCEPTIONS

The committee has defined a standard mechanism for exceptions thrown by Standard C++ library classes. The mechanism is documented in the December 1996 working paper.

The objective is sound. Exception handling is a powerful tool, defined by Margaret Ellis and Bjarne Stroustrup in *The Annotated Reference Manual* and refined and accepted by the committee. It is natural to use it in the Standard C++ library, and the committee has defined a solid and consistent method for throwing exceptions. If the committee's method proves to be a reliable, intuitive exception handling model, programmers will adopt it for use in their own designs. In *The Draft Standard C++ Library*, P.J. Plauger says about exception handling, "...the Standard C++ library has a moral obligation to set a good example."

The example it sets is clearly defined. Its essence is as follows:

- Exceptions thrown will be objects of classes.
- Exception classes are derived from a common base.
- The base class supports polymorphic members that describe the exception to the runtime system.

Remember from Chapter 14 that a *throw* with a publicly derived class as its parameter is caught by a *catch* handler with the base class as its parameter. The committee defined a hierarchy of exception classes based on that behavior. Figure 16.2 illustrates its configuration.

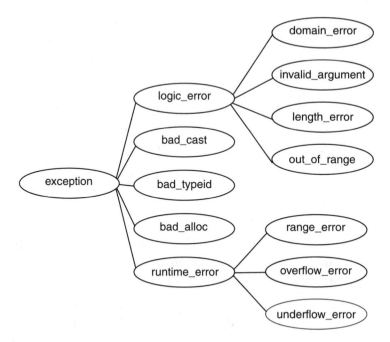

Figure 16.2 Standard C++ exception hierarchy.

It is generally agreed that programmers should follow the Standard C++ library example and model their own exceptions after this hierarchy. You should throw objects of these exceptions when appropriate or throw objects derived from the most appropriate of these exceptions depending on the requirements of your application. Table 16.9 lists the standard exceptions and explains their purpose.

Table 16.9 Standard C++ Exception Classes

Exception Class	Purpose
exception	The top-level base class from which all exceptions are derived.
logic_error	A base class that represents programming errors that violate logical conditions that should be detectable before the program runs.
domain_error [1]	A base class for exceptions that report violations of a precondition.
invalid_argument	A base class for exceptions that report invalid argument values passed to a function.
length_error	A base class for exceptions that report attempts to create objects greater than the largest possible object.
out_of_range	A base class for exceptions that report out-of-range argument values.
bad_cast	Thrown by the *dynamic_cast* operator to report bad casts of reference objects.
bad_typeid	Thrown for a *null* pointer argument to the *typeid* operator.
runtime_error	A base class that represents errors that are detectable only after the program is running.
range_error [2]	A base class for exceptions that report violations of a postcondition.
overflow_error	A base class for exceptions that report arithmetic overflow.
underflow_error	A base class for exceptions that report arithmetic underflow.
bad_alloc	A base class for exceptions that report failures to allocate memory.

[1] A precondition is one that exists before an operation is carried out. For example, when an operation cannot proceed because something in the system related to the operation's domain is not in a state required to support the operation, the program throws an exception derived from *domain_error.*

[2] A postcondition is one that exists as the result of an operation. For example, when an operation causes an invalid data condition to occur, the program throws an exception derived from *range_error.*

The *exception* class defines several member functions that derived classes can override. An important one to remember is the *what* function, which returns a pointer to an implementation-dependent string that identifies the exception. Exercise 16.37 illustrates how a C++ program can derive exception classes from the C++ Standard library *exception* class.

Exercise 16.37 *Deriving from the Standard* exception *class.*

```
#include <typeinfo>
#include <iostream>
#include <exception>
using namespace std;


class Bummer : public exception {
public:
    Bummer() : exception("Bummer") { }
};


int main()
{
    try {
        throw Bummer();
    }
    catch(exception& ex)  {
        cout << ex.what();
    }
    return 0;
}
```

SUMMARY

From the perspective of the working C++ programmer, the Standard C++ library is in a state of constant change, both because the committee is not finished with its work and because the current state of compiler implementation varies with respect to compliance with the proposed draft. By the time you read this, the committee will have convened again (scheduled for July 1997). The members will review more than 300 pages of public comments on the December 1996 draft, the document that I used as the basis for this edition of *teach yourself...C++*. Eventually, things will settle down, the committee will publish an approved standard specification, compilers will comply, and I can write the final edition of this work.

This chapter brings to a close your C++ lessons. Chapter 17 is a treatise on object-oriented programming from the view of the C++ programmer.

CHAPTER 17

Object-Oriented Programming

Object-oriented programming is a programming model—an approach to the expression of a computer program that emphasizes the data rather than the procedures. C++ includes features that support object-oriented programming. This chapter explains the model so that you, as a new C++ programmer, can associate what you have learned about the C++ language with the terms and concepts of object-oriented programming. You will learn about:

- Procedural vs object-oriented programming
- The four characteristics of an object-oriented program
- What an object is
- Abstraction
- Encapsulation
- Methods and messages
- Inheritance
- Polymorphism

As pervasive as object-oriented programming has become, many programmers still do not understand it. By using the exercises in this book you have acquired a working knowledge of C++. That experience alone has exposed you to the object-oriented paradigm. Having built and used C++ classes in class hierarchies, you have written object-oriented programs. There are, however, many terms in the object-oriented lexicon that this book has intentionally postponed until this discussion. Simply writing a C++ program does not qualify a programmer as an expert on object-oriented technology. There are rules and procedures to follow, and there are benefits to be gained by understanding and following the disciplines.

The traditional procedure-oriented programmer does not intuitively understand object-oriented programming. The notations and approaches to design and code are different from what you learned and used in the past. Furthermore, explanations such as this one do not usually complete your understanding of object-oriented programming. You need reinforcement—both from experience and from a feeling that there is something to be gained by using a new and different approach. Programmers might understand the concepts at the intellectual level and yet not accept them as a pragmatic approach to programming, simply because they have been writing good programs all along and see no compelling reason to tamper with success. For this reason, it is difficult to teach object-oriented programming, although it is not difficult to learn. Learning object-oriented programming is a process of discovery. Teaching it, therefore, becomes the management of that process.

Many programmers of the current generation have learned and accepted object-oriented programming as a better way to express software algorithms. Most of them started from the procedural paradigm, having programmed in traditional procedural languages such as FORTRAN, COBOL, and C. Those who make the switch become object-oriented advocates. Enough of them have done so that the rest of us cannot deny that there is something to it. You can take a lesson from the observation that once a programmer takes the plunge, he or she almost always becomes a convert. The best way to learn object-oriented programming is to try it.

THE BASICS

The first understanding of object-oriented programming is to be found in this design guideline:

The expression of an algorithm should model the application domain that it supports.

Or, expressed at a higher level:

The solution to a problem should resemble the problem.

A solution that follows these guidelines allows its observers to recognize its purpose without necessarily knowing in advance about the problem being solved. When you see a properly designed word processor, you intuitively understand that the problem being solved is one of capturing and manipulating textual data into an informational document. When you see a properly designed inventory management system, you recognize that its purpose is to maintain stock quantities, locations, and reorder points. You recognize those things because the designs resemble and therefore remind you of the problems that they solve.

Carrying this concept to a higher level of abstraction, you recognize that the purpose of a programming language is to express with algorithms the solution to a data processing problem. The techniques used in that expression determine how successfully the solution models its problem domain. Object-oriented programming is one of several different approaches to the expression of algorithms, and it is often misunderstood—primarily by those who do not use it.

PROCEDURAL PROGRAMMING

In the classic approach to programming, a programmer designs a set of data structures followed by functions and procedures to process the data. This approach is called *procedural programming* because it starts with the procedures. We came to think of programming in this way because that is how programming was done for 40 years.

Procedural programming does not always deliver a solution that resembles the problem, however, because it emphasizes the functions rather than the data—the procedures rather than the objects. Furthermore, procedural programming does not encourage the programmer to separate and hide from one another the procedures related to different data objects. Programmers have long known that those practices are worthwhile, but most procedural programming languages do not encourage them.

OBJECT-ORIENTED PROGRAMMING

The world and its applications are not organized into values and procedures separate from one another. Problem solvers in other crafts do not perceive the world that way. They deal with their problem domains by concentrating on the objects and letting the characteristics of those objects determine the procedures to apply to them. To build a house, grow a tomato, or repair a carburetor, first you think about the object and its purpose and behavior. Then you select your tools and procedures. The solution fits the problem.

The world is, therefore, object-oriented, and object-oriented programming expresses computer programs in ways that model how people perceive the world. Because programmers are people, it is only natural that your approach to the work of the world reflects your view of the world itself. We have not, however, universally learned how to do that. The crafts of carpentry, farming, and mechanics are centuries old, beginning in cultures that lacked technology. The objects and objectives of those trades were understood long before the development of the technologies that support them. Computer programming is relatively new. We are still forming its disciplines, and the technologies are developing faster than we can adjust.

The Object-Oriented Program

An object-oriented program has four fundamental characteristics:

- *Abstraction* defines new data types.
- *Encapsulation* gathers all of a data type's representation and its behavior into one encapsulated entity.
- *Inheritance* derives new data types from existing ones and forms them into hierarchies of classes.
- *Polymorphism* specializes the behavior of a derived data type.

Object-oriented programming uses a vocabulary of such terms in ways that are unfamiliar to procedural programmers. You hear these terms used frequently in discussions of object-oriented programming. Here is a more comprehensive list of object-oriented terms:

abstract base class

abstract data type

abstraction

base class

class

derived class

encapsulation

implementation and interface

inheritance

instance

instantiate

message

method

multiple inheritance

object

polymorphism

subclass

superclass

Now let's use some of those terms. The object-oriented programmer defines an *abstract data type* by *encapsulating* its *implementation* and *interface* into a *class*. *Inherited* abstract data types are *derived subclasses* of *base* classes. Within the program, the programmer *instantiates objects* of classes as *instances* and sends *messages* to the objects by using the class's *methods*.

Confused? Don't be concerned; it all makes sense soon enough, and you have already done all those things when you worked with the exercises in this book. The object-oriented programming community uses these terms universally. Therefore, when object-oriented programmers say "encapsulate," for example, you know that their meaning is consistent with the way others use it. When programmers acknowledge that a program is "object-oriented," you know that the program contains abstraction, encapsulation, inheritance, and polymorphism and that it defines abstract data types, instantiates objects, and sends messages to the object's methods. The discussion that follows draws on your experience with C++ to explain these terms.

The Object

The first question that most procedural programmers ask is, "What are the objects in object-oriented programming?" The second question is, "What should be the objects in my design?" These questions reflect this more revealing one: What is it about object-oriented programming that sets it apart from and makes it better than traditional procedural programming? Early writings on the subject effectively explained object-oriented programming to those who already understood it, but their explanations were sometimes too abstruse for newcomers to fathom, and they did not always justify the paradigm as an improved way to express algorithms.

Simply stated, an object is an instance of a data type; in other words, it is what procedural programmers call a *variable*. The program in Figure 17.1. declares two objects. The first object is a simple integer; the second object is of an abstract data type.

Figure 17.1 A Program with Two Objects

```
void f()
{
    int ndays; // an instance of an int
    Date cdt;  // an instance of an ADT
    // ...
}
```

Throughout this book you have been declaring objects—instances of the classes that you designed in the exercises. In your prior experience with other programming languages you declared objects when you declared variables. So what are the objects? They are the variables that you declare. What should be the objects in your object-oriented design? Anything that you build as a class will be the data type of an object.

Abstraction

Abstraction is the definition of an abstract data type; the definition includes the data type's representation and behavior. An abstract data type is a new type. It is not one of the primitive data types that are built into the programming language. The *int, long,* and *float* data types are primitive C++ data types. Their data representations and behavior are known to the compiler. For example, an integer data type's format—its representation—and response to arithmetic, assignment, and relational operators—its behavior—are defined as a part of the C++ language.

An abstract data type, however, is not known to the language; the C++ programmer defines the type's format and behavior in a class. For example, the calendar date class used in some of the exercises in earlier chapters is an abstract data type. The compiler and the computer do not know about calendar dates. Programmers have always had to define the behavior of dates by designing structures and functions or by using canned functions from published libraries. The Standard C library has several such date definitions, but they are defined with functions and structures and not with classes. When you define a C++ calendar date class such as the one in Figure 17.2, you express its format and behavior in one design entity. It has month, day, and year data members. It might even support arithmetic and relational operations.

Figure 17.2 *An Abstract Data Type (ADT)*

```
class Date  {
    int month, day, year;
public:
    Date(int mo, int da, int yr);
    int operator+(int n);
    // ...
};
```

Having declared a Date class, you can declare an object that has the type of the *Date* class; you can add an integer value to the object, subtract from it, compare it with other objects, assign it to other date objects, and assign values to it, all depending on which methods have been provided and which operators have been overloaded. A C++ program declares instances of abstract data types in the same way it declares instances of primitive data types. Refer again to Figure 17.1. The declaration of the *cdt* object is an instance of an abstract data type.

The term *instantiate* is used by object-oriented programmers for convenience. When an object-oriented program declares an instance of a data type, the program has instantiated an object, whether the data type is primitive or abstract. The program in Figure 17.1 instantiates the *ndays* and *cdt* objects.

Encapsulation

If abstraction defines a C++ class, encapsulation designs it. A programmer encapsulates the data representation and behavior of an abstract data type into a class, giving it its own implementation and interface. An encapsulated design hides its implementation from the class user and reveals its interface. Figure 17.3 is an example of an encapsulated class.

Figure 17.3 Encapsulation

```
class Date  {
// --- the class implementation
private:
    int month, day, year;
// --- the class interface
public:
    Date(int mo, int da, int yr);
    Date operator+(int n);
    // ...
};
```

The implementation of a class, which consists of the private data members and private member functions, is essentially hidden from the using program. The *month, day,* and *year* data members in Figure17.3 are the class's implementation. A user of the class does not care about the details of an implementation—only that it works. The class designer could totally change the implementation—perhaps changing the date representation to a long integer count of days—and the using programs, once recompiled and relinked with the new class implementation, would be unaffected.

The interface, which is visible to the user of the class, consists of the public members, which are usually member functions. The class user reads and modifies values in the data representation by calling public member functions. The class interface in Figure17.3 consists of the constructor, which contains initialization parameters, and an overloaded addition operator, which presumably allows the user of the class to compute and return a new *Date* objeect by adding an integral number of days to an existing *Date* object.

To use the abstract data type defined in Figure 17.3, a programmer makes assumptions about the interface based on its appearance and the programmer's understanding of C++ syntax. If the programmer is not the class's author, those assumptions could be invalid if the class interface design is not intuitive. In the case of Figure 17.3, most programmers would assume that the overloaded addition operator adds an integer to a *Date* object and returns another Date object with the result. Figure 17.4 illustrates how the class interface should work.

Figure 17.4 *An Intuitive Class Interface*

```
void f()
{
    Date dt(6,29,92);
    dt = dt + 30;  // should now be 7/29/92
}
```

Designing an intuitive class interface is not automatic. The C++ language provides the tools for you to do a proper job, but nothing in the language enforces good design. The class author can use unnecessarily clever techniques that obscure the meaning of the interface. An object-oriented design is not a good design by default. Learning C++ does not turn a poor programmer into a good one.

Experienced C++ programmers generally agree on certain design standards for C++ classes. The data members are usually private and constitute most of the implementation. The interface consists mostly of member functions that hide the access to the data members. The interface is generic in that it is not bound to any particular implementation. The class author should be able to change the implementation without affecting the using programs. These apparent rules are only guidelines, however. Sometimes you need to step around them to achieve some purpose. The fewer times you do that, the stronger your design.

Methods and Messages

Method is another name for C++ member functions. Methods may be constructors, destructors, procedures, and overloaded operators. They define the class's interface. The constructor and overloaded plus operator in Figure 17.3 are methods.

A message is the invocation of a method, which, in C++, is the same thing as calling the member function. The program sends a message to an object, providing arguments for the method's parameters, if there are any.

Various kinds of methods are characterized by how they support the class definition. There are functional methods, data type methods, and implicit conversion methods. Note that this delineation and these terms are coined here for convenience and are not part of the official object-oriented lexicon. They define different levels of support that C++ provides for class design.

Functional Methods

Figure17.5 shows three methods added to the *Date* class.

Figure 17.5 Functional Methods

```
class Date  {
    // ...
public:
    // ...
    void Display();          // display the date
    void AdjustMonth(int m); // +/- m months
    int DayOfWeek() const;   // return 0-6 = Sun-Sat
};
```

The three methods in Figure 17.5 illustrate three typical kinds of methods. The first method tells the object to do something, in this case display itself. The class's implementation knows how to display the object's data representation. The programmer who uses the class is unconcerned about the details of the implementation.

The second method tells the object to change itself, in this case to adjust its month data value up or down by the integer argument in the method's parameter. Once again, the programmer who uses the class does not care how the object stores the month value or what algorithm adjusts the month, only that it works.

The third method is one that returns a value, in this case the day of the week represented by the object's current value.

The methods in Figure17.5 define behavior related to the functional properties of the class. The class is a calendar date, and you want it to behave like a date.

Data Type Methods

Data type methods make a class act like a primitive data type by giving it the properties similar to those of a primitive data type. These properties are usually implemented as overloaded operators in the class interface. Figure 17.6 shows methods that compare dates, assign them to one another, and do some arithmetic on them.

Figure 17.6 Data Type Methods

```
class Date  {
    // ...
public:
    // ...
    // ---- arithmetic operators
    Date operator+(int n);
    Date operator-(int n);
    int operator-(Date &dt);
    // ---- assignment operators
    Date& operator=(Date &dt);
    // ---- relational operators
    int operator==(Date &dt);
    int operator!=(Date &dt);
    int operator<(Date &dt);
    int operator>(Date &dt);
};
```

Implicit Conversion Methods

The C++ language handles implicit conversion of intrinsic data types. If you write an expression with an *int* when the compiler expects a *long*, the compiler knows how to make the conversion and does so quietly. If, however, you write an expression when the compiler expects an abstract data type, and you provide a different data type intrinsic or abstract, the compiler does not know how to deal with that. Similarly, if the expression expects an intrinsic data type and you use an abstract data type, the compiler does not know what to do. In either case, unless you have provided implicit conversion methods, the compiler issues an error message and refuses to compile the program.

You can add implicit conversion methods to a class so that the compiler knows how to convert from one data type to another. The conversion constructor function constructs a data type to an abstract data type, and the member conversion function returns a data type converted from the type of the class in which the member conversion function is a member. When you code an expression in which the compiler expects to see something other than what you provide as just described, the compiler executes one of your implicit conversion methods to convert the data type. This is an example of a method that you do not explicitly call (or send a message to) from within your program. It executes as the result of the implicit call inferred by the compiler by its interpretation of your expression. Your program implies a call to the method by the context in which it uses data types in an expression.

Figure 17.7 shows two implicit conversion methods added to the Date class. The first method converts an *int* data type to a *Date* object that is being constructed. Note that if the constructor function in Figure 17.7 was declared with the *explicit* qualifier, it would not function as an implicit conversion method. It could be used only as an explicit constructor to instantiate a *Date* object from an *int* argument.

Figure 17.7 Implicit Conversion Methods

```
class Date  {
    // ...
public:
    // ...
    Date(int n);    // conversion constructor
    operator int(); // member conversion function
};
```

The second method in Figure 17.7 converts a *Date* data type to an *int* object and returns that object to the sender of the message (invoker of the method, caller of the function, however you prefer to say it). The conversions are not restricted to converting between abstract data types and primitive data types. You can convert between different abstract data types in the same manner. For example, you might have a *Date* class and a *JulianDate* class, and the same principles apply.

Member Functions

Having just learned about methods and messages in detail, you soon find that the terms themselves are not used much in C++ circles. The terms come from the object-oriented lexicon and reflect the syntax of pure object-oriented programming languages such as SmallTalk and Eiffel. Most C++ programmers prefer to call member functions rather than send messages through methods, which are essentially the same thing. Nonetheless, you should understand the terminology, because you will encounter the object-oriented terms.

Inheritance

A class can inherit the characteristics of another class. The original class is called the *base* class, and the new class is called the *derived* class. You also hear these classes called the *superclass* and the *subclass*. The word *subclass* is sometimes used as a verb to mean the act of inheriting.

The derived class inherits the data representation and behavior of the base class except where the derived class modifies the behavior by overloading member functions. The derived class also may add behavior that is unique to its own purpose.

A program can instantiate objects of a base class as well as those of a derived class. If the base class is an *abstract base class*—one that exists only to be derived from—the program may not instantiate objects of the base class.

Inheritance is the foundation of most object-oriented designs, and it is often ill applied or overapplied. Some programmers get carried away with the power of inheritance, and C++ can offer some surprises to the unwary designer. Many designs use inheritance to solve problems that would be better supported by a different approach, usually by embedding an object of the original class as a data member in the new class rather than deriving the new class from the original one. Despite this warning, inheritance is a powerful feature. When properly used, it offers a rich design capability to the object-oriented programmer.

Single Inheritance

The C++ inheritance mechanism lets you build an orderly hierarchy of classes. When several of your abstract data types have characteristics in common, you can design their commonalities into a single base class and separate their unique characteristics into unique derived classes. That is the purpose of inheritance.

For example, suppose that a personnel system maintains information about employees. Employees are people, and people have common characteristics: name, address, date of birth, and so on. Yet the system might record different kinds of employees; managers, project workers, and support personnel might be recorded differently. Therefore, you could design a base class of employees that stores in each object of the base class the name, address, Social Security number, and date of birth of an employee. Then you could derive separate classes for managers, project workers, and support personnel. Each of the derived classes would inherit the characteristics of the employee class and would have additional characteristics unique to itself. For example, the manager class might include an annual incentive bonus data member that other employee classes do not have. The project worker class could have a list of project assignments. The support personnel class could record overtime hours worked.

Multiple Inheritance

A derived class can inherit the characteristics of more than one base class. This technique is called *multiple inheritance.* Not all object-oriented programming languages support multiple inheritance, and many experts assert that it is both unnecessary and dangerous. Nonetheless, C++ supports multiple inheritance, and there are times when you might find it an effective way to express class relationships.

You recall that the effectiveness of a programming language can be measured in its ability to model the problem domains that it supports. The objects in the world reflect membership in multiple-inheritance hierarchies, and programmers are called upon to write programs to model those objects. A sofa bed is a sofa and it is a bed, both of which are items of furniture. An amphibious airplane is a boat and an airplane, both of which are vehicles. A company car is an asset and a vehicle, but a leased car is a vehicle but not an asset, and cash is an asset, and on and on.

Class Relationships

Object-oriented designers strive to use inheritance to model relationships in which the derived class *is a kind of* the base class. A car *is a kind of* vehicle. An engineer *is a kind of* employee, which *is a kind of* person. This relationship is called, colloquially, the *ISA* relationship.

Inheritance is not appropriate for relationships where one class has an instance of another. An employee *has* a date of birth. A department *has* a manager. This relationship is called the *HASA* relationship. Instead of using inheritance, the class that has an object of another class embeds the object as a data member. The HASA relationship is appropriate when the embedded object is singular and belongs to the class that embeds it. An employee's date of birth belongs to that employee. Even when another employee has the same birthday, each one has a private copy of the data element.

A third relationship exists when a class uses the methods of another class. This relationship, called the *USESA* relationship, is usually implemented with an embedded pointer or reference in the using class to the used class. You would use this relationship when objects of the using class share the services of an object of the used class. The objects of the two classes exist in separate spaces, but those of one class depend on the presence of those of the other class.

Polymorphism

Polymorphism exists when a derived class specializes the behavior of its base class to meet the requirements of the derived class. A C++ base class uses the *virtual* member function to specify that overriding member functions in derived classes have polymorphic behavior with respect to that method.

If a derived class overrides a base class method and if the base class method is not a virtual function, then the overriding behavior is effective only when the compiler is dereferencing a pointer, reference, or object of the derived class itself. If the object's pointer or reference refers to the base class, then the base class method has precedence. Such behavior is not polymorphic. However, if the base class method is virtual, then the compiler selects the overriding derived class method regardless of the type being dereferenced by the compiler.

Suppose, for example, that the support staff class in this discussion were further decomposed into derived classes that represented the various kinds of support personnel. You could have typists, corporate pilots, chauffeurs, maintenance personnel, instructors, and so on. The system measures skill levels differently for each of these disciplines, yet there is a requirement for a general-purpose skill index for the base support class. Each derived class exhibits different behavior for data entry and retrieval of the skill index, but some parts of the system invoke the skill method without knowing which kind of support personnel object is involved. The polymorphic skill method would modify the class's behavior at runtime based on the type of the derived class.

SUMMARY

The object-oriented programming model is a rich medium for the expression of the data formats and functions of an application. It is not necessary, however, for C++ programmers to immerse themselves in the object-oriented passion. The availability of improved design and programming methods does not automatically outdate the traditional approaches. C++ has the facility to support the basics of object-oriented programming while permitting the programmer to use traditional procedural programming where it seems appropriate. C++, in fact, encourages that approach. By supporting traditional C flow control of nested functions, C++ allows you to leverage your existing investment in mature and useful C function libraries. Furthermore, C++ does not force you to create a pure object-oriented hierarchical data structure in which every data type descends from one generic root base object. Instead, C++ allows you to build a number of class hierarchies representing the various problem domains that your application might deal with. There can be classes that define the data structures of the application's functional purpose; there can be classes that supply general-purpose container data structures such as strings, lists, queues, and so on; there can be framework classes that integrate your application with a particular user interface; there can be classes that encapsulate the processes of your particular problem domain. All these classes can co-exist independently of one another in a system of hierarchies integrated by you into an object-oriented application.

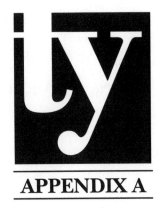

APPENDIX A

Using Quincy 97

Quincy 97 (hereinafter called Quincy) is an integrated development environment (IDE) that integrates a programmer's editor, compiler, and debugger into one Windows 95 application. Quincy uses the gnu-win32 port of the GNU C and C++ compilers and is intended to be used as a teaching environment rather than as an application development tool. Much more comprehensive development tools exist. Quincy does not attempt to replace them.

Quincy is integrated with the exercises in this book. A special **tyC++** tool button launches a table of contents window that opens the exercise program source-code files associated with an exercise in the book. This Appendix tells you how to use Quincy to run these exercises and to write programs of your own so that you can experiment with the lessons that this book teaches.

Although Quincy runs under Windows 95, it does not support the development of Windows 95 GUI programs. All Quincy programs are text-based console applications. Quincy is a tool for teaching the C++ language and not a tool for teaching Windows programming.

This Appendix assumes that you already know how to run Windows 95 and its applications. If you do not, I recommend my book *teach yourself... Windows 95, 3rd Edition*, 1997, MIS:Press.

INSTALLING QUINCY

To install Quincy, follow these steps:

1. Put the CD-ROM into your CD-ROM drive.

   If you have Autorun enabled on your Windows 95 PC, the Setup program launches automatically. If Autorun is not enabled, follow these steps:

1. Choose the **Run** command on the Windows 95 Start menu.

2. Enter **E:\setup** in the **Open** text field. (Substitute your CD-ROM drive letter for E.)

3. Click **OK**.

Figure A.1 shows the Setup program running.

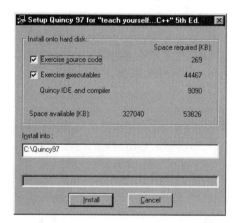

Figure A.1 *The Setup program.*

Check the options to specify whether you want to install the exercises and their executables. Here are your choices:

- You can leave the exercise source code and executables on the CD-ROM drive. You can run and step through the exercises, but you cannot modify and recompile them because you cannot write to the CD-ROM. To experiment with an exercise, you must manually move its source code to the hard drive and work with it from there.

- You can install the exercise source code without the executables, in which case you must compile each exercise before you can run it. The Quincy 97 debugger expects to find the executables in the same subdirectory as the program's source code.

- You can install the source code and executables to your hard drive, in which case you can do anything you want. This option requires a lot of hard drive space.

The Setup program calculates the amount of hard drive space required and compares it to the amount available. If not enough space is available, Setup reports that problem and does not continue.

Click **Install** when you are ready. The progress bar just above the command buttons indicates the Setup program's progress as it copies files.

UNINSTALLING QUINCY

To uninstall Quincy, follow these steps:

1. Open the Quincy 97 submenu on the Start/Programs menu.
2. Click the **Uninstall Quincy** command to run the Uninstall program shown in Figure A.2.
3. Cilck **Yes**.

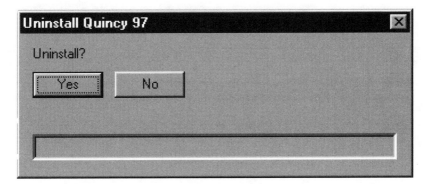

Figure A.2 *The Uninstall program.*

Or you can do this:

1. Open the Windows 95 Control Panel.
2. Run the Add/Remove Programs applet.
3. Select the Quincy 97 entry.
4. Click **OK** to run the Uninstall program shown in Figure A.2.
5. Click **Yes**.

STARTING QUINCY

There are two ways to start Quincy. The first approach has two steps:

1. Open the Quincy 97 submenu on the Start/Programs menu.
2. Click the **Quincy 97** command.

Or you can do this:

1. Double-click the **Quincy 97** icon that the Setup program optionally added to your desktop.

Quincy always loads the source-code files from your most recent Quincy session. Figure A.3 shows the Quincy application window with a source-code file loaded and ready to go.

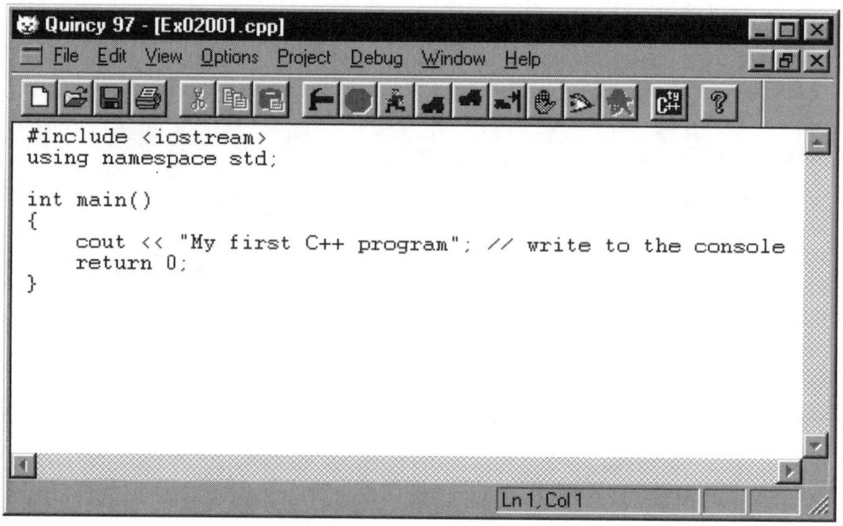

Figure A.3 The Quincy application window.

EXITING QUINCY

To exit from Quincy, follow these steps:

1. Choose the **Exit** command on the File menu.
2. Or click the **X** button in the upper-right corner of the application title bar.
3. Or press **Alt+F4**.

If any documents have been changed and not saved, a dialog box asks whether you want to save them before exiting. The dialog box asks the question once for each modified document.

EXERCISE PROGRAMS

Quincy is integrated with the exercise programs in this book. To proceed through the exercises as you read this book, do one of the following:

1. Click the **tyC++** button on the toolbar.
2. Or press **F3**.
3. Or choose the **Tutorial Exercises** command on the Help menu.

Any of these actions opens the Exercises dialog box shown in Figure A.4.

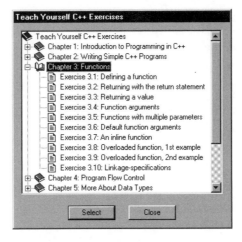

Figure A.4 *The Exercises dialog box.*

To load a specific exercise into Quincy, follow these steps:

1. Open the Exercises dialog box as just explained.
2. Click the + icon next to a book icon to open the chapter that contains the exercise you want to view.
3. Double-click the page icon that corresponds to the exercise.

Quincy loads the source-code files associated with that exercise into its document windows. Some exercises involve the Watch window. Using the Exercises dialog box to launch an exercise sets watch variables and opens the Watch window when you load the exercise. See "Watching Variables" later in this Appendix. This approach also sets Quincy's build options to match the exercise. See "Setting Options" later in this Appendix.

RUNNING A PROGRAM

To run a program that is loaded into Quincy's editor, follow these steps:

1. Click the **Run** tool button (the one with the little man running).
2. Or Press **F9**.
3. Or choose the **Run** command on the Debug menu.
4. If the program is out of date—if the source-code file has been changed so that it is newer than the executable—a dialog box asks first whether you want to compile the program. If you respond by clicking **Yes**, Quincy launches the compiler and runs the program only when a successful compile has completed.

Before running the program, Quincy creates a console window, which serves as standard console input and output for the program. You read text from and type text into that window as if you were running the program from a DOS command line. Figure A.5 shows a console window with a program that has run to completion.

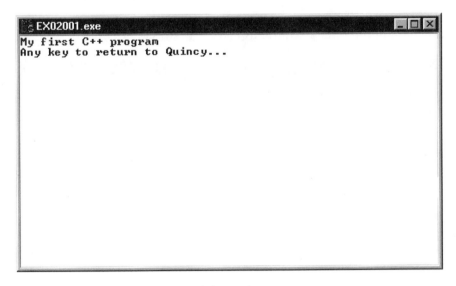

Figure A.5 *A running program.*

Quincy always displays the message "Any key to return to Quincy..." in the console window to give you time to read the output before Quincy closes the console. Type a key to close the window and return to the Quincy IDE.

STEPPING THROUGH A PROGRAM

You can step through a program in three ways: by single-stepping, by stepping over a function call, and by stepping to the cursor location.

Single-Stepping

Single-stepping executes the program one source-code line at a time. To single-step, follow these steps:

1. Click the **Step** tool button (the left-pointing shoe icon that is on the floor).
2. Or press **F7**.
3. Or choose the **Step** command on the Debug menu.

If Quincy has not already started the program, it does so first by opening the console window. Then Quincy executes instructions to the next line of executable source code, stops there, and displays a green bar on the next line to be executed in the editor window as Figure A.6 shows.

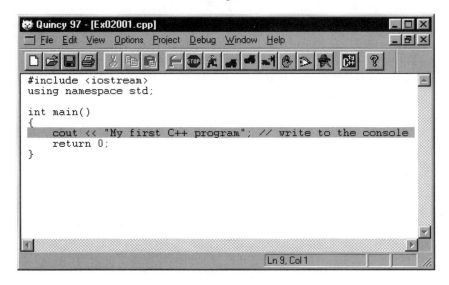

Figure A.6 *Stepping through a program.*

Each successive step executes the marked line of source code. If the source-code line is a statement that reads keystrokes from the console, you must select the console as the active window and make the data entry that the program is expecting before proceeding. If the statement writes to the console, the display shows in the console window after you make the step. When the last statement of the program has been stepped, select the console window and enter that last keystroke (Figure A.5) to close the console window.

Stepping over a Function Call

Stepping over a function call executes the function call but does not step into its source code. Use this command when you do not want to step through a function in your program. Perhaps you are satisfied with how that function is working and you do not want to spend time stepping through its source code.

To step over a function call, follow these steps:

1. Click the **Step Over** tool button (the raised shoe icon).
2. Or press **F8**.

3. Or choose the **Step Over** command on the Debug menu.

Quincy executes the function call and stops on the next statement following the function call. If, however, the function contains a breakpoint (see "Breakpoints" later in this Appendix), Quincy stops at the breakpoint instead.

Stepping to the Cursor Location

Stepping to the cursor location runs the program and breaks at the source-code statement where the keyboard cursor is positioned. Use this procedure to set a temporary breakpoint when the source-code line is in view.

To step to the cursor location, follow these steps:

1. Position the cursor on the line you want to step to.
2. Click the **Step To Cursor** tool button (the small right-pointing shoe icon that faces a vertical bar).
3. Or press **F10**.
4. Or choose the **Step To Cursor** command on the Debug menu.

Quincy runs the program from its current state and stops when the program arrives at the selected line of code. If, however, the function contains a break-point (see "Breakpoints" next), Quincy stops at the breakpoint instead.

BREAKPOINTS

Breakpoints are lines of code where you want to stop during a debug run to observe the progress of the program. This operation is similar to stepping to the cursor location except that you can set multiple breakpoints and they persist throughout the program's execution until you reset them.

Figure A.7 shows a breakpoint set in a program.

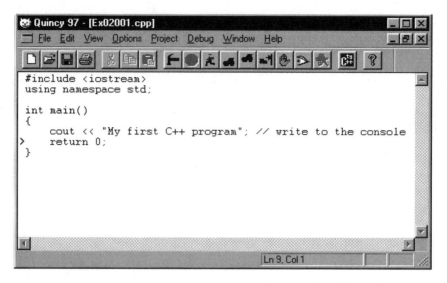

Figure A.7 *Breakpoint set.*

The tiny red angle bracket in the left margin of the source-code line indicates that a breakpoint is set. You can set multiple breakpoints in a program across several source-code files.

Setting a Breakpoint

To set a breakpoint, follow these steps:

1. Put the keyboard cursor on the line of code where you want a breakpoint.
2. Click the breakpoint tool button (the one with the hand), press **F2**, or choose the **Breakpoint** command on the Debug menu.

When a Breakpoint Occurs

When you run the program, Quincy interrupts execution when the program arrives at a source-code line that has a breakpoint. The green stepping bar is set on the breakpoint statement. You can examine and modify variables, set watch variables, and step or continue running starting at the breakpoint statement.

Clearing a Breakpoint

To clear a breakpoint, follow these steps:

1. Put the keyboard cursor on the line of code where the breakpoint is.
2. Click the breakpoint tool button (the one with the hand), press **F2**, or choose the **Breakpoint** command on the Debug menu.

Clearing All Breakpoints

To clear all breakpoints, choose the **Clear Breakpoints** command on the Debug menu. This command clears all programmed breakpoints.

EXAMINING AND MODIFYING VARIABLES

When a program is executing but the IDE has control—at a breakpoint or after a step—you can examine the values in variables that are in scope and modify their contents. To examine a variable, follow these steps:

1. Click the **Examine** tool button (the one with the shadowy spy face).
2. Or press **Ctrl+E**.
3. Or choose the **Examine** command on the Debug menu.

Any of these actions opens the Examine dialog box shown in Figure A.8.

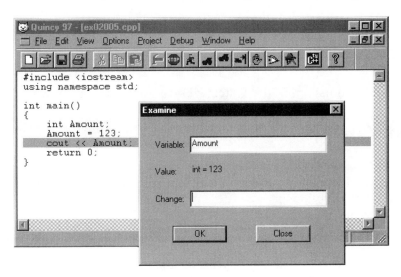

Figure A.8 Examining a variable.

4. Type the name of a variable that is currently in scope into the **Variable** field.

5. Click **OK**. The dialog box displays the type and current value of the variable. If the variable is not in scope, the dialog box displays the ?? token.

To modify the variable's value before proceeding, follow these steps:

1. Tab to the **Change** field.

2. Enter a new value from the keyboard.

3. Click **OK**. The new value is displayed. When you continue running the program, the variable has the new value stored in it.

To close the Examine window and return to the IDE, click **Close**.

WATCHING VARIABLES

You can watch the values of variables while stepping through a program by opening Quincy's Watch window and programming variables to watch.

Opening the Watch Window

To open the Watch window, follow these steps:

1. Click the **Watch** tool button (with the eyeball icon).

2. Or press **Ctrl+W**.

3. Or choose the **Watch** command on the Debug menu.

Any of these actions opens the Watch window shown in Figure A.9.

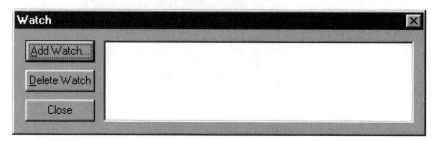

Figure A.9 The Watch window.

Adding a Watch Variable

To add a watch variable, follow these steps:

1. Click the **Add Watch** button.

This action opens the Add Watch dialog box shown in Figure A.10.

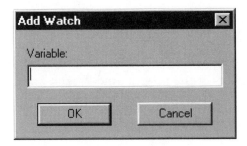

Figure A.10 *The Add Watch dialog box.*

2. Enter the identifier of the variable you want to watch in the Variable field.

3. Click **OK**.

The variable name is added to the Watch window's list. As you step through the program, the Watch window displays the variable's current value, as Figure A.11 shows.

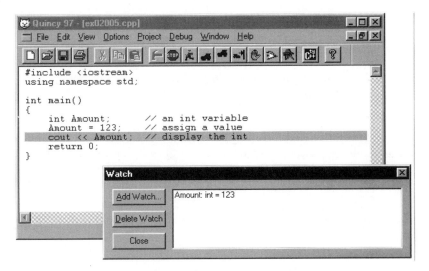

Figure A.11 *The variable's current value.*

Deleting a Watch Variable

To delete a watch variable from the Watch window, follow these steps:

1. Select the variable you want to delete by clicking it.
2. Click the **Delete Watch** button.

Closing the Watch Window

To close the Watch window, click the **Close** command. Closing the Watch window does not delete any of the programmed watch variables.

Reopening the Watch Window

You can reopen the Watch window at any time as described earlier in "Opening the Watch Window" or by choosing the **Watch Window** command on the View menu.

STOPPING A PROGRAM

To stop a program in progress before it has run to completion, follow these steps:

1. Click the **Stop** tool button (the stop sign icon).
2. Or select the **Stop** command on the Debug menu.
3. Or press **Ctrl+C** when the program is displaying text or waiting for the keyboard. This option terminates Quincy along with the running program and is unpredictable.
4. Or click the **X** icon at the right end of the console window's title bar. Windows 95 displays a dialog box asking whether you really want to do that. This option usually terminates Quincy along with the running program. It appears to lock up Windows 95 for a few seconds while it figures out that it is supposed to close the console window.

It is best not to use steps 3 or 4 but to use the **Stop** command or **Stop** tool button instead.

If a program has run to completion, its console window remains open with the "Any key to return to Quincy…" message displayed (Figure A.5). Select the console as the active window by clicking anywhere in it, and press the **Enter** key to close the window and return to Quincy's IDE.

WRITING NEW PROGRAMS

You write a new program by building a source-code file, setting options for the program, saving the program to disk, and then compiling the program. First you must create a new file.

Creating a Source-Code File

To create a source-code file from scratch, follow these steps:

1. Click the **New** tool button (the leftmost tool button with an icon showing a page with its corner turned down).

2. Or choose the **New** command on the File menu.

Quincy opens the New dialog box shown in Figure A.12.

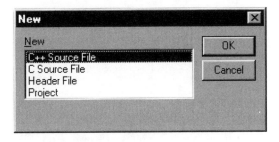

Figure A.12 *The New dialog box.*

3. Select the kind of source-code file you are building. A C++ file will be saved with the **.CPP** file extension and will be compiled by the C++ compiler. A C file will be saved with the **.C** file extension and will be compiled by the C compiler. A header file will be saved with the **.H** extension to include in your C and C++ source-code files.

4. Click **OK**.

Quincy creates an empty text file with the name **Textn**, where **n** is the next available number for Quincy to assign to a text file. You will probably want to change the name to something more meaningful when you save the file. This file has not yet been saved to disk. You cannot compile the program until you have saved the source-code file.

5. Use the standard Windows 95 text editing commands to write your program.

Saving a Source-Code File

Before you can compile and test your program, you must save it to disk. Before you can include a header file in another source-code file, you must save the header file to disk.

To save the source-code file, follow these steps:

1. Click the **Save** tool button (the one with the diskette icon).

2. Or press **Ctrl+S**.

3. Or choose the **Save** command on the File menu.

   If the source-code file was saved earlier, Quincy writes the current version over the old one. If the source-code file is a new one that you have not yet saved, Quincy opens the Save As dialog box shown in Figure A.13.

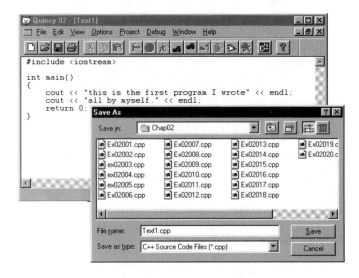

Figure A.13 *Saving a file.*

4. Enter the source-code file name in the **File name** field. You can omit the extension. Quincy uses the extension selected in the **Save as type** dropdown listbox.

5. Ensure that the Save As dialog box is positioned at the Windows 95 folder where you want to save the source-code file. If it is not, use the dialog box to navigate to the correct folder.

6. Click the **Save** button.

NOTE Remember when you save header files to put them in the same folder as source-code files that include them with the *#include "file.h"* notation. If you save the header files in a different folder, the source-code files that include them must use the *#include <file.h>* notation, and Quincy's options must be set to tell Quincy where to find such header files. (See "Setting Options" later in this Appendix.)

Using Save As

You can save an existing file that was saved earlier and give it a different name by choosing the **Save As** command on the File menu to open the Save As dialog box. Follow the procedure just described under "Saving a Source-Code File" beginning with step 4. The original file is not changed by this procedure.

Working with Multiple Source-Code Files

Quincy is a Windows 95 multiple document interface (MDI) application. This means that you can open and work with more than one source-code file at a time. Figure A.14 shows Quincy in its MDI configuration.

Figure A.14 *Quincy in its MDI configuration.*

If your program involves more than one translation unit—that is, a combination of multiple C files, C++ files, and libraries—you must organize the program into a Project before you can link the translation units and run the program. See "Quincy Projects" later in this Appendix.

BUILDING A PROGRAM

Quincy works with programs built from a single source-code file or from a Quincy Project that includes a number of source-code and library files. We'll discuss building a program from the single source-code file here. Then we'll discuss Quincy Projects.

Setting Options

There are several options for the way the program is to be compiled and the way Quincy is to run it from within the IDE. You set these options before compiling and running the program. Quincy remembers the option settings from session to session.

If you are working with a Quincy Project (see "Quincy Projects" later in this Appendix), the options settings are stored in the Project file.

If you are using Quincy with the tutorial exercises as described in "Exercise Programs" earlier in this Appendix, the tutorial command files set the options that each exercise uses even when no Project file is involved.

To set Quincy's options, follow these steps:

1. Choose the **Options** menu command. Quincy opens the Options dialog box shown in Figure A.15.

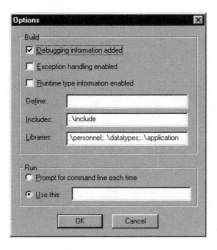

Figure A.15 *The Options dialog box.*

2. Check the **Debugging information added** check box if you want to use the IDE to step through the program or set breakpoints in the source code display when you debug the program.

3. Check the **Exception handling enabled** check box if your program uses C++ exception handling (try/throw/catch).

4. Check the **Runtime type information enabled** check box if your program uses the *dynamic_cast* or *typeid* operator. Any source-code file that uses these operators should include the Standard C++ **<typeinfo>** header file.

5. Enter in the **Define** field any preprocessor macros that the program needs. Whatever you type here will be treated as if you put it at the front of the source code as the arguments to a *#define* preprocessor directive with this exception: to define a global symbol with a value, use an equals sign (=) as shown here:

```
VERSION=2.5.
```

The example just shown compiles as if the source-code file included this statement:

```
#define VERSION 2.5
```

If you need more than one macro, separate them in the **Define** field with semicolons as shown here:

```
NDEBUG;VERSION=2.5
```

6. Enter paths to folders where the preprocessor can search for header files specified with the *#include <file.h>* directive. Separate the paths with semicolons. You can use relative paths or fully qualified paths. The preprocessor searches the paths in the order you enter them here. If the header file is not in one of these paths, the preprocessor searches the compiler's INCLUDE subdirectories.

7. Enter paths to folders where the linker can search for library files that a Project file includes. (See "Quincy Projects" later in this Appendix.) Separate the paths with semicolons. You can use relative paths or fully qualified paths. The linker searches the paths in the order you enter them here. If a library file is not in one of these paths, the linker searches the compiler's LIB subdirectories.

8. If the program does not read command line arguments, select the **Use This** radio button in the Run group, and clear the edit box.

9. If the program reads command line arguments, you can select **Use This** and enter the command line arguments in the edit box. Alternatively, you can select the **Prompt For...** radio button. Quincy will prompt you for command line arguments whenever you run the program.

Building the Program

To build the program, follow these steps:

1. Select the program's source-code file in the editor if the editor includes multiple source-code files.

2. Click the **Build** tool button (the one with the hammer icon).

3. Or press **F6**.

4. Or choose the **Build** command on the Project menu.

Quincy launches the compiler programs to preprocess, compile, assemble, and link the program into an executable.

Interrupting a Build

You can interrupt a build at any time by following this procedure:

1. Click the **Stop** tool button (the one with the stop sign icon).

2. Or choose the **Stop** command on the Project menu.

Quincy displays the dialog box shown in Figure A.16.

Figure A.16 Stopping a build.

Successful Build

If Quincy can build the program without errors, the build process terminates normally and you can proceed with running and debugging the program.

Unsuccessful Build

If the build involves errors or warnings, Quincy opens the Error and Warning Messages dialog box shown in Figure A.17.

Figure A.17 *The Error and Warning Messages dialog box.*

If the dialog box lists only warning messages, which are clearly labeled as such, the build completed and the program can be executed. You should strive, however, to write programs that compile cleanly—with no warnings.

If the dialog box lists any error messages, the build did not complete.

When you double-click any message in the dialog box, Quincy makes the editor the active window and moves the cursor to the offending source-code line.

Quincy tries to keep the messages concise and uncluttered. The messages are generated by the GNU compiler, however, and some of them involve more information than Quincy displays. If you do not understand a message, click the **Full Display** button. Quincy opens the Windows 95 Notepad applet with all the message content in a text file.

Compiling a Source-Code File

You can compile a source-code file without building an executable program. Sometimes you do this just to see whether the source-code file has any errors. To compile a source-code file, follow these steps:

1. Choose the **Compile** command on the Project menu.

2. Or press **F5**.

Quincy compiles the program and stops before launching the linker. You can review errors and warnings as described earlier.

QUINCY PROJECTS

A program that uses more than one translation unit must be built from a Quincy Project, which is a file that lists the source-code files and library files that the compiler and linker use to build the executable program.

You also use a Project to build a library file, which is a collection of compiled modules that can be linked into a program.

Setting Up a Project

To establish a Project, follow these steps:

1. Click the **New** tool button (the leftmost tool button with an icon showing a page with its corner turned down).

2. Or choose the **New** command on the File menu.

   Quincy opens the New dialog box shown earlier in Figure A.12.

3. Select the **Project** entry in the New dialog box.

4. Click **OK**.

Quincy opens the New Project dialog box shown in Figure A.18.

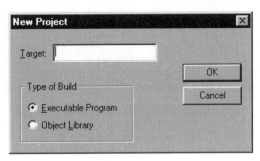

Figure A.18 *The New Project dialog box.*

5. Enter the name of the target in the **Target** field. The target is either an executable program or an object library. Enter the file name with no file extension.

6. Select either the **Executable Program** or the **Object Library** radio button. Click **OK**.

Quincy creates an empty Project file with the name **Projn**, where **n** is the next available number for Quincy to assign to a Project file. You will probably want to change the name to something more meaningful when you save the file. This file has not yet been saved to disk. You cannot build the program until you have saved the Project file.

Saving the Project

To save the Project file, follow these steps:

1. Ensure that Quincy's options are compatible with the target that the project builds. See "Setting Options" earlier. Library files are usually built with debugging information disabled. Executable files that include library files must have the paths to those files programmed into Quincy's options.

2. Click the **Save** tool button (the one with the diskette icon).

3. Or press **Ctrl+S**.

4. Or choose the **Save** command on the File menu.

   If the Project file was saved earlier, Quincy writes the current version over the old one. If the Project file is a new one that you have not yet saved, Quincy opens the Save As dialog box shown in Figure A.19.

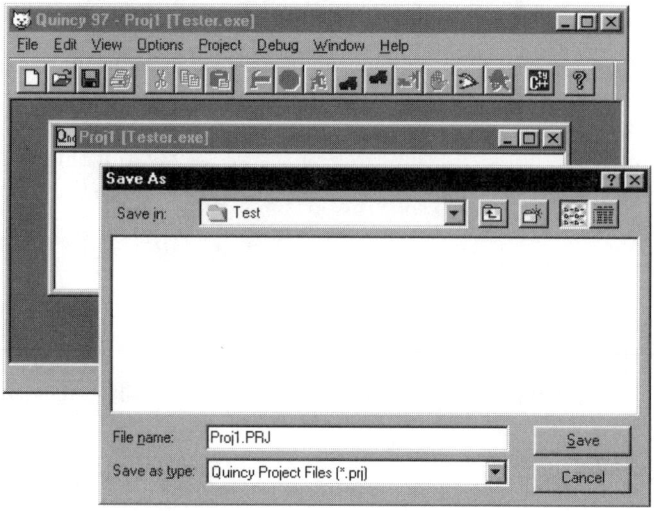

Figure A.19 *Saving a Project.*

5. Enter the Project name in the **File name** field. You can omit the extension. Quincy uses the extension selected in the **Save as type** dropdown listbox.

6. Ensure that the Save As dialog box is positioned at the Windows 95 folder where you want to save the Project file. A Project file must be in the same folder as its source-code files. Library files can be in other folders. Use the dialog box to navigate to the correct folder.

7. Click the **Save** button.

Adding Files to a Project

A Project file consists of a list of source-code files and, optionally, library files. The source-code files must be in the same folder with the Project file. The library files can be elsewhere.

To add a file to a Project, follow these steps:

1. Select the Project file as the active window.

2. If the Project already has files, select the file in front of which you want to insert the new files. If you want to append files to the list, select no files in the Project window. (To deselect a file, click anywhere in the empty part of the window.).

   The order of the files is important when you use libraries that refer to each other's object files. The linker makes only one pass. If you have circular references, you might need to list a library file more than once in the Project file.

3. Press the **Ins** key.

4. Or choose the **Insert File(s)** command on the Project menu.

   Quincy opens the Insert File(s) dialog box shown in Figure A.20.

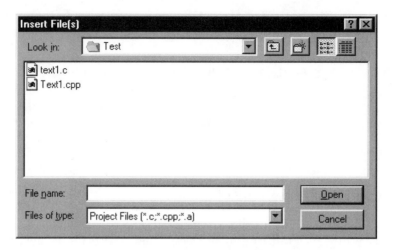

Figure A.20 *The Insert File(s) dialog box.*

5. Select one or more files from the list. If you are adding C or C++ source files, they must be in the same folder that contains the Project file. If you are selecting a library file, which has the extension **.A**, you can get it from any folder as long as Quincy's options have been set to permit the linker to find the library.

6. Click the **Open** button to add the selected files to the Project.

Remember that an executable Project must include one and only one source-code file with a *main* function.

N O T E

Deleting files From a Project

To delete files from a Project, follow these steps:

1. Select the file(s) to be deleted in the Project window.

2. Choose the **Delete File(s)** command on the Project window.

3. Or press the **Del** key.

    Quincy asks whether you really want to delete the files.

4. Click **Yes**.

Building a Project

To build a Project's target, follow these steps:

1. Select the Project file or one of its source-code files.
2. Click the **Build** tool button (the one with the hammer icon).
3. Or choose the **Build** command on the Project menu.

This procedure is a conditional "make" operation. This means that Quincy recompiles the source-code files that have changed since the previous build.

To rebuild all source code components of a project, select the **Rebuild All** command on the Project menu. This procedure recompiles all the source-code files listed as part of the Project and then links the executable target or builds the library target.

PRINTING THE SOURCE CODE

To print a source-code file, follow these steps:

1. Load the source-code file into the editor.
2. Select the source-code file as the active window.
3. Choose the **Print Setup** command on the File menu to set up your printer.
4. Click the **Print** tool button (the one with the printer icon) or choose the **Print** command on the File menu.

RUNNING QUINCY-COMPILED PROGRAMS WITHOUT THE IDE

Quincy's Setup program configures Quincy to run programs from within the IDE. Programs that Quincy compiles can execute only if a file named **CYG-WIN.DLL**, which is a part of the gnu-win32 port of the GNU compiler, is available. The normal Quincy setup configuration ensures that the DLL is available when you execute compiled programs from the IDE. However, if you try to run the programs from a DOS box, you will probably get the Windows 95 error message shown in Figure A.21.

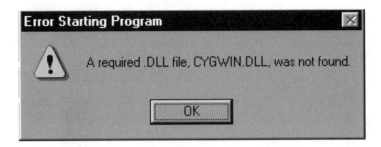

Figure A.21 *Running programs from a DOS box.*

To run Quincy-compiled programs from outside the IDE, do one of the following:

1. Copy **CYGWIN.DLL** from Quincy's BIN folder to the folder where the executable program is.

2. Or copy **CYGWIN.DLL** to the Windows\System folder.

3. Or put Quincy's BIN folder into the path.

Glossary

This glossary defines C++ and object-oriented programming terms.

abstract base class

A class definition that is always a base class for other classes to be derived from. No specific objects of the base class are declared by the program. A C++ abstract base class is one that has a pure virtual function, a protected constructor, or a protected destructor.

abstract data type

Also called ADT. A user-defined data type built as a C++ class. The details of implementation are not necessarily a part of the ADT. See also "intrinsic data type" and "concrete data type."

abstraction

Defining an abstract data type by designing a class. Also called "data abstraction."

address

An expression that returns the memory address of a variable or function.

algorithm

The formula or procedure by which a set of program instructions performs a defined task.

anonymous object

An internal, temporary object created by the compiler.

application

A program or group of programs that combine to support a defined, user-related function, such as payroll, inventory, accounting, and so on.

applications program

As opposed to "systems program." A program that is developed for a specific purpose within an application.

argument

The value passed to a function. Its type must match that of the function's corresponding parameter as declared in the function's prototype. See "parameter."

array

A group of variables of the same type organized into a table of one or more dimensions.

ASCII

American Standard Code for Information Exchange. The 8-bit system for encoding digits, the alphabet, special characters, graphics characters, and certain control values.

assignment

A statement that places the value of an expression into a memory variable.

associativity

The order in which operands in an expression are evaluated: left-to-right or right-to-left. Associativity is determined by the operator.

automatic variable

A local variable that does not retain its value when it goes out of scope. Each recursive execution of functions has its own copy of automatic variables.

base class

A class from which other classes derive characteristics. All the characteristics of the base are inherited by the derived class. Also called "superclass."

binary operator

An operator, such as +, that has two operands.

Boolean logic

The system of logic that applies the AND, OR, and XOR operators to two bitwise operands.

breakpoint

A debugging procedure in which the program's execution is stopped at a specified statement in the source code so that the programmer can examine the program's state.

byte

An 8-bit quantity used to store a character value or an integer in the signed range -128 to 127 or unsigned range 0 to 255.

cast

A parenthesized expression with only a type. It tells the compiler to convert the expression that follows to the type in the parentheses. Also called a *type-cast.*

character

An 8-bit value that represents one of the units in the computer's character set.

class

A user-defined data type that may consist of data members and member functions.

class hierarchy

A system of base and derived classes.

code

Computer instructions encoded in machine, assembly, or a high-level language. To write code.

comment

An informational statement in a program. The comment provides program documentation for the reader of the code. It reserves no memory and has no effect on the program's execution. C language comments begin with /* characters and end with */ characters. They may span several lines and they do not nest. C++ language comments begin with // and continue to the end of the line.

compiler

A program that reads high-level language source code and generates object code.

concrete data type

A user-defined or library data type complete with interface and implementation. The CDT is meant to be instantiated as an object and is not intended to be used solely as a base class.

condition

An expression that returns a true or false value.

console

The computer's keyboard and screen.

constant

A memory object with a defined value that cannot be changed while the program is running.

constructor

The function executed by the compiler when the program declares an instance of a class. See also "destructor."

control structures

The building blocks of structured programming: sequence, selection, and iteration. The sequence control structure is the sequential expression of imperative statements. The selection control structure is the *if-then-else* decision process. The iteration control structure is the *while-until* loop mechanism. Others are the *for* iteration and the *switch-case* selection control structures.

cursor

A screen pointer that tells the user where the next keystroke will be echoed. When the system uses a mouse, an additional cursor points to the current mouse position.

data abstraction

See "abstraction."

data member

A data component of a class. It may be any valid data type, including instrinsic data types, class objects, pointers, and references.

data type

The definition of a datum—its implementation and behavior. See also "intrinsic data type" and "user-defined data type."

database

A collection of data files loosely integrated to support a common application.

debugger

A systems program that helps a programmer debug an applications program. The debugger traces the program's source code and supports breakpoints, watchpoints, and the examination and modification of memory variables.

decision

The process whereby a program alters the statement execution sequence by testing a condition.

declaration

The program statement that associates an identifier with what it identifies. A declaration can declare a variable, specify the format of a structure, declare an external variable, or declare a function or subroutine's return value and parameter list. A declaration may or may not reserve memory.

definition

The program statement that defines the existence of a variable or function. A definition reserves memory for the item. The definition sometimes doubles as the item's declaration.

derived class

A class that inherits some of its characteristics from a base class. Also called a "subclass."

destructor

The function executed by the compiler when a declared instance of a class goes out of scope. See also "constructor."

dimension

The number of elements in an array. When the array is multidimensional— as in an array of arrays—the secondary dimension is the number of array elements in the array.

DOS

The dominant disk operating system for PCs. Also called PC-DOS and MS-DOS. Other operating systems are OS/2, Unix, and Windows NT.

editor

A utility program with which a programmer creates and modifies source code and other text files.

element

One entry in an array of variables.

encapsulation

The activity of defining a class with its data members and member functions encapsulated into the definition. Encapsulation implies an implementation, which is hidden from the class user, and an interface, which is visible to the class user.

error message

A message that the program displays to tell the user that an error has occurred in the processing.

escape sequence

Two-character combinations coded into string and character constants that begin with a backslash character and compile to a one-character value that usually cannot be represented by a single character code in the context of the constant.

exception

The signal that a program raises (throws) when it senses a condition that must interrupt the current procedure. Another part of the program, one that has already run and is higher in the call stack, can intercept (catch) and process the exception.

executable code

The assembled (or compiled) and linked code that is loaded into the computer and executed. In a source program, executable code is distinguished from code that declares objects and function prototypes and defines object formats.

expression

A grouping of one or more constant and variable references, function calls, and relational, logical, and arithmetic operators that form to return a numerical or pointer value.

external data

Data objects that are declared external to any procedure. They are accessible to all procedures within their scope. See also "global data."

extraction operator

The overloaded >> operator that reads (extracts) values from an input stream. See also "insertion operator."

field

A single entity of data, usually one item of a data type. Collections of fields form files in a database. A field is also called a *data element.*

file

A collection of records of a common format in a database.

file scope

The scope of variables and functions that may be accessed only from within the translation unit. Macros, static functions, and static external variables have file scope.

firmware

Software encoded into a read-only memory (ROM) integrated circuit.

floating-point number

A number used to represent very large and very small numbers and nonintegral values.

free store

The C++ heap. A dynamic memory pool that programs use to allocate and release temporary memory buffers.

friend

A function that has access to the private members of a class but that is not a member function of that class. The class definition declares the function to be a *friend*.

function

A program procedure that may return a value and may accept one or more arguments. A function consists of a function header and a function body.

function body

The program statements that constitute the local declarations and executable code of a function definition.

function header

The first statement in a function definition. It specifies the function's return type, identifier, and parameter list.

global data

External data objects that are declared to be within the scope of the entire program.

global scope

The scope of variables and functions that are accessible to all translation units in the program.

goto

A statement that abruptly and unconditionally modifies the execution flow to proceed from a remote labeled statement. The *goto* statement specifies a source-code label that matches one attached to an executable source-code statement elsewhere in the function.

graphical user interface (GUI)

A common user interface model that uses the graphics capabilities of the screen to support the "desktop" metaphor. A GUI provides generic menu and dialog box functions. Programs written to run under a GUI tend to have the same visual appearance to the user. Windows 95 is the most popular GUI.

header source files

Other source files that a program source file includes when it compiles. Header files typically contain things such as global declarations that independently compiled translation units need to see.

heap

A large, system-controlled buffer of memory from which the program can dynamically allocate and deallocate smaller memory buffers. See also "free store."

hexadecimal

Base-16 numerical notation. The digits are 0–9, A–F.

hierarchy

See "class hierarchy."

identifier

The name of a variable, macro, structure, or function.

implementation

The private members of a class. The implementation defines the details of how the class implements the behavior of the abstract base type. See also "interface."

information hiding

An object-oriented and structured programming technique in which data representations and algorithms are not within the scope of those parts of the program that do not need to access them.

inheritance

The ability for one class to inherit the characteristics of another class. The inherited class is said to be derived from the base class. Also called "subclassing."

initializer

An expression specified as a variable's first assigned value when the variable comes into scope.

inline function

A function that the compiler compiles as in-line code every time the function is called.

input/output redirection

A command line option when you run a program that redirects standard input and output to disk files.

insertion operator

The overloaded << operator that writes (inserts) values to an output stream. See also "extraction operator."

instance

A declared object.

instantiate

Declare an object of a data type.

integer

A whole number; a positive or negative value without decimal places.

integrated development environment (IDE)

A programming system that integrates a source-code editor, language translator (compiler or interpreter), linker, and debugger into one package.

interactive

An operating mode in which the user communicates with the program by using the keyboard and mouse during the program's execution.

interface

The public members of a class, which define the class user's interface to the class's data and its behavior. Usually implemented as member functions. See also "implementation."

interpreter

A programming language processor that executes the program by interpreting the source code statements one statement at a time. Interpreters are contrasted with compilers, which compile the source-code into linkable object code.

intrinsic data type

A data type known to the compiler, as compared to a "user-defined data type."Intrinsic data types in C++ are *bool, char, wchar_t, int, float,* and *double*. The integer types may be further qualified as *long, short, signed,* and *unsigned*. The *double* type may be further qualified as *long*. There are also pointer and reference variables, which refer to objects of specific types. Data aggregates may be organized as arrays of like types and as classes, structures, and unions of varying types. Also called "primitive data type."

iteration

One of the three control stuctures of structured programming. (The other two are "sequence" and "selection.") Iteration is the control structure wherein the program repeats a sequence zero or more times a some tested condition within the sequence or within a statement that controls the loop causes the program to cease repeating the sequence and, consequently, to exit from the loop. The *while, do...while* and *for* statements support iteration in C++.

keyword

A word that is reserved by the C++ programming language. Typical keywords are *if, else,* and *while*.

label

An identifier followed by a colon that names a program statement. The *goto* statement specifies the label associated with the statement that will execute next.

library

A file of relocatable object programs. Applications reference external identifiers in the library and link their object code files with the library. The linker pulls the object files from the library that contain the referenced external identifiers.

linkage specification

Notation that tells the C++ compiler that a function was or is to be compiled with the linkage conventions of another language.

linker

A systems program that builds an executable program file from a specified group of relocatable object code files. The relocatable object code files can stand alone, or they can be selected from a library.

local scope

The scope of automatic and static variables that are declared within a function body or as parameters in the function header.

local variable

A variable that is defined in a statement block and that is not in the scope of outer statement blocks or other functions.

loop

A sequence of one or more program statements that iterate—execute repetitively—while or until a specified condition is true. See also "iteration."

lvalue

An expression that can be dereferenced to modify memory. It can exist on the left side of an assignment. See also "rvalue."

macro

A statement that assigns source-code meaning to an identifier. A macro may have arguments.

manipulator

A value that a program sends to a stream to tell the stream to modify one of its modes.

member

A component of a class, either a data member or a member function. Also a variable within a structure or union.

member function

A function component of a class, also called a "method." A member function may be virtual.

memory

The internal storage medium of the computer. In a PC, semiconductor memory is divided into read-only memory (ROM) and random-access memory (RAM).

menu

An interactive program's screen display of selections from which the user may choose. Each selection corresponds to an action that the program will take.

message

A message is the invocation of a class's member function in the name of a declared object of the class. The message is said to be sent to the object to tell it to perform its function. The message includes the function call and the arguments that accompany it.

method

A method in C++ is a member function of a class. Programs send messages to objects by invoking methods.

multiple inheritance

The ability of a derived class to inherit the characteristics of more than one base class.

multitasking

An operating system model where multiple programs run concurrently.

multiuser

An operating system model in which multiple users share the processor. Each user runs independently of the other users. Users can run the same or different programs concurrently.

namespace

The logical scope in which names are declared and are unique. Names in an inner namespace can override names in an outer namespace. Code in an inner namespace can reference overridden names by using the scope resolution operator. Two objects in the same namespace cannot have the same name.

object

A declared instance of a data type, including standard C++ data types as well as objects of classes.

object code

The machine language code that an assembler or compiler generates from source code. To produce executable code, object code must be linked by the linker program with other object code files and with library object code files.

object database

A collection of persistent objects.

octal

Base-8 number system. The digits are 0–7.

operand

The variables and function calls that an expression uses with operators to produce its value.

operating system

The master control program that operates the computer. It maintains the file system and provides a command interface with the user to execute utility and application programs. See also "DOS."

operator

The code token that represents how an expression uses its operands to produce its value.

overloaded function

A function that has the same name as one or more other functions but that has a different parameter list. The compiler selects the function to call based on the types and number of arguments in the call.

overloaded operator

A function that executes when a C++ operator is seen in a defined context with respect to a class object.

overriding function

A function in a derived class that has the same name, return type, and parameter list as a function in the base class. The compiler calls the overriding function when the program calls that function in the name of an object of the derived class. If the function in the base class is virtual, the compiler calls the derived class's function even when the call is through a pointer or reference to the base class. See also "pure virtual function."

parameter

The declaration of a data item that a function uses to receive arguments that are passed to the function. This declaration includes the item's type and name and appears in the function's declaration block at the beginning of the function. When the parameter appears in the function's prototype, the parameter's name may be omitted. See "argument" and "prototype."

parameter

The declaration in a function's parameter list of a variable that the function expects to be passed to it. This declaration includes the variable's type and identifier and appears in the function's declaration. See "argument" and "prototype."

parameter list

The list of parameter types and names in a function declaration block. Also, the same list, which may exclude the names, in a function prototype.

parameter list

The comma-separated, parenthetical list of parameter variable declarations in a function header. It specifies the types and identifiers of the function's parameters.

persistence

The ability of an object to succeed its creator and to subsequently exist in space other than the space in which it was created.

persistent object

An object that exhibits persistence.

platform

A loosely applied term to mean the operating system or the programming environment. The computer itself, such as the "PC platform" or the "Macintosh platform." The operating environment, such as the "DOS platform" or the "Windows platform." The software development environment of a programming language, such as the "Visual C++ platform" or the "SmallTalk platform."

pointer

A variable that can contain the address of functions or other variables. The item pointed to can be referenced through the pointer.

polymorphism

The ability for methods in a class hierarchy to exhibit different behavior for the same message depending on the type of the object for which the method is invoked and without regard to the class type of the reference to the object.

precedence

The property that determines the order in which different operators in an expression are evaluated.

preemptive multitasking

A multitasking operating system model that does not require handshakes from the running programs. The operating system preempts the running program to allow others to run. Programs are given time slices within which they can run before they are preempted. Programs of higher priority can preempt programs of lower priority at any time.

preprocessor

A program that reads source code and translates it into source code suitable for the compiler. The preprocessor defines and resolves macros, includes other source-code files, and causes specified lines of code to be included or deleted based on conditional expressions.

primitive data type

See "intrinsic data type."

private class members

Members of a class for which access is granted only to the class's member functions and to *friend* functions of the class.

program

A collection of computer instructions that execute in a logical sequence to perform a defined task. To write a program.

program flow control statement

A statement that controls the flow of execution. The *if, do, while, for, else, break, continue,* and *goto* statements are program flow control statements

proper programming

A programming model in which procedures have one entry point at the top, one exit point at the bottom, and no endless loops.

protected class members

Members of a class that are private except to member functions of publicly derived classes.

prototype

The definition of a function's name, return type, and parameter list.

prototype

The declaration of a function's name, return type, and parameter list.

public class members

Members of a class to which access is granted to all functions within the scope of an object of the class.

pull-down menu

A menu that pops down, usually from a menu bar, on top of the screen display. After the user makes a menu selection, the menu pops up to uncover the displays that it obscured.

pure virtual function

A virtual function in a base class that must have a matching function in a derived class. A program may not declare an instance of a class that has a pure virtual function. A program may not declare an instance of a derived class if that derived class has not provided an overriding function for each pure virtual function in the base.

RAM

Random access memory. Volatile semiconductor memory. Most of the PC's internal memory is RAM.

random file

A file with fixed-length records that can be accessed in random sequence by addressing the record number.

real number

A number represented in a program with digits and a decimal point. See also "floating-point number."

real-time

The ability of a program to respond to external events when they happen. The program's execution may not delay its reaction to those events. A spacecraft's guidance system uses real-time processing. Also refers to a program's ability to emulate events within time constraints that match the user's perception of the passage of time. A flight simulator is an example of such a real-time program.

recursion

The ability of a function to call itself directly or indirectly from functions that it calls.

reference

A variable name that is an alias for another variable.

reference, pass by

Pass a pointer to the actual argument. The called function acts upon the caller's copy of the argument. See also "value, pass by."

relocatable object code

Compiled or assembled object code with relative, unresolved memory address references. The references are resolved by the linker program when it builds an executable program from one or more relocatable object files.

reusable code

Functions that perform utility and general-purpose operations to be used by many unrelated programs.

ROM

Read-only memory. Nonvolatile semiconductor memory. The PC's BIOS is stored in ROM. A program may not change the values written in ROM, and the values persist when power is turned off.

rvalue

An expression that cannot be on the left side of an assignment because it represents a value that might not be taken from a memory location. See also "lvalue."

scope

The range of source code that can access an identifier. An external identifier typically is in scope within the source-code file in which the object is declared. In C++ the scope extends from the position of the declaration to the end of the file. A global identifier's scope extends to all of the program's source-code files. A local identifier is in scope only within the statement block in which it is declared.

selection

One of the three control stuctures of structured programming. (The other two are "sequence" and "iteration.") Selection is the control structure wherein the program changes the sequential program flow based on the true/false value of a tested condition. The *if...else* and e*lse if* statements support selection in C++.

sequence

One of the three control stuctures of structured programming. (The other two are "selection" and "iteration.") Sequence is the control structure wherein program statements follow one another in top-down sequence.

sequential file

A file of fixed- or variable-length records that are accessed in the sequence in which the records occur in the file.

shareware

A technique for marketing software in which users try the programs first and pay for them only if they want to continue using them.

side effects

The behavior of a macro that references an argument more than once. If multiple evaluations of an expression can change its meaning or imply unneccessary overhead, the expression is said to have side effects when it is used as an argument to such a macro.

source code

Assembly or high-level programming language code statements.

stack

A memory buffer from which the system allocates space for function arguments and automatic variables.

Standard C

The C language as defined by the ANSI X3J11 Committee.

Standard C++

The C++ language as defined by the ANSI X3J16 Committee.

standard input/output devices

The device files that are usually assigned to the keyboard and screen but that may be redirected to disk files.

statement

A C++ language body of code that is terminated with a semicolon.

statement block

A group of statements that starts with a left brace ({) and ends with a right brace (}).

storage class

The manner in which a variable is stored in memory, as *auto, extern, static,* or *register.*

stream

A category of character-oriented data files or devices in which the data characters exist in an input or output stream.

string constant

A null-terminated, variable-length array of characters coded within an expression surrounded by double quotes.

structure

A record format consisting of one or more objects of multiple data types.

structured programming

A programming model that uses the three control structures: sequence, selection, and iteration. Structured programming has been extended to include the principles of modular programming.

subclass

See "derived class."

subclassing

See "inheritance."

subscript

An integer value used in an expression to reference an element of an array.

superclass

See "base class."

systems program

As opposed to "applications program." A program, such as an operating system, that supports the computer system rather than the functional application.

test

The application of a condition to alter the sequence of instruction execution. The *if* and *while* control structures are tests.

this

A pointer that exists in all nonstatic member functions. The *this* pointer is a pointer to an object of the class. It points to the object for which the function is being executed.

top-down design

Designing a program beginning at the highest level of execution and proceeding downward. The programmer designs the program's entry point and the calls to lower procedures. Each design of a lower procedure decomposes the design into lower and more detailed levels of abstraction until the final design at the lowest level is an expression of the program's algorithms.

translation unit

One independently compiled source-code unit consisting of the C or C++ source file and all included headers.

type

The type of a program constant or variable, which can be of a primitive or an abstract data type.

type conversion

The conversion of one type to another. The compiler has built-in type conversions, and a class may define its own conversions for converting from an object of the class to another type and from another type to an object of the class.

type qualifier

A qualifying keyword in a variable declaration that specifies whether the variable is *const* or *volatile.*

type-safe linkage

A technique that ensures that functions and function calls in separately compiled program modules use consistent parameter lists.

typecast

See "cast."

unary operator

An operator, such as *sizeof,* that has only one operand.

user interface

The interactive dialog between the program and the user. In the early days of the PC, user interfaces were invented or contrived by the programmer for each new program. That is why each spreadsheet, word processor, and so on, had its own unique command structure. Users had to learn a different procedure for each program. Contemporary programs are written to run within operating environments, such as Windows, that support a common user interface.

user-defined data type

A data type that the programmer builds by using *struct, union,* or *typedef.* See also "intrinsic data types."

utility program

A program that performs a utility function in support of the operating environment or the file system. The MS-DOS CHKDSK program is a utility program that tests the integrity of the file system.

value, pass by

Pass the value of argument. The called function acts upon its own copy of the argument, leaving the caller's copy intact. See also "reference, pass by."

variable

An object in memory in which the value can be modified by the program at any time.

virtual function

A member function in a class from which other classes may be derived. If the derived class has a function with the same name and parameter list, the derived class's function is always executed for objects of the derived class. See also "pure virtual function" and "overriding function."

watchpoint

A debugging procedure in which the debugger watches a memory variable for a specified value or a specified expression for a true condition. When the watchpoint condition is satisfied, the debugger stops the program's execution at the point where the condition became true.

white space

Spaces, newlines, and tab characters in a source-code text file.

Bibliography

Cargill, Tom, *C++ Programming Style*, 1992, Addison-Wesley

Coplien, James O., *Advanced C++ Programming Styles and Idioms*, 1992, Addison-Wesley

Eckel, Bruce, *Thinking in C++*, 1995, Prentice Hall

Ellis, Margaret A. and Stroustrup, Bjarne, *The Annotated C++ Reference Manual*, 1990, Addison-Wesley

Koenig, Andrew, editor, *Working Paper for Draft Proposed International Standard for Information Systems—Programming Language C++*, December 1996, ANSI Document Number X3J16/96-0225, WG21/N1043

Koenig, Andrew and Moo, Barbara, *Ruminations on C++*, 1997, Addison-Wesley

Murray, Robert B., *C++ Strategies and Tactics*, 1993, Addison-Wesley

Mussar, David R. and Saini, Atul, *STL Tutorial and Reference Guide*, 1996, Addison-Wesley

Myers, Scott, *Effective C++*, 1992, Addison-Wesley

Myers, Scott, *More Effective C++*, 1996, Addison-Wesley

Nelson, Mark, *C++ Programmer's Guide to the Standard Template Library*, 1995, IDG Books

Plauger, P.J., *The Draft Standard C++ Library*, 1995, Prentice Hall, Inc.

Plauger, P.J., *The Standard C Library*, 1992, Prentice Hall, Inc.

Stepanov, Alexander and Lee, Meng, *The Standard Template Library*, 1994, ANSI Document Number X3J16/94-0095

Stevens, Al, *C++ Database Development 2nd Edition*, 1994, MIS Press

Stroustrup, Bjarne, *The C++ Programming Language Second Edition*, 1991, Addison-Wesley

Stroustrup, Bjarne, *The Design and Evolution of C++*, 1994, Addison-Wesley

INDEX

#define, 90, 202, 215, 240
#define
  # stringizing operator, 249
  ## concatenating operator, 250
#elif, 255
#else, 254
#endif, 90, 252
#error, 256
#if, 252
#if defined, 253
#ifdef, 90, 254
#ifndef, 254
#include, 15, 239, 430
#line, 257
#pragma, 258
#undef, 252

8080 microprocessor, 4

<cassert>, 216
<cctype>, 199, 218
<cerrno>, 219
<cfloat>, 28
<cmath>, 100, 220
<complex>, 616
<csetjmp>, 221
<cstdarg>, 72, 224
<cstdio>, 226
<cstdlib>, 93, 110, 112, 179, 199, 226,
  602
<cstring>, 7, 177, 230
<ctime>, 233, 290
<ctype>, 178
<fstream>, 587, 600
<iomanip>, 167, 249, 574, 581
<iostream>, 15, 73, 226, 424, 570, 581
<stdlib.h>, 93
<string.h>, 93
<string>, 93, 564
<typeinfo>, 558

__cplusplus, 90

A

abort, 228, 527
abs, 615
abstract base class, 395, 436, 649, 681
abstract data type, 10, 641, 643, 681
abstraction, 640, 642, 681
access specifier, 271
access specifier
  private, 271, 278
  protected, 271, 400, 405
  public, 271, 278
acos, 221
address, 81, 153, 682
address constant, 32
address-of operator, 156, 159, 170,
  590

ALGOL, 3
algorithms, 622, 682
allocation of dynamic array, 190
allocation of fixed array, 189
American National Standards
  Institute, 5
and, 560
and_eq, 560
anonymous object, 312, 682
anonymous union, 145
ANSI, 5
API, 455
application, 682
application framework, 455
application programming interface,
  455
applications program, 682
arg, 615
argc, 186
argument, 8, 69, 77, 80, 682
argument, function call, 81
argv, 186
arithmetic operators, 38
array, 112, 147, 682
array
  allocation of dynamic array, 190
  allocation of fixed array, 189
  bounded, 490
  character, 152
  dimension, 112, 148
  elements, 147
  initializing, 148
  multidimensional, 150, 160
  of class objects, 328
  of pointers, 174
  of structs, 149
  subscript, 113, 148
arrays vs pointers, 159
ASCII, 2, 682
asctime, 234
asin, 221
assert, 216, 490, 514
assignment, 8, 23, 34, 316, 682
assignment operators, 47
assignment operators, overloading,
  378
assignment vs equality, 44
associative containers, 620
associativity, 47, 54, 55, 682
AT&T Bell Laboratories, 3, 5
atan, 221
atan2, 221
atof, 227
atoi, 199, 227, 602
atol, 227
auto, 22, 129
auto-decrement operator,
  overloading, 380

auto-increment operator,
  overloading, 380
automatic variable, 683

B

bad, 599
bad_alloc, 633
bad_cast, 550, 633
bad_typeid, 633
base class, 392, 397, 649, 683
BASIC, 2, 4, 10, 21, 62, 65, 110, 152,
  262, 431, 564
BCPL, 3
begin, 623
behavior, 10, 261, 264, 644
binary arithmetic operators,
  overloading, 369
binary files, 600
binary operator, 683
bitand, 560
bitor, 560
bitwise logical operators, 41
bitwise shift operators, 42
block, 9, 12, 17, 96
bool, 22
Boolean logic, 683
bounded array, 490
break, 105, 113
breakpoint, 683
built-in type, 22
byte, 683

C

C language
  compared to C++, 7
  relevance, 6
c_str, 568
calculator program, 195, 222, 533
call by reference, 208
calloc, 227
case, 104
cast, 683
catch, 7, 518
catch handler, 518
catch-all handler, 524
ceil, 221
cerr, 21, 63, 570
cfront, 5
char, 23, 29, 569
character, 29, 683
character array, 152
character constant, 29
cin, 21, 39, 60, 63
class, 10, 22, 260, 275, 641, 683
class template, 486
class template specialization, 504
class
  and the heap, 339

assignment, 316
behavior, 10, 264
bypassing derived member function
    override, 410, 438
common root base, 422
const member function, 303
constructor, 272, 283
conversion constructor, 288, 292
conversion functions, 288
data member, 10, 279
declaration, 276
default constructor, 285
default constructor argument, 284
derived classes, multiple, 411
deriving from derived class, 416
destructor, 272
enum member, 435
explicit constructor, 299
friend, 278, 305
friend classes, 306
friend function, 280, 310
getter member function, 302
hierarchy, 392, 420, 445, 683
hierarchy vs hierarchical database,
    421
implementation, 10, 264
inheritance, 392
initializer, 279
inline member function, 281
interface, 10, 264
invoking conversions, 295
member, 278
member conversion functions, 290
member function, 10, 265, 280
method, 10
mutable data member, 361, 557
object-oriented design, 280
overloaded assignment operator,
    317
overloaded constructor, 285
overriding member function in
    derived class, 408, 470
parameter initialization list, 406, 420
public static member, 339
pure virtual function, 436
reference data member, 354
scope of object, 281
setter member function, 302
specialized member, 405
static data member, 333
static member, 333
static member function, 336
this, 320
unique member function in derived
    class, 407
virtual destructor, 450
virtual function, 280, 435, 452
vptr, 453
vs structure, 272
vtbl, 452
classes, 259
classes
  complex, 615

ifstream, 590
ios, 569
iostream, 7
istream, 425, 570
istringstream, 612
istrstream, 602
less<T>, 625
ofstream, 588
ostream, 61, 424, 570
ostringstream, 612
ostrstream, 607
string, 7, 431, 564
stringstream, 612
strstream, 610
strstreambuf, 602
classic C, 4
clear, 568, 606
clog, 570
COBOL, 2, 10, 65, 262
code, 684
comma operator, 53
comma-separated declarations, 37
command line arguments, 186
comments, 14, 17, 93, 684
compiler, 684
compl, 560
complex, 615
compound assignment, 49
concrete data type, 440, 684
condition, 97, 684
conditional operator, 51
conj, 615
console, 684
console input/output, 60
const, 22, 134, 176, 210, 212, 358, 555
const member function, 303
const pointer, 177
const reference parameter, 210
const_cast, 555
constant, 684
constants, 29
constants
  address, 32
  character, 29
  decimal, 31
  floating, 32
  hexadecimal, 31
  integer, 31
  octal, 31
  string, 32, 153
constructor, 272, 283, 684
constructor
  base class, 406
  base class arguments, 407
  conversion, 288, 292
  copy, 350
  default, 285, 420
  default and arrays, 329
  default arguments, 284
  derived class, 406
  explicit, 299
  order of execution, 406, 468
  overloaded, 285

parameter initialization list, 356
container adaptor, 619
container classes, 486
continue, 114
control structures, 9, 684
conversion constructor, 288, 292
conversion functions, 288
copy constructor, 350
cos, 221
cosh, 221
cout, 15, 21, 60, 61
CP/M, 4
ctime, 234
cursor, 685

D

data abstraction, 259, 261, 265, 423,
    427, 685
data abstraction, specialization, 396
data member, 10, 279, 685
data representation, 260, 644
data type, 685
database, 685
debugger, 685
dec, 61, 571, 581
decision, 685
declaration, 9, 276, 685
decrement operator, 45
default, 105, 285
default arguments, 284
default constructor, 285
default constructor argument, 284
default function argument, 82
definition, 9, 685
delete, 7, 188, 339
delete, overloading, 343
delete[], overloading, 347
deque, 619
derived, 641
derived class, 392, 404, 686
derived classes, multiple, 411
deriving from derived class, 416
destructor, 272, 287, 314, 686
destructor
  and class object arrays, 331
  order of execution, 468
  virtual, 450
difftime, 234
digraph, 560
dimension, 686
do...while, 108
do...while vs while, 109
domain_error, 633
DOS, 686
double, 22, 28
downcasting
  objects, 553
  pointers, 548, 553
  references, 550, 553
Dr. Dobb's Journal, 540
dynamic memory allocation, 181
dynamic_cast, 548, 558

E

EBCDIC, 2
editor, 686
EDOM, 219
EDRANGE, 219
element, 686
Ellis, Margaret, 631
else, 101
else if, 102
empty, 568
empty parameter list, 7, 12, 72
encapsulation, 265, 640, 644, 686
end, 623
end-of-file, 591
endl, 103, 581
ends, 581, 608
entry and exit points, 12, 67
enum, 146
enum member, 435
eof, 591, 599
equality operator, 99
equality vs assignment, 44
errno, 219, 514
error message, 686
escape sequence, 29, 686
exception, 633, 687
exception handling, 7, 10, 200, 223,
  347, 513
exception specification, 523
exception
  standard exceptions, 631
  uncaught, 527
  unexpected, 523
exceptions
  bad_alloc, 633
  bad_cast, 550, 633
  bad_typeid, 633
  domain_error, 633
  exception, 633
  invalid_argument, 633
  length_error, 633
  logic_error, 633
  out_of_range, 633
  overflow_error, 633
  range_error, 633
  runtime_error, 633
  underflow_error, 633
executable code, 687
exit, 74, 228
exp, 221
explicit constructor, 299
expression, 9, 34, 97, 687
extern, 123, 131
extern "C", 89, 92
extern "C++", 92
external data, 687
external variable, 122
extraction operator, 39, 590, 687
extraction operator, overloading, 424,
  570, 583

F

fabs, 221
fail, 599
false, 22
field, 687
file, 687
file input/output, 587
file scope, 126, 687
fill, 575, 582
find, 567, 627
finite state machine, 171
firmware, 687
first, 630
fixed notation, 578
float, 28
floating constant, 32
floating point number, 28, 688
floor, 221
flush, 571, 581
for, 9, 110
for, declaration within, 113
FORTRAN, 2, 10, 262
forward reference, 308
free, 7, 179, 227
free store, 688
freeze, 609
friend, 278, 305, 688
friend classes, 306
friend function, 280, 310
friend functions, nonmember, 312
function, 14, 688
function body, 688
function call operator, overloaded,
  625
function header, 688
function object argument, 625
function pointer, 169
function template, 507
function
  address return, 167
  argument, 8, 69, 77, 80
  as its own prototype, 73
  calling, 73
  declaration, 17
  default argument, 82
  defining, 73
  empty parameter list, 7, 12, 72
  header, 68
  inline, 84
  inline vs #define, 246
  name, 68
  parameter, 8, 69
  parameter list, 7
  parameter, unnamed, 82
  pointer argument, 164
  pointer to, 169
  prototype, 7, 8, 9, 70
  recursion, 193
  return, 8
  return type, 12, 68
  return value, 76
  returning from, 74

statement body, 68
struct argument, 141
struct return, 141
unnamed prototype parameter, 70
variable paramenter list, 72
void parameter list, 7
void return, 71, 74
functional programming, 422, 448
functions, 8, 67
functions
  abort, 228, 527
  abs, 615
  acos, 221
  arg, 615
  asctime, 234
  asin, 221
  assert, 216, 490, 514
  atan, 221
  atan2, 221
  atof, 227
  atoi, 199, 227, 602
  atol, 227
  bad, 599
  begin, 623
  c_str, 568
  calloc, 227
  ceil, 221
  clear, 568, 606
  conj, 615
  cos, 221
  cosh, 221
  ctime, 234
  difftime, 234
  empty, 568
  end, 623
  eof, 591, 599
  exit, 74, 228
  exp, 221
  fabs, 221
  fail, 599
  fill, 575, 582
  find, 567, 627
  floor, 221
  free, 7, 179, 227
  freeze, 609
  get, 584, 590
  getline, 586, 590
  gmtime, 234
  good, 599
  imag, 615
  insert, 625, 627
  isalnum, 218
  isalpha, 218
  isdigit, 218
  islower, 218
  isprint, 218
  isspace, 218
  isupper, 218
  length, 567, 568
  localtime, 88, 235, 290
  log, 221
  log10, 221

longjmp, 7, 200, 221, 514
malloc, 7, 179, 227
max, 507
memset, 233
min, 507
mktime, 235
norm, 615
open, 596
polor, 615
pow, 100, 221
precision, 582
printf, 224
put, 582
qsort, 509
rand, 110, 228, 512
rdbuf, 595, 602, 608, 610
read, 587, 590
real, 615
rfind, 567
seekg, 592, 606, 611
seekp, 592
set_terminate, 529
set_unexpected, 523
setf, 579, 582
setjmp, 7, 200, 221, 514
sin, 221
sinh, 221
sort, 625
sqrt, 221
srand, 112, 228
str, 608, 610
strcat, 232
strcmp, 231
strcpy, 176, 232
strlen, 231
strncat, 232
strncmp, 232
strncpy, 232
system, 228
tan, 221
tanh, 221
tellg, 593
tellp, 593
terminate, 527, 529
time, 88, 235, 290
tolower, 218
toupper, 178, 218
unexpected, 523
unsetf, 579, 582
va_arg, 225
va_end, 226
va_start, 225
what, 634
width, 572, 582
write, 582, 589

G

genericity, 10
get, 64, 584, 590
getline, 586, 590
getter member function, 302
global data, 688

global namespace, 15, 544, 546
global scope, 9, 122, 688
global scope resolution operator, 125, 544
gmtime, 234
GNU compiler, 3, 16, 26, 89, 105, 187, 485, 529, 547, 596, 601, 616, 653
gnu-win32, 3, 653
good, 599
goto, 9, 116, 688
goto
    advisability of usage, 119
    C++ vs C, 117
    invalid use of, 117
graphical user interface (GUI), 689
grep, 547

H

HASA relationship, 651
header source files, 689
headers
    <cassert>, 216
    <cctype>, 199, 218
    <cerrno>, 219
    <cfloat>, 28
    <cmath>, 100, 220
    <complex>, 616
    <csetjmp>, 221
    <cstdarg>, 72, 224
    <cstdio>, 226
    <cstdlib>, 93, 110, 112, 179, 199, 226, 602
    <cstring>, 7, 177, 230
    <ctime>, 233, 290
    <ctype>, 178
    <fstream>, 587, 600
    <iomanip>, 167, 249, 574, 581
    <iostream>, 15, 73, 226, 424, 570, 581
    <stdlib.h>, 93
    <string.h>, 93
    <string>, 93, 564
    <typeinfo>, 558
    user-defined, 362
heap, 181, 188, 227, 689
heap exhaustion, 191
Hewlett-Packard Laboratories, 616
hex, 61, 571, 581
hexadecimal, 689
hierarchy, 689

I

IBM PC, 4
IDE, 3, 653
identifier, 19, 689
if, 23, 97
if, declaration within, 105
if...else, 101
ifstream, 590
imag, 615
immediate values, 29

implementation, 10, 261, 264, 641, 689
improper programming, 76, 101
increment operator, 45
indenting style, 96
information hiding, 689
inheritance, 392, 640, 641, 649, 689
inheritance, justification, 395
initializer, 9, 57, 279, 690
initializer
    function call, 79
    sequence of execution, 79
inline, 84
inline function, 690
inline member function, 281
inline vs #define, 246
inplementation, 644
input/output redirection, 690
insert, 625, 627
insertion operator, 21, 690
insertion operator, overloading, 424, 570
instance, 690
instantiate, 641, 643, 690
int, 22, 26
integer, 690
integer constant, 31
integrated development environment, 3, 653
integrated development environment (IDE), 690
interactive, 690
interface, 10, 261, 264, 641, 644, 690
International Standards Organization, 5
interpreter, 691
intrinsic data type, 691
intrinsic type, 22
invalid_argument, 633
invoking conversions, 295
ios, 569
ios::app, 598
ios::ate, 598
ios::beg, 593
ios::binary, 593, 600
ios::boolalpha, 580
ios::cur, 593
ios::dec, 580
ios::end, 593
ios::fixed, 578, 580
ios::hex, 580
ios::in, 598
ios::internal, 580
ios::lef, 580
ios::left, 576
ios::nocreate, 598
ios::noreplace, 598
ios::oct, 580
ios::out, 598
ios::right, 580
ios::scientific, 578, 580
ios::showbase, 580

ios::showpoint, 580
ios::showpos, 580
ios::skipws, 580, 584
ios::stdio, 580
ios::text, 600
ios::trunc, 598
ios::unitbuf, 580
ios::uppercase, 580
iostream, 7
iostream library, 569
ISA relationship, 650
isalnum, 218
isalpha, 218
isdigit, 218
islower, 218
ISO, 5
isprint, 218
isspace, 218
istream, 425, 570
istringstream, 612
istrstream, 602
isupper, 218
iteration, 9, 106, 691
iterator state
  dereferenceable, 622
  past-the-end, 622
  singular, 622
iterator
  bidirectional, 621
  forward, 621
  input, 621
  output, 621
  random access, 621
  reachable, 622

J
Java, 465
jmp_buf, 221, 516
jumping, 116
justification, output format, 576

K
K&R, 4, 14, 70
Kernighan and Ritchie, 14
Kernighan, Brian, 4
keyword, 691
keywords, 7, 20

L
label, 116, 691
length, 567, 568
length_error, 633
less<T>, 625
libraries, object, 10, 409, 444, 540
library, 692
linkage-specification, 89, 692
linked list, 326, 486, 494
linker, 409, 444, 540, 692
linking C and C++ program modules,
  89
list, 619

literals, 29
local scope, 123, 692
local variable, 692
localtime, 88, 235, 290
log, 221
log10, 221
logic_error, 633
logical operators, 40
long, 22, 26
long double, 22, 28
longjmp, 7, 200, 221, 514
loop, 692
looping, 106, 113
lvalue, 35, 158, 692

M
Macintosh, 60
macro, 215, 240, 692
main, 8, 11, 14, 17, 67, 68, 186
main, default parameters, 69
main, return type, 69
main, variations, 18
malloc, 7, 179, 227
mangled name, 88
manipulator, 692
manipulators, 61
manipulators
  dec, 61, 167, 571, 581
  endl, 103, 581
  ends, 581, 608
  flush, 571, 581
  hex, 61, 167, 571, 581
  oct, 61, 167, 571, 581
  resetiosflags, 581
  setbase, 581
  setfill, 581
  setiosflags, 249, 576, 581
  setprecision, 577, 581
  setw, 167, 249, 573, 581
  ws, 581
map, 621, 627
max, 507
member, 278, 693
member conversion functions, 290
member function, 10, 265, 280, 645,
  649, 693
member pointer operator, 163
memory, 693
memory architecture, 188
memset, 233
menu, 693
message, 646, 693
method, 10, 645, 693
methods
  data type, 647
  functional, 646
  implicit conversion, 647
MFC, 455
Microsoft, 6
Microsoft Foundation Classes, 455
min, 507
mktime, 235

MS-DOS, 4, 69, 87, 600
multimap, 621
multiple base classes, 466
multiple inheritance, 392, 417, 465,
  650, 694
multiple inheritance, ambiguities, 471
multiset, 620
multitasking, 694
multiuser, 693
mutable data member, 361, 557

N
name, 68
name function, 557
name mangling, 88
namespace, 540, 694
namespace
  alias, 543
  definition, 541
  explicit qualification, 542, 546
  unnamed definition, 545
  using declaration, 15, 542
  using directive, 543
namespaces
  global, 15, 544, 546
  std, 15, 93, 100, 546
NDEBUG, 216, 493
nested blocks, 12, 76, 96
new, 7, 188, 339
new, overloading, 343
new[], overloading, 347
newline, 30
norm, 615
not, 560
not_eq, 560
Notepad, 10
NULL, 226

O
object, 262, 642, 694
object code, 694
object database, 694
object libraries, 10, 409, 444, 540
object-oriented design, 280
object-oriented design, pure, 422
object-oriented programming, 5, 8,
  448, 640
objects, 8, 553
oct, 61, 571, 581
octal, 694
ofstream, 588
open, 596
opening a file, 597
openmode, 595, 598
operand, 694
operating system, 694
operator, 290, 694
operator keywords, 560
operators
  !, 40
  !=, 43

#, 249
##, 250
%, 38, 39
%=, 47
&, 41, 156, 159, 170, 201, 590
&&, 40
&=, 47
() overloaded, 625
*, 38, 154, 156, 168, 201
*=, 47
+, 38
+ overloading, 370
++, 45, 157
++ overloading, 380
+=, 47
+= overloading, 378
,, 37, 53
-, 38
—, 45
— overloading, 380
-=, 47
->, 163
-> overloading, 386
., 138
..., 72, 224, 524
/, 38
/=, 47
:, 406
::, 125, 280, 410, 471, 544
<, 43
< overloading, 378
<<, 21, 42, 61
<< overloading, 424, 570
<<=, 47
<=, 43
=, 34, 47
==, 43, 99
== overloading, 378
== vs =, 44
>, 43
>=, 43
>>, 39, 42, 590
>> overloading, 424, 570, 583
>>=, 47
?:, 51, 57, 110
[] overloaded, 625
[] overloading, 384, 491
^, 41
^=, 47
and, 560
and_eq, 560
bitand, 560
bitor, 560
catch, 7, 518
compl, 560
delete, 7, 188, 339
dynamic_cast, 548, 558
in expressions, 37
new, 7, 188, 339
not, 560
not_eq, 560
or, 560

or_eq, 560
reinterpret_cast, 554
sizeof, 181
static_cast, 552
throw, 7, 347, 517, 519
try, 7, 517
typeid, 557
xor, 560
xor_eq, 560
{, 17
|, 41
|=, 47
||, 40
}, 17, 18
~, 41
or, 560
or_eq, 560
order of evaluation, 54
OS/2 Presentation Manager, 60
ostream, 61, 424, 570
ostringstream, 612
ostrstream, 607
out_of_range, 633
overflow_error, 633
overloaded, 285
overloaded assignment operator, 317
overloaded constructor, 285
overloaded function, 85, 694
overloaded operator, 695
overloaded operator function
    friend, 375, 426, 429
    member, 370
    nonmember, 373, 426
overloaded operators, 365
overloading
    assignment operators, 378
    auto-decrement operator, 380
    auto-increment operator, 380
    binary arithmetic operators, 369
    delete, 343
    delete[], 347
    extraction operator, 424, 570, 583
    insertion operator, 424, 570
    new, 343
    new[], 347
    pointer-to-member operator, 386
    relational operators, 376
    subscript operator, 384
    unary minus operator, 382
    unary plus operator, 382
overriding function, 695
overriding member function in
    derived class, 408, 470

P

pair<T1,T2>, 630
parameter, 8, 69, 695
parameter initialization list, 356, 406,
    420
parameter list, 7, 695
parameterized data type, 10, 485
Pascal, 2

pass by reference, 81, 154
pass by value, 81
PDP-11, 3
PDP-7, 3
persistence, 695
persistent object, 695
PL/1, 262
platform, 696
Plauger, P.J., 366, 631
pointer, 81, 153, 696
pointer vs reference, 212
pointer-to-member operator,
    overloading, 386
pointer
    arithmetic, 156
    assigning to, 154
    const, 177
    downcasting, 548, 553
    function argument, 164
    size of, 155
    to array of pointers, 174
    to const variable, 176
    to function, 169
    to intrinsic type, 154
    to pointer, 172
    to struct, 163
    upcasting, 552
    void, 179
pointers vs arrays, 159
polor, 615
polymorphism, 453, 640, 651, 696
postcondition, 633
pow, 100, 221
precedence, 48, 54, 56, 696
precision, 582
precision, output format, 577
precondition, 633
predicate, user-defined, 627
predicates, 625
preemptive multitasking, 696
preprocessing directive, 15, 238
preprocessing directives
    #define, 90, 202, 215, 240
    #elif, 255
    #else, 254
    #endif, 90, 252
    #error, 256
    #if, 252
    #if defined, 253
    #ifdef, 90, 254
    #ifndef, 254
    #include, 15, 239, 430
    #line, 257
    #pragma, 258
    #undef, 252
preprocessor, 237, 696
primitive data type, 696
printf, 72, 224
priority_queue, 620
private, 271, 278
private base class, 405
private class members, 696

problem domain, 420, 445
procedural programming, 8, 262, 272, 422, 639
procedure, 71
program, 697
program flow control, 9
program flow control statement, 697
project file, 445
proper programming, 76, 101, 697
protected, 271, 400, 405
protected class members, 697
prototype, 7, 8, 9, 70, 697
public, 271, 278
public base class, 393, 405
public class members, 697
public static member, 339
pulldown menu, 697
pure virtual function, 436, 697
put, 582

Q

qsort, 509
queue, 620
quick sort function template, 509
quicksort algorithm, 509
Quincy 97, 2, 187, 653

R

RAM, 697
rand, 110, 228, 512
random file, 698
random number generator, seeding, 112
range_error, 633
rdbuf, 595, 602, 608, 610
read, 587, 590
read/write files, 595
real, 615
real number, 698
real-time, 698
recursion, 85, 193, 208, 698
recursive descent, 193, 208, 537
reference, 81, 200, 698
reference data member, 354
reference vs pointer, 212
reference, pass by, 698
reference
  class member, 203
  const parameter, 210
  downcasting, 550, 553
  extern, 203
  function parameter, 204, 206
  initializing, 203
  returning, 210
  returning auto, 212
  upcasting, 552
register, 22, 133, 153
reinterpret_cast, 554
relational operators, 43
relational operators, overloading, 376
relocatable object code, 698

resetiosflags, 581
return, 8, 18
return type, 12, 68
return value, 76
returning from a function, 74
reusable code, 698
reverse_iterator, 630
rfind, 567
Ritchie, Dennis, 3, 4, 540
ROM, 698
RTTI, 557
runtime type information, 557
runtime_error, 633
rvalue, 35, 699

S

scanf, 72
scientific notation, 578
scope, 122, 699
scope of object, 281
scope resolution operator, 125, 280, 410, 471
scope
  file, 126
  function parameters, 123
  global, 9, 122
  hiding, 124
  identifier, 79
  local, 79, 123
  vs lifetime, 128
second, 630
seekg, 592, 606, 611
seeking, 592
seekp, 592
selection, 9, 97, 699
sequence, 9, 699
sequence containers, 618
sequential file, 699
set, 620, 627
set_terminate, 529
set_unexpected, 523
setbase, 581
setf, 579, 582
setfill, 581
setiosflags, 249, 576, 581
setjmp, 7, 200, 221, 514
setprecision, 577, 581
setter member function, 302
setw, 249, 573, 581
shareware, 699
shell programs, 69
short, 22, 26
side effects, 56, 219, 508, 699
signed, 27
sin, 221
single inheritance, 404, 649
sinh, 221
sizeof, 181
smanip, 581
sort, 625
source code, 699
specialized member, 405

sqrt, 221
srand, 112, 228
stack, 188, 192, 208, 620, 700
Standard C, 5, 700
Standard C Library, 215
Standard C++, 700
standard error stream, 63
standard input stream, 63
standard input/output devices, 700
standard output stream, 21, 61
Standard Template Library, 616
state variable, 171
statement, 700
statement block, 700
statement body, 68
statement
  block, 9, 12, 17, 96
  defined, 9
  label, 116
  nested blocks, 12, 76, 96
  termination, 12
static, 22, 123, 126, 130
static data member, 333
static member, 333
static member function, 336
static_cast, 552
std namespace, 15, 93, 100, 546
stdio function library, 7
STL, 616
STL programming model, 618
storage class, 129, 700
storage class
  auto, 22, 129
  extern, 123, 131
  register, 22, 133, 153
  static, 22, 123, 126, 130
  typedef, 185
str, 608, 610
strcat, 232
strcmp, 231
strcpy, 176, 232
stream, 700
streampos, 594
string, 7, 32, 431, 564
string constant, 21, 32, 153, 700
string constant, adjacent, 33
string
  assigning, 565
  comparing, 566
  concatenating, 565
  construction, 565
  extracting substrings, 566
  overloaded [] operator, 566
  searching, 567
stringstream, 612
strlen, 231
strncat, 232
strncmp, 232
strncpy, 232
Stroustrup, Bjarne, 5, 273, 545, 631
strstream, 610
strstreambuf, 602

struct, 22, 97
struct argument, 141
struct return, 141
struct tm, 88, 233
struct
  initializing, 138
  member, 137
  struct member, 139
  variable, 137
structure, 136, 700
structure member operator, 138
structure vs class, 272
structured programming, 9, 700
subclass, 641, 649, 701
subclassing, 392, 701
subroutine, 71
subscript, 701
subscript operator, overloaded, 625
subscript operator, overloading, 384, 490
superclass, 649, 701
switch...case, 104
system, 228
systems program, 701

T

tan, 221
tanh, 221
tellg, 593
tellp, 593
template, 10, 485
template member function
  specialization, 506
template
  bounded array, 490
  class template, 486
  class template specialization, 504
  function template, 507
  linked list, 486, 494
  quick sort function template, 509
  specialization, 504
  template member function
    specialization, 506
terminate, 527, 529
termination, 12
test, 701
text files, 600
this, 61, 320, 701
Thompson, Ken, 3
throw, 7, 347, 517, 519
throw, from within a catch handler, 525
time, 88, 235, 290
time_t, 88, 233, 290
tolower, 218
top-down design, 701
toupper, 178, 218
translation unit, 126, 701
trigraph, 20, 560

true, 22
try, 7, 517
try block, 517
type, 22, 702
type conversion, 58, 101, 702
type conversion
  function argument, 81
  function return value, 81
type qualifier, 702
type qualifier
  const, 22, 134, 176, 210, 212, 358, 555
  volatile, 22, 135
type-safe linkage, 88, 702
type_info
  name function, 557
typecast, 180, 183, 547, 702
typedef, 185
typeid, 557
types
  bool, 22
  char, 23, 29, 569
  double, 22, 28
  float, 28
  int, 22, 26
  long, 22, 26
  long double, 22, 28
  short, 22, 26
  signed, 27
  unsigned, 26
  wchar_t, 25, 569

U

unary minus operator, overloading, 382
unary operator, 702
unary plus operator, overloading, 382
underflow_error, 633
unexpected, 523
UNICODE, 2
union, 22, 136, 142, 274
union
  anonymous, 145
  initializing, 144
unique member function in derived
  class, 407
Unix, 3, 69, 87, 547, 600
unnamed function parameter, 82
unnamed prototype parameter, 70
unsetf, 579, 582
unsigned, 22, 26
upcasting
  pointers, 552
  references, 552
user interface, 702
user-defined data type, 136, 259, 261, 702
USESA relationship, 651
using declaration, 15, 542

using directive, 543
utility program, 703

V

va_arg, 225
va_end, 226
va_list, 225
va_start, 225
value, pass by, 703
variable, 22, 703
variable paramenter list, 72
variable
  external, 122
  initial value, 134
  lifetime, 128
  size, 22
vector, 619, 625
virtual, 400
virtual base class, 474
virtual destructor, 450
virtual function, 280, 435, 452, 703
virtual function override, 450
virtual function, call by reference, 449
Visual C++, 6, 612, 616, 617
void parameter list, 7
void pointer, 179
void return, 71, 74
volatile, 22, 135
vptr, 453, 590
vtbl, 452, 590

W

watchpoint, 703
wchar_t, 25, 569
WG21, 5
what, 634
while, 9, 106
while vs do...while, 109
white space, 16, 583, 703
width, 572, 582
Win32 API, 455
Windows 3.x, 4
Windows 95, 4, 6, 60, 600
Windows NT, 4, 600
write, 582, 589
ws, 581

X

X-Windows, 60
X3J11, 540
X3J16, 5, 16
xor, 560
xor_eq, 560

Z

Z80 microprocessor, 4